Touchstones of
Gothic Horror

ALSO BY DAVID HUCKVALE

Hammer Film Scores and the Musical Avant-Garde
(McFarland, 2008)

*James Bernard, Composer to Count Dracula:
A Critical Biography* (McFarland, 2006)

Touchstones of Gothic Horror

A Film Genealogy of Eleven Motifs and Images

DAVID HUCKVALE

McFarland & Company, Inc., Publishers
Jefferson, North Carolina, and London

LIBRARY OF CONGRESS CATALOGUING-IN-PUBLICATION DATA

Huckvale, David.
Touchstones of gothic horror : a film genealogy of eleven motifs and images / David Huckvale.
    p.   cm.
Includes bibliographical references and index.

ISBN 978-0-7864-4782-4

1. Horror films — History and criticism.
2. Motion pictures and literature.
3. Art and motion pictures.
I. Title.
PN1995.9.H6H76   2010   791.43'616409—dc22   2010021726

British Library cataloguing data are available

©2010 David Huckvale. All rights reserved

No part of this book may be reproduced or transmitted in any form or by any means, electronic or mechanical, including photocopying or recording, or by any information storage and retrieval system, without permission in writing from the publisher.

Front cover images ©2010 Shutterstock

Manufactured in the United States of America

*McFarland & Company, Inc., Publishers
Box 611, Jefferson, North Carolina 28640
www.mcfarlandpub.com*

To Gail-Nina Anderson

Acknowledgments

Many thanks to Marcus Hearn who provided many of the film stills reproduced in this book. The two Piranesi illustrations are reproduced courtesy of the Ministero per i Beni e le Attività Culturali. Thanks also to the Friends of Strawberry Hill, the staff of Oakley Court Hotel and Peter Buttle, the current owner of St. Botolph's Church in Shenley.

Table of Contents

Acknowledgments — vi
Introduction — 1

ONE. Stairways to Hell — 7
TWO. Sturm und Drang — 33
THREE. Ruins — 47
FOUR. Municipal Sublimity — 73
FIVE. Heaving Cleavage — 91
SIX. Living Pictures — 109
INTERLUDE. Werewolves — 134
SEVEN. Ornate Coffins — 146
EIGHT. Hegelian Horrors — 166
NINE. Ancient Egypt — 180
TEN. The Occult — 199
ELEVEN. Satire — 229

Chapter Notes — 243
Select Bibliography — 251
Index — 255

Introduction

Life at its most basic level is indeed horrific. We are born, a horror we can't remember; we die, a horror we can't record; and in between, life throws at us a myriad of terrors: the tyranny of authority, the anxiety of sex, the melancholy of loneliness, the betrayal of trust, the pain of illness and the fear of mutilation, to mention but a few. Only that peculiarly human quality of optimism has sustained us over centuries. We all hope to overthrow tyranny, negotiate sexual relations, transform the melancholy of loneliness into the consolation of solitude, find true friends, defeat illness and avoid accidents. Frequently we achieve some or most of these, but the fear that we won't be so lucky persists. Intelligence and perception provide no immunity, as it's often the case that the most intelligent and perceptive among us suffer the most. From the ancient Greeks to our own time, great art has so often been the analysis of great suffering. To some temperaments, life is nothing *but* suffering. Swedish playwright August Strindberg was one of these. "Life is so horribly ugly," he wrote in 1905, "we human beings so utterly evil, that if a writer were to portray *everything* he saw and heard no one could bear to read it.... Life is a punishment. A hell. For some a purgatory, for none a paradise. We are compelled to commit evil and to torment our fellow mortals."[1] Gothic horror agrees in part with such a bleak view of the world, but differs from Strindberg in its conventional opposition of evil with good, and it is usually good that wins.

This dualism was a key aspect of Hammer's Gothic films and the Universal horrors that preceded them. It was a view of the world held fast by Hammer's principal director, Terence Fisher, and Hammer's main star, Peter Cushing, in particular. Gothic horror films are consequently a deal more optimistic than the Swedish playwright. Cushing eloquently defended the Gothic genre with which he became so firmly associated in his second book of memoirs, in which he observed that "the producers of today's epics in this genre rely too much upon brutal savagery, explicit sex scenes, nudity, obscene language, special effects, and little or no characterisation." He explained that his fans were also "sickened by the general decadence offered to them in the name of entertainment, so different from that of yesteryear." He continued:

> Those older classics hold for them the delights of a joy-ride in the ghost train at a funfair, when boyfriends put their arms protectively around their sweethearts' shoulders, and although there may be some gasps and screams, they all know they'll come out safely into the sunlight again at the end of the journey, after a healthy "scare," and enjoy a good giggle together. They love the unbelievable being made believable, and, above all, the fact that good always prevails over evil.[2]

And this is the difference between Gothic horror and the more visceral type of slasher film with which Gothic has so little in common. Both deal with the uncomfortable realities of life and death, but the brutal nihilism of *The Texas Chain Saw Massacre* (dir. Tobe Hooper,

"Lo! Farinata there, who hath himself / Uplifted: from his girdle upwards, all / Exposed, behold him." On his face was mine / Already fix'd: his breast and forehead there / Erecting, seem'd as in high scorn he held / E'en hell." Gustave Doré's illustration from Canto X of "Hell" from Dante's *The Divine Comedy.*

1974), for example, has more in common with Strindberg's worldview than with *Dracula* and *Frankenstein*. Obviously, other genres deal with the darker side of the human condition in their own terms, but Gothic horror films, like fairy tales, myth and many of the operas that are based on fairy tales and myth, cut to the quick, dispensing with the prosaic realities of everyday life and the naturalistic restrictions of probability and reason. They articulate in symbolic terms our fear of, but simultaneous fascination with, the mysteries of life and death, and all those emotional and physical insecurities which we spend most of our lives trying to control.

Paradoxically, life acquires meaning and momentum only from our awareness of death's ultimate meaninglessness. If we were able to avoid death's horror, there would be no urgency to do anything, and inaction and stagnation would be the inevitable result. Art, by which we articulate emotion and create meaning, would have no function or justification without our knowledge of death. Such is the allegory of the Tree of Knowledge in the Garden of Eden. Our lives and culture are therefore largely conversations from the tomb, and in this respect we all resemble the character of Farinata degli Uberti and Cavalcante Cavalcanti, in the tenth Canto of Dante's "Inferno" from *The Divine Comedy*. These unfortunate individuals lie in fiery graves, which must remain unsealed until the Day of Judgment. Dante, in the company of Virgil, his guide through the underworld, speaks with Farinata who predicts Dante's future exile from Florence. In Dante's Christian worldview, such a horror was confined to Hell; but in our modern world, in which there is no longer the possibility of either Heaven or Hell, such hellish imagery is revealed as a metaphor of life's reality here on Earth. Gustave Doré's theatrical nineteenth-century interpretation of Dante's lines also connects Dante's fourteenth-century vision firmly to the kind of imagery and lighting effects we encounter in twentieth-century horror films, a genre that has so often been derided by those who regard an enthusiasm for such entertainments as a sign of immaturity. "Horror" is indeed primarily marketed to adolescents, but that's only because they are the ones who most powerfully share the difficulties endured by so many of the traditional horror film characters. Like the werewolf, adolescents experience the anxieties of physical change in puberty. Like the vampire, they are victims of the compelling attraction and dangers of sexual desire. Like Frankenstein's Monster, they too experience the emotional vulnerability of inexperience and the sometimes unsympathetic authority of parents and society at large. What we all have in common with these mythical characters is our fear of death, which is an even greater terror for those who have only just begun to live. For others, it sometimes seems to offer a refuge from the vicissitudes of existence. "To die, to be *really* dead," says Bela Lugosi's Dracula, "that must be glorious." Many a potential suicide must have thought the same. (Incidentally, as an example of how horror films encapsulate on a popular level the grand ideas that have inspired religion, philosophy and art, it would be hard to find a more resonant line. After all, is not Lugosi's Dracula expressing the same hope as the Buddhist who aims to avoid reincarnation and attain Nirvana? Is it not the same as the doctrine of the German philosopher Arthur Schopenhauer (1788–1860), who adapted Buddhist belief to his philosophical system of the renunciation of the Will? Is it not the same as the words Richard Wagner originally intended for Brünnhilde at the end of his mighty Ring cycle: "I close the open gates of eternal life behind me: to my chosen, most holy land, goal of the journey through this world, to where neither wish nor illusion dwell, I now go, freed from rebirth and rich in knowledge"?)[3]

The basic concerns that are articulated by horror films never leave us, even though we may come to more comfortable terms with them as we grow older. Death seems to be a joke made in rather poor taste to the individual who thinks himself somehow more sophisticated than Death, but the concerns of horror affect us all, even though we might try to laugh them to scorn when we feel they get in the way of our sense of dignity and respectability. The power of horror films, however, lies in the fact that they aren't concerned with respectability, for this allows them to discuss things that are often out of place in polite society. Horror films make our dreams and nightmares tangible. If they reveal things about ourselves that disturb us, or which we regard as infantile, we share the fate of Shakespeare's Caliban, raging at the ugliness of his own reflection, for, as Freud pointed out in *The Interpretation of Dreams*:

> Dreams ... admit impossibilities, they disregard knowledge which carries great weight with us in the daytime, they reveal us as ethical and moral imbeciles. Anyone who when he was awake behaved in the sort of way that is shown in situations in dreams would be considered insane. Anyone who when he was awake talked in the sort of way that people talk in dreams or described the sort of thing that happens in dreams would give us the impression of being muddle-headed or feeble-minded.[4]

However, the so-called horror genre is a large one, and it is one that can (and should) be subdivided. The term itself is unfortunate, and is the product of a misunderstanding. When the first wave of Hollywood horror films came to England in the 1930s, the troubling nature of the issues they discussed in their dreamlike way caused concern amongst the guardians of conventional morality. The emotional issues which high art had been discussing for centuries seemed somehow more immediate and troubling in the new medium of the cinema. There was a belief that such films would corrupt not only the young but also the uneducated. It was one thing to discuss these issues between the covers of a book or on the stage of an opera house (not, of course, that literature and drama have been immune to the blue pencil of the censor over the years), but the democratic nature of the cinema brought them to the general public in a more powerful and immediate manner than ever before. After all, cinema invented the idea of the "close-up."

So it was that the infamous "H" certificate was introduced by the British Board of Film Censors in 1932, in direct response to Tod Browning's *Dracula* and James Whale's *Frankenstein*, both released the previous year. What really upset the censors in the case of the latter film was the death of a little girl at the hands of Boris Karloff's Monster. The National Society for the Prevention of Cruelty to Children complained to the Home Office about this scene and it was deemed that something had to be done about it. Illogically, children under sixteen were consequently banned from seeing such films, even though they were hardly the ones who would be inspired by it to go out and persecute other children themselves. There were no restrictions on potential pedophiles. (As Christopher Lee once pointed out, "Children who can see my films—in countries where they don't get an 'X' certificate—are never afraid of me. They'll always come up and chat. To them, these films are fairy tales."[5]) Of course, both the NSPCC and the BBFC both rather missed the point regarding the *Frankenstein* scene in question, in which the Monster doesn't *deliberately* murder the little girl but drowns her quite unintentionally and is subsequently mortified when he realizes what he's done. Seeing the girl floating flowers on the surface of an idyllic lake, the affection-starved Monster, delighted that the girl isn't repelled by him, joins in the fun. He then throws the girl into the water in the same spirit, expecting her to float just as prettily. By cutting the second half of this scene, as the censors insisted, all manner of troubling motivations were consequently allowed to fill the resulting vacuum. Audiences of the edited version inevitably wondered what it was that the Monster had done to the child. Had he sexually assaulted her? As is so often the case, the censors made matters far worse by interfering.

The "H" certificate didn't last all that long. In 1951, it was officially replaced by the "X" certificate, but the damage had been done. Such films were now regarded as *horror films*, when, in fact, horror wasn't really the point. A far more appropriate categorization would have been a "G" certificate for Gothic. The subgenre to which Frankenstein's Monster, Dracula, the werewolves and mummies belong is light years away from that other department of the horror genre which concerns itself with serial killers of various kinds and entertainments that are primarily motivated by gratuitous violence. Indeed, if the word hadn't already been diluted into the genre of the love story, "R" for "Romantic" would have been an even better alternative to "H." When there was a season of Hammer screenings at the Barbican Centre in London in 1996, *The Evening Standard* review quite rightly stated, "This is romantic cinema that transcends genre"[6] while *The Guardian* claimed that Hammer films at their best "have a quality unmatched by horror films today."[7]

Boris Karloff hated the categorization of "horror" for the films in which he starred. As Christopher Lee recorded in his autobiography, Karloff much preferred the terms "macabre" and "fantasy."[8] Gothic is certainly concerned with death but it also has an additional and important aesthetic element running through it, which makes it a rather more complex form. The kind of films that Universal Studios made in the 1930s and '40s, along with the classic so-called "horrors" of Hammer from the late 1950s through to the mid–1970s, can trace their ancestry back to the distinguished tradition of late eighteenth-century Gothic romance, which in its purest form had little to do with actual horror. It was far more concerned with evoking extremes of emotion (particularly terror) by means of architectural and scenic setting, and to develop the reader's ability to appreciate the sublimity of nature, though aspects of horror later became a significant element within it. As such, it has a firm place in the history of the European Romantic movement. Gothic films, however, have even more in common with the literary development that grew out of Gothic, which was that aspect of the European Symbolist movement that flourished in the late nineteenth century and later developed into that became known as "decadent." We are thus able to locate the once proscribed "H" certificate films of Universal and the "X"-rated Hammer horrors (once famously derided as being "for sadists only"[9]) as aspects of a cultural tradition that was completely overlooked by the majority of their critics at the time.

It is the aim of this book to trace that connection by exploring aspects of its various component parts. On this Gothic Grand Tour we shall, among other things, be taking in the weather, architecture, eroticism, painting, philosophy, landscape, aesthetic theory, occultism, ancient Egypt and, most of all, literature; but to get in the appropriate mood, we'll begin with one of the most important motifs of Gothic romance: the staircase.

ONE

Stairways to Hell

It's a physical thing, horror. The first time you see Dracula, up at the top of the staircase, in silhouette—and the audience, the ones you want to laugh, start to laugh because they think they're going to see ... what? Instead, they see this very handsome man, the perfect host come down the stairs, into close-up. I did it this way, not just to tease the audience but to show them that the whole idea of evil is very attractive. It's one of the great cards that evil holds![1]

That was how director Terence Fisher explained his way with Hammer's first and arguably best Dracula film to movie historian Alan Frank. Though he mentioned Dracula's staircase twice, Fisher was more keen to point out the allure of evil than the importance of the stairs themselves. But staircases are, as we shall see, a very significant element in Gothic horror, and no production designer for such films should ignore them. As Fisher pointed out in that interview, Christopher Lee's count in Hammer's 1958 production of *Dracula* is first seen in silhouette at the top of what is in fact a relatively modest flight of stairs. Lee glides down these with his customary elegance, cloak flowing behind him, and the effect, as Fisher intended, is completely different to that created by Bela Lugosi in the 1931 Universal *Dracula*. Lugosi, that strange, hybrid actor, was given a much more impressive staircase on which to introduce himself: "I am ... *Dracula*," he says with his incomparably idiosyncratic pronunciation. "I bid you welcome." Well, Lee brought that line, and its delivery, up to date. "I am Dracula," he says, "and I welcome you to my house." Gone was Lugosi's musically eerie intonation, to be replaced by Lee's patrician, clipped and very British enunciation. The effect, as Fisher was very well aware, couldn't have been more different; but both performers still required a staircase on which to perform their now famous entrances. Hammer domesticated the one they provided for Lee, who would hardly have been able to skip so energetically down the mouldering steps of the one in the Universal film. Lugosi, however, lingered on every step of his staircase and, again unlike Lee, never got down to the bottom.

Bernard Robinson, Hammer's astonishingly inventive production designer, came up with Castle Dracula sets that were, by comparison with Lugosi's dusty pile, a domestic goddess' dream: not a cobweb in sight, everything polished and dusted, as though the National Trust had taken it over. One almost expects a gift shop and restaurant. Indeed, Harker's meal is all ready for him when he arrives, and a fire burns in the grate. Lugosi's castle, designed by the equally wonderful but very different Charles D. Hall, is a much more conventionally Gothic affair with plenty of archetypal pointed windows. We will be returning to those important architectural details in chapter three, but at the moment it is staircases that have our undivided attention. Hall's Dracula staircase is truly a marvel of Hollywood set design, which, along with his other Gothic interiors for director Tod Browning's oth-

Christopher Lee in *Dracula A.D. 1972* (dir. Alan Gibson, 1972).

erwise rather stodgy film, were notoriously squandered by the director. Only in the film's opening scenes was their mouldering majesty used to its full advantage.

"I am Dracula; and I bid you welcome." One is tempted to think that such a line would entirely lose its resonance and power if uttered on the level, but it's important to realize that in Bram Stoker's novel, in which those words first appeared, Dracula answers the door to Jonathan Harker in an almost suburban manner, far from Lugosi's theatrical pomp. He doesn't greet Harker at the top of the stairs; they appear a little later on, after a short walk along a passageway, but they are nowhere near as significant an element in the book as they are in the films based on it. Stoker's vampire does not wear a cape, but he does sport that famously unflattering mustache (after the handlebar manner of Vlad the Impaler on whom the character was to some extent based). So, in Stoker's book, Harker first gazes into Dracula's eyes on the same level: man to vampire, so to speak. This detail was reinstated by Fisher, who made Lee walk into a close-up so that we see him from Harker's (face-to-face) point of view while he's introducing himself. (Such verbal introductions are almost completely unnecessary as James Bernard's music here provides a more than sufficient calling card.) Despite this, Fisher couldn't resist introducing the silhouette of Dracula at the top of the stairs to begin with, for, as art historian Kenneth Clarke put it in his study *The Gothic Revival*, "there is always something dramatic about a staircase."[2] Gothic horror films usually agree with Lord Clarke, if they can afford to.

In MGM's *Dracula*-inspired *Mark of the Vampire* (dir. Tod Browning, 1935), Lugosi and Carroll Borland process along another, slightly less grand flight of cobweb-infested stairs, in that film's only really arresting scene of pure Gothic beauty. As the characters have very little else to do but wander about, stairs are a vital ingredient here. They give the couple's meanderings a momentum that's immeasurably aided by the fluid camerawork of James Wong Howe.

Such talk of "momentum" brings me to the highly influential ideas of the early twentieth-century Swiss stage designer Adolphe Appia (1862–1928), who demonstrated around the same time that Stoker was writing his most famous novel, that steps and different levels are an extremely effective means by which to generate what he called rhythmic space.[3] Appia believed that the old-fashioned way of presenting theater drama by means of painted flats towering over the bare boards of a monotonously level stage, cancelled out the three dimensional reality of the living actors. Actors, he believed, required similarly three-dimensional surroundings if the characters they played were to be convincing. Frustrated with the lavish but mostly two-dimensional naturalism of Wagner's music-dramas at the Bayreuth Festspielhaus, which Wagner had had specially built for the "ideal" productions of his works, Appia, who found little of the "ideal" about them, suggested that the painted flats of Wagner's forest foliage should be swept away and replaced with more abstracted, fully three-dimensional spaces comprising different levels. Later, at his workshop theater at Hellerau just outside Dresden, he experimented further with even more abstract spaces, which were connected by flights of steps. He also surrounded the whole performance area with screens of white muslin, through which a general diffused lighting could create different emotions and atmospheres. Wagner's widow, Cosima, who by then presided over the temple sacred to the memory of her beloved husband, refused to have anything to do with Appia's innovations, which she frostily compared to arctic landscapes[4]; but Appia's ideas eventually found their way beyond the Wagnerian music-dramas that originally inspired them, and into mainstream stage design. Other innovators were similarly at work around the same time. In England there was Edward Gordon Craig (1872–1966); in Germany, Leopold Jessner (1878–1945) lent his name to what became known as *Jessnertreppen*: stylized staircases that were to appear in the movies as well. As film historian Lotte H. Eisner explained,[5] early German cinema was full of staircases. Ghostly figures walk down distorted stairs in *Raskolnikov*, Robert Wiene's 1923 adaptation of Dostoyevsky's *Crime and Punishment*. Wiene had already put staircases into *The Cabinet of Dr. Caligari* (1919) where they dripped blood. (More accurately, the blood was painted onto them in stylized rivulets.) These stairs lead

Bela Lugosi in *Dracula* (dir. Tod Browning, 1931).

Bela Lugosi and Carroll Borland in *Mark of the Vampire* (dir. Tod Browning, 1935).

to the police cells where a prisoner is kept in chains, accused of a murder that was in fact perpetrated by Cesare, the somnambulist who is kept in the cabinet of the film's title. In *Der Golem* (dir. Paul Wegener, 1920), a staircase in the laboratory of Rabbi Lowe was made to resemble a giant ear. Stairs sweep down grandly in Fritz Lang's *Dr. Mabuse der Spieler* (1922) and *Metropolis* (1926). Banisters and balustrades cast threatening shadows in G.W. Pabst's *Pandora's Box* (1928), and staircases even lend themselves to the title of 1921's *Hintertreppen* ("Backstairs"), directed, appropriately, by Leopold Jessner himself.

German expressionism eventually found its way into Hollywood Gothic horror, bringing a new way with staircases to films such as Edgar G. Ulmer's *The Black Cat* (1934), which updated Gothic to Bauhaus-inspired modernism. In this film, open-tread stairs swirl up to Boris Karloff's bedroom. Indeed, the character Karloff plays is partly named after one of Germany's preeminent modernist architects, Hans Poelzig (1869–1936), who had designed the sets of Wegener's *Der Golem*. Open-tread, though less modernistic stairs appeared again in what art director Jack Otterson called "psychological sets" for *Son of Frankenstein* (dir. Rowland V. Lee, 1939). "I departed entirely from any known style of architecture," Otterson explained, but, of course, what he was doing was looking back to German expressionist cinema. Otterson hoped that what he came up with would "force an impression of a weird locale without intruding too strongly into the consciousness."[6] It was the way in which those sets were lit, casting such disturbing shadows everywhere, that made them truly weird, particularly the stairs, which tottered so precariously into the soundstage heights.

So, yes, there is something inherently dramatic about a staircase. Eisner said that she preferred to "leave it to the psychoanalysts to discover what repressions they please in this fondness for stairs,"[7] adding, in a footnote, that the Freudian psychoanalyst, Otto Rank (1884–1939), "claimed that staircases are 'representations of the sexual act,' while cellars and corridors stand for the female sexual organ."[8] Indeed, Freud himself regarded staircases in dreams as symbols of copulation:

> It is not hard to discover the basis of the comparison: we come to the top in a series of rhythmical movements and with increasing breathlessness and then, with a few rapid leaps, we can get to the bottom again. Thus the rhythmical pattern of copulation is reproduced in going upstairs. Nor must we omit to bring in the evidence of linguistic usage. It shows us that "mounting" [German "*steigen*"] is used as a direct equivalent for the sexual act.[9]

Karloff and Lugosi on the art deco stairs featured in *The Black Cat* (dir. Edgar G. Ulmer, 1934).

If we agree with Freud here, what better way could there be to introduce a sexual predator such as Dracula than on a staircase? The idea of height and corresponding *descent* might also imply Dracula's sexual power and authority. In Terence Fisher's *Dracula*, the way in which he uses the stairs to symbolize the vampire's power and authority (as well as the possible, though latent, homosexual element in Harker's relationship with Dracula) is made quite clear at the end of the scene in which Harker descends into the vault to stake Dracula and his vampire bride. Foolishly, Harker decides to deal with the female of the species before dispatching Dracula, who's lying dormant in his coffin waiting for sunset. After the woman has been transformed into an ancient hag by Harker's liberating stake, Harker senses a shadow behind him, and turns to see Dracula appear at the top of the steps that rise above his coffin. Dracula looks down, slams the door and seals Harker's fate. Why else would Fisher have had Dracula go to the rather pointless trouble of walking up the steps off-camera only to walk down them again if not to make a dramatic point? If Harker had merely turned around to face the count on the same level, the effect would have been much less impressive and the meaning behind that effect quite lost. That Fisher also has Dracula climb the stairs on his way to seduce Mina later in the film only strengthens a Freudian interpretation of this particular symbolism.

Altitude is a key aspect of the Gothic. Before its collapse in 1825, Fonthill Abbey, England's grandest Gothic folly, had once towered over the Wiltshire countryside. It was without doubt the most extravagant example of Gothic revival theatricality ever built. The man who paid for it, sugar millionaire, writer and connoisseur William Beckford (1760–1844), had been fascinated by towers since his childhood, but the extreme height of the central tower over the octagon hall of Fonthill ultimately led to the destruction of the whole project. It collapsed several years after Beckford had sold the Abbey, demolishing a large portion of the buildings beneath it. Undeterred, Beckford built another tower in Bath (this time in classical style), which still stands (one can even hire it for holidays). Both towers were testaments to his desire for *altitude*. This desire was what made Beckford choose the Gothic style for Fonthill. He wasn't so much in love with Gothic *per se* as with what it could do for him, for its principal elements (the vault and the pointed arch) are designed to attain and enclose extremities of height. In Beckford's oriental Gothic romance *Vathek* (1786), the penchant its eponymous hero shares with Beckford for high towers enables the fulfillment of his simultaneous desire to regard other human beings contemptuously as ants, crawling insignificantly beneath him. Height as Power: this is surely the reason for so many staircases in Gothic romance, and for so many castles being situated on craggy mountain peaks. Originally placed there for purely defensive purposes, the castle and its towers, as well as its staircases, eventually became psychological symbols of authority and power in fiction and film.

Hammer continued to use staircases (and castles on craggy outcrops) in their Dracula follow-ups. Though the castle set of the sequel *Dracula, Prince of Darkness* (dir. Terence Fisher, 1966) was also provided with stairs, they're less impressive than they were back in 1958, and neither does Christopher Lee's Dracula make his first appearance in the film on them. He first has to be very gruesomely resurrected, after which he appears on a rather diminutive flight of steps in the castle vault. Significantly, Barbara Shelley, as the originally frigid and timid Helen, *does* make her first entrance as a seductively unrepressed vampire on the main staircase above. Dracula himself rushes down them during the impressively staged fight scene later on.

Hammer's *Dracula Has Risen from the Grave* (dir. Freddie Francis, 1968) is set entirely outside Castle Dracula, so we don't get to see any staircases in there. The most dramatic

Fonthill Abbey, from John Rutter's *Delineations of Fonthill Abbey*, 1823 (photograph by the author).

"staircase" in that film, metaphorically speaking, is the steep and lengthy ascent of the mountain leading up to the castle itself, which is undertaken by Rupert Davies' monsignor and his nervous priest (Ewan Hooper); but as this scene is an excellent example of the kind of sublime scenery that is another crucial element in the genre of Gothic romance, we'll leave a discussion of it to chapter four. At the beginning of the film, however, there is a spiral staircase in the church which a mute altar boy (Norman Bacon) climbs before discovering one of Dracula's victims improbably suspended like the human clapper of a giant bell in the belfry. Though Dracula doesn't descend these stairs, the blood from his victim trickles down the bell rope that hangs next to them. If one felt inclined, one could use these images to expand upon Freud's staircase theory and interpret dripping blood, the holes in the floor of the belfry and the bell rope as sexual symbols as well.

A spiral staircase had also provided the title of Robert Siodmak's 1946 thriller about a mute girl who is terrorized in a creepy New England house. The serial killer of *The Spiral Staircase* is motivated to murder people with disabilities. "There's no room in the whole world for imperfection," he says, a foible which one could also interpret along Freudian lines as an expression of horror at the sexual act. If so, the image of a *spiral* staircase would seem even more appropriately a symbol of the vagina than any other kind of staircase, or cellar for that matter. Siodmak doesn't dwell on the staircase itself, but by using it in the film's title he certainly invested it with a particular significance.

Taste the Blood of Dracula (dir. Peter Sasdy, 1970), the next Hammer Dracula, uses the ready-made steps of Highgate Cemetery in London to lead up to the wholly imaginary deconsecrated church in which Dracula's disciples, egged on by the very flamboyant Ralph Bates in his most Byronic mode, bring the vampire back to life. The other significant staircase is situated in the Victorian home of Linda Hayden's Alice Hargood. When the dysfunctional Hargood family returns from church one Sunday morning, Alice hurries upstairs toward her room, but before she's halfway there, her father (played with domineering brutality by the excellent Geoffrey Keen) calls her back, demanding that she apologize for her behavior in church. He accuses her of "smiling and flirting" with her boyfriend Paul, and points out that she is "a sexually attractive young woman" who has been acting like "a harlot in God's house." All this sets up the sexual dynamics of his incestuous desire for her, which we witness later, and it seems appropriate, given the Freudian ideas discussed above, that all this should take place while Alice is halfway up the stairs. She soon runs up to the top and takes refuge in her bedroom, but later in the film, after secretly returning from a party which her father forbade her to attend, Mr. Hargood appears at her open bedroom door with a whip in his hand. Alice's bedroom is right at the top of the stairs, as a subsequent shot reveals to us, so Hargood (following Freud's theory) has already mounted them and now presumably intends to mount his own daughter as well. "I haven't whipped you since you were a little girl," he wistfully observes through his drunken haze. Alice escapes through the window; Hargood is too drunk to follow her and collapses in a stupor on the floor. By the time he regains consciousness, Alice has already encountered Dracula in the garden below, but Hargood has every intention of carrying out his threat and sets off down the stairs (though we only see him approach the top of the staircase before the film cuts back into the garden). By the time Hargood catches up with Alice, Dracula has hypnotized her and now commands her to murder her own father, which she does in a particularly brutal way that fully reveals the depths of her repressed hatred of him. If any proof were needed of the fact that horror films are able to express disturbing familial relationships in a way that would have been regarded as deeply shocking (particularly in the 1970s) if presented in a contemporary setting on prime-time television, one need look no further than *Taste the Blood of Dracula*.

Scars of Dracula (dir. Roy Ward Baker, 1970) was so feeble an entry in Hammer's Dracula saga, and so slipshod in its production values, that the interiors of Castle Dracula resemble a Gothic bungalow in which stairs would anyway be redundant. Most of the money apparently went toward constructing the exterior wall up which Christopher Lee's rather obvious double scampers, lending the film its only distinction (apart from the music of James Bernard) as that's exactly what Stoker's count did in the novel; but this does rather suggest that Dracula has no real need for stairs. That need is entirely ours. As an audience we need to experience the rhythmic space that Appia understood so well, to articulate the relationships between the characters presented to us.

In the democratic world of Hammer's *Dracula A.D. 1972* (dir. Alan Gibson, 1972) the only conventional staircase in sight is situated in Professor Van Helsing's modest Victorian villa in Chelsea, though Dracula does chase Van Helsing up another spiral staircase in the derelict Victorian Gothic church during the finale. (In the first *Dracula*, it had been Cushing who had chased Lee up the stairs of Castle Dracula. Now it's the other way around.) *The Satanic Rites of Dracula* (dir. Alan Gibson, 1973) appropriately replaced stairs with a Howard Hughes–style lift, which eerily elevates Van Helsing to Dracula's penthouse suite, an appropriate update of the time-honored staircase of old. Dracula's Chinese disciple Chin Yang (played by Barbara Yu Ling) is given Dracula's now outmoded staircase duties, appearing

Stairway to the Tombs from the Colonnade at Highgate Cemetery (photograph by the author).

at the top of a splendidly sweeping example in the Pelham House set in which the Satanic Rites of the title take place.

It's not just Hammer's Dracula films that feature staircases. Surprisingly, Terence Fisher completely wasted the impressive staircase that Bernard Robinson provided for *The Mummy* (1959). For once following in Tod Browning's cavalier footsteps regarding sets, Fisher squandered this staircase in a single brief shot, where it features merely as a background to the beautiful Yvonne Furneaux, who's running to the assistance of her husband (Cushing again) when the Mummy (Christopher Lee) breaks into his study. It would have been much more effective, surely, to have had the Mummy stomp down these stairs, rather than crash through the French windows, for as the scene stands there's no inequality of level in the encounter between the Mummy and the archaeologist. It was a lesson Michael Carreras learned when he directed the sequel, *The Curse of the Mummy's Tomb* (1964), in which he made sure that the Mummy makes full use of the stairs provided.

That's not to say that Fisher didn't understand the power of stairs, as we've already discussed. *The Brides of Dracula* (1960) didn't feature Dracula himself but the film nonetheless basks in the most impressive of all Bernard Robinson's highly impressive staircases for Hammer. It's flanked by flamboyant griffins and fully used by the actors who travel up and down it a great deal, most significantly when David Peel's Baron Meinster compels his bullied mama (played by Martita Hunt) to "come here, Mother," and of course she can't resist. The irony in the way this scene is staged is that the powerful figure remains on ground level while his victim is elevated above him at the top of the stairs. Such an inversion economically expresses this perverted mother-son relationship. After all, Baroness Meinster's true place *should* be on the stairs, but her decadent vampire son has undermined her authority. Hunt was virtually reprising her role as Miss Haversham in David Lean's 1946 film adaptation of Charles Dickens' *Great Expectations*, itself a somewhat Gothic tale. (Freda Jackson, who starred alongside Hunt in *Brides*, also appeared in *Great Expectations*, as Joe Gargery's wife.) Lean was keen to elaborate on these Gothic elements; as he recalled, the set designs of John Bryan were much influenced by German expressionism:

> The trees in the churchyard were carefully designed so that you could almost see a face in them. The churchyard was built in the studio and the church itself was about ten feet tall. The forced perspective looked perfectly natural, but unnatural too, and that was great. Nearly all the sets used the technique.[10]

Lean makes the opening graveyard scene, with those skeletal trees, sighing wind, and the terrifying apparition of Magwitch the convict (Finlay Currie) far more Gothic than it is in Dickens' novel, and as such it has a great deal in common with Universal and later Hammer horrors. When young Pip (Anthony Wager) first visits Miss Haversham in the creepy Satis House, Lean again emphasizes a Gothic atmosphere that Dickens only suggests. Dickens writes: "We went through more passages and up a staircase, and still it was all dark, and only the candle lighted us."[11] Lean extrudes this economic description into a sequence that lasts rather longer as Pip follows Estella (Jean Simmons) up an elaborately meandering staircase to the fatal room wherein Miss Haversham sits amidst her decaying wedding feast, her tangled hair resembling the snakes of a Gorgon who seems to have petrified *herself* into stone.

Speaking of which, Hammer was first to devote an entire film to the ancient Greek legend of the Gorgon. For some reason, John Gilling's script called the Gorgon in question Megaera, who, strictly speaking, was one of the Eumenides, or Furies. Like the Gorgons, the Eumenides were three in number (the other two were called Tisiphone and Alecto).

David Peel and Peter Cushing meet on Bernard Robinson's set for Chateau Meinster in *The Brides of Dracula* (dir. Terence Fisher, 1960).

However, the most famous Gorgon, and the only one who was mortal, was Medusa. (Her sisters were called Stheno and Euryale, and all three had snakes for hair, wings, claws and enormous teeth.) Directed by Terence Fisher, *The Gorgon* (1964) unfortunately suffered from less than satisfactory special effects, which let things down at the end, but these deficiencies were more than compensated for by Bernard Robinson's splendid sets for Castle Borski, wherein the Gorgon has her lair at the top of another important staircase. Again, one could interpret this in a Freudian manner, especially as the Gorgon is ultimately decapitated, an action which Freud was always keen to identify as a symbol of castration. In his posthumously published thoughts on that subject, he explained:

> Cutting off the head = castration. The terror inspired by Medusa is therefore the terror of castration, which is linked to something seen. From numerous analyses we know the occasion: it happens when a boy, who formerly refused to believe in the threat, sees female genitals. Probably adult genitalia surrounded by pubic hair, in principle the mother's.
> If the hair of Medusa's head is so often represented in art as snakes, this also arises from the castration complex, and surprisingly, as frightful as they are, they actually serve to modify the horror, for they replace the penis, whose absence causes such horror. A technical rule (called "compensation") is here confirmed: the multiplication of penis symbols means castration.
> The sight of Medusa's head makes one rigid with fear, turns the viewer into stone. The same

Oakley Court, where many of Hammer's Gothic horrors were filmed (photograph by the author).

source in the castration complex and the same emotional reaction! Growing rigid means erection, and so in the original situation it is the consolation of the viewer. He still has a penis, and confirms it through getting an erection.[12]

We'll be returning to the erotic aspects of *The Gorgon* in chapter five, but for now it's sufficient to point out that Hammer's Megaera apparently prefers to remain upstairs to ensure that her victims turn to stone as they ascend to her lair. That way, they can at least have a spectacular tumble back down again. As Sergei Eisenstein had proved in the famous Odessa Steps sequence of *Battleship Potemkin* (1925), it's so much more effective to die on a staircase than on the level. So completely did Eisenstein believe this to be the case, he deliberately distorted history to inject his central scene with a powerful dose of Appian "rhythmic space." The Odessa Steps massacre is not historical fact, but the impact of Eisenstein's famous sequence was so powerful that many people now think it is. Director John Hough Gothicized the Odessa Steps at the end of *Twins of Evil* (1971), the third film of Hammer's celebrated "Karnstein trilogy." There are two interesting flights of steps in this film, both of which suggest the influence of Eisenstein. The first one appears towards the end of the story as Count Karnstein and the evil, now undead twin of the title, Freda, attempt to make their escape from the castle. The steps are revealed behind a door, shrouded in quantities of atmospherically drifting mist. Freda makes her way up them, only to meet the puritan vampire hunter Gustav Weil at the top; he promptly decapitates her, providing a host of Freudian interpretations. Weil was played by Peter Cushing, who later recalled his own spectacular death scene in that film, with "a hatchet buried in my back causing me to hurtle over the edge of a balcony, plunging to the stone-flagged floor 30-odd feet below (do I hear someone say 'a stunt man did that?'—if so, ten out of ten whoever you are, but I did top and tail that happy landing myself—just the free fall bit in the middle was left to some other

The main entrance of Oakley Court, as featured in Hammer's *The Brides of Dracula* (photograph by the author).

brave body)."[13] What Cushing failed to recall was that he came to rest on a flight of steps, which in their more modest way echo the rather more majestic ones in Eisenstein's famous film.

Twenty-eight years earlier, Cushing had appeared in that veritable riot of cinematic staircases that is Laurence Olivier's *Hamlet* (1948), playing the role of Osric, the flamboyant "waterfly" who judges the final fatal duel. He wasn't the only actor in the film who went on to make an impression in subsequent Gothic horrors. Christopher Lee was also on the set and apparently shouted "Lights!" at the end of the Players' scene, though he was standing in the dark at the time.[14] Terence Morgan, who played Laertes, later portrayed the immortal brother of an Egyptian pharaoh in Hammer's *The Curse of the Mummy's Tomb*. Felix Aylmer, the Polonius in Olivier's film, played Cushing's father in Terence Fisher's *The Mummy*, and Niall MacGinnis, whom Olivier cast in the small role of a sea captain, would become the much more frightening occultist in *Night of the Demon* (dir. Jacques Tourneur, 1957). Of course, these are just coincidences. Actors take what work they can find, but with its castle, ghost, revenge plot and obsession with death, *Hamlet* is in many ways the ultimate Gothic drama. As Hamlet himself says, at the end of Act III, Scene 2:

The main staircase of Oakley Court, now a luxury hotel (photograph by the author).

> 'Tis now the very witching time of night,
> When churchyards yawn and hell itself breathes out
> Contagion to this world: now could I drink hot blood,
> And do such bitter business as the day
> Would quake to look on.[15]

Olivier seemed determined to make his film of *Hamlet* as Gothic as possible; he succeeded to such an extent that, as the theater historian Bernard Grebanier put it, "In order to allow the camera to play lovingly with all that stonework at Elsinore, all those staircases, the raging sea, and especially, and oh so subtly!, Gertrude's bed, [Olivier] had to omit about a third of the play."[16] If staircases really do signify copulation, there's an awful lot of it going on in Olivier's film. Flights of steps shrouded in mist dominate it. Indeed, they open the proceedings, Olivier's camera prowling up and down them, and along the empty corridors of Elsinore in a manner that may have influenced Terence Fisher's eerie tracking shots through the interior of Castle Dracula in *Dracula, Prince of Darkness*. One might also compare Olivier's opening tracking shots with Sacha Vierny's languid camerawork at the beginning of Alain Resnais' *L'Année dernière à Marienbad* (*Last Year at Marienbad*, 1961). Vierny's camera does little else than linger on its architectural surroundings, as we shall see in chapter eight, when the Gothic elements of this film will be considered in more detail. As if to back up Freud's psychosexual interpretation of stairs, Olivier confessed to having been influenced by Ernest Jones' Oepidal analysis of *Hamlet*. Olivier's direction keeps the camera returning to Queen Gertrude's bed, the curtains of which are swept back in such a way as to leave a triangle of black shadow hovering over it which it might not be too fanciful to regard in the same manner as Hamlet's later obscene pun to Ophelia: "Do you think I meant country matters?"[17] Well, Olivier certainly seems to want us to think of the shadow over the bed as the female pudenda, and he emphasizes both this and the incestuous theme by having Hamlet later walk up a flight of "sexually" winding stairs before going to see his mother in that bedchamber. "Mother, Mother, Mother," Hamlet repeats, though that repetition is pure Olivier, not Shakespeare. Then he reverts to the text, asking with sinister ambivalence: "Now, mother, what's the matter?" Olivier's delivery here, together with the preceding staircase, may well also have been in Terence Fisher's mind when staging the equally Oedipal scene in *The Brides of Dracula* mentioned above.

Olivier's Elsinore is very like Ann Radcliffe's *Hamlet*-infused castle in *The Mysteries of Udolpho* (1794), even though the architectural style of the former is severely Romanesque rather than Gothic. In its general *cinematic* style *Hamlet* was greatly influenced by the example of German expressionist film. The swooping camera of Olivier's photographer, Desmond Dickinson, often shoots scenes from above and then moves down towards a close-up, or pulls dramatically away from close-ups, as in the scene in which Claudius and Laertes discuss

The vestibule of Oakley Court (photograph by the author).

their plot to kill Hamlet. In this instance the dialogue is divided up into three sections, each of which begins with a close-up of the plotters before the camera pulls back into the colonnaded passages that surround them. Some of these columns are incised with zigzag decorations that remind one of Paul Gerd Guderian's costume designs in Fritz Lang's *Die Nibelungen* (1922–24). The moment in the Gravedigger's scene when the shadow of Hamlet's head neatly covers the disinterred skull of Yorick is just the same kind of technique used by F.W. Murnau toward the end of *Nosferatu*, when the shadow of the vampire's hand clenches into a fist over Ellen's heart.

Hamlet's Ghost would no doubt have been disapproved of by the ultimately rational Mrs. Radcliffe, that sort of supernatural happening being much more to the taste of her rival novelist, Matthew Lewis. For Shakespeare, however, the supernatural world was a very real one, even though he does sow some doubt as to the true nature of the Ghost. Olivier makes this doubt even more overt in his film. That *something* appears on the battlements is presumably in no doubt as the soldiers, Marcellus, Barnado and Francisco, also see it, as does Horatio, but the ghost doesn't *say* anything until it gets Hamlet on his own. Olivier's Hamlet climbs yet more steps for this supernatural interview, which takes place on the topmost turret of the castle, and then Olivier gives the Ghost his own voice (disguised by being slowed down on the soundtrack). The use of Olivier's voice here suggests that what the Ghost is saying might well have been *imagined* by Hamlet, as a kind of mental confirmation to himself of his own suspicions about the usurper, his uncle Claudius. (On other occasions, usually for soliloquies, the camera moves in over the back of Hamlet's head to imply that we are entering Hamlet's mind.) By suggesting, in this way, that it is Hamlet's mind that is speaking rather than the Ghost (whatever the Ghost is), Olivier is able to emphasize the doubt about the Ghost's true nature that Shakespeare expresses in the lines:

> Be thou a spirit of health or goblin damn'd
> Bring with thee airs from heaven or blasts from hell,
> Be thy intents wicked or charitable,
> Thou comest in such a questionable shape
> That I will speak to thee[.][18]

This doubt is central to the play for it goes some way towards explaining why Hamlet delays so long in executing his revenge upon Claudius. He has to be sure he is right, that he has not been led astray by a demon (or, more rationally, merely by his own suspicions).

Having said that, Olivier, for all his psychologizing, gives the Ghost as much Gothic punch as possible. Electronic effects combine on the soundtrack with a heartbeat and William Walton's music to create an atmosphere that's worthy of any Universal horror film. The expressions of apprehension on the faces of the characters, and the swirling mist that surrounds them, also belong firmly in the Gothic horror tradition. The shaky zoom towards the bewildered Hamlet at the moment of the Ghost's arrival is the only occasion in the entire film in which things go out of focus to heighten Hamlet's dizzy sense of fear. (Olivier and Dickinson were devotees of so-called "deep focus," a technique that allows foreground, middle-ground and background to remain in sharp focus simultaneously.)

However, as *Great Expectations* demonstrated, not all Gothic films are concerned with the overtly supernatural. Indeed, as I've already mentioned, the late eighteenth-century Gothic romances of Ann Radcliffe actively shunned supernatural solutions. Radcliffe was adamant that everything, no matter how apparently unearthly it might seem, should ultimately be explained by rational means. Daphne du Maurier's much later Gothic romance *Rebecca* (1938) follows in this tradition. She suggests nothing overtly supernatural beyond the "presence" of the dead Rebecca de Winter, but there are many other Radcliffian elements at work here. Significantly, from our point of view, there's an important staircase scene in the 1940 Alfred Hitchcock film adaptation of the story. Du Maurier herself makes scant reference to the staircase, which leads up to Rebecca's bedroom. The only description of it in the novel is the narrator's description: "I began to walk upstairs. My heart was beating in a queer excited way."[19] For the film, Hitchcock went to a great deal of trouble to show us Joan Fontaine's journey up a very impressive staircase, his composer Franz Waxman raising the pitch of his brooding strings accordingly as the camera travels up towards the forbidden chamber. (Max Steiner, Waxman's contemporary in Hollywood, took a similar but rather less subtly executed approach in the scene from *King Kong* [dir. Merian C. Cooper and Ernest B. Schoedsack, 1933] when the tribal chief, realizing he's been filmed by Robert Armstrong's Carl Denham, impressively descends a gigantic set of steps in his advance towards the intruders. Steiner made sure that his descending scale accurately synchronized with every footstep, a technique known in the business as "Mickey Mousing.")

Stairs also played their Gothic part in *Dragonwyck* (dir. Joseph L. Mankiewicz, 1946), in which Vincent Price's Nicholas Van Ryn murders his first wife because she can't bear him a son. When his second wife (played by Gene Tierney) does manage to deliver a son, he dies soon after birth, so Nicholas plans to dispense with her too. His wife's maid also has a limp, which doesn't augur well for her, given Nicholas' horror of deformity. But he then begins to hide in a tower at the top of his creepy mansion, and when Tierney decides to flush him out, Mankiewicz makes sure his camera lovingly tracks her passage up another shadow-infested staircase. The turret room has, of course, a tall Gothic window in it, and when Tierney enters, Price rises from his couch like a vampire from his tomb. "I wasn't expecting you," he says, in one of his best screen performances. "It must have taken a great deal [of courage] to make this pilgrimage up to the mysterious tower room.... Tell me, are you disappointed in what you find here? I'm sure you expected velvet drapes and heathen idols, an altar for human sacrifices at least." His problem is nothing quite so exotic, however, for he is no more than a drug addict who retreats to his tower to indulge his opium dreams. As Jonathan Rigby aptly described the whole wonderful affair, "*Dragonwyck* is Poe all the way, though seen through the prism of a Mills & Boon romance."[20]

If one wishes to add Gothic resonance to one's hero, one should always make sure that he appears at the top of the stairs. That's what Leslie Banks did in *The Most Dangerous Game* (dir. Ernest B. Schoedsack, 1932) in which he plays the murderous Count Zaroff, whose passion is to hunt human beings and mount their severed heads alongside his other trophies. Immaculate in white tie and tails, he strongly resembles Lugosi's Dracula, but without the order and candlestick. (Instead he waves a long cigarette around, which we needn't be too Freudian about.) Freud would no doubt have found plenty to keep him busy in Harry Kümel's *Daughters of Darkness* (1970), in which Delphine Seyrig plays a modernized incarnation of Countess Elizabeth Bathory, who is not merely interested in bathing in virgins' blood to stay young but is also a literal vampire. The deserted Belgian hotel in which the claustrophobic, languid action takes place perhaps inevitably features a very grand staircase leading from the foyer to the bedrooms above, and Kümel was very keen to exploit both its dramatic potential and Gothic associations. So too was Stephen Volk, who wrote the screenplay for Ken Russell's film *Gothic* (1986). Volk specifically had Christopher Lee's first entrance as Dracula in mind when he instructed Gabriel Byrne's Lord Byron to appear at the top of the stairs in the building that stood in for Villa Diodati, the birthplace of Mary Shelley's novel *Frankenstein*. Film versions of Shelley's story can never resist staircases either: from the timeworn steps in James Whale's Gothic windmill and tower in the first two Universal *Frankenstein* films, to Kenneth Branagh's adaptation called *Mary Shelley's Frankenstein* (1994). The latter includes a truly gigantic, curving staircase which was dangerously deprived of its banister in homage, surely, to both Charles D. Hall's similarly denuded steps in the shamefully underused Carfax Abbey sets of Tod Browning's *Dracula*, and to Roger Furse and Carmen Dillon's principal castle set for Olivier's *Hamlet*.

How else could Gloria Swanson's Norma Desmond have made her final descent into Salomé insanity at the end of *Sunset Blvd.* (dir. Billy Wilder, 1950) other than down another curving flight? For that matter, could Bette Davis have killed Claude Rains' arrogant composer in *Deception* (dir. Irving Rapper, 1946) any more dramatically than by shooting him on a staircase, its balustrade casting sumptuous Warner Brothers shadows on the adjacent pearly white wall. Rains falls to his death Eisenstein-style while his parrot (apparently deaf to the sound of Davis' pistol shot) sits peacefully on its perch above. Though *Deception* isn't a Gothic horror film, the stairs add that element of kinetic excitement about which Appia knew so much.

This brings us (along with Claude Rains) to the bottom of all these stairs, and to the first Gothic staircase that led to all the others. The genealogical descent of such spiraling escalation can indeed be traced back to the origin of Gothic romance as a genre, for it was at the eighteenth-century Gothic fantasy castle, Strawberry Hill, at Twickenham on the banks of the River Thames, that staircases first acquired their Gothic resonance. Strawberry Hill was built by the writer and "man of feeling," Horace Walpole (1717–1797). Impressive and innovative though it was, it would have been dwarfed by Beckford's Fonthill Abbey. Indeed, Beckford hated it, calling it a Gothic mousetrap, but Strawberry Hill was the first important building of the eighteenth-century Gothic revival. Having completed it, Walpole enjoyed nothing so much as wandering through its mock medieval interiors. It was apparently the staircase of his mansion (replete with a ceiling of gold stars on a blue background) that inspired Walpole to dream a curious dream:

> I waked one morning in the beginning of last June [1764] from a dream, of which all I could recover was, that I had thought myself into an ancient castle (a very natural dream for a head filled like mine with Gothic story) and that on the uppermost banister of a great staircase I saw a gigantic hand in armour.[21]

Walpole immediately set to work to write a story around it, eventually completing the world's first Gothic novel, *The Castle of Otranto*, which he published under a pseudonym only a few months later. Though there have been no film adaptations of Walpole's novel, one British horror film in particular seems indebted to Walpole's idea of an out-of-scale object bringing terror in its wake. The film in question is *Night of the Eagle* (dir. Sidney Hayers, 1962), a supernatural thriller in the tradition of the classic ghost story writer M.R. James. In it, Peter Wyngarde plays a skeptical college lecturer who is terrorized by a gigantic eagle that pursues him along the corridors of the institution at which he works. The principal of this college turns out to be a practicing witch, and she doesn't like the idea that Wyngarde's character might be about to threaten her position, so she uses her magical powers to bring to life the stone eagle that sits over the entrance of the college. At least, she is able to make Wyngarde *think* it has come to life, and in one of the film's most impressive sequences, the giant bird breaks through the main door and chases Wyngarde down a corridor. The intrusion of a giant version of something normally much smaller is a common device in science fiction, but *Night of the Eagle* places such a phenomenon in the more Walpolean Gothic setting. (The college isn't in Gothic Revival style but is nonetheless a riot of pointed gables,

Exterior of Strawberry Hill (photograph by the author).

crocket-like chimney stacks and, inside, one or two Tudor arches amongst the predominantly Romanesque ones.)

Long before *Night of the Eagle*, however, artists had taken their cue from Walpole's staircase mania. That nineteenth-century master of the sublime and apocalyptic landscape, John Martin (1789–1854), was keen to use staircases in his illustrations to Milton's *Paradise Lost*. Milton's Satan was the model for all the Gothic anti-heroes and subsequent Byronic villains who modeled themselves on them,[22] and when designing his response to Milton's description of Satan viewing obedient angels on their way to Heaven, Martin envisaged an enormous flight of steps up which the angels made their way to paradise like mall shoppers on a celestial escalator. Gustave Doré (1832–1883) took a similar approach when illustrating the story of Jacob's vision for his 1865 edition of *The Bible*, and both illustrations were no doubt in the mind of Alfred Junge, the set designer of *A Matter of Life and Death* (dir. Michael Powell and Emeric Pressburger, 1946) when he was constructing the equally gigantic moving stairway to Heaven that is one of that film's most striking images.

If staircases indeed represent sexuality, they are also places of *encounter*. After all, Harker (or Renfield, in the Tod Browning version) first encounters Dracula's perhaps ambivalent and certainly demonic eroticism on a staircase. As William Hughes Mearns' little rhyme puts it, "Yesterday, upon the stair, I met a man who wasn't there."[23] Dracula, who can walk through cobwebs (at least until the tidier and more corporeal Christopher Lee took over the role), is only ever half there. A famous still of Lugosi on the stairs of Castle Dracula shows him to be transparent, incorporeal and elemental. It was for these reasons, as well as the Gothic heritage it brought with it, that the crucial encounter between two incestuous and ruthlessly separated twins in Hammer's *Demons of the Mind* (dir. Peter Sykes, 1972) takes place on a staircase. Originally a straightforward werewolf tale, Christopher Wicking's evolving script for this late-vintage Hammer film increasingly

Top: Stairwell of Strawberry Hill, the birthplace of the Gothic novel. *Bottom:* Stairwell ceiling of Strawberry Hill (photographs by the author).

"And he dreamed, and, behold, a ladder set up on earth, and the top of it reached to heaven: and, took a behold, the angel of God ascending and descending on it" (Genesis, Chapter 28, verses 10–17). Gustave Doré, Jacob's Ladder, from Dore's *Bible* illustrations (1866).

Illustration of Jacob's Dream from *The Family Devotional Bible*, ed. the Reverend Matthew Henry, London, John Tallis and Company, 1860, facing p. 58. Painting by Thomas Stothard 1755–1834, engraved by Robert Wallis.

distanced itself from that rather obvious myth in favor of a more psychoanalytical account of the psychopathically incestuous love of Emil (Shane Briant) for his sister Elizabeth (Gillian Hills). The lugubrious, turreted Victorian pile in which they have their first encounter after a period of separation isn't strictly speaking a Gothic edifice, but the staircase inside is used in an entirely Walpolean manner. Director Sykes went to the trouble of setting up several rather complicated points of view on these stairs to help articulate the siblings' mutual desire for each other, a desire that is watchfully restrained by their father (Robert Hardy) and well-meaning though relentless nurse (Yvonne Mitchell).

In this film, the stairs lead us up to the echoing and sterile corridors of the upper floor, where the siblings are locked away in their separate chambers, but stairs can also lead us in the opposite direction, of course, down to the depths. Cellars in Gothic fiction invariably imply forbidden territory: either secrets (guilty or otherwise), repressed desires (Freud's vagina symbolism again) or psychological regressions. In *Blood from the Mummy's Tomb* (dir. Seth Holt, 1971) an open-tread wooden staircase leads down to a cellar wherein the tomb of an evil Egyptian queen called Tera has been reassembled by an Egyptologist with the interesting name of Fuchs (played by Andrew Keir). Director Holt could have had Mark Edwards' knowingly named character, Tod Browning, overhear the conversation between Corbeck (James Villiers) and Margaret (Valerie Leon) that takes place in this cellar, while merely standing by the upper door. Instead, Holt decided to exploit not only the more dramatically effective but also the highly symbolic possibilities of stairs instead. At risk of being betrayed by a creaking joist, Tod cat-creeps down as Corbeck explains to Margaret what's been going on in the, until then, rather complicated plot. Here is yet another staircase encounter and one that is also charged with considerable sexual tension, for Tod only now realizes that his relationship with Margaret is under threat. Corbeck has begun to take her away from him, just, indeed, as Tera will continue to do as the story unfolds. When the conversation between Corbeck and Margaret reaches its peak, Tod strikes a match and lights a cigarette, a traditionally phallic gesture that attempts to put Corbeck in his place.

"I suppose you heard all that?" Corbeck snaps.

"I did, some of it," Tod replies, later agreeing that Tera has some kind of power.

"Good, I'm glad we don't have to convince you," Corbeck sneers, having poured scorn on Tod's academic investigations into what Corbeck calls "parapsychology, the paranormal plane. Telekinesis: The Modern Approach." This cellar is the heart of the film, the place where Tera is ultimately reincarnated, just as the vault in *Dracula* is another place of resurrection and immolation. (Dracula also takes up residence in the cellars of Hammer's *Dracula* and *Dracula Has Risen from the Grave.*)

It seems that Hammer films are connected by a subterranean network of cellars. Peter Cushing's most ruthless incarnation as Frankenstein in *Frankenstein Must Be Destroyed* (dir. Terence Fisher, 1969) also chooses a cellar in which to conduct his experiments in brain transplantation. When the police call, the psychological symbolism of cellars as places of guilty secrets is made explicit as we see Simon Ward as the baron's unwilling assistant, pretending to decorate the stair banisters, having papered over the door leading down to the cellar laboratory.

In *The Curse of the Mummy's Tomb*, Hammer put their Mummy in a cellar which provided handy access to the sewers wherein the film's (presumably rather smelly) finale takes place, and all these examples follow the time-honored tradition of earlier Gothic cinema. Universal's *The Black Cat* had also placed the devil worshippers below stairs, along with Boris Karloff's collection of previous wives, embalmed, as they are, in glass cases for con-

The Stairway to Heaven in *A Matter of Life and Death* (dir. Michael Powell, Emeric Pressburger, 1946).

venient viewing. Ulmer's film was an art deco extravaganza. In Amicus' *Dr. Terror's House of Horrors* (dir. Freddie Francis, 1965), a humble coal cellar proves to be the resting place of a werewolf called Cosmo Waldemar. Architect Jim Dawson (Neil McCallum) discovers Waldemar's coffin while making alterations to the house he sold to a certain Mrs. Biddulph (Ursula Howells), who turns out to be a werewolf herself. Far better that he should have remained upstairs.

One of Hammer's most powerful uses of cellar imagery occurs in "The Silent Scream" (dir. Alan Gibson, 1980), an episode from the TV series *The Hammer House of Horror*, in which Peter Cushing plays an ex–Nazi who has perfected a means of training humans beings through fear, like animals. He ensnares an ex-convict in the cellar of his innocent-looking pet shop, but eventually ends up imprisoned himself. By contrast, in *The Ghoul* (dir. Freddie Francis, 1975), Cushing kept his monster upstairs. The Ghoul of the title, the degenerate son of theologian Dr. Lawrence (Cushing), feeds on the flesh of passing strangers. After the Ghoul has ritually slaughtered them in the bedroom, the corpses are then carved up in the kitchen by Gwen Watford's sinister Ayah, who efficiently preserves her choice cuts in a barrel of salt for future meals. Corrupted beyond redemption while in India with his father, the Ghoul (played by Don Henderson) still wears a sarong (blood-stained, of course) even in the middle of chilly English marshland, but as the vegetarian Dr. Lawrence keeps the place so warm, western dress (especially when consuming the flesh of damsels in distress) does seem somewhat superfluous. This ghoul is the same kind of character as *The Beast in the Cellar* (dir. James Kelley, 1970) whom we later learn is the brother of two middle-aged ladies (played by Flora Robson and Beryl Reid) who have incarcerated him there to prevent him from having to enlist during the second world war. He'd have been far better off on the front line, having by now turned into a ravening beast. That all these monsters are differentiated from the normal everyday world by environments either elevated or subterranean aptly demonstrates the powerful psychological power of staircases, which in horror always lead to hell.

Two

Sturm und Drang

The prelude to full-blooded German Romanticism in the nineteenth century was a movement known as *Sturm und Drang*. It borrowed its name from a play about the American War of Independence, written in 1776 by the German playwright Friedrich Maximilian Klinger (1752–1831). All the leading minds of the day were caught up in its liberating aesthetic. Goethe, Schiller, Herder and Rousseau in literature and Haydn, C.P.E. Bach, Mozart and Beethoven in music (to name but eight of *Sturm und Drang*'s greatest exponents) experimented with its proto–Romantic issues: freedom, individualism, the irrational, the expression of personal emotion, despair, fear, even eroticism, all those things, indeed, which had been regarded with some suspicion in the Age of Reason that had preceded and now mingled with it. As the new eighteenth-century movement progressed, Gothic novelists added an extra dose of the sublime and supernaturalism to the mix. By this time the gigantic soufflé of the Romantic generation had burst out of the European oven and overwhelmed everything. It was appropriate that the movement was called "Storm and Stress." The emotions it discussed were certainly stressful, and the way in which they were conveyed was certainly stormy, but was it so very different from the manner in which the passions had been expressed before?

As Ann Radcliffe was very much aware, many elements of the kind of Gothic fiction with which she had so much success had been created by Shakespeare. Indeed, she was very keen to be compared with the Immortal Bard, and regularly quoted from him in the epigrams she placed beneath the chapter headings in her novels. Sometimes she deliberately wrote scenes that echoed Shakespearean situations, as, for example, in *The Mysteries of Udolpho* (1794), when Emily hears the wicked Montoni with his henchmen in the castle hall below her chamber:

> She distinguished, till a late hour, the distant carousals of Montoni and his companions—the loud contest, the dissolute laugh and the choral song, that made the halls re-echo.[1]

This seems to be a direct reference to Act I, Scene 4 of *Hamlet*, when Hamlet explains the sound of trumpets and ordnance to Horatio while they are waiting for the Ghost on the battlements of Elsinore:

> The king doth wake to-night and takes his rouse,
> Keeps wassail, and the swaggering up-spring reels;
> And as he drains his draughts of Rhenish down,
> The kettle-drum and trumpet thus bray out
> The triumph of his pledge.[2]

When Mrs. Radcliffe's novel *The Romance of the Forest* (1791) was performed as a play at Covent Garden in 1794 under the title *Fontainville Forest*, Drury Lane, the other legitimate

"[T]here came I, / Pierced in the throat, fleeing away on foot, / And bloodying the plain. Here sight and speech / Fail'd me; and, finishing with Mary's name, / I fell, and tenantless my flesh remain'd." Gustave Doré illustration (1867) for Canto V of the "Pugatorio" from Dante's *The Divine Comedy*.

theater at the time, felt that the only way to lure crowds away from Covent Garden was to put on a production of Shakespeare's *Macbeth*.³ Mrs. Radcliffe was certainly thought to be as good as Shakespeare by many of her fellow writers. Thomas De Quincey called her "the great enchantress."⁴ John Keats, in a letter to his friend John Hamilton Reynolds, advised him to

> Buy a girdle — put a pebble in your mouth — loosen your braces — for I am going among scenery whence I intend to tip you the Damosel Radcliffe — I'll cavern you, and grotto you, and waterfall you, and wood you, and water you, and immense-rock you, and tremendous-sound you, and solitude you. I'll make a lodgment on your glacis by a row of Pines, and storm your covered way with bramble Bushes.⁵

In *Childe Harold's Pilgrimage*, Lord Byron left no doubt as to the literary standing of Mrs. Radcliffe in a stanza that discusses his love of Venice. (Unlike Byron, Mrs. Radcliffe had never been to Venice but her descriptions of it were perhaps even better than the real thing.)

> I loved her from my boyhood: she to me
> Was as a fairy city of the heart,
> Rising like water-columns from the sea,
> Of joy the sojurn, and of wealth the mart;
> And Otway, Radcliffe, Schiller, Shakespeare's art
> Had stamp'd her image in me, and even so,
> Although I found her thus, we did not part,
> Perchance even dearer in her day of woe,
> Than when she was a boast, a marvel, and a show.⁶

Anonymous illustration for Byron's "Ode on Venice" from a nineteenth century edition of *Byron's Poetical Works.*

We've already explored the Gothic qualities of *Hamlet*, and one could obviously isolate similarly Gothic elements in *Macbeth*, but Shakespeare is at his most consistently Gothic in his use of bad weather as an expression of the turmoil felt by his characters. This is the metaphoric device which the Victorian art critic John Ruskin described in his monumental *Modern Painters* as the "pathetic fallacy." No Gothic film would be complete without a thunderstorm, and Shakespeare certainly put storms center stage to create similar effects. Both *Macbeth* and *The Tempest* start with thunder and lightning even before any words have been spoken, and Shakespeare brings on a storm at the beginning of Act II of *Othello* as he stirs the action of the play itself: the storm at sea, that brings Desdemona to Cyprus, anticipates the terrible storm of jealousy that will lead to Othello's murder of her there. King Lear's speech, when he finds himself destitute on a windswept moor, is the ultimate use of storm imagery to express the passions:

> Blow, winds, and crack your cheeks! rage! blow!
> You cataracts and hurricanoes, spout
> Till you have drench'd our steeples, drown'd the cocks!
> You sulphurous and thought-executing fires,
> Vaunt-couriers to oak-cleaving thunderbolts,
> Singe my white head! And thou, all-shaking thunder
> Strike flat the thick rotundity o' the world![7]

Storms also play their part in Radcliffe's repertoire of Gothic effects. She never overdoes them, preferring for the most part to allow her heroines ample opportunities to admire glorious sunsets, but when a storm *is* needed, she happily obliges. In *The Romance of the Forest* Pierre de la Motte has to go into exile due to his financial embarrassment; to reflect his state of mind, the weather is appropriately "dark and tempestuous":

> The "pitiless pelting" of the storm, which, at this time, beat with increasing fury upon La Motte, inclined him to give up the attempt of proceeding further till day-light.[8]

Later in the story, the heroine, Adeline, "almost wished to have witnessed the tremendous effect of a thunder storm in these regions"[9] so that she could compare its effect with those she has no doubt read about in the pages of Edmund Burke. She is not disappointed, for on the following page, Mrs. Radcliffe provides us with a particularly spectacular example:

> It was evening when they came within view of the lake, which the travellers rejoiced to see, for the storm so long threatened was now fast approaching; the thunder murmured among the alps; and the dark vapours that rolled heavily along their sides heightened their dreadful sublimity. La Luc would have quickened his pace, but the road winding down the steep side of a mountain made caution necessary. The darkening air and the lightnings that now flashed along the horizon terrified Clara, but she withheld the expression of her fear in consideration of her father. A peal of thunder, which seemed to shake the earth to its foundations, and was reverberated in tremendous echoes from the cliffs, burst over their heads.[10]

The delightful terror of thunderstorms obviously appealed to musicians of the Romantic period not only because the sound of a storm so readily lends itself to musical imitation but also because storms provided an excellent metaphor for so much that was encapsulated in the word "Romantic": violence, terror, pantheism, sublimity and so forth. Beginning with the storm in Beethoven's Sixth Symphony (the "Pastoral"), one could compile a catalogue of musical storms that owe their inspiration to the literary tradition of the sublime. Rossini included storms in his operas *The Barber of Seville* (1816), *La Cenerentola* (1817) and *William Tell* (1829). For Berlioz, however, the storm in the famous *William Tell* Overture wasn't anywhere near as impressive as Beethoven's for, in his opinion, "the musician is always in evidence.... Beethoven on the other hand has known how to reveal himself wholly to the attentive listener: it is no longer an orchestra that one hears, it is no longer music, but rather the tumultuous voice of the heavenly torrents blended with the uproar of the earthly ones, with the furious claps of thunder, with the crashing of uprooted trees, with the gusts of an exterminating wind, with the frightened cries of men and the lowing of the herds. This is terrifying, it makes one shudder, the illusion is complete. The emotion that Rossini arouses in the same situation falls far short of attaining the same [effect]."[11]

Considering that highly charged description, Berlioz's own musical storm in his *Symphonie fantastique* (1830) seems curiously understated, but no less atmospheric in its own way. It occurs in the third movement ("Scène aux champs") for which he created a novel effect of distant rumbling thunder by using a quartet of timpani each tuned to a different pitch. (James Bernard was also to use this musical effect in the courtroom scenes of *Frankenstein Created Woman* [dir. Terence Fisher, 1967], though the only brewing storm in that situation is the array of emotions on display.) Liszt, one of Bernard's favorite composers, also wrote a storm for the piano ("Orage") in the first book of his *Années de pèlerinage* (1855), while Wagner's overture to *Der Fliegende Holländer* (1843) must surely rank as one of the windiest pieces of music ever written. The same composer's god of thunder, Donner, summons a storm at the end of the first *Ring* cycle opera *Das Rheingold* (1869); the second *Ring* opera, *Die Walküre* (1870), also opens with a storm. After all that, it was hardly surprising that Richard Strauss, who continued the Wagnerian tradition into the twentieth century, should have composed a spectacular storm of his own in his *Alpensinfonie* (1915). Replete with wind machine, it's perhaps the most realistic musical impression of Nature's most dramatic effect, and the true fulfillment of Berlioz's tempestuous effusion in response to Beethoven. Strauss was much more sanguine about it, having composed it merely to fill in the time while waiting for an opera libretto. It apparently gave him "less pleasure than shaking maybugs off trees."[12] Admirer of Nietzsche that he was, he originally intended to call it *The Antichrist*, "because in it there is: moral purification by means of one's own strength, liberation through work, worship of glorious, eternal nature,"[13] but he no doubt realized that such a title would have been misunderstood and so chose a less inflammatory one. Though Strauss' musical style went on to inspire a host of Hollywood film scores, he disliked the cinema personally and never considered writing for it (an odd prejudice for such a money-obsessed composer). In 1941, however, he did *appear* in a film version of the Alpine Symphony, which intercut shots of him conducting with appropriate mountain views.

None of these musical storms would have existed had it not been for the literary aesthetic that promoted a particular way of looking at this natural phenomenon, and as the Gothic tradition developed, storms became increasingly significant. A particularly violent one appears in the fourth chapter of Charles Maturin's Gothic romance *Melmoth the Wanderer* (1820):

> [T]he evening came on, prematurely darkened by clouds that seemed surcharged with a deluge. Loud and sudden squalls of wind shook the house from time to time, and then as suddenly ceased. Towards night the storm came on in all its strength; Melmoth's bed was shaken so as to render it impossible to sleep. He "liked the rocking of the battlements," but by no means liked the expected fall of the chimneys, the crashing in of the roof, and the splinters of the broken windows that were already scattered about his room. He rose and went down to the kitchen, where he knew a fire was burning, and there the terrified servants were all assembled, all agreeing, as the blast came roaring down the chimney, they never had witnessed such a storm, and between the gusts, breathing shuddering prayers for those who were "out at sea that night."[14]

This storm introduces us to Melmoth, the immortal wanderer of the title. Like Wagner's Flying Dutchman, this doomed, demonic anti-hero could hardly arrive any other way, washed up on shore after a shipwreck, in a manner which fellow Irish writer Bram Stoker must surely have remembered when writing his own storm sequence in *Dracula*:

> The wind roared like thunder, and blew with such force that it was with difficulty that even strong men kept their feet, or clung with grim clasp to the iron stanchions. It was found necessary to clear the entire piers from the mass of onlookers, or else the fatalities of the night would have been increased manifold. To add to the difficulties and dangers of the time, masses of sea-fog came drifting inland — white, wet clouds, which swept by in ghostly fashion, so dank and damp and cold that it needed but little effort of imagination to think that the spirits of those lost at sea were touching their living brethren with the clammy hands of death, and many a one shuddered as the wreaths of sea-mist swept by. At times the mist cleared, and the sea for some distance could be seen in the glare of the lightning, which now came thick and fast, followed by such sudden peals of thunder that the whole sky overhead seemed trembling under the shock of the footsteps of the storm. Some of the scenes thus revealed were of immeasurable grandeur and of absorbing interest — the sea, running mountains high, threw skywards with each wave mighty masses of white foam, which the tempest seemed to snatch at and whirl away into space; here and there a fishing-boat, with a rag of sail, running madly for shelter before the blast; now and again the white wings of a storm-tossed sea-bird.[15]

Stoker may also have recalled Shelley's poem "A Vision of the Sea" (1820):

> The vessel, now tossed
> Through the low-trailing rack of the tempest, is lost
> In the skirts of the thunder-cloud: now down the sweep
> Of the wind-cloven wave to the chasm of the deep
> It sinks, and the walls of the watery vale
> Whose depths of dread calm are unmoved by the gale,
> Dim mirrors of ruin, hang gleaming about [...]
> The intense thunder-balls which are raining from Heaven
> Have shattered its mast, and it stands black and riven.
> The chinks suck destruction. The heavy dead hulk
> On the living sea rolls an inanimate bulk,
> Like a corpse on the clay which is hungering to fold
> Its corruption around it.[16]

This is exactly the kind of storm imagery we find in Christopher Isherwood's adaptation of Mary Shelley's *Frankenstein*, which was originally made for television and later released as *Frankenstein — The True Story* (dir. Jack Smight, 1973). The title might lead us to expect a faithful adaptation of the novel, which it is not, but it is true in the sense that it attempts to relate the historical personages of the haunted summer of 1816 when the story was written, to characters in the novel. Unfortunately, the opening scenes which recreated the Geneva house party (uniting Percy and Mary Shelley with, among others, Lord Byron and Dr. Polidori) were cut from the finished film. Consequently, we lose Isherwood's illuminating conceit in which Byron becomes Clerval (both roles played by David McCallum), Shelley becomes Frankenstein (Leonard Whiting), Mary Shelley becomes Elizabeth Frankenstein (Nicola Pagett) and James Mason's Polidori remains Polidori throughout, but becomes the equivalent of Ernest Thesiger's Dr. Pretorius in *Bride of Frankenstein*. In Isherwood's version of events, Polidori creates a beautiful female creature called Prima (played by Jane Seymour), who has the misfortune of having her head pulled off by Michael Sarrazin's maltreated Creature. Towards the end of the film, Frankenstein attempts to escape his creation by setting sail for pastures new, but the Creature follows, as does Polidori. During a storm

"Though here and there the hapless mast and shroud / Mark the sad gulf where half a kingdom slips." Drawing by E. M. Wimperis (engraved by W. Thomas), for the poem "Truth" by J.S.W. in *The Quiver, an Illustrated Magazine for Sunday and General Reading,* Vol. III, London, Cassell, Petter, and Galpin, 1868, p. 233.

at sea, Polidori is struck by lightning (a nicely ironic touch as he is not only terrified by lightning but also prides himself on a more sophisticated, purely chemical means of inducing life into his creature. (In this version, Frankenstein's is the product of sunlight rather than storm.) The Creature takes command of the ship and steers it to the North Pole, where Isherwood, loosely following Mary Shelley's plot, brings creator and created to their doom, crushed beneath an avalanche of snow and ice.

As a young man, Shelley had also enthusiastically devoured Gothic romances, as he explained in the fifth stanza of his "Hymn to Intellectual Beauty" (1816):

> While yet a boy I sought for ghosts, and sped
>   Through many a listening chamber, cave and ruin,
> And starlight wood, with fearful steps pursuing
>   Hopes of high talk with the departed dead.[17]

He had written two Gothic romances of his own in his youth and storm imagery plays its part in both of them. We only have to read three pages before a storm appears in the first of these, *Zastrozzi* (1810). The second, *St. Irvyne, or The Rosicrucian,* plunges immediately into

> Red thunder-clouds, borne on the wings of the midnight whirlwind, floated, at fits, athwart the crimson-coloured orbit of the moon; the rising fierceness of the blast sighed through the stunted shrubs, which, bending before its violence, inclined towards the rocks whereon they grew: over the blackened expanse of heaven, at intervals, was spread the blue lightning's flash; it played upon the granite heights, and, with momentary brilliancy, disclosed the terrific scenery of the Alps, whose gigantic and misshapen summits, reddened by the transitory moonbeams, were crossed by black fleeting fragments of the tempest-clouds. The rain, in big drops, began to descend, and the thunder-peals, with louder and more deafening crash, to shake the zenith, till the long-protracted war, echoing from cavern to cavern, died, in indistinct murmurs, amidst the far-extended chain of mountains.[18]

Thunder was one of Shelley's favorite images, and similar Gothic storms feature in much of his poetry. In *The Witch of Atlas* (1824) for example, he writes:

> [T]he outer lake beneath the lash
>   Of the wind's scourge, foamed like a wounded thing,
> And the incessant hail with stony clash
>   Ploughed up the waters, and the flagging wing
> Of the roused cormorant in the lightning flash
>   Looked like the wreck of some wind-wandering
> Fragment of inky thunder-smoke[.][19]

There is so much sea storm imagery in Shelley's work that it seems his fate of drowning in a sea storm was inevitable. With hindsight, his writing indeed has a terrible sense of premonition about it. Even his early poem *The Revolt of Islam* (1817) has a storm at sea:

> Hark! 'tis the rushing of a wind that sweeps
>   Earth and ocean. See! the lightnings yawn
> Deluging Heaven with fire, and the lashed deeps
>   Glitter and boil beneath: it rages on,
>   One mighty stream, whirlwind and waves upthrown,
> Lightning, and hail, and darkness eddying by.[20]

Sea storms were for most of the time well beyond Hammer's budgets. *The Lost Continent* (dir. Michael Carreras, 1968) had one, but none of the company's Dracula pictures managed to put out to sea. A brief but effective sea storm on board ship formed part of

Tod Browning's 1931 *Dracula* but audiences had to wait until the BBC mounted its own television production of Stoker's novel in 1977 before an adaptation of *Dracula* got the sea storm it really deserved. Before the '70s were out, John Badham mounted an even more spectacular storm for his version of Stoker's novel starring Frank Langella in the title role, in which the count meets his end at sea, hoisted into the deadly sunshine on a flagpole. It's again symptomatic of Hammer's original approach to Gothic that not only was there no sea storm in their first *Dracula*, but also no thunder on the soundtrack. The 1958 *Dracula* takes place in fine weather throughout — yet another way Terence Fisher attempted to distance himself from the Gothic clichés of Hollywood horrors (though it has to be said that the 1931 *Dracula* is similarly un-thunderous). Of course, things changed with Hammer's Dracula sequels, thunder and lightning fulfilling in them exactly the same function they had had in the works of Shelley, Radcliffe and Shakespeare. That function was what Shelley, in his *Hymn to Intellectual Beauty*, had called "awful LOVELINESS" and which Edmund Burke had defined as the sublime pleasure of terror (see chapter four).

One of Hammer's most sublime storm scenes occurs in *Dracula Has Risen from the Grave*, in which Rupert Davies' Monsignor Muller travels to Castle Dracula to exorcise it. He carries a giant crucifix from the local church up the mountain and secures it to the giant doors of the castle. Then, with traditional bell, book and candle (the tinkle of the bell sounds particularly vulnerable against James Bernard's sepulchral underscore) he begins to intone the Latin service of exorcism. This authentic touch adds a powerful sense of dignity, dread (and imminent catastrophe) to the proceedings:

> *Exorcizo te, immundissime spiritus, omnis incursio adversarii, omne phantasma, omnis legio, in nomine Domini nostri Jesu Christi eradicare, et effugare ab hoc plasmate Dei. Ipse tibi imperat, qui te de supernis caelorum in inferiora terrae demergi praecepit. Ipse tibi imperat, qui mari, ventis et tempestatibus imperavit.*

The Latin here summons a similar kind of demonic *frisson* to that of the plainsong melody of the "Dies Irae" sequence, which composers such as Harry Robinson often incorporated into their scores for Hammer horrors. (Indeed, the subsidiary theme of Bernard's main title music for *Dracula Has Risen from the Grave* also echoes the "Dies Irae" melody.) However, before the monsignor can complete his ceremony, a storm (symptomatic of the wrath of God or the Devil — or both) grows to such a tempest of thunder and wind that the candle is extinguished and his words are drowned out by the sound effects. Hammer intercut their shots of lightning from stock footage, as usual, but the novel use of filters by director Freddie Francis and cinematographer Arthur Grant add a suitable sense of weirdness to this impressive scene that introduces the resurrection of Dracula from his icy grave a few moments later.

Of course, storms had a more functional part to play in so many film adaptations of Frankenstein, for without them the Creature could not have been brought to life. We've discussed some exceptions to this: Cushing's Frankenstein often relies on surgery, while Leonard Whiting's Frankenstein used sunlight. Mary Shelley does not mention a storm in her famously muted passage about the animation of the Creature. All she allows Frankenstein to say is, "It was on a dreary night of November that I beheld the accomplishment of my toils,"[21] and November is hardly the most likely time of year in which to experience a thunderstorm. All Frankenstein lets us know of the process is that "I collected the instruments of life around me, that I might infuse a spark of being into the lifeless thing that lay at my feet,"[22] and it was this spark of life which was amplified into the full-blown electric storm of the 1931 *Frankenstein*; director James Whale was no doubt influenced by Percy Shelley's own fascination with thunder and lightning. As Mary used the novel to present a critique of male Romantic idealism (an idealism that brings nothing but death and disaster in its wake), it was an obvious correlation to make. Shelley indeed saw himself as a storm, and in his "Ode to the West Wind" (1820) expressed the wish to share the power of a storm wind to transform the world from a place of tyranny to a paradise of liberty:

> Angels of rain and lightning: there are spread
> On the blue surface of thine aëry surge,
> Like the bright hair uplifted from the head
>
> Of some fierce Maenad, even from the dim verge
> Of the horizon to the zenith's height,
> The locks of the approaching storm.
>
> …
>
> Drive my dead thoughts over the universe
> Like withered leaves to quicken a new birth![23]

Unfortunately, like Frankenstein, Shelley's dreams of changing the world failed, and yet the urgency of his message remains undimmed. His obsessive sense of union with the Promethean power of storms was nicely captured in *Gothic* (1986), Ken Russell's cinematic interpretation of the events of the haunted Geneva summer of 1816. During a storm, Shelley (played by Julian Sands) is discovered cavorting naked on the parapets of the Villa Diodati communing with the thunderbolts. While Peter Cushing never stripped off in such a manner, one might say that his approach to the role of Frankenstein was also informed by the boundless optimism and determination of Shelley. It was certainly in marked contrast to Colin Clive's presentation of Frankenstein as an unbalanced neurotic in James Whale's two earlier Frankenstein films. Clive's Frankenstein is even bullied into taking up his scalpel by Dr. Pretorius in *Bride of Frankenstein*. One could never imagine Cushing succumbing to such an indignity. Neither can one really imagine Clive convincingly reading the last steely lines of Shelley's "Ode to the West Wind":

> Scatter, as from an unextinguished hearth
> Ashes and sparks, my words among mankind!
> Be through my lips to unawakened earth
>
> The trumpet of a prophecy! O, Wind,
> If Winter comes, can Spring be far behind?[24]

One *can*, however, imagine Cushing imbuing these lines with the appropriate, utterly committed and ruthless idealism that he brought to Frankenstein. It was an approach which combined all that Shelley understood by the term "Romantic" with the efficiency of a "modern" middle-class professional, exactly the type of person, indeed, to whom Harold MacMillan was referring when claiming that voters "had never had it so good" in 1950s Britain. Cushing himself recognized this, pointing out that despite the title of his third portrayal of the role in *The Evil of Frankenstein* (dir. Freddie Francis, 1964), the baron was ruthlessly idealistic rather than downright evil.[25] That's a little hard to swallow in his most sadistic manifestation in *Frankenstein Must Be Destroyed* (dir. Terence Fisher, 1969) but it certainly holds for the others.

Cushing played a rather more benevolent and absent-minded scientist in *The Creeping Flesh* (dir. Freddie Francis, 1972). As Emmanuel Hildern, he unwittingly resurrects the fossilized remains of an ancient skeleton he's discovered on a field trip, and it turns out to be

The product of a storm: Boris Karloff as the Monster in *Frankenstein* (dir, James Whale, 1931).

the embodiment of evil. At first the evil is controlled: he wipes water over the skeleton's bony finger and when it starts to rejuvenate, he promptly chops it off. Then he discovers that such a resurrection has been prophesied: the ancient fossil is the storm god and it is a storm that will revive him. When Christopher Lee, playing Cushing's ruthlessly ambitious brother, steals his sibling's great discovery, his coach is involved in an accident during a violent thunderstorm and the skeleton is subjected to a thorough drenching. Now fully restored to life, it makes its way back to Cushing's home to exact revenge. Our last glimpse of poor Emmanuel Hildern shows us that he too is missing a finger.

Long before this late flowering of British Gothic cinema, American horror films had also been thunderous (and soggy) affairs. After the storms of James Whale's Frankenstein films, the storms of Universal Studios became increasingly sublime. *Son of Frankenstein* is awash with storms, which drench the dripping umbrellas of the villagers who greet Basil Rathbone's Frankenstein and his family at the railway station. Winds howl around the stylized Gothic castle, whose weird and wonderful staircase has already been discussed, and lightning streaks the skies beyond the windows of the baronial study. *The Black Cat* also begins with a storm that's so violent it causes a landslide and forces the romantic leads, in the company of Bela Lugosi, to finish their bus journey to Boris Karloff's art deco mansion on foot. A landslide similarly features in James Whale's even more sodden *The Old Dark House* (1932), the soundtrack of which is a veritable catalogue of storm effects: lashing rain, rolling thunder and every kind of wind one could imagine. There are howling gales, eerie moanings and literal curtain-raisers whenever a window or door is opened. The sound of wind is virtually continuous throughout, and is used in such a musical manner that there is no need for an underscore, which Whale sensibly eschews. The sound effects provide all the atmosphere required for this macabre farce about a mad Welsh family who takes in a group of strangers, lost in the storm. When we follow Raymond Massey's Philip Waverton upstairs to the mysterious bedroom wherein the ancient head of the household, Sir Roderick Femm, lies in bed, the wind is muted to create a truly disturbing, eerie moan. Before that, Melvyn Douglas as Roger Penderel parodies the song "Singin' in the Rain" as the car that drives him through a torrentially wet Wales gets stuck in a flood; Gloria Stuart as Margaret Waverton complains of feeling like a drowned rat, and there's some kidding about the cliché "raining in buckets." Even when dealing with science fiction the following year, Whale couldn't resist a snowstorm to open his production of *The Invisible Man* (1933), and neither could William Wyler in the mildly Gothic romance *Wuthering Heights* (1939).

Actors in horror films have to be prepared to be thoroughly soaked, often under considerable makeup. Fredric March's Mr. Hyde revels in a cloudburst in Rouben Mamoulian's adaptation of *Dr. Jekyll and Mr. Hyde* (1931). His simian features respond to the rain in an almost orgasmic manner, and his subsequent promenade through the drenched passageways of Victorian London is truly the Gothic equivalent of Gene Kelly's dance routine in *Singin' in the Rain* (dir. Stanley Donen, 1952).

But rain is, of course, more often depressive in its effect. In one of the stories by Ray Bradbury which were adapted in *The Illustrated Man* (dir. Jack Smight, 1969), "The Long Rain" which endlessly pelts the surface of Venus drives two shipwrecked astronauts to suicide. "It pounds you, the rain," says Rod Steiger's space commander, echoing the sentiments expressed in Somerset Maugham's earlier tale "Rain," which is set in Samoa. "If only it would stop raining for a single day it wouldn't be so bad," says Dr. Macphail, in this very different story, which nonetheless exploits the same depressive effect of relentlessly wet weather. Maugham describes the rain as "unmerciful and somehow terrible.... It did not pour, it flowed. It was like a deluge from heaven, and it rattled on the roof of corrugated iron with a steady persistence that was maddening. It seemed to have a fury of its own. And sometimes you felt that you must scream if it did not stop, and then suddenly you felt powerless, as though your bones had suddenly become soft; and you were miserable and hopeless."[26] Though "Rain" is not Gothic, its use of bad weather is. Following Maugham's

Boris Karloff and Bela Lugosi in *Son of Frankenstein* (dir. Rowland V. Lee, 1939).

example, Bryan Forbes' *Séance on a Wet Afternoon* (1964) also included a reference to precipitation in its title. The film concerns a fake medium (played by Kim Stanley) whose husband (Richard Attenborough) kidnaps a girl to give his wife an opportunity to help the police locate the girl by "psychic means" and thus gain the recognition she craves. The atmospheric presentation of the psychic's gloomy mansion lends this thriller its Gothic credentials, but its most impressive section is perhaps its main title sequence. Accompanied by John Barry's evocative Raindrop Prelude, we are shown various people leaving a séance and walking home through deserted suburban streets during an afternoon shower. The muted melancholy mood here belongs to a tradition that began with Poe in the famously dank introductory sentence of "The Fall of the House of Usher":

> During the whole of a dull, dark, and soundless day in the autumn of the year, when the clouds hung oppressively low in the heavens, I had been passing alone, on horseback, through a singularly dreary tract of country...[27]

Forbes' title sequence could, indeed, have been based on this passage, Poe's reference to riding on horseback notwithstanding.

So central are storms (particularly the thunderous variety) to Gothic tradition it was inevitable that Ken Russell should have included one in the climax of *Lisztomania* (1975), his wildly inventive biopic of Franz Liszt. In this underrated film, Russell intriguingly portrays Richard Wagner (played by Paul Nicholas) as a vampire who feeds musically off Liszt's own compositions (a very good way of pointing out what was no less than the truth). "I need your music to make my creations live!" Wagner hisses at Liszt through bared Hammer horror-style fangs. Russell then has the Abbé Liszt (played by Roger Daltrey) exorcise the Meister of Bayreuth with a flame-throwing piano which also blasts out Liszt's *Totentanz*, a series of variations for piano and orchestra based on the "Dies Irae" plainchant melody mentioned earlier. Appropriately enough, all this takes place during a highly Gothic thunderstorm that summons memories of every horror film ever made.

But there is more to Gothic than thunderstorms and staircases. Ruins are important too, as we shall see during our exploration of them in the next chapter.

Three

Ruins

It's rather surprising to discover on a close viewing of Hammer's Gothic horror films that there are relatively few that exploit the atmospheric potential of ruins. I'll be exploring why this might be the case later. For the moment, though, a few words on ruins themselves are in order, and we'll begin by returning to the opening of the second chapter of Ann Radcliffe's novel *The Romance of the Forest*. It begins with a page of supreme description, which is a virtual blueprint for all the literary and cinematic Gothic ruins that followed in its wake:

> He approached, and perceived the Gothic remains of an abbey: it stood on a kind of rude lawn, overshadowed by high and spreading trees, which seemed coeval with the building, and diffused a romantic gloom around. The greater part of the pile appeared to be sinking into ruins, and that, which had withstood the ravages of time, shewed the remaining features of the fabric more awful in decay. The lofty battlements, thickly enwreathed with ivy, were half demolished, and become the residence of birds of prey. Huge fragments of the eastern tower, which was almost demolished, lay scattered amid the high grass, that waved slowly to the breeze. "The thistle shook its lonely head; the moss whistled to the wind." A Gothic gate, richly ornamented with fret-work, which opened into the main body of the edifice, but which was now obstructed with brush-wood, remained entire. Above the vast and magnificent portal of this gate arose a window of the same order, whose pointed arches still exhibited fragments of stained glass, once the pride of monkish devotion. La Motte, thinking it possible it might yet shelter some human being, advanced to the gate and lifted a massy knocker. The hollow sounds rung through the emptiness of the place. After waiting a few minutes, he forced back the gate, which was heavy with iron work, and creaked harshly on its hinges.
>
> He entered what appeared to have been the chapel of the abbey, where the hymn of devotion had once been raised, and the tear of penitence had once been shed; sounds, which could now only be recalled by imagination — tears of penitence, which had been long since fixed in fate. La Motte paused a moment, for he felt a sensation of sublimity rising into terror — a suspension of mingled astonishment and awe!
>
> ...The deepening gloom reminded La Motte that he had no time to lose, but curiosity prompted him to explore further, and he obeyed the impulse. As he walked over the broken pavement, the sound of his steps ran in echoes through the place, and seemed like the mysterious accents of the dead, reproving the sacrilegious mortal who thus dared to disturb their precincts.[1]

Radcliffe, acknowledging her debt to the father of Gothic romance Horace Walpole, prefaced all this with a quotation from Walpole's *The Mysterious Mother*:

> How these antique towers and vacant courts
> Chill the suspended soul! Till expectation
> Wears the face of fear: and fear, half ready
> To become devotion, mutters a kind
> Of mental orison, it knows not wherefore.
> What kind of being is circumstance![2]

Gustave Doré illustration from *Les Contes de Perrault*, 1863.

Three. Ruins

The epigram demonstrates where Radcliffe is coming from, but her subsequent passage sensationally shows us where she's going. One can obviously draw comparisons with Charles D. Hall's sumptuously ruinous set for Universal's 1931 Castle Dracula. It too is "thickly enwreathed in ivy," "half demolished," and the residence, if not of birds of prey, then certainly of Universal Studio's bats. The full view of the set also reminds one of Radcliffe's words later in the passage above, that speak of "the nave of a great church," with "one window, more perfect than the rest."[3] It is as if Hall had this particular passage in mind when designing his celebrated scenes.

Bela Lugosi in *Dracula* (dir. Tod Browning, 1931).

Hammer rarely went quite so far. Bernard Robinson recycled the screen of Gothic arches that featured in the original *Dracula* for the ruins required by *The Hound of the Baskervilles* (dir. Terence Fisher, 1959), in which some of James Bernard's music from *Dracula* is also reprised, but these ruins were hardly very majestic. Far more so was Don Mingaye's set for the derelict Victorian church of St. Bartolph's in *Dracula A.D. 1972*. It was also rather more in the spirit of Radcliffe, which is rather ironic, given the film's intention to update the Dracula story. This church not only gave Mingaye an opportunity for Gothic arches but it also served to remind its original audience of the fate suffered by so many deconsecrated Victorian churches in the Britain of the 1970s. By the mid–Victorian period, Gothic had left its playful origins at Strawberry Hill far behind. Soon after Strawberry Hill came the perpendicular theatricality of William Beckford's Fonthill Abbey which we have already mentioned. After its final collapse in 1825, what remained of Fonthill became a very impressive Gothic ruin for several years until all the rubble was eventually cleared away. Beckford, who had sold the place some five years before, now had only memories of this grandest of Gothic follies. His description of its (too rapid) construction is itself a masterpiece of Gothic frisson:

> It's really stupendous, the spectacle here at night — the number of people at work, lit up by lads; the innumerable torches suspended everywhere, the immense and endless spaces, the gulph below; above, the gigantic spider's web of scaffolding — especially when, standing under the finished and numberless arches of the galleries, I listen to the reverberating voices in the stillness of the night, and see immense buckets of plaster and water ascending, as if they were drawn up from the bowels of a mine, amid shouts from subterranean depths, oaths from Hell itself, and chanting from Pandemonium or the synagogue....[4]

After Fonthill, the Gothic style increasingly became the architectural embodiment of Victorian moral rectitude. Under the watchful eye of its greatest champion Augustus Welby Pugin (1812–52), who designed most of the interiors of the Palace of Westminster in London, along with a great deal more elsewhere, Gothic became regarded as the most virtuous, because most Christian architectural style. Pugin regarded Gothic as far superior to the "pagan" associations of Renaissance style with its classical idioms, and along with the art critic John Ruskin, he believed that Gothic was the preeminent style in which to build all buildings, In his highly influential chapter "The Nature of Gothic" in *The Stones of Venice* (1853), Ruskin passionately argued that it was "not only the best, but the *only rational* architecture, as being that which can fit itself more easily to all services, vulgar or noble."[5] It was largely as a consequence of Ruskin's immense influence that so many nineteenth-century British town halls, those symbols of Victorian civic pride, and the many

The Guildhall, Northampton, designed between 1861 and 1864 by E. W. Godwin (photograph by the author).

Top, left: Main entrance to Strawberry Hill. *Top, right:* A staircase in the Guildhall. *Bottom:* Gothic chimney in the Great Parlour at Strawberry Hill (photographs by the author).

T. Raffles Davison, "The Grand Staircase," Manchester Town Hall, designed by Alfred Waterhouse, from *An Architectural and General Description of the Town Hall, Manchester* (ed. William E. A. Axon), Manchester and London, Abel Heywood & Son, 1878, p. 10.

T. Raffles Davison, "The Waiting Hall," Manchester Town Hall, designed by Alfred Waterhouse, from *An Architectural and General Description of the Town Hall, Manchester* (ed. William E. A. Axon), Manchester and London, Abel Heywood & Son, 1878, p. 8.

The 1992 extension to the Guildhall, designed in modern Gothic style by Stimpson Walton Bond (photograph by the author).

churches the Victorians built in order to strengthen the spine of Anglican Christianity in the wake of Darwin, were decorated and fenestrated with Gothic pointed arches. That Ruskin was often horrified by the way in which modern architects interpreted his noble medieval/Venetian ideals, didn't stop the buildings from being built.

The problem was that there were so many different ways of interpreting exactly what Gothic was. When a new church was commissioned, there was often confusion as to which type of Gothic should be adopted. Arbiters of taste in this department gathered around what was known as the Camden Society, and of the three basic types of Gothic, as originally defined by architect Thomas Rickman in 1817 (Early English, Decorated and Perpendicular), the Camden Society favored Decorated (a term largely defined by the elaborate tracery in Gothic windows of this type). In his study of *The Gothic Revival,* Kenneth Clarke thought this choice "was certainly the worst style for the Gothic Revival. Either of the other two styles was preferable. Early English needed very little detail which an ordinary craftsman could not manage; perpendicular was infinitely the most adaptable of medieval styles and the only one which had been widely applied to civil architecture. But the very simplicity of Early English meant a lack of those ecclesiological details which were the essential part of Camdenian doctrine."[6]

Even more unfortunate for these Victorian Gothic churches was that they had become profoundly unfashionable by the 1960s. One of their vast number, St. Clement's Church in Leeds suffered the same fate as so many of its fellows and was demolished in 1975, three years after the release of *Dracula A.D. 1972*. The wood carving, stone and stained glass ended up as landfill and the site eventually resembled the derelict wasteland in which Caroline Munro's severed head was discovered in that film. Mingaye's set for the derelict St. Bartolph's Church was therefore doubly melancholic: it exuded the traditional Radcliffean ambience of a Gothic ruin but also played on the audience's awareness of a Victorian heritage that was being ruthlessly demolished all around them by developers and modernist architects. (London's famous Victorian Highgate Cemetery might have suffered a similar fate had not the Friends of Highgate Cemetery come to its rescue in 1975. A few years before the involvement of FOHC, the cemetery had been used by Amicus for the main title sequences of two of its compendium horror films, *Tales from the Crypt* (dir. Freddie Francis, 1971) and *From Beyond the Grave* (dir. Kevin Connor, 1973), suggesting a similar yearning for the Victorian past that was in danger of being swept away forever.)

Dracula A.D. 1972 obviously dispensed with the lovingly recreated Victorian settings of Hammer's earlier films, though Mingaye did furnish Professor Van Helsing's study in a suitably dignified manner with antiques and oil paintings, and filled the elegantly curving bookcase with appropriate volumes on the occult sciences. It's fun trying to identify these (a pleasure reserved for chapter ten), along with the aspects of interior decor and *bric-a-brac* in Hammer's other films. Over the years, Peter Cushing was provided with some fascinating studies and places of work. One of the most interesting from our point of view can be found in *The Gorgon* where Cushing's Dr. Namaroff inhabits a room decorated with William Morris' "Daisy" wallpaper. That particular design was first made commercially available in 1864, so by the time of *The Gorgon*, which is set in 1910, Morris' design would presumably have had time to penetrate the indeterminate, middle–European locale of Vandorf where the action takes place; and it's further evidence of set designer Bernard Robinson's marvelous attention to detail. It's also revealing to note Hammer's delight in Victorian settings at a time when the reputation of Victorian art had reached its nadir amongst the arbiters of taste in the art establishment. That masterpiece of High Victorian painting, Frederic, Lord Leighton's *Flaming June*, for example, was discovered on a market

Gothic revival tomb at Kensal Green Cemetery, London (photograph by the author).

"Read me the lines that lie / Along that sunset sky." Drawing by E. M. Wimperis (engraved by W. Thomas), for the poem "A Reverie" by A. B. in *The Quiver, an Illustrated Magazine for Sunday and General Reading,* Vol. III, London, Cassell, Petter, and Galpin, 1868, p. 873.

Anonymous illustration (engraved by W. Thomas) of Winchester Cathedral, in *The Quiver, an Illustrated Magazine for Sunday and General Reading,* Vol. III, London, Cassell, Petter, and Galpin, 1868, p. 769. Winchester contains excellent examples of Early English, Decorated and (particularly in the nave) Perpendicular Gothic. Jane Austen is buried there.

Anonymous illustration (engraved by W. Thomas) of the Abbey Church of Iona in *The Quiver, an Illustrated Magazine for Sunday and General Reading,* Vol. III, London, Cassell, Petter, and Galpin, 1868, p. 641. The church had been left in ruins for centuries before its restoration in 1910. This illustration, lit by moonlight, was obviously informed by the spirit of Gothic romance.

Gothic revival tomb at Highgate Cemetery, London (photograph by the author).

Gothic revival tomb at Kensal Green Cemetery, London (photograph by the author).

trader's stall somewhere in Chelsea in 1963 — only the year before *The Gorgon* was released. It was selling for around £50 at the time, but no one seemed to want it. It was eventually acquired by art dealer Jeremy Maas who attempted to persuade museum directors to care for the painting, but no one was interested. It was eventually purchased by Luis Ferré, then the governor of Puerto Rico, which is where it remains to this day.[7] It's one of the ironies of history that Victorian art could fall into such contemptuous neglect by the art establishment at the same time that a highly successful film company was producing such beautifully mounted Victorian Gothic horror stories for an enthusiastic general public, and it reflects the complicated response there was to the social (and architectural) upheaval experienced by most British towns and cities at that time. These films were popular precisely because they offered a sense of stability and certainty in an increasingly unstable and uncertain world. For all the excitement of the swinging sixties, Rodgers and Hammerstein's *The Sound of Music* sold more records than anything by The Beatles. Most people wanted reassuring traditional values at this time of bewildering social change, and this explains the revival of interest in Victoriana that took place alongside the destruction of so much Victorian architecture (to say nothing of Victorian morality). While the young made fun of Victorian values, they also flirted with Victorian bric-a-brac. The Beatles themselves reflected the fashion trend for Victoriana on the cover of their *Sgt. Pepper* album. So did Michelangelo Antonioni, in the scene in *Blow Up* (1966) in which David Hemmings' photographer buys a propeller in an antique shop. Before Hemmings makes his eccentric purchase, Antonioni is keen to show us as much antique shop Victoriana as possible. Intriguingly, the shop manager is played by Susan Brodrick, who would later appear in the role of prim and proper (and very Victorian) Susan Spencer in *Dr. Jekyll and Sister Hyde*.[8]

Gothic revival tomb at Kensal Green Cemetery, London (photograph by the author).

As well as its Daisy wallpaper and Victorian interiors, *The Gorgon* also features Robinson's splendidly ruined set for the interior hall of Castle Borski, which at first sight seems to resemble the ruins of Radcliffe's *Romance of the Forest*, though the traditionally Gothic and ecclesiastical elements are largely missing here. Having said that, Robinson's trademark Solomonic or barley-sugar columns are very noticeable here, and they carry their own ecclesiastic and occult symbolism. This can be traced back to the rather vague Biblical descriptions of the two columns, called Boaz and Jachin, which stood on either side of the entrance to the Temple of Solomon in Jerusalem. We learn about the names in the second book of *Chronicles*, chapter III, verse 17, while the second book of *Kings*, chapter XXV, verse 17, describes them as being made of brass. So too was "the wreathen work, and pomegranates upon the chapter round about." Éliphas Lévi explained the occult significance of Boaz and Jachin as symbolizing "the procreative struggle between man and woman, for, according to the law of Nature, the woman must resist the man, and he must entice or overcome her. The active principle seeks the passive principle, the *plenum* desires the void, the serpent's jaw attracts the serpent's tail."[9]

Top: The Greek Revival Anglican Chapel, designed in 1836 by John Griffith, at Kensal Green Cemetery, London (photograph by the author). Griffith's chapel appears in *Theater of Blood* (dir. Douglas Hickox, 1973). *Bottom:* William Morris' "Daisy" wallpaper design, 1864.

No one, however, knows what these columns really looked liked. It's often thought that the barley-twist which characterizes Solomonic columns as we know them today more probably was derived from Trajan's column in Rome, but the barley-twist form also appears in Byzantine architectural decorations. We can only speculate. We do know, however, that in the fourth century, Constantine the Great brought examples of barley-twist columns to Rome and installed them in the altar of the original basilica of St. Peter. It was thought that Constantine's gift originally came from Solomon's temple — not the original one, which was destroyed by the Babylonians in 257 B.C., but the second temple. It's unlikely that they came from either. They probably originated in Greece, but the important thing was that this kind of column became firmly associated with the Temple of Solomon[10] and because of their connection with St. Peter's in Rome, it seemed logical to Bernini that Solomonic columns should support that sculptor's famous Baldacchino there, which was completed in 1633. Bernini's columns set a fashion, and soon the use of Solomonic columns became widespread. Surprisingly, given that Solomonic columns were rare in British architecture, they also form part of the interior decoration of St. Mary's Church in Whitby. (In its churchyard, Dracula first attacks Lucy in Stoker's novel.) Predominantly, however, they were associated with Catholic Europe and this was why they weren't so popular in Protestant England.

I think it's significant that Robinson should emphasize Solomonic columns over Gothic arches in so many of his designs for Hammer's Gothic films, for his choice raises the interesting question of just how Gothic Hammer was. By using an architectural motif that was associated with Catholic Europe, Robinson was helping to articulate Hammer's connection with the symbolist and decadent movements, both of which were focused on Catholic France. We'll be dealing with this subject in more detail in chapter seven.

Hammer's most Radcliffian Gothic moment wasn't in a film but rather in what was originally a vinyl LP record, issued by EMI in 1974. Over a mix of atmospheric sound effects and the sepulchrally resonant music of James Bernard, Christopher Lee intoned a Dracula story specially written by ex–*Doctor Who* writer Don Houghton (who had also scripted Hammer's two modern-dress Dracula films). The ruinous Gothic mood which this recording manages so powerfully to achieve, largely depends on the interaction of these elements, and sometimes, the sound effects alone translate into purely sonic terms the mood of Rad-

St. Mary's Church, Whitby (photograph by the author).

cliffe's *The Romance of the Forest*. The following lines from Radcliffe are closely replicated on the recording:

> La Motte, thinking it possible it might yet shelter some human being, advanced to the gate and lifted a massy knocker. The hollow sounds rung through the emptiness of the place. After waiting a few minutes, he forced back the gate, which was heavy with iron work, and creaked harshly on its hinges.[11]

The following extracts from Houghton's script for the Hammer *Dracula with Christopher Lee* LP demonstrate the considerable influence of Radcliffe's marvelous invention on an example of popular Gothic entertainment from the mid–1970s. A coach carrying a man and a woman on the eve of their wedding loses a wheel near Castle Dracula. As the coachman inspects the damage, the girl wanders to the side of the road, attracted by a light she can see through "the curtain of trees" (which we can compare with the "brushwood" of Radcliffe). Eventually the girl sees "the grey bulk of a silent, towering castle," the windows of which stare down "like eyeless sockets." Like La Motte, the girl is drawn by curiosity into the Gothic space within:

> The hall was vaulted like a lofty crypt. And at the far end was a wide, winding stairway, guarded at its foot by two stone pillars.
>
> It was not the gloom of the place that sent a shiver of dread clutching at her heart. It was the atmosphere, the scent of death that pervaded the damp air, the sour smell of decay. It clung to the floor and the walls.[12]

Later, the girl's fiancé, hearing a scream, hurries down to the vaulted hallway, and eventually finds himself in a mausoleum, where he stakes Dracula through the heart. The supernatural horror elements here are, of course, quite un–Radcliffean, but the use of ruins to evoke sublime shudders of unease and terror (the castle's windows are described as "dead, hollow, sightless") is the same.

A similar, though more subtle use of ruins to achieve a mood of unease occurs in Hammer's *The Witches* (dir. Cyril Frankel, 1966), in which Alec McCowan's character, Alan Bax, is set up as a red herring. He's actually a harmless failed priest, but he is presented as a possible psychopath. As such, he takes the new headmistress of the village school, Miss Mayfield (played by Joan Fontaine), to the ruins of the village church. It seems odd that the church is ruined, as Alan wears a dog collar, but his failure to enter the

Whitby Abbey (photograph by the author).

priesthood and his harmless fantasy of pretending to be a priest haven't yet been explained. The fact that the villagers have no need for a church because they practice witchcraft under the leadership of Alan's apparently benign sister, Gwen, also isn't revealed until much later. The image of the ruined church representing a no longer relevant way of life was, incidentally, reprised for the same basic reasons in *The Wicker Man,* (dir. Robin Hardy,1973).

Hammer's most impressive ruins feature in *The Vampire Lovers* (dir. Roy Ward Baker, 1970), which begins with one of the most atmospherically photographed Gothic set pieces in all of Hammer's output. The film is set in 1794, a prime Gothic vintage, as that was the year in which *The Mysteries of Udolpho* was first published. It's probably as well to reproduce Mrs. Radcliffe's description of Castle Udolpho here, as it had such an influence on what followed:

Douglas Wilmer as Baron Hartog, Jon Finch as Carl Ebhardt and George Cole as Morton in the final scene of *The Vampire Lovers* (dir. Roy Ward Baker, 1970).

[T]he gothic greatness of its features, and its mouldering walls of dark grey stone, rendered it a gloomy and sublime object. As [Emily] gazed, the light died away on its walls, leaving a melancholy purple tint, which spread deeper and deeper, as the thin vapour crept up the mountain, while the battlements above were still tipped with splendour.... The gateway before her, leading into the courts, was of gigantic size, and was defended by two round towers, crowned by overhanging turrets, embattled, where, instead of banners, now waved long grass and wild plants, that had taken root among the mouldering stones, and which seemed to sigh, as the breeze rolled past, over the desolation around them. The towers were united by a curtain, pierced and embattled also, below which appeared the pointed arch of an huge portcullis, surmounting the gates[.][13]

Scott MacGregor's set for Castle Karnstein in *The Vampire Lovers* achieves a remarkably similar mood to Radcliffe's description here, elaborating, as it does, on Sheridan Le Fanu's somewhat pithier description of Karnstein Castle in the film's literary source "Carmilla" from *In a Glass Darkly*:

[T]he towers and battlements of the dismantled castle, round which gigantic trees are grouped, overhung us from a slight eminence.
In a frightened dream I got down from the carriage, and in silence, for we had each abundant matter for thinking; we soon mounted the ascent, and were among the spacious chambers, winding stairs, and dark corridors of the castle.[14]

The fact that both Udolpho and Karnstein castles are ruins is an important element of their Gothic effect. *The Vampire Lovers* begins with a scene that Le Fanu leaves until the end of "Carmilla," when a Woodman tells of how a Moravian aristocrat came to the castle to destroy the vampire that haunted it:

"[H]e watched until he saw the vampire come out of his grave, and place near it the linen clothes in which he had been folded, and then glide away towards the village to plague its inhabitants.
"The stranger, having seen all this, came down from the steeple, took the linen wrappings of the vampire, and carried them up to the top of the tower, which he again mounted. When the vampire returned from his prowlings and missed his clothes, he cried furiously to the Moravian, whom he saw at the summit of the tower, and who, in reply, beckoned him to ascend and take them. Whereupon the vampire, accepting his invitation, began to climb the steeple, and as soon as he had reached the battlements, the Moravian, with a stroke of his sword, clove his skull in twain."[15]

Tudor Gates' screenplay faithfully transfers all this to the screen, the only difference being that the vampire, who turns out to be female rather than male, brushes her exposed bosom against the aristocrat's crucifix just before he chops off her head. Gates also gives the Moravian (played by Douglas Wilmer) a name, the Baron Hartog. Hartog duly plunges through swirling mist, climbs winding staircases and waits for his quarry against Gothic windows, illuminated by a flambeau that's flaming in a sconce behind him. It's all very different from the majority of Hammer's Dracula films, where the castle is invariably in apple-pie order, and in this respect, *The Vampire Lovers* has far more in common with Charles D. Hall's sets for the 1931 Universal *Dracula*. (In fact, only three of Hammer's seven Dracula films feature ruins. *Taste the Blood of Dracula* and *Dracula A.D. 1972* explore the potential of a derelict Victorian church, while *Scars of Dracula* has a rather unconvincing ruin of Castle Dracula itself.)

The ruins of Karnstein Castle were again seen in the sequel, *Lust for a Vampire*, the following year, but Don Mingaye's designs for it were nowhere near as evocative as MacGregor's in the earlier film, and neither was David Muir's photography up to the standard of Moray Grant in *The Vampire Lovers*. Perhaps most at fault was director Jimmy Sangster, who failed to extract the required atmosphere from his cast and crew. The last in the trilogy,

Twins of Evil, set the proceedings further back in time, in the seventeenth century, so the castle is consequently restored to its former glory. That's appropriate from the point of view of literary history, as the contemplation of ruins only became fashionable (at least from a picturesque/sublime/Gothic Revival point of view) somewhat later in the middle of the eighteenth century.

In the early part of the eighteenth century, ruins were regarded as symbols of man's vanity, what Christopher Woodward, in his study on the subject, calls the Ozymandias complex.[16] Woodward is referring here to Shelley's poem written in 1818:

> I met a traveller from an antique land
> Who said: Two vast and trunkless legs of stone
> Stand in the desert ... Near them, on the sand,
> Half sunk, a shattered visage lies, whose frown,
> And wrinkled lip, and sneer of cold command,
> Tell that its sculptor well those passions read
> Which yet survive, stamped on these lifeless things,
> The hand that mocked them, and the heart that fed:
> And on the pedestal these words appear:
> "My name is Ozymandias, king of kings:
> Look on my works, ye Mighty, and despair!"
> Nothing beside remains. Round the decay
> Of that colossal wreck, boundless and bare
> The lone and level sands stretch far away.[17]

Woodward also notes Diderot's thoughts on ruins:

> Everything vanishes, everything perishes, everything passes away, the world alone remains, time alone continues.[18]

This is precisely the sentiment expressed by the immortal Ayesha in Rider Haggard's novel *She*. The explorer, Holly, is being given a personal tour of Ayesha's establishment of caves that were created thousands of years earlier by the inhabitants of an ancient civilization:

> "Thou seest, O Holly," she said, "this people founded the city, of which the ruins yet cumber the plain yonder, four thousand years before this cave was finished. Yet, when first mine eyes beheld it two thousand years ago, it was even as it is now. Judge, therefore, how old must that city have been! And now, follow thou me, and I will show thee after what fashion this great people fell when the time was come for it to fall."[19]

Holly is then shown an inscription on one of the cave walls:

> Kôr is fallen! No more shall the mighty feast in her halls, no more shall she rule the world, and her navies go out to commerce with the world. Kôr is fallen! and her mighty works and all the cities of Kôr, and all the harbours that she built and the canals that she made, are for the wolf and the owl and the wild swan, and the barbarian who comes after.[20]

In Hammer's adaptation of *She* (dir. Robert Day, 1965), Ursula Andress' Ayesha stands on the balcony of her palace and shows the ruins of the ancient city of Kôr to Leo Vincey (John Richardson), Holly (Peter Cushing) and Job (Bernard Cribbins):

AYESHA: Was there ever a greater civilization than the Egyptian? And look where it ended: in this volcanic crater. But my world will not end. It will begin again, here.
HOLLY: And you will be its queen. You're not the first person in history to have such a dream of supreme power, and I don't expect you'll be the last.

Unfortunately, the cost of constructing the ruins of an ancient city was considerably beyond Hammer's means, and so we are given instead a reasonably convincing *trompe l'oeil*

Bernard Cribbins as Job, Peter Cushing as Major Holly, Ursula Andress as Ayesha and John Richardson as Leo Vincey survey the ruins of an ancient city in *She* (dir. Robert Day, 1965).

painting of all the ruined columns of Kôr. Despite this visual shortcoming (which, after all, was not so apparent when the film was released, audiences not having been spoiled by CGI technology) this scene, via Haggard's novel, directly connects us to the early eighteenth-century aesthetic of ruins.

Ruins as a kind of melancholy *memento mori* became increasingly fashionable around the middle of the eighteenth century for much the same reason that "picturesque" and "sublime" views became so enthusiastically sought after and described. The causes were a mixture of the decline of religious belief, a distaste of emerging industrial change, and a sense that modernity was undermining the values which a past and "better" age had enshrined. Paintings of ruins became the height of fashion, their executants being known as "ruinistes." The greatest of them was the French artist Hubert Robert (1733–1808), who studied for twelve years with Giovanni Battista Piranesi (1720–1778) in Italy, the spiritual home of the ruin. Piranesi had devoted the majority of his energies to recording the ruins of Roman antiquity in his etchings, and ruins now also became the subject of paintings in their own right, as opposed to being put merely in the background for effect and mood. Robert's *Imaginary View of the Grand Gallery of the Louvre in Ruins* (1796) was the first painting to depict a still-existing building in ruins. Robert knew the Louvre well as he was Keeper of the King's Pictures there, but none of these pictures survive in his painting where only three masterpieces remain untouched: the Apollo Belvedere, a bust of Raphael and the "Slave" of Michelangelo. To understand why Robert painted such a strange work, we have to put it into historical context. Robert had almost been guillotined during the French revolution, but had been saved at the last minute, rather like Baron Frankenstein at the beginning of Hammer's *The Revenge of Frankenstein* (dir. Terence Fisher, 1959), due to being confused with a namesake who was executed in his place. Having lived through such an upheaval, he no doubt felt that art was the only certainty in a very uncertain world; but ruins were also thought, by some, to be more beautiful than intact buildings. Woodward reminds us of the country curate, poet and painter John Dyer who wrote in 1724:

> There is a certain charm that follows the sweep of time, and I can't help thinking the triumphal arches more beautiful now than ever they were, there is a certain greenness, with many other colours, and a certain disjointedness and moulder among the stones, something so pleasing in their weeds and tufts of myrtle, and something in them altogether so greatly wild, that mingling with art, and blotting out the traces of disagreeable squares and angles, adds certain beauties that could not be before imagined, which is the cause of surprise no modern building can give.[21]

As the eighteenth century gave way to the nineteenth, the past became increasingly a place of benediction. When, in the early nineteenth century, Felix Mendelssohn rediscovered the music of J.S. Bach (who had become a kind of musical ruin after decades of neglect), he found a voice from another age that spoke somehow more humanely, more spiritually, and more virtuously than any music of the present. Consequently, Mendelssohn began writing in the manner of Bach, as did his friend Robert Schumann, who recalled Mendelssohn's enthusiasm for the music of the Baroque master:

> The *cantus firmus* was hung with wreathes of golden leaves, and flooded with a spirituality that prompted you to confess: "If life were to deprive me of hope and faith, this single chorale would replenish me with both."[22]

Melrose Abbey. Illustration drawn by H. Melville (engraved by R. Stains), reproduced in "The Steel Plate Edition" of Sir Walter Scott's *The Monastery*, London, George Routledge & Sons, 1877, facing page 115.

The Priory of St. Ruth. Illustration drawn by H. Melville (engraved by G. Presbury), reproduced in "The Steel Plate Edition" of Sir Walter Scott's *The Antiquary*, George Routledge & Sons, 1877, facing page 224.

Richard Wagner composed an entire opera about the glories of musical tradition as epitomized by Bach (*Die Meistersinger von Nürnberg*, 1868), and he deliberately chose stories of ancient saga and legend as the subject matter for his other music dramas. Antiquarianism thrived. Sir Walter Scott's novel *The Antiquary* (1816) and others from his Waverley series abound in ruined abbeys and tales of past ages. The past began to come alive in a way it never had before. Landscape too was viewed as an aid to memory of the past, both geological and cultural. Ramond de Carbonnières wrote in 1793 that a site "has a sentimental as well as a geological history: the buried strata of the past are directly evoked by the sensations of the present."[23]

As an example of what de Carbonnières meant, we need look no further (though this is already quite far enough as it's a fairly remote location) than Fingal's Cave in the Hebrides, which soon became one of the unmissable sights on the itinerary of any self-respecting eighteenth-century tourist. James MacPherson's infamous literary hoax of 1765, in which he claimed to have rediscovered the ancient Celtic poems of Ossian, gave added charm to this spectacular cave with its weird basalt columns. With the cult of all things Scottish, in the early nineteenth-century, created largely by the success of Sir Walter Scott's novels, Fingal's Cave became even more popular. Mendelssohn visited the place on his tour of Scotland, and the experience inspired his Hebrides Overture, subtitled "Fingal's Cave" just in case audiences weren't sure of the exact location the music is meant to suggest.

The aesthetics of ruins also informed Werner Herzog's 1979 remake of Murnau's *Nosferatu*. Herzog shows Castle Dracula in a more ruinous state than Hammer or even Universal ever chose to do, at least from the outside. (Inside, things seem to be in reasonable order apart from a broken pane of glass or two in the window casements, but the general effect is one of desolation.) As we shall see in the next chapter, the German Romantic painter Caspar David Friedrich (1774–1840) inspired many of the landscapes that play such an integral role in Herzog's film, and Friedrich himself was also fascinated by ruins. In particular, he was obsessed with the ruins of Eldena Abbey, a former Cistercian monastery near the town of Griefswald in Mecklenburg-Vorpommern, Northern Germany, which he painted many times and which also formed the basis of his most "Gothic" painting, *Abtei im Eichwald* ("Abbey in an Oakwood," 1809–10). As Brigitte Buberl points out, for the Romantic artist, "[the] effort of imagination necessary to visualize the building complete generated a more credible image of Christian truth than an intact cathedral would have done."[24] For German Romantic painters, cathedrals and Gothic ruins were part of a longing for the past, and consequently for a period when it was felt that mankind was in closer touch with nature and religion. Friedrich Schlegel (1772–1829), who famously described architecture as

Isabelle Adjani as Lucy Harker, Klaus Kinski as Dracula and director Werner Herzog on the set of *Nosferatu the Vampyre* (1979).

"frozen music," also believed that the effect of Gothic architecture was the same as that which we experience when viewing natural beauty:

> From a distance, with all its countless towers and turrets, the whole looks not unlike a forest; but when one steps somewhat closer, the whole organism seems more like a monstrous crystallization. In a word, these miraculous works of art in their organic infinity and inexhaustible profusion of form, resemble nothing so much as the works of nature itself. The impression, at least, is the same.[25]

The German Romantic artist's fascination with the Gothic cathedral either intact or in ruins, arose from the enthusiasm across Europe in the mid–nineteenth century for an idealized revival of the Middle Ages, which we have already touched upon regarding the Gothic Revival in England. It was particularly strong in Germany because it represented German unity (Germany itself was not unified as a country until 1871). Brigitte Buberl explains that this enthusiasm "ultimately gave rise to magical, unreal images that served a mystical enthusiasm."[26] This is the tradition in which Herzog's *Nosferatu* is rooted. The "unreal" ruins in this film are not merely picturesque, they convey an echo of that "mystical enthusiasm" and, as we shall see, indicate the way in which Herzog presents the vampire legend of Dracula as a German Romantic *Liebestod*. This is not to deny that the ruins also convey their traditionally Gothic, melancholy associations of the past. Clouds rush overhead in stop-motion photography, emphasizing how rapidly the passing of time must seem to a vampire who is already centuries old. Like Ayesha, Klaus Kinski's Dracula is immune to time but also hungry for love. During their tour of the ancient mummies in the caves of Kôr, Haggard's Ayesha had shown Holly two mummies embraced in death, which causes Holly to imagine who they might have been in life:

> "Behold the lot of man," said the veiled Ayesha, as she drew the winding sheets back over the dead lovers, speaking in a solemn, thrilling voice, which accorded well with the dream that I had dreamed: "to the tomb, and to the forgetfulness that hides the tomb, must we all come at last! Ay, even I who live so long. Even for me, O Holly, thousands upon thousands of years hence; thousands of years after thou hast gone through the gate and been lost in the mists, a day will dawn whereon I shall die, and be even as thou art and these are."[27]

When Kinski's Dracula is drawn down in a similar embrace by the self-sacrificing Lucy at the end of Herzog's film, the image of two mummies locked together in death is also suggested. Herzog emphasized this image by changing the way in which Dracula is destroyed. In Murnau's film, the daylight made him dematerialize into a puff of smoke. By contrast, Herzog shows the vampire curled up on the floor, a grotesque cross between a contorted mummy and a dead insect. Like Ayesha, the Nosferatu also dies. Though it's unlikely that Herzog was looking in the direction of Hammer's 1965 film of *She*, the way Kinski doubles up in his death agonies is indeed comparable to the manner in which Ayesha emerges from the cold blue flame that takes her immortality away at the end of that film.

All horror film monsters end up dead. After all they *are* dead and they "belong dead," as Karloff's monster put it in *Bride of Frankenstein*. Ruins are their natural habitat, or at least so one would think; but as I've already suggested, so many of Hammer's films dispense with ruins, and we need to keep that perhaps surprising anomaly in mind for a few chapters more before we'll be ready to discuss in more detail some possible reasons why that may have been the case. Meanwhile, it's time to explore the particular kind of scenery we find in Gothic romance, a pilgrimage that will first take us to deepest Buckinghamshire in the south of England.

Four

Municipal Sublimity

Hammer's most favored outdoor location enjoys the splendidly sinister name of Black Park. From that name alone, one imagines something as Teutonic and foreboding as the Black Forest or as mysterious and threatening as the wooded foothills of the Carpathian Mountains. No doubt Hammer would still have used it if it had been called White Park, or even Deer Park, but those names would have been quite wrong. Black Park is exactly the kind of name to suggest the never-never lands of Hammer Horror.

In fact, Black Park is a modest place, popular with families and dogs on Sunday afternoons. Cared for by Buckinghamshire County Council, it's open for all to enjoy, and to those who have never watched a Hammer film it seems innocuous enough. It does offer some atmospheric vistas, however, which take on added significance if one's nights have been spent watching what Hammer made of them. There's a tree-lined lake, several forested avenues, a few gently rising slopes, a glade or two, and some open heathland, all of which, if photographed from the right angle by an imaginative director, can easily persuade an audience that they are a long way away from this overcrowded corner of southeast England. The principal attraction of Black Park for Hammer was its proximity to their studios at Bray on the banks of the River Thames. It's only about six miles from Bray and from Oakley Court, Hammer's handy, ready-made Gothic pile on the opposite side of the river. It's also positively on the doorstep of Pinewood Studios. If one required larger vistas, rural Buckinghamshire offered other possibilities. Indeed, many of Rank's biggest stars lived in Buckinghamshire (Dirk Bogarde for one), occupying various residences in Amersham and Beaconsfield. The village of Denham, once home to Denham Studios, is only three miles from Black Park too.

Not a trace of the once sprawling film studios of London Film Productions remains at Denham now. Sir Alexander Korda's dream of making Denham Studios the envy of the world were sadly short-lived; but memories persist. Buckinghamshire and neighboring Hertfordshire, home of Elstree Studios, were once the backlot of British films. Amersham (which Hammer's special effects director Ian Scoones liked to call Hammersham), along with Great Missenden, provided useful country town settings for the company (particularly in its television episodes). Indeed, in its latter years Hammer set up shop at Hampden House just outside High Wycombe, now a popular venue for wedding parties. Bray itself featured in Hammer's *The Quatermass Xperiment* (dir. Val Guest, 1955). The Dashwood Mausoleum at West Wycombe and, just over into Hertfordshire in the East, St. Botolph's Church in Shenley provided memorable settings for Hammer's last great film, the occult thriller *To the Devil a Daughter* (dir. Peter Sykes, 1974). Buckinghamshire therefore provided a significant element of Britain's image abroad (to say nothing of how the British liked to see themselves), and humble Black Park became a particularly influential stretch of municipal woodland, affecting the dreams of millions of people across the world.

It was, of course, essential that the views offered by Black Park were carefully framed, and the approach of Hammer's directors to these sylvan views can be traced back to the eighteenth-century ideas of the Reverend William Gilpin (1724–1804), who invented the term "picturesque." This once new idea wasn't dreamed up in Gilpin's study but was the result of his own practical explorations of the great outdoors. He began touring Britain in 1768 and by 1776 he'd taken in Norfolk, Kent, Essex, South Wales, the Wye Valley, the Lake District, North Wales, the South Coast, the west of England and the Highlands of Scotland. He was truly one of the first tourists of the British Isles—an activity that's so commonplace these days, it's hard to imagine just how unusual and innovative Gilpin was.

Before the first stirrings of the Romantic movement in the middle of the eighteenth century, savage scenery was of no interest to anyone of cultivated taste. Nature was regarded as a place of toil, not of beauty, the pursuit of which took place in towns, where *artifice* reigned supreme. It had been quite acceptable, indeed *de rigueur*, for gentlemen to experience the cultural pleasures of a European Grand Tour, but it was considered quite another thing to look for enlightenment and aesthetic pleasure on one's own doorstep, and it would have been considered particularly eccentric to look for them in mere scenery. However, with the rise of industrialism along with the sense that urban life corrupted rather than ennobled the human spirit, the British countryside was reassessed.

Around the same time in France, the philosopher Jean-Jacques Rousseau (1712–78) had similarly been arguing for a return to nature. In his educational treatise *Emile* (1762), he claimed that it is better "to breathe the fresh air of the country than the foul air of the town":

Oakley Court seen from the River Thames (photograph by the author).

Men are not made to be crowded together in ant-hills, but scattered over the earth to till it. The more they are massed together, the more corrupt they become. Disease and vice are the sure results of over-crowded cities. Of all creatures man is least fitted to live in herds. Huddled together like sheep, men would very soon die. Man's breath is fatal to his fellows. This is literally as well as figuratively true.

Men are devoured by our towns. In a few generations the race dies out or becomes degenerate; it needs renewal, and it is always renewed from the country. Send your children to renew themselves, so to speak, send them to regain in the open fields the strength lost in the foul air of our crowded cities.[1]

Of course, financial considerations prevented the majority from doing this. Only the very wealthy had been able to afford the Grand Tour, and no one in their right mind would try to suggest that the working poor could ever have afforded the kind of "picturesque" tour of England encouraged by Gilpin. But for those who *could* afford it (and for a British person, touring Britain then, as now, was cheaper than going abroad), the idea of setting off to enjoy the fresh air of one's own countryside suddenly became fashionable.

Top: Black Park. Crossroads featured in *Dracula, Prince of Darkness* (dir. Terence Fisher, 1966). *Bottom:* Black Park. Woodland vista featured in *Vampire Circus* (dir. Robert Young, 1971) (photographs by the author).

Gilpin did not suggest that the countryside was without its faults. To respond fully to what nature had on offer, one had, like the director of a Hammer horror film in Black Park, to view the prospect from the correct point of view and to make sure it was appropriately framed, just like a picture: hence the term "picturesque." Indeed, in the visual arts, the way that artists used landscape in their paintings began to change around this time. Rather in the manner that ruins had been used as mere backgrounds before becoming themselves the subject of paintings, as mentioned in the previous chapter, the function of landscape in paintings had previously been to provide a backdrop for something else: a heroic story from a classical legend, for example. Landscape was *generalized*, not *individualized*. In the early nineteenth century, a new kind of landscape emerged: the "portrait" landscape, which focused on a specific place as a way of discussing an emotion, mood or idea. Landscape now became *subjective*. As German playwright Friedrich von Schiller (1759–1805) put it:

OBSERVATIONS,

ON

SEVERAL PARTS OF ENGLAND,

PARTICULARLY THE

MOUNTAINS AND LAKES

OF

Cumberland and Westmoreland,

RELATIVE CHIEFLY TO

PICTURESQUE BEAUTY,

MADE IN THE YEAR 1772.

By WILLIAM GILPIN, A.M.
PREBENDARY OF SALISBURY; AND VICAR OF BOLDRE IN
NEW-FOREST, NEAR LYMINGTON.

THE THIRD EDITION, IN TWO VOLUMES.
VOL. II.

LONDON:
PRINTED FOR T. CADELL AND W. DAVIES, STRAND.
1808.

Title page of Gilpin's *Observations on Several Parts of England*.

There are two ways that Nature without living creatures can become a symbol of the human: either as representations of feelings or as representations of ideas.[2]

The musicologist Charles Rosen adds:

> What Schiller demands is that the poet and the artist show us the correspondence between the sensuous experience of Nature and the spiritual and intellectual workings of the mind.... [P]ortrait-landscapes had no subject — they conveyed feelings and ideas like music, without reference to history or myth, merely by the arrangement of the elements of nature on canvas.... In the extraordinary triumph of landscape, we can see both painter and poet using elements of Nature — foliage, rocks, mountains and, above all, the unifying power of light — the way a musician uses harmonies and motifs.[3]

One might also say that the Gothic filmmaker uses these elements of Nature (light is even more important in the cinema) to help convey mood and atmosphere though, admittedly, within the context of a story. Without the appropriate setting, however, the story would lose all its significance, and in this respect it is the *settings* and the musical accompaniments of the kind of films this book is discussing that are by far the most important elements in them. The story and the characters, it could be argued, are merely excuses for the creation of mood through setting and musical accompaniment.

Black Park (photograph by the author).

To promote his cause, Gilpin issued various books and prints such as *Picturesque Tours* in 1782, but not everyone shared his enthusiasm for the great outdoors. Dr. Johnson, for example, found the Scottish Highlands less than inspiring:

> They exhibit very little variety; being almost wholly covered with dark heath, and even that seems to be checked in its growth. What is not heath is nakedness, a little diversified by now and then a stream rushing down the steep. An eye accustomed to flowery pastures and waving harvests is astonished and repelled by this wide extent of hopeless sterility.[4]

Perhaps the problem was that Dr. Johnson was looking at things from quite literally the wrong point of view. As Gilpin himself put it:

> Nature is always great in design; but unequal in composition. She is an admirable colourist; and can harmonize her tints with infinite variety, and inimitable beauty; but is seldom so correct in composition, as to produce a harmonious whole. Either the foreground, or the background, is disproportionate: or some awkward line runs across the piece: or a tree is ill-placed; or a bank is formal: or something or other is not exactly what it should be. The case is, the immensity of nature is beyond human comprehension. She works on a *vast scale*; and, no doubt, harmoniously, if her schemes could be comprehended. The artist in the meantime, is confined to a span. He lays down his little rules therefore, which he calls the *principles of picturesque beauty*, merely to adapt such diminutive parts of nature's surfaces to his own eye, as come within its scope.[5]

Gilpin was not impressed by Tintern Abbey, later made famous by William Wordsworth:

> Though the parts are beautiful, the whole is ill-shaped. No ruins of the towers are left, which might give form, and contrast to the wall, and buttresses and other inferior parts. Instead of this, a number of gabel-ends hurt the eye with their regularity; and disgust by the vulgarity of their shape. A mallett judiciously used (but who durst use it?) might be of service in fracturing some of them.[6]

Film directors regularly dare to use Gilpin's imagined mallet, not literally, of course, but by means of framing their shots to cut out anything that might spoil the effect they're seeking.

There were other factors in European society that contributed to the aesthetic change of heart of which Gilpin was an example. Critics often suggest that the Lisbon Earthquake of 1755 was an important trigger of the Romantic movement, for it caused such a profound shock to established Christian faith. The question "How could God have so punished so devout a city?" was on everyone's lips at the time, and doubts emerged whether God still existed, if He had ever existed at all. This crisis of faith displaced the established way in which humanity's religious instincts were channeled, and it was then that Nature began to fill the void. For many intellectuals, Good and Evil now became embodied in Nature itself, and pantheism became increasingly fashionable. The term "pantheism" was coined in 1705 by the radical Irish thinker John Toland (1670–1722), but pantheism had been "invented" much earlier by the Dutch philosopher Baruch (or Benedictus) Spinoza (1632–77), who claimed that there is only one substance in the universe, and he described that substance as *Deus sive natura* (God or Nature). Spinoza was therefore somewhat ahead of his time, and we'll be returning to his ideas in chapter ten when we will discuss aspects of occultism.

Whereas Spinoza's ideas had horrified his own contemporaries, individuals in the latter half of the eighteenth century happily began to worship at the shrine of Nature rather than in a church; but differing slightly from Spinoza's idea, the new Romantic pantheism regarded Nature as both demonic and divine. It could both redeem and destroy. It could overwhelm you, and as such it *terrified*. Fear was one of the most powerful watchwords of this new Romantic movement. According to Goethe (whom Kenneth Clarke points out was only six at the time of the Lisbon earthquake), "Never before ... has the Demon of Fear so quickly and so powerfully spread horror throughout the land."[7] However, by using Gilpin's method of framing, one could tame the demonic in Nature and gain aesthetic pleasure by so doing. One Dr. John Brown did just this, as his remarks on Keswick in the Lake District suggest:

> Instead of a meagre rivulet, a noble living lake adorned with every variety of wooded islands ... on the opposite shore, you will find rocks and cliffs of stupendous height, hanging over the lake in horrible grandeur, the woods climbing up their steep and shaggy sides, where mortal foot never yet approached; on those dreadful heights the eagles build their nests: a variety of waterfalls are seen pouring from their summits, and tumbling in vast sheets from rock to rock in rude and terrible magnificence[.][8]

"Stupendous, horrible, dreadful, terrible": these evocative adjectives are what Gothic romance and Gothic horror are all about, and they now bring us to the related subject of the sublime in landscape, as it was defined by the one-time Member of Parliament for Bristol and scourge of the French Revolution, Edmund Burke. Born in 1729, Burke was only 28 when he wrote his famous *A Philosophical Enquiry into the Origin of Our Ideas of the Sublime and Beautiful* in 1757. It was exactly the right time to have written it: only two years after the Lisbon earthquake and only eight years before Horace Walpole had his dream about the giant hand on the staircase at Strawberry Hill. He wasn't the first person to discuss this particular subject, which goes back to a work attributed to Longinus, the Greek teacher from the first (or third) century A.D. But in the middle of the eighteenth century, the sublime seemed a particularly relevant topic. Longinus' treatise *On the Sublime* is concerned with the sublimity, or "grandeur," of rhetoric. In it, he explains that

> the effect of elevated language is, not to persuade the hearers, but to entrance them; and at all times, and in every way, what transports us with wonder is more telling than what merely persuades or gratifies us.... [A] well-timed stoke of sublimity scatters everything before it like a thunderbolt, and in a flash reveals the full power of the speaker.[9]

By the middle of the eighteenth century the word "sublime" had grown to mean more than just rhetorical grandeur. Evolving from Longinus' metaphor of the thunderbolt, the emphasis of the word changed to include many other phenomena, particularly those of Nature, which were most powerfully imbued with the spirit of fear that Goethe had talked about. Longinus had discussed how the sublime "uplifts our souls; we are filled with a proud exaltation and a sense of vaunting joy,"[10] and it was how these emotions could be conjured by natural scenery in particular that concerned eighteenth-century aestheticians and poets. As they became increasingly interested in the emotional consequences of the Lisbon earthquake and the Godless universe it implied, they became even more in thrall to the emotionally redemptive or demonic aspects of Nature.

The skeptical age in which Burke found himself, caused him to discuss pantheistic ideas using secular language. Just as Sir Isaac Newton had systemized the universe, Burke felt that it should be possible to codify human emotions in the same manner. In his comparison of the sublime and the beautiful, he pointed the way to that combination of the terrifying and the erotic, which was to find expression in Hammer horror films of the mid–twentieth century. For Burke, the erotic was an aspect of the beautiful, while terror was an aspect of the sublime. Here is Burke on sensual beauty:

> Whoever compares his state of mind, on feeling soft, smooth, variated, unangular bodies, with that in which he finds himself, on the view of a beautiful object, will perceive a very striking analogy in the effects of both; and which may go a good way towards discovering their common cause. Feeling and sight in this respect, differ in but few points. The touch takes in the pleasure of softness, which is not primarily an object of sight; the sight on the other hand comprehends colour, which can hardly be made perceptible to the touch; the touch again has the advantage in a new idea of pleasure resulting from a moderate degree of warmth.[11]

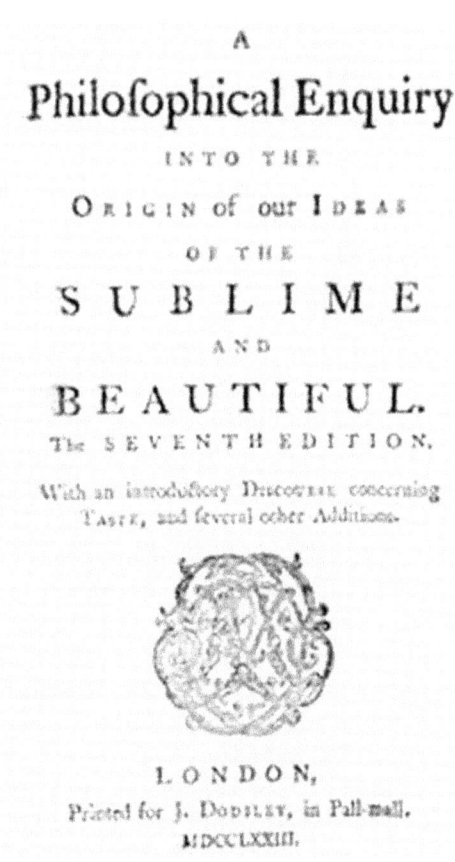

Title page of Edmund Burke's *A Philosophical Enquiry.*

And here is Burke, in the most famous passage of the book, on the sublime:

> Whatever is fitted in any sort to excite the ideas of pain, and danger, that is to say, whatever is in any sort terrible, or is conversant about terrible objects, or operates in a manner analogous to terror, is a source of the *sublime*; that is, it is productive of the strongest emotion which the mind is capable of feeling. I say the strongest emotion, because I am satisfied the ideas of pain are much more powerful than those which enter on the part of pleasure.[12]

Combine both these passages, mix them with a dash of blood, and one has the recipe for Hammer's success. That, at least, that was Hammer's intention. On paper its ideas were certainly a combination of the erotic and the sublime, but Hammer, mainly because of the economically efficient manner in which its films were made, created a generally picturesque aesthetic to *imply* the sublime. It's films were confined to studio sets or to Black Park; no matter how sublime the dreams of Hammer's screenwriters, the company could never afford genuine Alpine scenery or even Lakeland crags. The carefully composed and lushly evocative views of Black Park were subjected to variations on the same picturesque theme from *The Curse of Frankenstein* in 1957 to *Vampire Circus*, directed fifteen years later by Robert Young. Occasionally, matte shots were intercut into the proceedings to suggest a more Alpine context for their Buckinghamshire hoaxes. There is an Alpine view in *The Curse of Frankenstein*, and a nestling Alpine village in *Dracula Has Risen from the Grave*. The foothills of the mountain on which Castle Dracula perches amidst craggy outcrops in this latter film were created in the studio. The effect is not entirely convincing, but it's far more sublime than anything Black Park could have offered. Dracula's castle itself is a model, rather a good one, which one particularly sublime shot presents to us with the toiling figure of Rupert Davies' crucifix-burdened monsignor superimposed upon it.

Glimpses of castles either real (on somewhat grainy library footage) or specially made miniatures, attempt to give the impression that these films were shot in genuinely sublime locales, but all too often these additions after the fact rather jar against the tight angles and eye-level sylvan views that were at Hammer's disposal in Black Park. That's not to deny that wonders were achieved in this respect. The prologue to *The Brides of Dracula* makes Black Park's lake look positively miasmic and threatening as never before (or since, for that matter). Peter Sasdy also made it shimmer as though several times bigger than it is during a tryst between the rejuvenated countess (Ingrid Pitt) and her young lover Imré Toth (Sandor Elès) in *Countess Dracula* (1971), and it looks particularly ominous in the prologue of *Taste the Blood of Dracula*. A well-photographed forest could, after all, be anywhere in Europe, and this was the great appeal of Black Park to cost-conscious purveyors of Gothic fantasy.

In such scenes, Hammer indeed managed to evoke many of Burke's categories of the sublime, even though more often than not they remained picturesque. Burke's categories were extensive. They included "Terror," of course, "Obscurity" ("how greatly night adds to our dread, in all cases of danger"[13]), "Power" ("[the sublime] comes upon us in the gloomy forest, and in the howling wilderness, in the form of the lion, the tiger, the panther,"[14] and, one might add, the werewolf, the vampire and the mummy), "Vastness" ("A perpendicular has more force in forming the sublime, than an inclined plane"[15]), "Magnitude in Building," "Sound and Loudness," "Pain and Fear," even "The Cries of Animals" ("Listen to them," says Count Dracula, "the children of the night. What music they make!"). Burke again anticipates the cinema, and what Peter Cushing himself described as the "ghost train" effect[16] of Gothic horror in particular, by emphasizing that *genuine* horror and pain aren't at all the point here:

"Between the sunny April showers / The swallows dart, the wild bee hums." A picturesque landscape drawn by E. M. Wimperis (engraved by W. Thomas) to illustrate W. Thornbury's poem "The Warning" in *The Quiver, an Illustrated Magazine for Sunday and General Reading,* Vol. III, London, Cassell, Petter, and Galpin, 1868, p. 537.

When danger or pain press too nearly, they are incapable of giving any delight, and are simply terrible; but at certain distances, and with certain modifications, they may be, and they are delightful, as we every day experience.[17]

Many of Burke's ideas derived from Milton's *Paradise Lost*, as Burke himself acknowledged. In this passage, describing Satan's expulsion from Heaven, we have all the categories of the sublime listed above (excepting the cries of animals):

> Him the almighty Power
> Hurled headlong flaming from th' ethereal sky,
> With hideous ruin and combustion, down
> To bottomless perdition, there to dwell
> In adamantine chains and penal fire
> ...
> At once, as far as angels' ken, he views
> The dismal situation waste and wild;
> A dungeon horrible, on all sides round,
> As one great furnace, flamed; yet from those flames
> No light, but rather darkness visible
> Served only to discover sights of woe,
> Regions of sorrow, doleful shades, where peace
> And rest can never dwell, hope never comes,
> That comes to all; but torture without end
> Still urges, and a fiery deluge, fed
> With ever-burning sulphur unconsumed.[18]

So much of *Paradise Lost* has a direct influence on Gothic horror. The opening of Hell's doors in Book II, for example, is not only an example of Burke's "Magnitude in Building" but also suggests the doors of many a vampire's castle:

> [T]hen in the keyhole turns
> Th' intricate wards, and every bolt and bar
> Of massy iron or solid rock with ease
> Unfastens: on a sudden open fly
> With impetuous recoil and jarring sound
> The infernal doors, and on their hinges grate
> Harsh thunder, that the lowest bottom shook
> Of Erebus.[19]

It was Ann Radcliffe who truly popularized the aesthetics of the sublime and the beautiful. As Hammer films were later to demonstrate, Radcliffe believed that the sublime and the beautiful could complement each other. (For Burke, they remained contrary and mutually exclusive qualities.) Radcliffe also contrasted the sublime with the ridiculous, sending herself up to some extent by means of the garrulous servants she includes in her plots. She thus anticipated the subgenre of the horror film satire, with which we will be dealing in chapter eleven. The three painters who had by far the greatest influence on Radcliffe's imagery were Claude Gelée (Lorrain, 1600–82), Salvator Rosa (1615–73) and Nicholas Poussin (1594–1665). Indeed, Claude's painting *Landscape with Psyche Outside the Palace of Cupid*, also known as "The Enchanted Castle," unwittingly looks forward to the Castle of Udolpho itself, not to mention all the other castles of Gothic literature and film; but the three artists traditionally expressed different kinds of view. Claude represented what Burke categorized as "The Beautiful," Rosa represented "The Sublime" and Poussin, "The Grand." Radcliffe's approach to landscape in her novels compares and contrasts all three. Her biographer Rictor Norton points out that the octagonal pavilion in the grounds of Chateau-le-

Blanc in *The Mysteries of Udolpho* has six windows from which six different kinds of landscape may be viewed: forest scenery, sublime scenery, picturesque scenery, beautiful scenery, the grand and the horrific.[20] It is the Gothic heroine's main duty to develop her aesthetic capability in order to respond correctly to these various kind of landscape. Indeed, Radcliffe's heroines all compose their own poetic responses to wherever they happen to find themselves, despite the dangers of banditti or the activities of unscrupulous villains going on around them.

Radcliffe's descriptions of sublime Alpine scenery were acknowledged at the time to be unequalled, though many have subsequently imitated her achievements. Here, for example is a passage from *The Mysteries of Udolpho*:

> Over these crags rose others of stupendous height, and fantastic shape; some shooting into cones; others impending far over their base, in huge masses of granite, along whose broken ridges was often lodged a weight of snow, that, trembling even to the vibration of a sound, threatened to bear destruction in its course to the vale. Around, on every side, far as the eye could penetrate, were seen only forms of grandeur — the long perspective of mountain-tops, tinged with ethereal blue, or white with snow; vallies of ice, and forests of gloomy fir.[21]

We can trace even the thinnest of threads that link the influence of Radcliffe on mainstream Romanticism (and thence to Hammer horror). Norton intriguingly identifies an influence that projects both forward to the poet Percy Shelley (and hence Mary Shelley's *Frankenstein*) and back to Gilpin, via a single line in Radcliffe's earlier novel *The Romance of the Forest*: "Beauty sleeping in the lap of horror." Shelley borrowed this image from Radcliffe and put it in his philosophical poem *Alastor; or the Spirit of Solitude,* where it reads: "It was a tranquil spot, that seemed to smile/Even in the lap of horror."[22] Radcliffe's line was itself derived from Charles Avison, the organist of St. Nicholas church in Newcastle upon Tyne. He used it to describe Derwentwater in the Lake District, in a letter to William Gilpin, but he wrote "Lying" rather than Radcliffe's judicious alternative of "sleeping,"[23] which Shelley further changed to "smile." Beauty (in the form of well-endowed young ladies) and Horror (in its many contrasting forms) were, of course, the principal selling points of Hammer films.

It's revealing to compare all that with Shelley's poem "Mont Blanc." It was written in 1816, the same year in which his wife's novel *Frankenstein* was conceived, and it contains elements of Radcliffean sublimity *par excellence*:

> In the wild woods, among the mountains lone,
> Where waterfalls around it leap for ever,
> Where woods and winds contend, and a vast river
> Over its rocks ceaselessly bursts and raves.
>
> II
>
> Thus, thou, Ravine of Arve — dark, deep Ravine —
> Thou many-coloured, many-voicèd vale,
> Over whose pines, and crags, and caverns sail
> Fast cloud-shadows and sunbeams: an awful scene[.]
> ...
> Dizzy Ravine! and when I gaze on thee
> I seem as in a trance sublime and strange[.][24]

Frankenstein too contains its fair share of Alpine sublimity:

> The path, as you ascend higher, is intersected by ravines of snow, down which stones continually roll from above; one of them is particularly dangerous, as the slightest sound, such as even speaking in a loud voice, produces a concussion of air sufficient to draw destruction upon the head of the speaker. The pines are not tall or luxuriant, but they are sombre, and add an air of

severity to the scene. I looked on the valley beneath; vast mists were rising from the rivers which ran through it, and curling in thick wreaths around the opposite mountains, whose summits were hid in the uniform clouds, while rain poured from the dark sky, and added to the melancholy impression I received from the objects around me.[25]

Such graphic descriptions were bound eventually to find their way into visual images. In the paintings of John Martin we have the most sensational response to Burke's ideas and Milton's inspiration as any. Martin illustrated *Paradise Lost* in the most cinematic terms, as we have already seen regarding staircases in chapter one. His picture of Adam and Eve leaving the Garden of Eden even seems to anticipate the feeling one has on leaving a cinema. Light still shines from the door of heaven, the show is still going on inside, but all is dark outside. On leaving the dream world of the cinema, we, like Adam and Eve are confronted with uncomfortable (and often raining) reality. Sometimes confused with his brother Jonathan, who burned down York Minster in a fit of insanity, John Martin wasn't mad himself. It was Jonathan (called "Mad Martin") who was sent to a lunatic asylum. John, by contrast, was apprenticed as a glass and china artist but eventually attained huge success with his Cecil B. DeMille–style canvas *Belshazzar's Feast* in 1821. Despite the immense popularity of that painting, and the fact that he was showered with awards from continental Europe, Martin wasn't so successful with England's artistic powers-that-be, who found his work too theatrical, too sensational, too much, indeed, like those qualities identified by disdainful critics of Gothic horror.

Martin specialized in sublime scenery. His figures were never very convincing, but they weren't the point of the exercise. Like the special effects–driven film industry of today, Martin's figures were merely the motivation of the landscape and the sublime events that took place in it. Paintings such as *The Destruction of Sodom and Gomorrah* (1852) and *The Great Day of His Wrath* (1851–53) were widescreen cinematic visions. The scenery didn't have to be realistic. Indeed, Martin's 1817 painting based on Thomas Gray's poem "The Bard" is meant to be set in Wales. It shows the ancient Druidical Bard pouring scorn on the invading English army of Edward I, but no Welsh mountains, not even in the most patriotic of Welshmen's imagination, ever looked as impossibly sublime as Martin's. The Bard is placed centrally at the viewer's eye level, halfway up the canvas on a craggy, virtually Alpine outcrop (the similarity to Radcliffe's and the Shelleys' Alpine imagery is very apparent here). The Bard is quite out of scale with his surroundings, a giant really, while the invading soldiers are mere insects down below in the bottom right hand corner, as insignificant as Vathek's minions when viewed from the top of his tower. It is Nature who is the principal character here, as it is in all Martin's works.

It was the same mixture of sublime terror and pantheism that informed the *Schauerromantik* aesthetic of nineteenth-century German art and music. Nature became supernatural in Carl Maria von Weber's *singspiel*, *Der Freischütz* (1821). Johann Friedrich Kind's description of the famous "Wolf's Glen" at the end of the second act of his libretto for this sensational cornerstone of German Romantic opera is a veritable compendium of sublime terrors, which somehow seems to gain in gloom if read in the original German:

> Furchtbare Waldschlucht, grösstenteils mit Schwarzholz bewachsen, von hohen Gebirgen rings umgeben. Von einem stürzt ein Wasserfall. Der Vollmond scheint bleich. Zwei Gewitter sind von entgegengesetzter Richtung im Anzug. Weiter vorwärts ein vom Blitz zerschmetterter, verdorrter Baum, inwendig faul, so dass er zu glimmern scheint. Auf der anderen Seite, auf einem knorrigen Ast, eine grosse Eule mit feurig rädernden Augen. Auf anderen Bäumen Raben und andere Waldvögel.

[*A terrible woodland glen largely planted with pines, and surrounded by high mountains. A waterfall rushes down from one of them. The full moon shines wanly. Two thunderstorms are brewing from opposite directions. Nearer to us a tree struck by lightning and withered, decayed inside so that it seems to glow. On a gnarled branch at the other side sits a huge owl with fiery, circling eyes. Crows and other woodbirds on other trees.*][26]

The musical means by which Weber amplifies this sublime setting include the kind of effects beloved of many a horror film composer: tritones, tremolo strings, clarinets in their lowest, most sinister register, diminished seventh chords, incantations and melodrama (i.e., spoken dialogue over musical underscore), and imitative tone painting. As the hero, Max, watches Caspar forge his magic bullets and hold them up to the light of the moon, various supernatural phenomena occur, for which Weber provides musical equivalents. The first bullet causes the woodbirds to flutter down from their trees and form a circle. The second bullet summons a black boar, which runs across the stage. With the third, a storm wind stirs the trees, and so on, until we have experienced fiery wheels, ghostly huntsmen, and a gigantic storm, which brings the scene to a close.

Der Freischütz made a gigantic impression on Wagner, who was fascinated by what he called "its spooky plot." His subsequent confession that the "excitement of horror and fear of ghosts constitute a singular factor in the development of my emotional life"[27] suggests that he would also have been a fan of horror films (if not a composer of their scores) had he lived in the twentieth century. Wagner's *oeuvre* overflows with evocations of sublime Nature. *Der Ring des Nibelungen* not only features the storms already mentioned, but also endless forests, rocks and rivers. The first of the four music-dramas in the cycle begins in the River Rhine, before moving up to the mountaintops and down into subterranean mines. *Die Walküre*, the second, presents a sequence of savage scenery, ending with Brünnhilde's rock surrounded by magic fire. *Siegfried* is set almost entirely in the brooding Teutonic forests, where Fafner the dragon lurks in the darkness, while the corrupt civilization of *Götterdämmerung* is ultimately destroyed by being deluged by the overflowing Rhine. Nature is more important than humanity in the *Ring*, and many of the nature effects in Wagner's music derive from Weber's example in *Der Freischütz*. Wagner was also inspired by the musical landscapes of Mendelssohn in works such as the Hebrides Overture and *Die schöne Melusine*, along with much from his father-in-law Franz Liszt, whose fascination with supernaturalism was just as strong as his own. Liszt dealt with the sublime in nature in his tone poem *Ce qu'on entend sur la montagne* and the piano pieces that made up book one of the *Années de Pèlerinage*, while his associate, the now rather less well-known Joachim Raff, devoted an entire symphony, subtitled *Im Walde*, to the German Romantic forest. He wrote another dedicated to the Alps (*In der Alpen*), while Schumann's *Waldscenen* for piano presented nature imagery on a more modest scale.

A modest scale is hardly how one would describe the symphonies of Gustav Mahler, but his ambition to create a "gigantic hymn to the glory of every aspect of creation"[28] required the largest possible forces. He described his gigantic Third Symphony as a work in which "the whole of nature finds a voice."[29] When conductor Bruno Walter came to visit Mahler in his Alpine retreat at Steinbach in the Salzkammergut, he looked up at the mountains. "No need to look up there," Mahler said, "I've composed all that already."[30] Richard Strauss' *Alpensinfonie* of 1915, mentioned in chapter two, was, therefore, the culmination of the German obsession with sublime, pantheistic Nature which, via German cinema in the 1920s, paved the way for later Gothic horror films. However, the actual location of such landscape isn't anywhere near as important as the way in which one responds to it. One way of explaining this is to compare two landscapes from different countries but written at the peak of the Romantic movement. The first comes from James Fenimore Cooper's *The Last of the Mohicans* (1826):

> The river was confined between high and cragged rocks, one of which impended above the spot where the canoe rested. As these, again, were surmounted by tall trees, which appeared to totter on the brows of the precipice, it gave to the stream the appearance of running through a deep and narrow dell. All beneath the fantastic limbs and ragged tree-tops, which were, here and there, dimly painted against the starry zenith, lay alike in shadowed obscurity. Behind them, the curvature of the banks soon bounded the view, by the same dark and wooded outline; but in front, and apparently at no great distance, the water seemed piled against the heavens, whence it tumbled into caverns, out of which issued those sullen sounds, that had loaded the evening atmosphere. It seemed, in truth, to be a spot devoted to seclusion, and the sisters imbibed a soothing impression of security as they gazed upon its romantic, though not unappalling beauties.[31]

Such writing (except for the reference to a canoe) is not really American at all. It is, rather, an example of a universal Romantic landscape aesthetic. Compare the above passage with the typically savage scenery of Walter Scott's first Waverley novel, set in Scotland:

> Advancing a few yards, and passing under the bridge which he had viewed with so much terror, the path ascended rapidly from the edge of the brook, and the glen widened into a silvan amphitheatre, waving with birch, young oaks, and hazels, with here and there a scattered yew. The rocks now receded, but still shewed their grey and shaggy crests rising among the copsewood. Still higher, rose eminences and peaks, some bare, some clothed with wood, some round and purple with heath, and others splintered into rocks and crags. At a short turning, the path, which had for some furlongs lost sight of the brook, suddenly placed Waverley in front of a romantic waterfall. It was not so remarkable either for great height or quantity of water, as for the beautiful accompaniments which made the spot interesting. After a broken cataract of about twenty feet, the stream was received in a large natural basin filled to the brim with water, which, where the bubbles of the fall subsided, was so exquisitely clear, that although it was of great depth, the eye could discern each pebble at the bottom.[32]

This passage, despite the wonders it did for the Scottish tourist trade, is similarly part of the idealized landscape of international Romanticism, and could just as easily be situated in Norway, Germany or even Italy. Indeed, Scott gives the game away when, a few sentences later, he writes, "Here, like one of those lovely forms which decorate the landscapes of Poussin, Waverley found Flora gazing on the waterfall."[33] The imagery here is not so much based on any particular place as on a particular aesthetic, in which the paintings of Poussin also reside. In a very real sense, the actuality of Romantic literary landscape is irrelevant. Often the best descriptions of real places have been written by authors who had never visited them. By basing their imaginative descriptions of landscape on secondary sources rather than on first-hand experience, the resulting imagery is far more emotionally resonant and psychologically meaningful. Bram Stoker's descriptions of Transylvania are not only more dramatic than the actuality, they are also more appropriate to the narrative:

> Beyond the green swelling hills of the Mittel Land rose mighty slopes of forest up to the lofty steeps of the Carpathians themselves. Right and left of us they towered, with the afternoon sun falling full upon them and bringing out all the glorious colours of this beautiful range, deep blue and purple in the shadows of the peaks, green and brown where the grass and rock mingled, and an endless perspective of jagged rock and pointed crags, till these were themselves lost in the distance, where the snowy peaks rose grandly.... There were dark, rolling clouds overhead, and in the air the heavy, oppressive sense of thunder. It seemed as though the mountain range had separated two atmospheres, and that now we had got into the thunderous one.[34]

Hammer may only have been able to imply such natural sublimity with its picturesque, municipal means, but Werner Herzog's 1979 remake of F.W. Murnau's *Nosferatu* uses scenery in the truly sublime manner of Burke (and, as we shall see, provides a striking visualization of Stoker's "two atmospheres"). Herzog, for whom no arduous discomfort was too great when turning his visions into reality, took his cast and crew into genuine locations, just as Murnau had done with his original film, though in Herzog's case the locations were rather grander (his advantages of color and stereo sound notwithstanding). Herzog's resulting images understandably have far more to do with the sublime portrait landscapes of Caspar David Friedrich than with John Martin, and Herzog's view of the entire story is also specifically Germanic. To understand the sublime aesthetic of Friedrich, which Herzog recreates on film, it's important to realize that the gaze of the German Romantic artist is more often than not turned *inward* rather than outward. Friedrich said:

A romantic waterfall in Scotland (photograph by the author).

> Close your bodily eye, that you may see your picture first with the eye of the spirit. Then bring to light what you have seen in the darkness, that its effect may work back on others, from without to within.[35]

Friedrich's paintings are landscapes of the soul, a particularly Germanic way of looking at things, as we have seen with regard to the aforementioned quotation by Schiller. As the expressionist (as opposed to impressionist) artist Ernst Ludwig Kirchner would later say:

> The Latin takes his forms from the object as it exists in nature. The German creates his form in fantasy, from an inner vision peculiar to himself. The forms of visible nature serve him as symbols only ... and he seeks beauty not in appearance but in something beyond.[36]

In Friedrich's paintings, Nature often threatens to overwhelm the human beings he occasionally includes in his landscapes. It's true that this is also something that happens in Martin's approach to landscapes, but there is a stillness in Friedrich that is lacking in the far more theatrical Martin. Friedrich is more interested in evoking eternity and infinity in his landscapes. Darkness and mist fascinated him. For Burke, "obscurity" was sublime because it increases our sense of dread and danger. For Friedrich it had a more spiritual implication. He felt that "when a region is cloaked in mist, it appears greater and nobler: it enriches the imagination and intensifies expectancy, like a girl wearing a veil."[37]

Friedrich, the pantheist, aims to be transcendentally absorbed in both the divine and the demonic via Nature. His painting *Mist in the Elbe Valley* (1821) was interpreted not only as a study of Nature but also as a specifically Christian allegory. The foreground of the painting represents the world in which we live and breathe, but when we penetrate the mist, we enter the world beyond material existence.

Herzog puts this principle right at the heart of *Nosferatu*. As did Murnau before him, Herzog set the action in the Biedermeir period, the period of Friedrich himself, to emphasize the connection his film has with Friedrich's aesthetic. After Jonathan Harker (played by Bruno Ganz) has made his way through moist pastures and forested hillsides, and climbed Romantic waterfalls, all photographed in Friedrich's landscape manner, he rests at the top of a mountain. As he sits down to admire the view, one cannot help being reminded of the standing figure in Friedrich's seminal Romantic painting *Der Wanderer über dem Nebelmeer* (1818). The Wanderer in that painting has his back to the viewer, just as Harker also faces away from the camera. Harker looks around at the gathering clouds above, and we hear that epitome of Romantic nature music, the Prelude to Wagner's music-drama *Das Rheingold* (1869), swell out from the soundtrack. The clouds swirl around the last vestiges of daylight and eventually engulf it entirely, signifying that Harker has entered what Stoker called the "thunderous atmosphere" in the passage from *Dracula* quoted above. He is now in the demonic realm of the vampire, or, in the terminology of Friedrich's *Mist in the Elbe Valley*, he has left the foreground and has now penetrated the veil of clouds. He thus enters a world beyond material existence, a world inhabited by the Romantic artist: the world of insight, wisdom and dreams.

Harker then makes his way along a path cut into the side of a rock, which runs alongside a rushing stream. The view recalls the sublime imagery of Shelley's *Alastor; or The Spirit of Solitude*:

> ... Calm, he still pursued
> The stream, that with a larger volume now
> Rolled through the labyrinthine dell; and there
> Fretted a path through its descending curves
> With its wintry speed. On every side now rose
> Rocks, which, in unimaginable forms,
> Lifted their black and barren pinnacles
> In the light of evening, and, its precipice
> Obscuring the ravine, disclosed above,
> Mid toppling stones, black gulfs and yawning caves,
> Whose windings gave ten thousand various tongues
> To the loud stream.[38]

Though Murnau's film and Herzog's remake are obviously based on Stoker's *Dracula*, the emphasis in both films has shifted. Landscape has become far more important than it ever was in the novel or in any other film adaptation of the story. Landscape had been used as an indicator of mood in previous Dracula films, certainly, as well as an instrument of sublime effects, but it had always remained a backdrop to the narrative. Herzog, by contrast, places landscape center stage. Herzog's Dracula lives not only beyond the forest (the literal meaning of the word "Transylvania") but also beyond the mist, and the continual references in the film to German Romantic landscape traditions suggests to us that we should approach this vampire tale in a particular manner, to prepare us for the very significant way in which the film ends.

It was Murnau who changed the emphasis of the original story by introducing into it the very German idea of the *Liebestod*, whereby a woman's love redeems the tortured male vampire through a form of symbolic death. Herzog went one stage further by giving Klaus Kinski's Dracula several lines that leave us in no doubt about how he wishes us to view this tragic character. Kinski's Dracula is unutterably *sad*: so very different from the theatrical menace of Lugosi or the athletic, dignified hauteur of Lee. Kinski's Dracula longs to experience the human warmth that Harker and Lucy enjoy together. The insight of centuries (a metaphor if ever there was one, for the perceptive wisdom of the true artist) is a sterile thing indeed compared with mortal love. During the scene at Castle Dracula in which he discusses with Harker the property he is buying in England, Dracula explains:

> I am the descendent of an old family. Time is an abyss, profound as a thousand nights. Centuries come and go. To be unable to die is terrible. Death is not the worst. There are things more horrible than Death. Can you imagine enduring centuries, experiencing each day the same futile things?

Later in the film, when Dracula visits Lucy in her bedroom he confesses: "I wish I could partake of the love which is between you and Jonathan."

One might say that Herzog has interpreted *Dracula* along similar lines to *Lohengrin*, Wagner's Romantic opera of 1849, in which Lohengrin is presented as a metaphor, *par excellence*, of the Romantic artist. He is an individual who exists apart from ordinary humanity, tormented by his insight and in desperate need of the redemptive love of a woman. Lohengrin first appears on a boat pulled by a swan, having left the Castle of the Grail (another metaphor for artistic insight) to meet a loving woman. He agrees to marry her on condition that she never asks his name. He requires absolute trust from her, absolute devotion, as Wagner himself required of both his wives and anyone else who crossed his path; but the woman, Elsa, proves to be weak. She can't resist asking who he is, and Lohengrin, on telling her, has no alternative but to leave her. *Lohengrin* is therefore the most tragic of Wagner's operas, even though Lohengrin's departure *does* restore Elsa's brother to the world. (The brother had been transformed, by the evil Ortrud, into the swan that pulled Lohengrin's boat. His disappearance was what caused the whole tragedy in the first place, for Ortrud had accused Elsa of murdering her own brother, and it was to champion Elsa's cause that Lohengrin first appeared on the scene.)

Given the comparisons between this opera and Herzog's *Nosferatu*, it's not at all surprising that Herzog eventually went on to direct a production of *Lohengrin* at the 1988 Bayreuth Festival, in which he created sublime nature tableaux of a similar intensity to those we find in *Nosferatu*. In one of the settings Herzog worked on with his designer Henning von Gierke, the effect of tidal waters being pulled by the gravitational force of a rising and setting moon was suggested. Herzog used real water, so that its lapping could be heard blending with Wagner's music in a manner similar to the blending of naturalistic sound effects with symphonic underscore in a film. He also envisaged the conceit that the theater itself was situated in the center of an imaginary circle of stones, and that the *Gerichtseiche*, or "judicial oak tree," which Wagner mentions in his stage directions for Act I, and beneath which Elsa the heroine is to be tried for murder, was growing through the center of the theater auditorium itself. He suggested this imaginary tree by showing the audience its branches hanging down below the proscenium arch, thus emphasizing the central importance of Romantic nature imagery in his production. Significantly, concerning what we have already said about such symbolism, Lohengrin's first appearance in Act I and later departure at the end of Act III took place through a swirling tunnel of mist. As Alan Hollinghurst wrote in his review of this production for *The Times Literary Supplement*,

> *Lohengrin* is enacted in a world of miraculously conjured light and cloud, moon, mist, stars and snow. Lohengrin himself arrives and departs not in a boat but through the swirling funnel of a tornado—we are in the realm of weather rather than of miracles.

> Herzog's view of the opera is not so much Christian as post–Christian…. He shows us Brabant reverting to a state of nature, hungry for belief, but shelterless and disillusioned. He reads the legendary tenth century in terms of our own. His triumph is to convey this bleakness not through the routine anachronism of modern Wagner stagings but through a return to German Romantic art itself.[39]

At the end of both Murnau's and Herzog's *Nosferatu*, Lucy, Harker's wife, voluntarily sacrifices herself to save her community. She has read that only a woman pure in heart can defeat the vampire if she manages to keep him by her side until dawn. This is exactly what Lucy succeeds in doing. Realizing the Nosferatu's desperate hunger not just for blood but also for love, she encourages him to drink her own blood until dawn, when the vampire is destroyed, and consequently redeemed.

The idea of a *Liebestod* is totally alien to Stoker's novel, and to all the Universal and Hammer adaptations of it. Hammer did flirt with various forms of sympathetic symbolism in their presentation of Dracula. In *Dracula Has Risen from the Grave*, the title of which is heavy with Messianic import, Dracula weeps tears of blood, while at the end of *The Satanic Rites of Dracula* he is even given a Christlike crown of thorns to wear during his immolation. But he is never *redeemed* by love, no matter how sorry we are encouraged to feel for him. In Wagner's Romantic operas, however, the idea of *Liebestod* is ubiquitous. His *Flying Dutchman* (1843), which is a vampire tale in all but fangs, ends with the heroine, Senta, hurling herself into the waves to redeem the tortured, immortal, and virtually undead Flying Dutchman of the title. *Tristan und Isolde* (1865) contains the most celebrated *Liebestod* of all. Indeed, the whole opera is a *Liebestod* in which the two main characters aim to achieve complete union with each other through a kind of psychologically transformative death. At the end of *Götterdämmerung* (1876), the last of the four music-dramas that make up Wagner's *Der Ring des Nibelungen*, Brünnhilde commits suicide not only to achieve eternal union with her beloved Siegfried but, also like Lucy in Herzog's *Nosferatu*, to redeem her corrupted society. Kundy, the schizophrenic seductress of Wagner's last opera *Parsifal* (1882), also achieves redemption through death, as well as helping to restore the health of the decadent kingdom of the Grail by acknowledging Parsifal as its new leader. Even before Wagner, in 1816, E.T.A. Hoffmann (1776–1822) had composed an opera based on the legend of Undine, the water sprite who falls in love with a human being. The libretto he also wrote for this work contains one of the earliest appearances of the word *Liebestod*, but he could have had no idea of how pervasive it was to become. Undine has her human lover "zum reinen Liebestod erkoren," chosen for pure love-in-death. Herzog's Dracula might also have said the same of Lucy, and vice versa.

Five

Heaving Cleavage

Having raised the subject of the *Liebestod*, it now seems a good moment to explore eroticism from a Gothic point of view. Jung's definition of that aspect of the potentially destructive feminine principle, which he called the anima, is a redefinition of what had long been known as the *femme fatale*. Hollywood horror films of the 1930s had very few of them, two notable exceptions proving the rule. Carroll Borland, that archetypal Goth in *Mark of the Vampire*, was the most influential of them. Gloria Holden in *Dracula's Daughter* (dir. Lambert Hillyer, 1936) was the other. One should perhaps add Anna May Wong's portrayal of Fu Manchu's daughter Ling Moy in *Daughter of the Dragon* (dir. Lloyd Corrigan, 1931), but Warner Oland's Fu Manchu still had the upper hand in that film, and anyway Fu Manchu exists only on the outer fringes of Gothic horror. In the first two films, the social mores of the time at which they were made forbade the overt presentation of their *femmes fatales'* more interesting sexual natures. Borland's character was supposed to have had an incestuous affair with her father (Count Luna, as played by Bela Lugosi), while Holden's daughter of Dracula was originally to have demonstrated distinct lesbian proclivities. Hints of these idiosyncrasies are all that remain: with a meaningful expression in her flaming eyes, Holden hypnotizes a woman found on the streets. Count Luna, on the other hand, wanders about with an unexplained bullet wound on his forehead (incestuous guilt having caused him to commit suicide and thus become a vampire; but it's all a hoax anyway, as the final scene of the film rather disappointingly reveals).

Prudery and prejudice may well explain the fact that the majority of the monsters from the golden age of Hollywood were male. Film noir, however, abounded with *femmes fatales,* but they were never supernatural and their heterosexuality was never in any doubt. They existed for men, who still ruled the show. Things changed in the more permissive world in which Hammer films flourished. True, Hammer remained conservative (it was, after all, Frankenstein who Created Woman), and women were, of course, still victims of male desire. But Hammer not only made sex appeal more explicit, they also gave their women far more authority and power.

We can trace the sex element in Hammer's Gothic films back to the Gothic pornography of the Marquis de Sade (1740–1814), but it was really Matthew Lewis who pioneered the use of heaving cleavage to sell the product, so to speak. In this respect too, Lewis' *The Monk* was a kind of eighteenth-century Hammer horror film. Mario Praz, in his seminal study *The Romantic Agony*, highlights the following passage from that novel as an example of what he calls Lewis "awkward naïveté" when it came to sex scenes:

> She had torn open her habit, and her bosom was half exposed. The weapon's point rested upon her left breast: and, oh! that was such a breast! The moon-beams darting full upon it enabled

Gloria Holden and Otto Kruger in *Dracula's Daughter* (dir. Lambert Hillyer, 1936).

the monk to observe its dazzling whiteness: his eye dwelt with insatiable avidity upon that beauteous orb: a sensation till then unknown filled his heart with a mixture of anxiety and delight; a raging fire shot through every limb; the blood boiled in his veins, and a thousand wild wishes bewildered his imagination. "Hold!" he cried, in a hurried, faltering voice; "I can resist no longer! Stay then, enchantress! Stay for my destruction!"[1]

Praz felt that Lewis was "not skilled in voluptuous suggestion"[2] but mere "suggestion" was hardly the point. Lewis, like any exploitation film director, had no intention of leaving anything to the imagination of his readers. One is reminded here of the scene in Hammer's *Twins of Evil* in which Damien Thomas' Count Karnstein makes love to the vampire Mircalla, whom he has just summoned from the tomb. As they reach the climax of their ecstasy, Mircalla reaches out to fondle a candle in what Praz would no doubt call a similarly "naïve" manner as Lewis (though, as the above extract proves, Hammer's reliance on a candle as a phallic symbol pales into insignificance when compared with Lewis' imagination). The orgasmic, cross-eyed ecstasy of Yutte Stensgaard in *Lust for a Vampire* is perhaps closer to the spirit of Lewis. Of course, it was the promise of this sort of soft porn that made Hammer (and Lewis) so sensationally popular. Inevitably, not everyone at the time thought it in the best possible taste, and Lewis (again like Hammer) was accused of pandering to the lowest common denominator (which, to a large extent, he was). It was, however, his coupling of sex (no pun intended) with explicit supernaturalism that caused so much indignation from the great mistress of Gothic romance, Ann Radcliffe. This is ironic, as it had been Lewis' fevered reading of Radcliffe's *The Mysteries of Udolpho* that had inspired him to write his own novel. Mrs. Radcliffe replied with *The Italian* in which she reiterated her conviction that the genre she had done so much to develop was about terror rather than horror, and sensibility rather than sex (at least sex of the overtly titillating kind purveyed by Lewis). Most important of all, she again stressed the golden rule that all apparently supernatural events should always be explained by rational means, rather like Tod Browning's *Mark of the Vampire*, indeed.

Nonetheless, *The Monk*, like Hammer films at their peak, made a fortune. Also like Hammer, Lewis became a household name and was known as "Monk" Lewis wherever he went. If the cinema had been invented he would no doubt have turned his own novel into a screenplay. (That privilege had to wait until 1972 in a version directed by Ado Kyrou, which was based on a screenplay by Luis Buñuel.) Instead, Lewis became a playwright. His play *The Castle Spectre*, which followed hard on the heels of *The Monk*'s success, was as close as the eighteenth-century stage got to Hammer horror. It was among the first of a glut of melodramas which, again like Hammer, tumbled over one another to cash in on the craze for Gothic, and the way these plays were advertised anticipated Hammer too. Hammer always started each new project with a poster, often before they even had a script. In the early nineteenth century, the scripts for such melodramas were written well before the posters that advertised them were put up, but the posters did the same job as Hammer's lurid masterworks in this department, even though they had to rely on words rather than pictures. Public interest was obviously focused on the actors, but the posters also gave elaborate details of the scenery and effects to be expected. A poster for Edward Fitz-Ball's play *The Devil's Elixir* (one thinks of Hammer's *The Man Who Could Cheat Death*), listed the following:

> THE MYSTIC CAVERN
> OF THE SHADOW KING
> Francesco's Cell.
> THE RELIQUARY CHAMBER
> *In the Silver Palm Tree Monastery*
> THE EXTERIOR OF THE MONASTERY
> AND ITS DOMAINS
> *The Woodman's Hut and Forest.*
> The CASTLE of HARTZMERE,
> And Forest in the distance

That was just for Act One. Act Two boasted a Shrine, falling ruins and "THE DESTRUCTION OF THE DEMON."[3] *Frankenstein* and vampire plays were also popular. (Mary Shelley even saw an example of the former. "The story is not well managed," she reported, "but Cooke played [the Creature's] part extremely well.... I was much amused, and it appeared to excite a breathless eagerness in the audience."[4]) They were often linked, and shown in conjunction with comedies and farces in much the same way that cinemas used to provide a whole package for the evening: newsreels, an organist, B feature, cartoons and main feature. The presentation of the female body in such melodramas was, of course, nowhere near as explicit as Hammer would increasingly attempt, but as the above extract from *The Monk* proves, sex at this time was definitely a selling point.

Lewis was the godfather of heaving cleavage. One of *The Monk*'s many erotic scenes describes what we would now call "date rape." It's perpetrated by the monk of the title, Ambrosio, who is a positive Mount Vesuvius of repressed desire, capped by the snow-white mantle of virtue:

> He lifted her still motionless from the Tomb: He seated himself upon a bank of Stone, and supporting her in his arms, watched impatiently for the symptoms of returning animation.

Scarcely could He command his passions sufficiently, to restrain himself from enjoying her while yet insensible. His natural lust was increased in ardour by the difficulties, which had opposed his satisfying it....

Gradually He felt the bosom which rested against his, glow with returning warmth. Her heart throbbed again; Her blood flowed swifter, and her lips moved. At length She opened her eyes, but still opprest and bewildered by the effects of the strong opiate, She closed them again immediately. Ambrosio watched her narrowly, nor permitted a movement to escape him. Perceiving that She was fully restored to existence, He caught her in rapture to his bosom, and closely pressed his lips to hers. The suddenness of his action sufficed to dissipate the fumes, which obscured Antonia's reason....

He repeated his embraces, and permitted himself the most indecent liberties.[5]

The closest Hammer approached this kind of overt sexual activity was in the much-discussed rape scene, which proved to be so distressing for Peter Cushing and Veronica Carlson, in *Frankenstein Must Be Destroyed*. "That was very sad for both of us," Carlson admitted:

Terry Fisher was the same. They were trying to work out how to tear my nightgown off without exposing me because there was no nudity in my contract. I didn't want to be exposed. And every alternative was more vulgar than the last, and it was just the most horrendous thing. Peter and I discussed it at length very quietly together. Just him and me. We tried to argue about it but it wasn't any good. But I can remember Terry cut it short. He said, "Cut! That's enough." And he just turned away. And we stopped and Peter and I just stayed there and held onto each other. We felt very bad about it.[6]

Rape is, of course, implied in many other Hammer films, but it is never presented as lasciviously as in *The Monk*. Cleavage, however, was quite another matter, and it was an obvious selling point for Sir James Carreras, the managing director of Hammer. Carreras was determined to milk as many bosoms as offered themselves for inspection, but as mentioned earlier, this isn't to suggest that Hammer always reduced their leading ladies to subservient sex symbols.

In *Frankenstein Created Woman*, Christina, the "Woman" of the title, is egged on by the male brain that the baron has put inside her to dispatch the three aristocratic hooligans who sent the original owner of her new brain to the guillotine. Susan Denberg plays Christina as a psychopathic doll, not really aware of what she's doing. She snares each of her victims with a *Playboy* pout before plunging her phallic dagger into their unfeeling hearts. (It's important to realize that her body is also exacting its own revenge upon them, as all three cruelly mocked its deformities before the baron straightened it out.) She's a kind of Salome figure, and a rather more powerful one than the waxwork of Salome which Peter Cushing encountered in *The House That Dripped Blood* (dir. Peter Duffell, 1971). A serial man-eater, Christina performs her equivalent of Salome's Dance of the Seven Veils three times before she's overcome by the horror of her crimes and hurls herself over a cliff.

Salome, as we recall from the fourteenth chapter of the *Gospel According to St. Matthew*, danced before Herod in exchange for the head of John the Baptist, and Christina's resemblance to Salome reaches its peak in a scene towards the end of the film in a scene which shows her addressing the severed head of Hans (whose brain now lives on inside her own skull). She has propped this gruesome object on the finial of her bedroom mirror, from where it stares down inspirationally. At other times, however, she keeps the head in a hatbox, lavishing over it all the care attention of Salome over the head of Jokanaan.

I have kissed thy mouth, Jokanaan. I have kissed thy mouth. There was a biter taste on thy lips. Was it the taste of blood...? But perchance it is the taste of love.... They say that love hath a bitter taste.... But what of that? What of that? I have kissed thy mouth, Jokanaan.[7]

Publicity photo of Veronica Carlson.

Christina's connection to the decadent aesthetic of Oscar Wilde, from whose *Salome* play those words come, is even stronger. Originally written in 1891 in French for one of the theater's most decadent *femmes fatales* Sarah Bernhardt, the play was later transformed into Richard Strauss' even more sensational opera in 1905. Echoes of the music Strauss composed for Salome's final moments in that work appropriately suffuse Franz Waxman's score for the scenes in *Sunset Blvd.* in which Gloria Swanson's Norma Desmond descends her Gothic staircase, already mentioned in chapter one. *Sunset Blvd.*, indeed, opened the way for Hammer's series of psychological shockers starring veteran Hollywood actresses. The films were called "mini–Hitchcocks" by Sir James Carreras but they should really have been called "mini–Clouzouts" as they were all based, one way or another, on Henri Clouzout's classic thriller *Les Diaboliques* (1955). Perhaps it was to be expected that a French director should have decided to cast women as the murderers rather than as the victims; after all, the term *femmes fatales* is a Gallic expression. But by the time *Les Diaboliques* was made, the social position of women (thanks to the effects of World War II) had radically changed. One no longer needed to mythologize the *femme fatale*. She could now wear modern fashions, drive a car, smoke cigarettes *and* be utterly diabolical as well. In *Les Diaboliques*, two women decide to murder the boorish headmaster of a rather dreary boarding school. One of the women is the headmaster's wife. The other, her accomplice, is one of the staff. We eventually discover, however, that the wife has been duped by both her accomplice and her husband. Terrorized by the apparent return of her husband after she thought him safely dispatched, the wife ultimately witnesses his gruesome resurrection and suffers a fatal heart attack. This is exactly what the headmaster and the other woman have planned, for we now learn that they are lovers and have arranged the whole thing.

Screenwriter Jimmy Sangster exploited this basic scenario for the plots of his five intriguing thrillers for Hammer. The first of these, *Fear in the Night* (dir. Jimmy Sangster, 1972), has Ralph Bates terrorizing Judy Geeson. The film even shares the school setting of *Les Diaboliques*, and we shouldn't forget Joan Collins in prime nutcracker mode as Bates' lover and accomplice. Together they hope to make it look as though Geeson's character has killed Peter Cushing's headmaster. The headmaster is married to Collins' character and she and Bates hope to inherit his money. The second, male-motivated, Hammer mini–Hitchcock is *Maniac* (dir. Michael Carreras, 1963), which concerns an acetylene-torch murderer played by Donald Houston. The protagonist of Hammer's earlier attempt at this sort of thing, *The Snorkel* (directed by Guy Green, 1958, with a screenplay by Peter Myers), was also male; but for all the others, women are either guilty accomplices or perhaps less culpably deranged.

In *Nightmare* (dir. Freddie Francis, 1964), Jennie Linden is set up by her guardian and his girlfriend who contrive to get her to murder the wife of a psychiatrist. Posing as a nurse, this girlfriend proves to be quite the opposite of caring as she callously exploits Linden's paranoia. She terrorizes her by wandering around the house wearing a rubber mask, the very image, we later learn, of the psychiatrist's wife (played by the statuesque Clytie Jessop). When Linden is introduced to the genuine article, she is so overcome with terror that she plunges the knife that was intended to cut her birthday cake into the wife's stomach instead. Linden is put into an asylum and the guardian and his girlfriend think they've got away with it, along with Linden's money; but things don't work out quite as they had intended.

Paranoiac (dir. Freddie Francis, 1963) similarly features a powerful woman for whom murder is not too high a price to protect her unbalanced son, while in Hammer's *Taste of Fear* (dir. Seth Holt, 1961), Ann Todd is after the inheritance of Susan Strasberg and sets about getting it in as similarly ruthless a manner as Hammer's other *femmes fatales*. Christopher Lee, meanwhile, provided a useful but ultimately unconvincing red herring. (Lee regarded this as one of his best roles, though it's hard to see why.)

There were other Hammer thrillers which, though not based on *Les Diaboliques*, nonetheless featured strong women. In *Fanatic* (dir. Silvio Narizzano, 1965), Tallulah Bankhead plays an evangelical Christian whose moral zeal derives from a desire to wipe out the decadence of her past life. Meeting an unbeliever in the form of Stefanie Powers, she decides to lock her up in her crumbling mansion until she sees the light. Rather more psychologically complex was *The Nanny* (dir. Seth Holt, 1965) in which Bette Davis brilliantly portrayed the deranged nanny of the title, who is trying to come to terms with her guilty secret. We eventually learn that she accidentally drowned the little girl in her care, distracted by the news that her own neglected daughter has died from an abortion. Even more problematical is her relationship with the little girl's elder brother Joey (William Dix), who knows what happened.

Hammer also adventurously experimented with all manner of female anti-heroes. Following Roger Vadim's odd and uneven version of Sheridan Le Fanu's vampire tale "Carmilla" in 1960 (*Et mourir de plaisir* being inaccurately translated as *Blood and Roses* for its worldwide release), Hammer decided to hang Ingrid Pitt in their Gothic gallery as the star of *The Vampire Lovers*, which was based on the same source. This was both fortunate and unfortunate. No one could deny that Pitt is very pleasing on the eye as well as being an accomplished

Ingrid Pitt in *Countess Dracula* (dir. Peter Sasdy, 1971).

actress, but she was perhaps already too old for this role as a nubile teenager and much better suited to that of Elizabeth Bathory in Hammer's *Countess Dracula*. She was cruelly deprived of her own voice in this by the film's director, Peter Sasdy, so we get only half of her performance here. Her German-Polish accent would have been so much more powerful and appropriate to this story than the very proper English diction of the actress who dubbed her. Based on historical fact, *Countess Dracula* can't resist adding a supernatural element that tries to convince us that bathing in virgins' blood isn't merely an egomaniac's delusion but really can restore youth and beauty. Even so, Sasdy plays his tale more as a historical epic than as supernatural Gothic. Thanks to the impressive castle sets left over from *Anne of the Thousand Days* (dir. Charles Jarrott, 1969), there's a majesty and spaciousness about the film lacking in equally ambitious but less fortunate Hammer productions. This helped no end, especially in the final scenes in which the countess, about to be married to her horrified fiancé, suddenly grows old again and stabs him with her knife. Where does this action take place? On an impressive staircase, of course, a fact which has somehow managed to escape from chapter one.

Countess Dracula was Hammer's last female monster. It first appeared seven years earlier as *The Gorgon*—that ultimate anima role, epitomizing, as this character does, many a well-known quotation and cliché: "Hell hath no fury like a woman scorned," "If looks could kill" and so forth. It's one thing to chop off heads (that psychological metaphor of castration, previously discussed) but quite another to turn people to stone. Most of the Gorgon's victims are male in Hammer's version, though she's not fussy and starts off Gorgonizing an artist's female model. It is, however, significant that most of the victims are male because this film, one of Hammer's most poetic, is a kind of female version of the Beauty and the Beast story. In Jean Cocteau's even more poetic treatment of that legend (*La Belle et la bête*, 1946), the main thrust of the allegory concerns the process by which a young man learns to control his bestial impulses (and all that this implies from a sexual point of view) in order to win the girl. In *The Gorgon*, we see a woman struggling with her anima to allow men to love her. In this respect, the film follows the approach to the subject that was conveniently laid out for it by Shelley in his poem "On the Medusa of Leonardo da Vinci in the Florentine Gallery" (1824). Shelley describes Leonardo's sculpture of Medusa in ambivalent terms. "Its horror and its beauty are divine," he says. "Upon its lips and eyelids seems to lie/Loveliness," that famous "tempestuous loveliness of terror," indeed. "Yet," Shelley points out, "it is less the horror than the grace/Which turns the gazer's spirit into stone."[8]

Fully to convey this duality, Hammer's Carla, possessed by the spirit of the snake-headed terror, and the Gorgon herself are played by two actresses: Barbara Shelley and Prudence Hyman respectively, though they're meant to be the same being. Shelley manages to combine emotional vulnerability with a certain frigid beauty, which is exactly what's needed for Carla. She is loved by two men. The first, Dr. Namaroff (played with smolderingly subdued intensity by Peter Cushing), knows what's wrong with her but won't tell her. The second lover, Paul (played by Richard Pascoe), at first has no idea of Carla's split personality problems, and when he eventually finds out he doesn't really want to know. Both are ultimately destroyed by the spirit of the Gorgon—an unusual situation for a Hammer film in which the romantic leads are usually saved at the end. It's up to Christopher Lee's crusty academic to dispatch the Gorgon, which is appropriate as he's far more interested in examining shards of pottery than in admiring women.

Although Hammer makeup artist Roy Ashton based his designs for the Gorgon on Benvenuto Cellini's Head of Medusa,[9] the result wasn't as effective as Percy Shelley in conveying the

> Hairs which are vipers, and they curl and flow
> And their long tangles in each other lock,
> And with unending involutions show
> Their mailèd radiance, as it were to mock
> The torture and the death within[.][10]

The petrified victims of the Gorgon (particularly the demise of Michael Goodcliffe's Professor Heitz) were more convincing, resembling, in their swiftness and verisimilitude, H. P. Lovecraft's description of similarly petrified figures in "The Man of Stone," the tale on which he collaborated with Hazel Heald in 1932. Set in the Adirondack Mountains in New York State, "The Man of Stone" is a revenge story in which a mad sculptor, fascinated by the occult, discovers how to turn people and animals to stone by means of an infusion of calcium and barium salts. He petrifies his wife's dog as a sadistic test, then turns his wife's lover to stone, but is prevented from doing the same to his wife, who finds out what he's planning and hoists him with his own petard. She leaves an account of how she traps him and funnels the fatal mixture down his throat. "In ten minutes I knew he was solid stone. I could not bear to touch him, but the tin funnel *clinked* horribly when I pulled it

Prudence Hyman in the title role of ***The Gorgon*** (dir. Terence Fisher, 1964).

out of his mouth."[11] But if sexual jealousy is the motivation of Lovecraft's tale, it's more a matter of sexual disavowal in *The Gorgon*. Not having assimilated her own sexuality, Carla ends up destroying the things she tries to love. She is both Belle *and* Bête, and her frigidity reaches its ultimate form when she is decapitated as the Gorgon herself, a female castration indeed. All Carla wants to do is run away from rather than confront her problem. She urges

Paul to leave with her after their moonlight assignation in, how appropriate, a graveyard. Their love is doomed to destruction so long as she ignores the Gorgon within her, until she unites the beautiful, well-behaved but unfulfilled Carla with the potentially destructive anima of the Gorgon and thus becomes a completely integrated psyche, or what Jung would call "individuated."[12] Namaroff fears this outcome as it means he will lose his control over Carla, which is why he tries to keep the truth from her. Paul sees her only as a beautiful woman, a kind of mother figure. He has already lost his father to the Gorgon, while his artist brother, horrified by the death of the model at the beginning of the film, has hanged himself. Paul's mother isn't mentioned, but her absence seems to be filled by Carla's appearance in his life. At one point he even says that having lost his father and brother he doesn't care what happens to himself (which does indeed suggest that he has no mother left alive either). Carla replies, "I care what happens to you," but in the end both Paul and Namaroff pay the price for their blindness. The anima has its revenge upon them as well. (One could say that anima was the cause of Maegaera/Medusa's problems in the first place. The original Gorgon legend explains that Medusa had once been a beautiful maiden but was transformed into a Gorgon by Athena as a punishment for having been caught *in flagrante delicto* with Poseidon in one of Athena's temples.)

Paul eloquently fulfills the criteria of the male victim of a *femme fatale* as described by Mario Praz. He is

> usually a youth [who] maintains a passive attitude; he is obscure, and inferior either in condition or in physical exuberance to the women, who stands in the same relation to him as do the female spider, the praying mantis, &c., to their respective males: sexual cannibalism is her monopoly.[13]

Drawing our attention to the Italian novelist and poet Gabrielle D'Annunzio (1863–1938), Praz uses a quotation from that author's classic novel of decadence, *Trionfo della morte* ("The Triumph of Death," 1894) to typify this kind of predatory *femme fatale*. D'Annunzio's hero, Giorgio, is musing on the object of his obsessive infatuation:

> "Cruelty lurks hidden in her love," he thought. "There is something destructive in her, which becomes the more evident the more violent her orgasm...." And he saw again in memory the terrific, almost Gorgon-like vision of her as she had often appeared to him, when, convulsed by a spasm or inert in final exhaustion, he had looked at her through half-closed eyelids.[14]

Praz traces this type of *femme fatale* back via Swinburne, Baudelaire and Shelley, to Matthew Lewis and the Marquis de Sade. This literary journey also takes Praz past the aesthetic writings of Victorian critic Walter Pater (1839–94), whose famous description of Leonardo da Vinci's *Mona Lisa* has even more significance if read in tandem with Shelley's poem on Leonardo's *Medusa*:

> She is older than the rocks among which she sits; like the vampire she has been dead many times, and learned the secrets of the grave; and has been a diver in deep seas, and keeps their fallen day about her; and trafficked for strange webs with Eastern merchants [...]. The fancy of a perpetual life, sweeping together ten thousand experiences, is an old one; and modern philosophy has conceived the idea of humanity as wrought upon by, and summing up in itself, all modes of thought and life. Certainly Lady Lisa might stand as the embodiment of the old fancy, the symbol of the modern idea.[15]

The same could be said of Rider Haggard's immortal woman, Ayesha, in his novel *She* (1887). Hammer hired Ursula Andress to portray Ayesha in their adaptation of the story. Whether by accident or design, the main theme for it, based on the syllables of the name

Ay-Esh-A, is identical to Franz Liszt's setting of the words "ewig Wiebliche" from Goethe's lines "Das ewig Weibliche/zieht uns hinan" ("the eternal feminine leads us on").[16] These words bring the second part of *Faust* to a close, and Liszt decided to set them to music as a way of concluding his own Faust Symphony, which is based on that drama. Ayesha is most certainly an eternal woman, in the sense that she has acquired physical immortality, like the vampire. But also, on a deeper level, she represents the immutability of the anima. Her love crosses centuries and is terrible. Like Carla, she is a mixture of frigid beauty and barbaric violence and, like all Hammer's female vampires, her unleashed sexuality and consequent power over men, is seen as both dangerous and alluring by the men who cross her path. Like the women in Hammer's mini–Hitchcocks, she plots her way to her ultimate desire, luring Leo Vincey to her palace beyond the Mountains of the Moon, by means of maps, rings, visions and sheer will power; but she is also vulnerable.

In this respect she resembles the *femme fatale* of Hammer's *The Reptile* (dir. John Gilling, 1966). Ayesha is vulnerable to the cold, in her case the cold blue flame which, when entered a second time, takes back its gift of immortality, bringing death instead. The cold is also the Achilles heel of the Reptile, otherwise known as Anna Franklin (played by Jacqueline Pearce). She is the unfortunate daughter of a doctor of theology (Noel Willman) who unwisely penetrated the secrets of a snake cult while on a research trip in the Far East. As a result, they have turned Anna into a shape-shifting snake woman by way of punishment. Somewhat like Carla in *The Gorgon* before her, Anna now suffers from a split personality. One minute she's an attractive young girl, the next, she turns into a hideous and deadly reptile. Of course, Hammer wasn't the first to deal with shape-shifting schizophrenic females. H.P. Lovecraft had collaborated on a story with Zealia Bishop called "Medusa's Coil" (published in 1939), in which the Gorgonesque *femme fatale* is called Marceline. She marries an American boy who takes her back to his family home in Missouri. There, the husband's friend, an artist of the decadent school, feels compelled to paint Marceline's portrait — a portrait that reveals the full horror of what she is and has been throughout the centuries. Marceline is eventually murdered by her husband, who scalps her snakelike hair, which promptly strangles the artist friend, coiling about his neck like a boa constrictor. The husband's father then buries all the bodies in a lime pit. When a visitor to his decaying mansion pumps twelve bullets into the canvas one night, overwhelmed with horror by what he has seen, the terrible Marceline comes back to life.

The cinema had also experimented with female shape-shifters quite some time before Hammer came along. Simone Simon had turned into a cat woman (or *had* she? Jacques Tourneur's 1942 film *Cat People* is tantalizingly ambivalent), and there have even been a couple of female werewolves: Nina Foch in *Cry of the Werewolf* (dir. Henry Levin, 1944) was one, Ursula Howells in *Dr.*

Jacqueline Pearce in the title role of *The Reptile* (dir. John Gilling, 1966).

Terror's House of Horrors another. But Hammer's *Reptile* has an even greater resonance than any of those because of its literary antecedents, which can ultimately be traced back to the serpent who tempted Eve in the garden of Eden. We needn't go quite so far back as that here, however. As with so much of his account of the Romantic *femme fatale*, Praz concentrates on Swinburne concerning the serpentine manifestation of the type, and quotes from Swinburne's *Notes on Designs of the Old Masters in Florence* in which the poet has been discussing some studies of female heads by Michelangelo:

> But in one separate head there is more tragic attraction…: a woman's, three times studied, with divine and subtle care; sketched and re-sketched in youth and age, beautiful always beyond desire and cruel beyond words; fairer than heaven and more terrible than hell; pale with pride and weary with wrong-doing; a silent anger against God and man burns, white and repressed, through her clear features. In one drawing she wears a head-dress of eastern fashion rather than western, but in effect made out of the artist's mind only; plaited in the likeness of closely-welded scales as of a chrysalid serpent…. Her eyes are full of proud and passionless lust after gold and blood; her hair, close and curled, seems ready to shudder in sunder and divide into snakes. Her throat, full and fresh, round and hard to the eye as her bosom and arms, is erect and stately, the head set firm on it without any droop or lift of the chin; her mouth crueller than a tiger's, colder than a snake's, and beautiful beyond a woman's. She is the deadlier Venus incarnate[.][17]

Swinburne continues his analysis with even more serpentine imagery: This woman is like Cleopatra, "not dying but turning serpent under the serpent's bite." Another drawing gives her "electric hair, which looks as though it would hiss and glitter with sparks if once touched." This hair is "wound up to a tuft with serpentine plaits and involutions; all that remains of it unbound falls in one curl, shaping itself into a snake's likeness as it unwinds, right against a living snake held to the breast and throat." Swinburne continues:

> This is rightly registered as a study for Cleopatra; but notice has not yet been accorded to the subtle and sublime idea which transforms her death by the aspic's bite into a meeting of serpents which recognise and embrace, an encounter between the woman and the worm of Nile, almost as though this match for death were a monstrous love-match, or such a mystic marriage as that painted in the loveliest passage of *Salammbô*, between the maiden body and the scaly coils of the serpent and the priestess alike made sacred to the moon[.][18]

What better description of Hammer's *The Reptile* than Swinburne's here of "the maiden body and the scaly coils of the serpent"? As Praz goes on to explain, "It is hardly necessary to point out how little Swinburne's imagination sticks to the drawings he is discussing: Michelangelo is translated into terms of Gautier,"[19] just as Hammer's *Reptile* turns Swinburne's idea into a popular horror film; but the connection is clear and certain. Swinburne was part of a long tradition when it came to snake-women. E.T.A. Hoffmann had preceded him in his famous tale "The Golden Pot" (1827) in which a young student, Anselmus, hears singing in the branches of an elder tree:

> [H]e looked up, and perceived three little snakes, glittering with green and gold, twisted around the branches, and stretching out their heads to the evening sun. Then, again, began a whispering and twittering in the same words as before, and the little snakes went gliding and caressing up and down through the twigs; and while they moved so rapidly, it was as if the elder-bush were scattering a thousand glittering emeralds through the dark leaves.
> "It is the evening sun sporting in the elder-bush," thought the Student Anselmus; but the bells sounded again; and Anselmus observed that one snake held out its little head to him. Through all his limbs there went a shock like electricity; he quivered in his inmost heart: he kept gazing up, and a pair of glorious dark-blue eyes were looking at him with unspeakable longing; and an unknown feeling of highest blessedness and deepest sorrow nearly rent his heart asunder.[20]

These snakes are the daughters of a mythical Salamander who, in typically Hoffmannesque style, has taken the human form of one Archivarius Lindhorst. The Salamander wants to find husbands for his three daughters, and has hopes of the student poet Anselmus "for who knows but a spark may fall in this or that young man's breast, and kindle a longing for the green snake; whom, on Ascension Day, under the elder-bush, he will forthwith seek and find?"[21]

Hoffmann's snakes are fascinating rather than fatal females, but they belong to the same genus as the snake woman of *The Reptile*, a genus which had previously attracted the attention of the Romantic poets Coleridge (1772–1834) and Keats (1795–1821). Their snake women are nowhere near as benign as Hoffmann's and they graphically anticipate what Hammer was to do with the story in 1966. Keats was himself aware of the potential popularity of a snake woman tale when he was writing his celebrated lyric *Lamia*, which was first published in 1820. In a letter to his brother George, Keats confessed that he believed his poem had "that sort of fire in it which must take hold of people in some way. Give them either pleasant or unpleasant sensation — what they want is a sensation of some sort."[22] Hammer was obviously of the same opinion. Keats drew his story from Robert Burton's *Anatomy of Melancholy* (1621), and it concerns a young Corinthian called Lycius, who is spellbound by the beautiful Lamia. He plans to marry her but only finds out what she is when his old tutor, Apollonious, spills the beans at the bridal feast. "And shall I see thee made a serpent's prey?" he asks. Thus unmasked, Lamia's beauty withers and with a dreadful scream she vanishes, leaving Lycius to die of a broken heart. Though it takes until the end of the poem for Lycius to find out the truth, the reader knows exactly who Lamia is from having read the prologue in which we learn how Hermes transformed a snake he encounters on his travels into a beautiful woman:

> Her head was serpent, but, ah, bitter-sweet!
> She had a woman's mouth with all its pearls complete:
> ...
> Her throat was serpent, but the words she spake
> Came, as through bubbling honey, for Love's sake[.][23]

Once transformed into a human being she becomes

> ... a maid
> More beautiful than ever twisted braid
> Or sigh'd, or blushed, or on spring-flowered lea
> Spread a green kirtle to the minstrelsy:
> A virgin purest lipp'd[.][24]

This image of "full-born beauty" is interesting to compare with Dr. Franklyn's despairing description of his daughter in the fiery denouement of *The Reptile*, when he explains how the whole tragedy happened.

> DR. FRANKLYN: She lies down there in the cavern. That vile thing underneath that blanket is my daughter, Anna — oh, not the Anna you know, not that lovely girl. *Not that lovely girl*, but a hideous parody of herself, a loathsome thing, using her body. My daughter! My lovely Anna! ... She was my only happiness, my dearest possession.

Coleridge's snake woman occurs in his 1797 poem "Christabel," which, unlike Keats' later serpent story, revels in a full-on Gothic setting:

> 'Tis the middle of night by the castle clock,
> And the owls have awakened the crowing cock

>   ...
>   Is the night chilly and dark?
>   The night is chilly, but not dark.
>   The thin gray cloud is spread on high,
>   It covers but not hides the sky.
>   The moon is behind, and at the full;
>   And yet she looks both small and dull.
>   The night is chill, the cloud is gray:
>   'Tis a month before the month of May,
>   And the spring comes slowly up this way.[25]

Wandering through the wood, Christabel, the daughter of a knight, comes across the snake woman Geraldine, who, like Anna Franklin in *The Reptile,* at first appears vulnerable and melancholy:

>   The lady strange made answer meet,
>   And her voice was faint and sweet: —
>   Have pity on my sore distress,
>   I scarce can speak for weariness[.][26]

It is in a similar mood that Anna introduces herself to her new neighbor Mrs. Spalding in *The Reptile.* Anna invites her and her husband Captain Spalding to dinner at the Franklin residence in a similarly faint and sweet voice. "*Please* say you'll come," she says, as if it's a matter of some urgency. Like Coleridge's Geraldine, she too is a "maiden most forlorn." Anna is kept prisoner by her father who dares not let her out for fear of the truth about her being discovered. At first we suspect Dr. Franklin of being the villain of the piece, but that role is reserved for Marne Maitland's splendidly saturnine Malay, whose mission it is to persecute Franklin and his daughter for the rest of their lives. Again like Coleridge's Geraldine, Anna understandably seeks human companionship, but she also needs physical warmth due to her reptilian nature, and the vital warmth of animals, which are her prey. Her room in the gloomy Franklin mansion (the exteriors of which were filmed at Oakley Court again) are filled with her "pets," kept in cages for convenient consumption. After dinner, Dr. Franklin suggests to Anna that she show these to Mrs. Spalding, while he takes a cigar with Captain Spalding in the sitting room. Mrs. Spalding follows Anna to her bedroom and a curious scene ensues which suggests that the captain's wife has another kind of attraction for Anna. This is later expressed through Anna's ardent attentions to the kitten she is given to stroke by the Malay servant. Mrs. Spalding is unnerved, as was Coleridge's Christabel during a subliminally lesbian moment in which Christabel undresses in front of her strange guest as they prepare for bed:

>   Her gentle limbs did she undress,
>   And lay down in her loveliness.[27]

It's not long before Geraldine, also undressing, reveals the true horror of what she is:

>   Beneath the lamp the lady bowed,
>   And slowly rolled her eyes around;
>   Then drawing in her breath aloud,
>   Like one that shuddered, she unbound
>   The cincture from beneath her breast:
>   Her silken robe, and inner vest,
>   Dropt to her feet, and full in view,
>   Behold! her bosom and half her side —
>   A sight to dream of, not to tell!
>   O shield her! shield sweet Christabel![28]

It's also worth comparing Roy Ashton's snake makeup for Jacqueline Pearce in Reptile mode,[29] with Coleridge's description of the serpentine characteristics of Geraldine:

> A snake's small eye blinks dull and shy;
> And the lady's eyes they shrunk in her head,
> Each shrunk up to a serpent's eye,
> And with somewhat of malice, and more of dread,
> At Christabel she looked askance![30]

Christabel now feels guilty for having been attracted to Geraldine, tempted by this snake of lesbian lust:

> [H]er girdled vests
> Grew tight beneath her heaving breasts.
> "Sure I have sinn'd!" said Christabel,
> "Now heaven be praised if all be well!"[31]

No more is made of the potentially lesbian encounter in Anna's bedroom, though the film's central set piece, in which Anna performs on the sitar before her father and her two guests, implies some disturbing emotional undercurrents. As the music becomes weirder and more hypnotic, Anna stares imperiously at her increasingly agitated father. No longer the submissive daughter, Anna begins to reveal her snake nature, much to the delight of the onlooking Malay servant. She is both a man hater and a maneater, and the resentment she feels for her father can also be translated into a hatred of men altogether. Significantly, Anna wants desperately to make friends with Mrs. Spalding rather than her husband, and doesn't succeed in killing/kissing her when, in Reptile mode, opportunity offers itself so to do.

Whatever the psychosexual undertow of *The Reptile*, Hammer made no bones about the lesbian content of their so-called Karnstein Trilogy, which put Christabel's "heaving breasts" in the spotlight. Ingrid Pitt was of the opinion that vampires "don't have any gender"[32] but Hammer was very keen to display the naked bodies of its female vampires, so obviously someone thought vampires enjoyed gender, and a consequent sexuality. The lesbian content of the Karnstein trilogy is so obvious it hardly needs pointing out. The misguided decision to add lyrics to Harry Robinson's music during the erotic swimming scene in *Lust for a Vampire* is now a firmly established part of Hammer folklore. "Strange love." Well, perhaps in 1970 lesbian vampires were considered almost as strange as mortal lesbians. At that time it was only possible to discuss such things in mainstream cinema within the context of a Gothic horror film. (It had taken until 1961, after all, for British cinema to discuss male homosexuality openly when Dirk Bogarde, never one to come out of the closet himself, bravely agreed to star in *Victim* [dir. Basil Dearden] as a gay lawyer who becomes the victim of blackmail. That the blackmailer is another gay in denial is all too obvious from the poster of Michelangelo's *David* on his bedsit wall.)

Critics often back their claims that horror films were able to go to sexual places out of reach to other genres by referring to the famous still of Yutte Stensgaard rising from her tomb in *Lust for a Vampire*, her exposed breasts drenched in blood as she bares her fangs as if about to indulge in some sort of demonic felattio; but nothing so explicit is shown on screen. We see Carmilla begin to rise from her tomb, certainly, but the shot ends before we see anything as graphic as that still. Such thrills, it seems, were permitted only to the promenaders of cinema lobbies where they were displayed under "Forthcoming Attractions."

Le Fanu hadn't been the first to write about Gothic lesbians. De Sade had included every kind of sexual permutation he could think of in his novels *The 120 Days of Sodom* (written in 1785) and *Justine* (1791), but even Ann Radcliffe had suggested such forbidden fruit in her more polite novels. In *The Italian*, for example, the heroine, Ellena, makes friends with a nun called Olivia. Their encounters are described by Radcliffe in a way which suggests that rather more than mere mutual respect is going on here:

> [T]he nun passed close by Ellena, who threw back her veil, and fixed upon her a look so supplicating and expressive, that the nun paused, and in her turn regarded the novice, not with surprize only, but with a mixture of curiosity and compassion. A faint blush crossed her cheek, her spirits seemed to faulter, and she was unwilling to withdraw her eyes from Ellena....
> "She is very handsome," said Ellena.[33]

When Ellena is rescued by her male lover Vivaldi, he is put rather in the shade during the passionate farewell between Ellena and Olivia:

> The fears of Ellena now gave way to affectionate sorrow, as, weeping on the bosom of the nun, she said "farewell! O farewel, my dear, my tender friend! I must never, never see you more, but I shall always love you[.]"[34]

Radcliffe's perceptive biographer, Rictor Norton, refers to Jane Spencer's observation that *The Romance of the Forest*, *The Mysteries of Udolpho* and *The Italian* all "end with defeat for the authoritarian male and the heroine's marriage to a feminized hero."[35]

Gothic horror has always appealed to outsider sexualities. Its narratives are primarily concerned either with the sexual oppression of persecuted heroines or the destiny of those ultimate outsiders, shunned by "normal" society, who form a veritable gallery of monsters. It is hardly surprising that the gay director James Whale should have identified so movingly with Mary Shelley's famous Creature, but never again, after *Bride of Frankenstein*, were so many homosexual references consciously to inform a so-called horror movie. Hammer continued to experiment with alternative sexualities and issues of gender in *Dr. Jekyll and Sister Hyde* (dir. Roy Ward Baker, 1971) in which the good doctor turns into a beautiful woman rather than a hideous travesty of a man. In a desperate attempt to explain what's happened to the innocent young girl who lives in the flat above his laboratory, he calls this alter ego his sister and thus approaches a kind of incestuous hermaphrodism. Mrs. Hyde, as played by Martine Beswick, is the ultimate anima stereotype, carrying a dagger in her black stockings and dispatching prostitutes with (in both senses of the word) gay abandon. The most intriguing scene occurs when Dr. Jekyll meets a young man called Howard (the brother of the innocent girl who lives upstairs). Howard (played by Lewis Fiander) has already encountered Mrs. Hyde and they have already expressed their physical attraction for each other in no uncertain terms. Mrs. Hyde is proving to be the dominant gender in Dr. Jekyll's psyche, so when the doctor meets Howard in the doorway of a ladies' outfitters, she comes temporarily to the surface. There's no physical change in Dr. Jekyll, but he looks longingly into Howard's eyes and languorously whispers his name. Howard is understandably disconcerted. It's the only moment of overt male homosexuality in the whole of Hammer's output (Dracula biting Johnny Alucard in *Dracula A.D. 1972* isn't really in the same league).

The dominant ideology of the time, which favored the female body over the male, still prevails, of course. So entrenched was it that it never occurred to Hammer to take male homosexuality as seriously as they took their lesbians. Only one horror film from the Hammer period presented an overtly male homosexual vampire. Intriguingly, this was in Roman Polanski's satire on Hammer's style (*The Kiss of the Vampire* [dir. Don Sharp, 1964] in par-

Martine Beswick as Mrs. Hyde in *Dr. Jekyll and Sister Hyde* (dir. Roy Ward Baker, 1971).

ticular) which is known alternately as *Dance of the Vampires* or *The Fearless Vampire Killers, or Pardon Me, Your Teeth Are in My Neck* (1967). Polanski himself played one of these vampire hunters (called Alfred) who finds himself in the splendidly Gothic castle of Count von Krolok (Ferdy Mayne) where he comes across the count's flamboyantly gay vampire son, Herbert (Iain Quarries). Much to Alfred's discomfort they discuss the arts of seduction together, using a handbook on the subject, which Alfred has been consulting for purely heterosexual purposes:

> HERBERT [*reading Alfred's book*]: "Seventieth way: Place the left arm around the shoulders of the loved one. [*He puts his left arm around Alfred's shoulder.*] Put the left hand on her left shoulder like a little birdie alighting on a branch." [*He does this.*] Good! Excellent! "Then, let an angel pass?" Shall we let an angel pass? "Once the angel has passed, bend the face towards the locks of the loved one and brush them with the lips." [*Bares his fangs. Alfred rams the book between them.*]

By this time Alfred has already realized that something isn't quite right about this particular individual, as there is no reflection of him in the mirror that hangs in his Gothic bedroom. The lack of a reflection, as is well known, implies the lack of a soul, but portraits in Gothic romance often have a life of their own and they invariably find it hard to stay in their frames, as we're just about to find out…

Six

Living Pictures

One of the most famous scenes in *The Mysteries of Udolpho* concerns a portrait that turns out not to be a portrait at all. The scene in question caused a great deal of excitement among the young women in Jane Austen's *Northanger Abbey*. Catherine Morland, Austen's impressionable heroine, confesses:

> [W]hile I have Udolpho to read, I feel as if nobody could make me miserable. Oh! the dreadful black veil! My dear Isabella, I am sure there must be Laurentina's skeleton behind it.[1]

Catherine is referring here to the scene in which Emily Saint Aubert enters a chamber in the mysterious castle of Udolpho and comes across a portrait covered with a black veil. Emily's servant, the garrulous Annette, knows nothing about the portrait but eagerly shares in the rumors appertaining to it:

> I have heard there is something very dreadful belonging to it — and that it has been covered up in black *ever since* — and that nobody has looked at it for a great many years — and it somehow has to do with the owner of this castle before Signor Montoni came to the possession of it[.][2]

When Emily eventually steels herself and does peer behind the veil, she sees something so terrible that Mrs. Radcliffe makes the reader wait until the very end of the novel for a full description. The implication, meanwhile, is that the villain of the piece, Montoni, has murdered the presumed sitter of the portrait, the castle's previous owner, Laurentini di Udolpho (which, in fact, he has not). A great many pages later, however, we are at last told the truth:

> It may be remembered, that, in a chamber of Udolpho, hung a black veil, whose singular situation had excited Emily's curiosity, and which afterwards disclosed an object, that had overwhelmed her with horror; for, on lifting it, there appeared, instead of the picture she had expected, within a recess of the wall, a human figure of ghastly paleness, stretched at its length, and dressed in the habiliments of the grave. What added to the horror of the spectacle, was, that the face appeared partly decayed and disfigured by worms, which were visible on the features and hands. On such an object, it will be readily believed, that no person could endure to look twice. Emily, it may be recollected, had, after the first glance, let the veil drop, and her terror had prevented her from ever after provoking a renewal of such suffering, as she had then experienced. Had she dared to look again, her delusion and her fears would have vanished together, and she would have perceived, that the figure before her was not human, but formed of wax. The history of it is somewhat extraordinary, though not without example in the records of that fierce severity, which monkish superstition has sometimes inflicted on mankind. A member of the house of Udolpho, having committed some offence against the prerogative of the church, had been condemned to the penance of contemplating, during certain hours of the day, a waxen image, made to resemble a human body in a state, to which it is reduced after death. This penance, serving as a memento of the condition at which he himself must arrive, had been designed to reprove the pride of the Marquis of Udolpho[.][3]

The image had long since been forgotten behind its black veil, however, waiting through the years to become one of Mrs. Radcliffe's most impressive red-herrings. The horror of the lifelike (or death-like) waxen image, here, is comparable to those exhibited by Madame Tussaud, who, coincidentally, began to trade under that name in 1795, the year after *The Mysteries of Udolpho* was first published. (Tussaud had, however, been exhibiting her effigies since 1770 and, as is well-known, collected notable heads severed during the French revolution as models for her grisly work. Her marriage to François Tussaud changed the name of the enterprise.) The thrill of standing close to lifelike but harmless effigies that are performing horrific deeds is another manifestation of Burke's opinion, "Whenever danger or pain press too nearly, they are incapable of giving any delight, and are simply terrible; but at certain distances, and with certain modifications, they may be, and they are delightful."[4] The "modifications" at work in the waxwork Chamber of Horrors are obvious. Why else would we pay good money to see an effigy of Adolf Hitler or Dr. Crippen? Stuffed animals also provide the opportunity to get up close and personal with something that might kill you if it were alive; but what if such effigies could come back to life? Therein lies the real thrill of such attractions (which is related to the *frisson* of an Egyptian mummy, staring out at us from across the centuries). We know that neither a wax effigy nor a mummy can come to life but we can imagine how we might feel if they could, and thus give ourselves agreeable gooseflesh in the process.

Waxworks have gone on to inspire several films in which such effigies either come to life or are created by insane artists. Paul Leni's *Das Wachsfigurenkabinett* of 1924 was the first significant example, in which, amongst other things, a waxwork of Jack the Ripper (played by Werner Krauss) comes to life. That was followed by *Mystery of the Wax Museum* (dir. Michael Curtiz, 1933), in which Lionel Atwill as mad waxwork sculptor Ivan Igor pours wax over the corpses of people he has murdered before adding them to his gallery of masterpieces. Vincent Price starred in the remake *House of Wax*, directed in 3-D by André de Toth in 1953, while *Carry on Screaming* (dir. Gerald Thomas, 1966) sent up the whole thing by having Kenneth Williams dunk pretty young women in his vat of wax to provide mannequins for boutiques, a process he introduced with the immortal words, "Frying tonight!" It was all a very apposite satire for the fashion conscious, heavily–Hammered 1960s. As *Carry On* producer Peter Rogers explained:

> Dear Jimmy Carreras used to say to me, "You make the comedy. I'll make the horror." It may be unfair that I tackled his line of business, but he was perfectly free to put "Matron Has Risen From the Grave" into production. I certainly wouldn't have minded![5]

Williams was apparently undead in *Carry On Screaming*, and required regular jolts of electricity to keep him going. He was made up to look like a travesty of Peter Cushing, but the characters played by Price and Atwill were both horribly disfigured, the audience being asked to believe that their normal faces were made of wax too. This gave Phantom of the Opera–style opportunities for horrible unmasking at the end, so one could claim that they were living works of art themselves.

Waxworks were only one part of the Gothic tradition of art and illusion invading so-called reality. Gothic romance has a long history of oil paintings coming to life. This idea first occurred in Walpole's *The Castle of Otranto*, when the villain of the piece, Manfred, is about to seduce Isabella:

> At that instant the portrait of his grandfather, which hung over the bench where they had been sitting, uttered a deep sigh and heaved its breast. Isabella, whose back was turned to the picture,

saw not the motion, nor knew whence the sound came, but started and said, Hark my lord! what sound was that? and at the same time made towards the door. Manfred, distracted between the flight of Isabella, who had now reached the stairs, and his inability to keep his eyes from the picture, which began to move, had however advanced some steps after her, still looking backwards on the portrait, when he saw it quit its pannel, and descend on the floor with a grave and melancholy air.[6]

This sort of thing soon became a cliché of horror tales, and it was eventually satirized by Gilbert and Sullivan in their Gothic operetta *Ruddigore* (1887). The hero of that work has inherited the family curse. He's known as Robin Oakapple but is really Sir Ruthven Murgatroyd (note the significant forename, derived from the eponymous hero of Polidori's *The Vampyre*). The curse compels him to commit a crime a day, but so far he's not been very wicked at all, and it's not long before the portraits of his ancestors step down from their frames to berate in withering terms his pathetic attempts at villainy. Gilbert's Gothic text is set in pseudo–Wagnerian manner by Sullivan, and the result (as happened in Polanski's *The Fearless Vampire Killers*) is rather more frightening than one might have expected:

> When the night wind howls in the chimney cowls, and the bat in the moonlight flies,
> And inky clouds, like funeral shrouds, sail over the midnight skies—
> When footpads quail at the night-bird's wail, and black dogs bay at the moon,
> Then is the spectres' holiday—then is the ghosts' high noon![7]

A variation on this theme took place twenty years after Ruddigore, when the great Russian choreographer Mikhail Fokine premiered his ballet *Le Pavillion d'Armide*, with music by Alexander Tchereprin, at St. Petersburg's Maryinsky Theatre in 1907. The plot concerns the Vicomte de Beaugency, who, in true Gothic style, takes refuge in a castle during a storm. The sinister owner of the castle escorts him to a garden pavilion where he invites the vicomte to sleep for the night, but the vicomte is fascinated by a tapestry of the sorcerer Armide that hangs there. He falls asleep and dreams that the characters of the tapestry come to life. When Armide herself steps down before him, he falls in love with her, and on awakening the following morning, the vicomte finds to his amazement that he is holding Armide's scarf. Looking at the tapestry more closely, he discovers that the scarf in the picture is missing, and he is so shocked by the realization that what he took for a dream actually happened, he falls lifeless to the ground, to the jubilation of the sinister owner of the castle, who is a sorcerer himself.

Henry James' ghost story "Owen Wingrave" (1892) also features pictures that come to life, though these, like those of *Ruddigore*, are oil portraits rather than tapestries. Owen is the last of a military family. His pacifist convictions compel him to abort his preparations for a military career, a decision that outrages his highly militant relations. He is accused of cowardice, and to prove his courage to his fiancée Kate, he agrees to spend a night in the haunted room of the family seat, which is where he encounters the ghosts. The following morning he is found dead. These supernatural happenings provided some effective visual elements in Benjamin Britten's operatic adaptation of the tale which was made specially for television in 1971. Only two years later, Amicus made *And Now the Screaming Starts* (dir. Roy Ward Baker), which was set in the vintage Gothic year of 1795. The main titles linger over the Victorian Gothic splendor of Oakley Court, filmed from the River Thames, which stands in (somewhat anachronously) for the ancestral home of the Fengriffen family. Ironically, this film makes far more use of the exteriors of Oakley Court than any Hammer film ever did, and very beautiful Baker makes it look too. Things turn ugly inside, however, when Stephanie Beacham as newlywed Catherine Fengriffen has a *Ruddigore* moment of her own. It takes place on the film's very elaborate staircase set (designed by Tony Curtis), which bears some relation to David Myerscough-Jones' sets for Britten's *Owen Wingrave* opera. Apparently it didn't cost anywhere near as much as one would think, but it certainly looks expensive. Even though this staircase scene would seem to be the province of chapter one, I've saved it until now because its real point of interest lies in the portraits that adorn the walls around the staircase rather than in the staircase itself, though it's obviously significant that this scene should be set on such a grand example. During a guided tour of her new husband's ancestors, Catherine's attention is attracted by one of Herbert Lom as Sir Henry Fengriffen, her husband's debauched and deceased grandfather. While she's staring at it, Douglas Gamley's score warns us to expect something nasty any minute, and sure enough, a bloody hand soon punches its way through the canvas. Later, an eyeless apparition with a bloody stump in place of its left hand drifts out of the portrait, dripping red hot Kensington Gore onto the floor. There's also a legend about the house that no one seems willing to talk about, but Rosalie Crutchley, who plays the housekeeper, takes pity on Catherine and fetches a book from the library. This has all the information Catherine needs to research the subject; but as the housekeeper is taking the book upstairs, the portraits start to rattle against the wall. When a vision of a severed hand appears before her, she has a fit and falls, Odessa Steps–style, to her death.

Top: Oakley Court roofs. ***Bottom:*** A room with a view: looking out from one of Oakley Court's windows (photographs by the author).

It's all too much for Catherine, who takes to her bed where she reads some suitably Gothic imagery from Milton's *Comus*:

Some say no evil thing that walks by night,
In fog, or fire, by lake, or moorish fen,
Blue meagre hag, or stubborn unlaid ghost,
That breaks his magic chains at curfew time,
No goblin, or swart faery of the mine,
Hath hurtful power o'er true virginity.[8]

Unfortunately, Catherine is now pregnant and so no longer immune from evil things that walk by night. As her paranoia is showing no signs of abating, Peter Cushing is called in as a psychiatrist called Dr. Pope, whose working methods have anticipated Sigmund Freud by a century. He tries to persuade Catherine that the legend of the Fengriffen family has unsettled her mind and that this is the cause of her hallucinations, as he interprets them. The legend itself concerns the wicked Sir Henry who was said to have exercised his *droit du seigneur* with the fiancée of his estate woodsman. When the woodsman protested, Sir Henry chopped off the unfortunate man's left hand. The curse on the Fengriffen family is said to date from that time, when it was laid upon Sir Henry's descendants by the woodsman himself, who vowed that the first child of the family's next virgin bride will be born deprived, like the woodsman, of its left hand, which is exactly what happens.

Related to the idea of portraits coming to life is the old chestnut of cutting away the eyes of a portrait to provide discrete peepholes through which one may conveniently spy on other people. This sort of thing happens in Hitchcock's *Psycho* (1960) and, rather more flamboyantly, in *Theatre of Death* (dir. Sam Gallu, 1966), in which the tyrannical director (played by Christopher Lee) of a Parisian theater specializing in Grand Guignol entertainments is first introduced to us while spying on his party guests using this time-honored technique. In fact, he stares through the eyeholes of his own portrait, although it's meant to be his father, who was obviously a dead ringer for the son.

A novel variation of this idea occurs in Ken Russell's *Gothic* (1986), in which the poet Shelley (played by Julian Sands) thinks he can see two eyes staring at him from the naked breasts of Claire Clairmont (Myriam Cyr). According to Dr. John Polidori, who was present at the occasion on which this scene was based, Shelley did indeed have just such a hallucination, though it was inspired by Byron's reading of Coleridge's *Christabel* rather than a fixation on Claire's breasts:

> Shelley, shrieking and putting his hands to his head, ran out of the room with a candle. Threw water in his face and after gave him ether. He was looking at Mrs S, & suddenly thought of a woman he had heard of who had eyes instead of nipples, which, taking hold of his mind, horrified him.[9]

Gothic also refers to Henry Fuseli's famous picture *The Nightmare* (1781), which was used in the film's advertising campaign. The latter caused a surprising degree of controversy at the time, as Derek Malcolm, film critic of *The Guardian*, recalled:

> The poster has a naughty-looking goblin perching on the elegant chest of Natasha Richardson and Virgin films have been told that it is not acceptable. So they have airbrushed the goblin out, leaving Natasha looking more relaxed but a little uncertain as to what is happening to her. All this seems rather silly since ... it is a pretty exact pastiche of a well-known Fuseli painting that's been perverting visitors to the Tate for some years, as Ken Russell pointed out at his Guardian lecture earlier in the week.

Paraphrasing the whole point of the book you are reading now, Malcolm continued:

> The point surely is that the original Fuseli is high art, likely to be gazed at only by nice middle-class people who can take it; while the poster is low cunning which might shock or possibly deprave and corrupt unfortunate commuters from the lower orders.[10]

Gothic horror films have always re-contextualized and thus democratized elements of high art, and that's one of the reasons why the genre has always existed in a twilight world of its own. Despite the supposedly liberating advent of post-modernism, it's still shunned by some critics, who often feel that horror films contaminate something they regard as far more important and significant.

The surrealist movement was always open to offers from the mass media. Think of Luis Buñuel's *Un Chien andalou* (1928), which was a cinematic warm-up for Salvador Dalí who went on to bring an extra *frisson* to the dream sequences of Alfred Hitchcock's *Spellbound* (1945). These feature stocking-topped card players, giant eyes, enormous scissors, and Gregory Peck being chased down a pyramid by a pair of disembodied wings. What more could any psychoanalyst ask for? The images which top and tail *The Creeping Flesh* were in surrealist mode too. They are meant to have been painted by Peter Cushing's deranged scientist, Emmanuel Hildern, and depict the vengeful monster of the story, to whom we'll be returning in the next chapter.

Popular cinema also democratized the expressionist movement in Robert Wiene's *The Cabinet of Dr. Caligari* (1919). In 1922, to prepare British audiences for this alien experience from a country with which they had been at war only a few years before, the distributors felt that a word or two of explanation was necessary to those who had not already been initiated into the mysteries of this strange new style. They pointed out that the aim of the film was to bring the style of expressionist painting to life. Two painters from the Der Stürm group, Walter Röhrig and Hermann Warm, were hired to create the angular distorted sets that made the film so memorable. Indeed, the film's design is its most important element, its preponderance of dagger-like shapes fully *expressing* the murderous intentions of Dr. Caligari himself.

We've already seen how Werner Herzog summoned echoes of the German Romantic landscapes of Caspar David Friedrich in *Nosferatu*. Indeed, the slow-motion footage of a bat in flight against a moonlit background is a vampire film version of Friedrich's sepia design *Eule vor dem Mond* ("Owl Before the Moon," 1836–37). The ship that brings Dracula to Harker's sleepy little town is also reminiscent of Friedrich's paintings of ships in full sail. Such references are part of a long tradition in German cinema. Murnau's original *Nosferatu* had, of course, attempted the same thing (though without the advantage of color). Friedrich had also informed various images in *The Student of Prague* (dir. Henrik Galeen, 1926). The famous still from that film, in which Werner Krauss' Scapinelli, umbrella in hand, gazes out beyond a contorted tree against a stormy sky, recalls Friedrich's *Mann und Frau den Mond betrachtend* ("Man and Woman Contemplating the Moon") from 1830–35.

It's to be expected from a director like Fritz Lang, who trained as an artist, that his films should be particularly informed by the visual arts. One of the most obvious references to fine art in *Metropolis* (1926) is the scene that tells the story of the Tower of Babel, the model of which in the film is directly inspired by Breugel's famous painting from 1563. *Metropolis* also contains, amongst all its art deco futurism, some typically German Gothic elements: in the home of the inventor Rotwang and in a scene that's set in a cathedral. The former has some telling Gothic arches, while the latter is the location for a nightmare scene in which statues of Death and the Seven Deadly Sins come to life. The medieval image of Death as a skeleton, playing a bone like a flute, has several parallels in nineteenth-century German art, particularly in the Alfred Rethel picture *Death as Assassin* (1848), in which Death plays his violin with a bone rather than a bow. Walter Schulze-Mittendorf's face mask for the Deadly Sin of "Zorn" (or "Anger") in the film also has certain features in common with the grotesque masks which Arnold Böcklin sculpted for Basle Art Gallery in 1871.

Other Lang films extend the range of references. One might even make a bid to compare the famous medieval sculpture of the Bamberg Rider, at Cologne Cathedral, with the celebrated shots of Siegfried on his white stallion in Lang's *Die Nibelungen* (1922–1924). In the same film, a shot of children dancing naked around a slender birch tree is reminiscent of the nineteenth-century German painter Hans Thoma's *Frülingsreigen* ("Spring Procession") of 1875, in which (fully clothed) children dance around a similarly delicate tree. This image was echoed again in Max Reinhardt's celebrated adaptation of Shakespeare's *A Midsummer Night's Dream* for Warner Brothers in 1935, along with several other references to Böcklin. For example, Mickey Rooney's Puck, emerging from underwater covered in weed, recalls Böcklin's sculpture *Der Froschkönig* (*The Frog King*), and Reinhardt was keen to echo Böcklin's painting from of a woman riding a unicorn, called *Das Schweigen des Waldes*

Max Schreck in *Nosferatu* (dir. F. W. Murnau, 1922).

("The Silence of the Forest," 1887). Non-German audiences of the movie wouldn't necessarily have picked up these artistic references, as all the artists I've mentioned so far have never become as popular outside Germany as they are with Germans themselves but they undoubtedly contribute to the atmospheric effect. By contrast, British and American directors rarely assumed that art references would be so easily identified, even if they were interested in doing such a thing, which wasn't often the case. *Dante's Inferno* (dir. by Harry Lachman, 1935) was an attempt to place Gustave Doré's nineteenth-century illustrations of Dante's epic poem in the context of a twentieth-century story about a ruthless carnival owner, but one has to wait until midway through the film before the carnival owner has the nightmare that is the cue for the Doré-inspired dream sequence. It's worth waiting for, however, for as Leslie Halliwell said, though the film is a "Curiously unpersuasive melodrama with a moral, ... the inferno sequence is one of the most unexpected, imaginative and striking pieces of cinema in Hollywood's history."[11]

A rather more integrated and far more compelling blend of fine art and cinema was made ten years later by RKO. Directed in 1945 by Mark Robson, *Isle of the Dead* was one of several rather cerebral horror films produced by Val Lewton, who had emigrated from Russian to America with his family in 1909 (the same year in which Rachmaninoff composed his own musical response to the painting by Arnold Böcklin that was to inspire Lewton's *Isle of the Dead*). Lewton's name was originally Vladimir Leventon and he had been fascinated and terrified by Böcklin's picture since early childhood. He had a famous aunt in Hollywood, the actress Alla Nazimova, who had left Russia in 1905, and for a while the family stayed with her. Vladimir wanted to write. He'd write *any*thing: prose, poetry, journalism, and he eventually made a career for himself in the film business, starting as a script editor for producer David O. Selznick. By then he'd changed his name to Val Lewton and was eventually

put in charge of RKO's horror film unit. The studio would come up with titles they thought would draw in the crowds and Lewton was told to produce them; but the studio didn't get quite what they expected. Lewton crafted some amazingly restrained and poetic films from titles as unpromising as *I Walked with a Zombie* (1943), which became a version of *Jane Eyre* set in Haiti and, moreover, featured Böcklin's *The Isle of the Dead* on the walls of one of its sets. Another film, *Bedlam* (1946), was inspired by an engraving by the eighteenth-century artist William Hogarth, which made the fact that the film was never granted a certificate in Britain rather ironic. There were many others, including *Cat People* (1942), *The Leopard Man* (1943), and *The Seventh Victim* (1943), all of which avoided obvious monsters and relied instead on atmosphere and suggestion to create their effects. Many had literary and cultural references far beyond the call of duty, and one of the most interesting was *Isle of the Dead*, which starred Boris Karloff as a grim but somehow simultaneously genial general of the Greek Army during the war between Greece and Turkey in 1912. A plague has followed the war and Karloff tells a journalist about the mysterious island where his wife, another victim of the war, is buried:

GENERAL PHERIDES: You saw that island off the shore? It's a cemetery, a burial place.
OLIVER DAVIS: I'd like to see the place. I'll go there tomorrow. I'd like to put some flowers on your wife's grave.
GENERAL PHERIDES: I'll give you that chance. I plan to go there tonight. I'll take you with me.
OLIVER DAVIS: Across the battlefield out there?
GENERAL PHERIDES: You mean it's dangerous for an old man? You forget I'm an old soldier as well. You take the lantern.

Karloff and his young friend row over to a recreation of Böcklin's most famous painting, which has already served as a backdrop for the film's main titles. On the island we are introduced to a group of unfortunate individuals who have been quarantined there. They share a house together, the main sitting room of which is decorated with another Böcklin painting: Böcklin's own self-portrait, in which a skeleton, playing a violin, looks over the artist's shoulder as a *memento mori*. Nothing much happens in the first part of the film, but gradually people start dying of the plague and we eventually learn that one character is terrified of being buried alive, which, of course, is just what happens to her. There are also rumors that the island is haunted by a kind of Greek vampire, though this is never made explicit. It was all part of Lewton's strategy of eerie suggestion.

Lewton wasn't the only person to have been haunted by the work of an artist who had once been the intellectual rage of Europe. Böcklin lived long enough to become a cult figure in his own lifetime, especially during the last years of the nineteenth century when the symbolist movement idolized his dreamy and atmospheric landscapes. The list of his admirers is impressive (and from the point of view of contemporary taste, astonishing). It includes Brahms (who visited Böcklin in 1887 in his Zurich studio), Hugo Wolf (who hung a reproduction of *The Isle of the Dead* on the wall of his study in Vienna), Max Klinger (who made an etching of *The Isle of the Dead*) and Ferdinand Keller (who painted another homage to the artist, his own version of *The Isle of the Dead*, luxurious with purple wisteria, which he called *The Tomb of Böcklin*). Giorgio de Chirico, Wassily Kandinsky, Salvador Dali, and Edvard Munch were also fans, as were Strindberg (who included a reference to *The Isle of*

Opposite, top: A scene from *Dante's Inferno* (dir. Harry Lachman, 1935). *Opposite, bottom:* "And, lo! there came / Two naked men, torn with briers, in headlong flight[.]" Gustave Doré illustration (1867) for Canto XIII of the "Inferno" from Dante's ***The Divine Comedy.***

Above: Poster for *Isle of the Dead* (dir. Mark Robson, 1945), showing a version of Böcklin's original picture at the bottom. *Opposite, top:* Boris Karloff and Marc Cramer in *Isle of the Dead* (dir. Mark Robson, 1945). *Opposite, bottom:* A reproduction of Böcklin's painting "The Isle of the Dead," competing with the shadows in *I Walked with a Zombie* (dir. Jacques Tourneur, 1943).

the Dead in his 1907 play *The Ghost Sonata*), Stefan George, Hugo von Hofmannsthal and Thomas Mann. Böcklin was made an honorary citizen of Zürich, the university of which also awarded him an honorary doctorate. There were torchlit processions on his birthday, and he was generally praised for having being the founder of a new, intensely yearned-for art, the aesthetic sublimity of which would stimulate the imagination and, through the rediscovery of mythology, bring people back into contact with the rejuvenative forces of nature. Wagner had been doing much the same thing with his music dramas, and, as Edvard Munch pointed out, Böcklin, like Wagner, gave the Germanic soul, in particular, exactly what it was searching for at the turn of the nineteenth century by making art a mystical event for the soul, turning it into a religious experience. As we've seen, Böcklin's predecessor in all this had been Caspar David Friedrich, whose landscapes of the soul opened the way to what the Belgian playwright and poet Maurice Maeterlinck (1862–1949) referred to as "a spiritual epoch."[12] German idealism hoped to make that epoch a reality, but unfortunately, such a yearning contributed to the first world war, and later came to a sticky end with the perversion of this idealistic dream by the Nazis. At the turn of the century, though, such ideals were respected across Europe, and had a particular resonance for German culture.

So what is Böcklin's most famous painting all about? For a start, the title *The Isle of the Dead* wasn't Böcklin's idea at all. That was dreamed up by an art dealer called Fritz Gurlitt, who realized that it's much easier to market a picture if you can call it something. Böcklin himself wasn't fond of titles, which he felt limited the viewer's response to the image, much as Chopin disliked titles for his waltzes and preludes. Instead, Böcklin gave the generic title of *Stimmungsbild* or "Mood Picture" to his dreamy landscapes, for there were many more than just *The Isle of the Dead*, which itself exists in several versions. The word "Stimmungsbild" itself went on to be highly influential, particularly in musical circles, where a host of musical *Stimmungsbilder* eventually filled the piano stools of European drawing rooms, most famously a collection of piano pieces by Richard Strauss. Böcklin would have been delighted to have inspired so much music because he too believed in what Wagner called *Gesamtkunstwerk* ("total work of art"), which synthesized the different arts into a unified whole.

The *Stimmungsbild* that became known as *The Isle of the Dead* was originally commissioned from Böcklin by a certain Maria Berna, later Countess of Oriola, who, in 1880, had visited Böcklin in Italy where he had lived for much of his professional life. Madame Berna had recently been widowed and asked Böcklin for a painting in memory of her husband — a painting, as she put it, with which "to dream by."[13] What Böcklin came up with took Europe by storm: a shrouded figure is being rowed to a mysterious island. An echo of Christ on the Mount of Olives perhaps? The Death of Religion or a Religion made out of Death? Is it belief that is being rowed to its tomb? Above, the sky is somber with storm-streaked purple clouds. Dark waters lap the stones of the gateway to the catacombs with the merest ripple. These are the tombs of the long departed, lost to memory with none but the dead to watch over their crumbling stones; and towering over all, like obelisks, the dark needles of cypress trees inject the sky with melancholy. None but the never-to-return come here.

Böcklin left viewers to come to their own conclusions as to the painting's meaning but there's no doubt that it caught the general spirit of the times. His art resonated deep within the consciousness of late nineteenth-century Europe, echoing a general sense of pessimism and cultural decline that was felt by artists and intellectuals and was persuasively articulated in particular by the writer Max Nordau in his book *Entartung* (Degeneration). In this highly influential book, Nordau argued that industrialization and modern urban life had alienated humanity from its spiritual needs, hence what he called the "symptoms" of man's spiritual hunger that he saw in the mysticism of the Pre-Raphaelites, the dreamy works of the Symbolist painters, the mythological regressions of Wagnerian music drama, the cult of decadence and aestheticism.

It was this general symbolist/decadent atmosphere that went on to inspire many of the sets and costumes in Francis Ford Coppola's extravagant *Bram Stoker's Dracula* (1992). However, whatever its other merits as a modern Hollywood horror film, it would be hard to find a presentation of the title character that is *less* like Bram Stoker's description of him. Coppola's title for this strangely overblown, self-conscious but often beautiful film is consequently rather misleading. Gary Oldman has many different manifestations as the vampire count. We first see him wearing a kind of Japanese Kabuki hairpiece and costume, but later he's rigged out in an outfit that recalls the jeweled geometric designs worn by the two figures in Gustav Klimt's painting *Der Kuss* ("The Kiss," 1907–08). Dracula's Transylvania castle, propped up by iron girders *à la* Gustave Eiffel, is based on a painting by the Czech symbolist František Kupka (1871–1957) called *The Black Idol* (1903). Back in England, various High Victorian paintings decorate the walls of the Hillingham Estate (Lord Leighton's *Flaming June* among them), while Lucy is presented as the kind of stylized woman favored by the art nouveau artist Alphonse Mucha (1860–1939). The headboard of her bed resembles the halo-like designs against which Mucha often placed his appealing maidens. Later, as Lucy grows weaker from her vampiric illness, she wears a gigantic white lace ruff. This not only refers to Mucha again, but also gives her the appearance of a frilled lizard when she is resurrected as a vampire. Dracula's three vampire brides were also made to resemble Mucha maidens. Coppola and his designers deliberately chose these symbolist images, even though they play no part in Stoker's novel. Costume designer Eiko Ishioka argued, like Coppola, that "the world that Dracula inhabits is familiar territory to the Symbolist imagination — whose artists, in the words of Moreau, 'hurl themselves into the abysses of bygone ages, into the tumultuous spaces of dreams and nightmares.'"[14] We'll be returning to this point in more detail in the next chapter.

In the early years of the twentieth century, many people saw the decadence of such imagery as symptomatic of an illness: an urgent summons for the regeneration not only of society but, more sinisterly perhaps, of mankind itself. Böcklin, with his mythological subject matter and brooding melancholy, became regarded by many as a spokesman for specifically Germanic cultural forces that the international industrial world was perceived to be destroying. Ironically, considering he lived in Italy for so many years and was actually Swiss rather than German, Böcklin was now appropriated for the cause of German nationalism, just as Wagner would form an integral part in the later catastrophes of twentieth-century German history.[15]

The horrors of the first world war, which were largely provoked by such idealistic German nationalism, were soon to turn the whole of Europe into an Isle of the Dead. At first, the war was greeted with hysterical approval. University students were encouraged to engage in this struggle for *Kultur* over *Civilization*:

> Students! The muses are silent. The issue is battle, the battle forced on us for German *Kultur*, which is threatened by the barbarians from the east, and for German values, which the enemy in the west envies us. And so the *furor teutonicus* bursts into flame once again. The enthusiasm of the wars of liberation flares, and the holy war begins.[16]

Those were the words of a rector of a Bavarian university; and many German students responded accordingly. When one of them said, "Poetry, art, philosophy, and culture are what the battle is all about,"[17] he was not alone. The artist Franz Marc went so far as to say:

> Let us remain soldiers even after the war…for this is not a war against an eternal enemy, as the newspapers and our honorable politicians say, nor of one race against another, it is a *European civil war*, a war against the inner invisible enemy of the European spirit.[18]

For the many of the German intelligentsia, the war was what they called an *innere Notwendigkeit*, a spiritual necessity. As the historian Modris Eksteins put it,

> It was a quest for authenticity, for truth, for self fulfillment, for those values, that is, which the avant garde had evoked prior to the war and against those features—materialism, banality, hypocrisy, tyranny—which it had attacked. The latter were associated particularly with England, and it was to be England, of course, who was to become Germany's most hated enemy after she entered the war on August 4.[19]

That spiritual necessity, however, failed to be achieved. There was no victory for German idealism, that idealism, which, among many other things, had found a metaphor in the dreamy landscapes of Arnold Böcklin. Idealism destroyed itself in war, the devastation of which Val Lewton's film so aptly conjured up on a much more modest budget. Though the specific war referred to in *Isle of the Dead* was the Balkan War of 1912, the film as a whole also reflected the far greater horrors of the first and second world wars, for when it first appeared in 1945 the atrocities of Nazism were still fresh in the minds of the audiences who first saw it.

Towards the end of the story, Boris Karloff's genially ruthless Greek army general succumbs like many of the other characters to the dreaded plague. Despite a change in the wind, it's all too late for him and he realizes that there is no escape from the Isle of the Dead:

> OLIVER DAVIS: General, the wind! Look! The wind has changed to the south. It's a *sirocco*! We'll be able to leave this place, and you can take command of your troops again.
> GENERAL PHERIDES: I've taken command for the last time.
> OLIVER DAVIS: Oh, come now, general, you'll feel a lot better after we leave this accursed island.
> GENERAL PHERIDES : I shall never leave the island.

And perhaps that is the secret meaning of Böcklin's mysterious painting. After all, there's no escape for anyone and each of us will one day make that journey far across the silent waters to those brooding cypress trees and timeless tombs. Death, as Böcklin's self-portrait reminds us, is always looking over our shoulder. Death is waiting within us. It is part of us.

The most famous portrait in film must, of course, be *The Picture of Dorian Gray* (dir. Albert Lewin, 1945), that elegant black-and-white rendition of Oscar Wilde's only novel, in which the portrait of Hurd Hatfield, who plays the title role, is unveiled to us in vivid Technicolor, before gradually corrupting as the immortal Dorian's somewhat ill-defined sins grow worse and worse. This portrait has no need of a skeleton peering over its shoulder for it *is* death, or at least it becomes the image of the death that Dorian himself manages to avoid until the end of the story. A rather more subtle way of using portraits to suggest duality occurs in J. Sheridan Le Fanu's Gothic novel *Uncle Silas* (1864), which pairs the evil Uncle Silas himself with his apparently benign brother, Austin Ruthyn. The story follows straightforward Gothic conventions: Austin is deceived into thinking that his dissolute and murderous brother Silas is a redeemed character, and therefore assigns him as the guardian of his daughter, Maud. Too late, he learns that Silas is not what he seems but is prevented from amending his will by a sudden heart attack. Maud is consequently terrorized by her seemingly benign uncle, who intends to kill her and thus inherit her estate. But, this being a Gothic novel, she is ultimately rescued and the forces of evil are overpowered. The psychological structure of the novel, however, makes it more interesting than its fairly conventional story would suggest.

W. J. McCormack argues that within the context of the book's Swedenborgian frame of reference, mirror images form a central aspect of the book as a whole, which presents an entire paradigm of reflections, oppositions and symmetries. As McCormack paraphrases him, Emanuel Swedenborg (1688–1772) was of the belief that after death, "the events of a man's life are repeated in his consciousness in order to reveal his real (and hidden) motivation and spiritual condition.... [The] recently dead do not know they are dead, and the living may be visited by angels whom they cannot distinguish from mortals. In such a framework, 'Austin' is the earthly existence of a soul whose real nature is exposed in the figure of 'Silas' who is constantly described in metaphors of death."[20] The structure of the plot emphasizes this duality. The first part of the novel concerns Austin, whose home is dominated by a portrait of Silas. When Austin dies, the action transfers to Silas' frightening Gothic pile, Bartram-Haugh, the opposite of what Austin seems to stand for, but which, in fact, is merely a metaphor for the darker side of his own personality. Instead of a portrait dominating the proceedings, Le Fanu employs the symbolic force of a large Bible given to Silas by his sanctimonious brother.

The film adaptation of *Uncle Silas* (dir. Charles Frank, 1947) carefully articulates the duality of Austin/Silas by means of Silas' portrait. In the novel, Maud describes this as having "a remarkable elegance and a delicacy in the features, but also a character of resolution and ability that quite took the portrait out of the category of mere fops or fine men." Maud comments on "that slender oval face, and a fire in the large, shadowy eyes, which were very peculiar, and quite redeemed it from the suspicion of effeminacy."[21] This curiously ambivalent description, suggesting moral decay while simultaneously seeming to deny it, is wonderfully captured by Derrick De Marney who plays the much older Silas in the film. (He, for instance, blows away a thick layer of dust from the Bible after professing to consult it on a regular basis.) The portrait of Silas itself, we are told, was painted many years before. The portrait in the film confirms this with the Regency fashion on display in it, but the face has far more in common with the features of Reginald Tate, who plays Austin Ruthyn. The film opens with a blank picture frame, over which the names of the film's three stars are superimposed, before the portrait of Silas itself fills the frame. By opening the film in this manner, screenwriter Ben Travers boldly prepares us for the following study in appearance and reality, image and illusion, oppositions, duality and ultimate synthesis.

As W.J. McCormack points out, Bartram-Haugh is hell,[22] but it is a hell in which Caroline/Maud is at first quite happy, whereas at Knowl she was often quite the opposite when confronted with her father's coldness and the grotesque horrors of the French governess who had been recommended to her father by Silas, and who is instrumental in Silas' plans to obtain Caroline's money. The contrasting worlds of Knowl, Austin's home, and Bartram-Haugh, Silas' home, are the central mirror images of the story. Knowl is an elegant Regency affair, where lightness, elegance and space dominate. Bartram-Haugh is far more Elizabethan, darker, far less comfortably furnished and even provided with a chiming clock that includes the sinister interval of a tritone (or augmented fourth, the well-known *diabolus in musica*) in its oft-repeated sequence. The first shot of Jean Simmons as Caroline (as

One of Ivan Le Lorraine Albright's paintings for *The Picture of Dorian Gray* (dir. Albert Lewin, 1945).

Maud is called in the film) shows her brushing away a spider's web. This is an apt symbol of her role in the story, for she is an innocent fly who is trapped in two webs: the sanctimonious, misguided idealism of her "good" father and the murderous hypocrisy of her wicked uncle. Austin is introduced to us in a severe manner, unsmiling, forceful, determined. Only later does he soften. At first sight we aren't sure what to make of him. Later, Dr. Bryerly (played by Esmond Knight), who knows the truth about Silas' character, accuses Austin of being "deceived by [his] own righteous simplicity," and, indeed, Austin's sanctimonious blindness, and his cold refusal to listen to Caroline's fears makes him no more sympathetic than Silas, who at least has the redeeming feature of being rather more human, in contrast to the cold pillar of morality that is his brother. (De Marney plays Silas as an old rogue for the most part, with only occasional flashes of evil.)

Unlike *The Picture of Dorian Gray*, there is nothing supernatural about the Gothicisms of *Uncle Silas*, but it was Edgar Allan Poe who anticipated both stories in his own very short story "The Oval Portrait" (1850). A combination of aestheticism, Gothic and supernaturalism, Poe's tale tells of a young artist who puts so much of his beautiful sitter into his portrait of her that when the painting is finished, the woman is discovered to be dead: quite literally a portrait from life.[23] "The Oval Portrait" was referred to in Jean Epstein's silent version of *The Fall of the House of Usher* (1928), in which Roderick Usher is seen painting a portrait of Madeline, whom Epstein unfortunately turns into Roderick's wife rather than his sister, thus removing the important incestuous element from the tale. (Roger Corman's 1960 *The Fall of the House of Usher*, starring Vincent Price, followed Epstein's approach and similarly featured paintings supposedly by Roderick himself, which formed the basis for the dream sequence.)

It's well known that so-called "primitive" peoples are wary of having their photograph taken. Capturing their image suggests to them that their soul is also being captured, in much the same way that the Oval Portrait absorbed the very life and soul of the sitter. Such a belief is related to voodoo and the other magical systems described by Sir James Frazer in *The Golden Bough* as "contagious" magic. This assumes "that things which have once been in contact with each other are always in contact."[24] He goes on to recount a Malay charm that works on this principle:

Vincent Price in *House of Usher* (dir. Corman, 1960).

> Take parings of nails, hair, eyebrows, spittle, and so forth of your intended victim, enough to represent every part of his person, and then make them up into his likeness with wax from a deserted bees' comb. Scorch the figure slowly by holding it over a lamp every night for seven nights, and say:
> "*It is not wax that I am scorching,
> It is the liver, heart, and spleen of So-and-so that I scorch.*"
> After the seventh time burn the figure, and your victim will die.[25]

We will be returning to voodoo practices in chapter ten, but the idea of combining voodoo with painting occurs in Amicus' *Vault of Horror* (dir. Roy Ward Baker, 1973). In the section of this film called "Drawn and Quartered," Tom Baker plays an artist who follows in Gauguin's footsteps by traveling to exotic climes for his inspiration. Instead of Tahiti or Polynesia he ends up in Haiti where a voodoo priest informs him that his painting hand has magical powers. The artist then puts these to good use to take revenge on the art critics who have blackened his name. One by one, he paints and then destroys their portraits. Each critic subsequently dies in his turn, but unfortunately the artist has also painted a self-portrait which is left to burn by accident, thus destroying himself as well.

This kind of story opens the path to that other kind of portrait which is the reflection. Portraits are obviously very closely related to mirrors, and mirrors have their own part to play in Gothic horror. Vampires cast no reflection in mirrors because there is no soul to reflect. Their existence is more of an illusion than a reflection. "It is a foul bauble of man's vanity," says Count Dracula in Stoker's novel,[26] before flinging Harker's shaving mirror out of the window. Certainly mirrors are symbols of vanity, as is powerfully expressed in the fairy tale "Snow White," in which the wicked queen asks her magic mirror, "Who is fairest of us all?" The queen's mirror is, however, far more than a mere looking glass. It is also a scrying glass, which, like the crystal ball, is used for clairvoyance and divination. So too is the mirror of the Lady of Shalott in Tennyson's poem:

> And moving thro' a mirror clear
> That hangs before her all the year,
> Shadows of the world appear.[27]

This interpretation of the mirror as a scrying glass was emphasized by the British artist Sidney Meteyard (1868–1947) in his painting *I Am Half Sick of Shadows*, which shows the Lady of Shalott falling asleep before her giant mirror, her needlepoint neglected. Tennyson's poem is also an allegory about the dangers inherent in introversion. More specifically, it discusses in allegorical manner the problems faced by Romantic ivory tower artists, who can only reflect upon the world rather than actively engage with it. (Meteyard's picture also presents the Lady of Shalott in a very languorous, enervated pose.) The implication is that too much isolation leads ultimately to emotional sterility.[28] When the Lady of Shalott looks *directly* at Camelot by leaving the loom at which she works her artist's thread, the mirror cracks "from side to side" and she cries, "The curse is come upon me."

As well as crystal balls and mirrors, naturally formed crystals have also been also used for scrying purposes. The earliest reference to scrying with crystals can be found in Exodus, chapter 28, verse 30, when the priest, Aaron, carries what the Bible calls "the Urim and the Thummin" ("Lights and Perfections"), which are usually interpreted as clairvoyance crystals. Of course, the application of such occult practices for any but the most advanced initiates was frowned upon by both the Jews and later by Christianity. As early as Deuteronomy (chapter 18, verses 10–11) we find the stricture "There shall not be found among you *any one* that maketh his son or his daughter to pass through the fire, *or* that useth divination, *or* an observer of times, or an enchanter, or a witch, Or a charmer, or a consulter with familiar spirits, or a wizard, or a necromancer."

Scryers usually work at night, when the distractions of the everyday world are less likely to disturb their concentration. As occultist Éliphas Lévi (1810–75) eloquently expressed it:

A particular phenomenon occurs when the brain is congested or over-charged by Astral Light; sight is turned inward, instead of outward; night falls on the external and real world, while fantastic brilliance shines on the world of dreams; even the physical eyes experience a slight quivering and turn up inside the lids. The soul then perceives by means of images the reflection of its impressions and thoughts. This is to say that the analogy subsiding between idea and form attracts in the Astral Light a reflection representing that form, configuration being the essence of the vital light; it is the universal imagination, of which each of us appropriates a lesser or greater part according to our grade of sensibility and memory. Therein is the source of all apparitions, all extraordinary visions and all the intuitive phenomena peculiar to madness or ecstasy.[29]

Horror films frequently use crystal balls as evocative props. Catherine Lacey stares into one as the old witch, Haiti, in *The Mummy's Shroud* (dir. John Gilling, 1967). Her very name connects the idea of a reanimated mummy with the zombies of voodoo. Rosalie Crutchley stares into another crystal ball as the clairvoyant Helen Dickerson in *Blood from the Mummy's Tomb*. To her considerable distress she see in it the mystical seven stars of Ursa Major that are Queen Tera's chosen constellation. Indeed, mummy movies are particularly fond of clairvoyance. Boris Karloff's Imhotep, in Universal's *The Mummy* (dir. Karl Freund, 1932), encourages Helen Grosvenor (Zita Johann) to stare into the swirling waters of an occult font in his creepy Cairo home as a way of showing the audience the necessary ancient Egyptian backstory and (in a sequence cut from the final print of the film) to show Helen her past lives over the centuries.

Boris Karloff as Imhotep shows his magic mirror to Zita Johann's Helen Grosvenor in *The Mummy* (dir. Karl Freund, 1932).

Magic mirrors, however, provide the genre with some rather more dramatically interesting opportunities. "Guardian of the Abyss" (dir. Don Sharp, 1980) demonstrates how a scrying glass can be used for clairvoyant purposes. It summons images of the demon Choronzon, whom occultist Charles Randolph (played by John Carson) aims to incarnate. It also informs him of the whereabouts of the girl he intends to sacrifice to the demon. It is, indeed, an all-seeing eye; and we'll be exploring that episode from Hammer's television series *Hammer House of Horror* in more detail in chapter ten.

The way many other Gothic and fantasy films employ mirrors is related to the weirdly esoteric conceit of Lewis Carroll in *Through the Looking Glass* (1871). When Alice decides to walk through the mirror, the glass goes "all soft like gauze" and it turns into "a sort of mist,"[30] which is exactly what happens when Orphée (played by Jean Marais) walks through the mirror in Jean Cocteau's updated version of the Orpheus and Euridice myth in *Orphée* (1949). The way one enters the underworld in this film is by putting on magic rubber gloves and stepping through a liquefying mirror. "Il ne s'agit pas de comprendre," says François Périer's Heurtebise, "il s'agit de croire." ("It is not necessary to understand, it is necessary to believe.") This novel method of transport was, however, anticipated by H. P. Lovecraft in the tale "The Trap" (1932), in which a schoolboy is sucked into a mirror where he finds everything reversed: colors, distance, and, when he eventually emerges, he even discovers that his internal organs have been moved around. The parallel universe is a fourth dimension made up of the scenes the mirror had reflected over the years, but there is nothing tangible there apart from the people who have similarly been trapped there. Everything (with the exception of a couple of pieces of furniture, transplanted there by the magician who created the mirror) is virtual. This magician was an eighteenth-century Danish occultist who found a way of entering the mirror to attain immortality; for once inside the mirror's alternative, eternal world, time cannot touch him.

The underworld of Cocteau's film is also an unnerving place but it is not a sinister trap. However, mirrors can often lead us down to Hell. At the beginning of Hans Christian Andersen's "The Snow Queen," a wicked demon makes a magic mirror that distorts and corrupts reality:

> [E]verything good and beautiful that was reflected in it shrank together into almost nothing, but whatever was worthless and looked ugly became prominent and looked worse than ever. The most lovely landscapes seen in this mirror looked like boiled spinach, and the best people became hideous, or stood on their heads and had no bodies; their faces were so distorted as to be unrecognizable, and a single freckle was shown spread out over nose and mouth.[31]

A similar thing occurs in Hammer's *Vampire Circus*. When an eerie circus troupe visit the plague-ridden town of Schtettel, one of the entertainments they offer is a Hall of Mirrors. At first these seem no more than harmlessly amusing distortions, but as each visitor progresses along the tented "hall" they discover that the mirrors contain reflections other than their own; as Orphée experienced in Cocteau's film, the mirror proves to be an entrance to another place. Those who are lured through the mirrors by the vampires find themselves in the vaults of Count Mitterhaus' castle where they are sacrificed on his tomb, so that fresh blood will eventually revive him.

The Looking Glass World of *Through the Looking Glass* is also a kind of underworld where Alice finds herself exploring the landscape of the unconscious. After all, the whole story is revealed to have been a dream in the end. As in a dream, everything seems normal but is also quite different from waking reality:

> Then she began looking about, and noticed that what could be seen from the old room was quite common and uninteresting, but that all the rest was as different as possible. For instance, the pictures on the wall next the fire seemed to be all alive, and the very clock on the chimney-piece (you know you can only see the back of it in the Looking-glass) had got the face of a little old man, and grinned at her.
> "They don't keep this room so tidy as the other," Alice thought.[32]

The world of the unconscious is not only a magical place but also a much more untidy place than the organized one of the rational everyday world.

Sometimes mirrors can lead us into nightmares. The mist that Alice noticed forming in the mirror returns in "The Gate Crasher," the first of the four stories in the Amicus film *From Beyond the Grave*. In it, David Warner plays Edward Charlton, who buys a mirror from an antique shop called Temptations, presided over by a sinister (and, we later learn, thoroughly demonic) shopkeeper played by Peter Cushing. Having hung his mirror over the mantelpiece of his well-appointed flat (exactly like the mirror in *Through the Looking Glass*), Charlton invites some friends around for a party. Looking at the mirror, one of the guests mentions that it "looks like something that belongs in a clairvoyant's parlor," and this casual comment inspires Charlton to hold a séance. "Concentrate!" he commands. "Just empty your minds." The séance raises a spirit which is trapped in the rising mist behind the mirror. Unfortunately, this entity now demands to be fed with blood sacrifices, and Charlton is compelled to commit several murders. He smashes the mirror in an attempt to free himself from the possession of the spirit but it is magically restored. The spirit grows strong enough to leave the confines of its mirror world and enter Charlton's blood-spattered living room, but in order to remain there he requests one final sacrifice: Charlton must change places with the spirit and enter the Looking Glass World, where he will await some future owner of the mirror to liberate him.

Through the Looking Glass is also a study of opposites and reversals. Time runs backwards; "Jabberwocky" is written in mirror-script, and only makes sense when Alice reads a reflection of the text. Carroll also experimented with space in *Alice's Adventures in Wonderland* (1865), wherein Alice became large in small spaces and tiny in large spaces. *Through the Looking Glass* continues to explore the relativity of size (Alice encounters a gnat the size of a chicken in chapter three) and there is also a significant element of time reversal. The White Queen, for example, screams in pain before pricking her thumb with a brooch and talks about the imprisonment of the king's messenger for a crime he has yet to commit. In both books, Carroll could be said to have anticipated Einstein's theory of relativity. Both books also predate Wagner's mystical music-drama *Parsifal* (1882), which not only has singing flower maidens (who resemble the singing flowers of *Through the Looking Glass*) but also contains the line "zum Raum wird hier die Zeit" ("Here time is one with space"),[33] which has also been seen as another precursor to Einstein's idea.

Horror films also use mirrors to play with the relativity of time and space. The "Haunted Mirror" segment of *Dead of Night* (dir. Robert Hamer, 1945) concerns a mirror that reflects an alternative reality. At first the mirror seems perfectly normal, just like the Looking Glass World of *Through the Looking Glass*, which Alice describes as follows:

> First, there's the room you can see through the glass— that's just the same as our drawing room, only the things go the other way. I can see all of it when I get upon a chair — all but the bit just behind the fire-place. Oh! I do so wish I could see *that* bit.[34]

In "Haunted Mirror," a man is given a mirror by his wife for his birthday. As he unwraps it, he sees a picture frame and asks his wife, "You haven't gone and had your portrait painted,

Sir John Tenniel's illustration of Alice entering the mirror in Lewis Carroll's *Through the Looking Glass* (1871).

have you?" "No," she replies, "I thought you'd like to look at yourself." Indeed, as the story unfolds, the man is forced to look hard at himself. Is he going mad? Is he the decent, loving man he took himself to be, or is he possessed by an evil spirit? At first he thinks it some sort of optical illusion. "All done by mirrors," his wife laughs, but as the visions persist he grows increasingly preoccupied and short-tempered. "Don't nag," he shouts at his wife, revealing a side of him that she hadn't seen before. He now tells her about what he can see

Peter Cushing as the proprietor of Temptations, the dangerous antique shop in *From Beyond the Grave* (dir. Kevin Connor, 1973).

in the mirror. "If I made an enormous effort of will," he explains, "the reflection used to change back to what it ought to be," but he now feels that the mirror room is trying to draw him into it. When his wife learns the history of the mirror, the haunting seems to be explained. Its previous owner strangled his wife in front of it in a fit of jealous rage before killing himself, and it's his bedroom that haunts the mirror. One could interpret the tale on a psychological level, the mirror reflecting hidden aspects of the haunted man's personality. After all, he is able *by an effort of will* to change the reflection back to normal. He even says, "The trouble's in my mind, not the mirror." Is he using the mirror as a scrying glass by means of his *enormous effort of will* or are we to believe the literal story of him being possessed by the spirit of the previous owner? The latter is strongly suggested in the final scenes when he coldly accuses his wife of being unfaithful and attempts to strangle her as the previous owner strangled his wife, but the mirror is smashed and the spell is broken.

Robert Louis Stevenson's short story about a murderous thief, "Markheim" (1885), begins with another mirror. Markheim plans to rob an antique shop. He pretends to be interested in making a purchase and is offered a mirror by the dealer. Markheim is horrified:

> "Why, look here — look in it — look at yourself! Do you like to see it? No! nor I — nor any man."
>
> The little man jumped back when Markheim had so suddenly confronted him with the mirror; but now, perceiving there was nothing worse on hand, he chuckled. "Your future lady, sir, must be pretty hard-favoured," said he.
>
> "I ask you," said Markheim, "for a Christmas present, and you give me this — this damned reminder of years, and sins and follies — this hand-conscience."[35]

Markheim kills the dealer and prepares to rob the shop but a strange figure appears; we may interpret him as either the devil or Markheim's conscience. Their conversation concerns morality and salvation. "Evil, for which I live," says the stranger, "consists not in the action but in character. The bad man is dear to me; not the bad act, whose fruits, if we could follow them far enough down the hurtling cataract of the ages, might yet be found more blessed than those of the rarest virtues."[36] Markheim undergoes a conversion, however. He realizes that he has wasted his life and repents. The figure now explains that there is a way of escaping the law. Even though the maid is returning, all he has to do is to kill her too and he can escape. Markheim instead confesses his guilt and attains spiritual salvation. By introducing this tale with a mirror, Stevenson provides us with a classic metaphor of the duality of character, a theme he would develop a year after "Markheim" in his much more famous story of duality, *Dr. Jekyll and Mr. Hyde* (1886). We all contain our mirror image within us. Only by looking at our reflections and acknowledging our contradictory natures can we hope to find salvation and attain psychological good health.

H. P. Lovecraft's short story "The Outsider" (1926) offers another mirror parable along these lines. The narrator of the tale has no idea who or what he is and doesn't realize why he causes such mayhem when encountering other people. He then see a hideous monster beneath a golden arch which turns out to be his own reflection in *"a cold and unyielding surface of polished glass."*[7] The parable here suggests that until we face up to what Jung called our shadow (those monstrous aspects of the subconscious), we will never know who we are. Lovecraft's Outsider remains an outsider, but at least he knows the truth.

Though not strictly speaking a Gothic horror film, *Arabian Adventure* (dir. Kevin Connor, 1979) was given Gothic credentials by the presence of Christopher Lee and Peter Cushing. Lee plays the evil magician Alquazar, who has split his own personality in two. His mortal body is wholly evil, while he keeps all that is good about him imprisoned in a magic mirror. The good Alquazar longs to be free but is forced to answer truthfully all the questions of the evil Alquazar, just like the magic mirror of the wicked queen in "Snow White." Characters in horror films frequently discover their altar egos in mirrors. In *Dr. Jekyll and Sister Hyde*, Dr. Jekyll transforms into his diabolical female self in front of a mirror (in an impressively executed shot that shows us the metamorphosis without the need of cuts or special effects). As Mrs. Hyde triumphs over her weaker "brother," she stabs the mirror with the dagger she also uses to murder the prostitutes who supply the female hormones that have given her life. The resulting image of her distorted reflection amidst the shards of the mirror provides a graphic metaphor of her split personality. A similar kind of image had appeared in *Corruption* (dir. Robert Hartford-Davis, 1967) when Sue Lloyd as Lynn Nolan examines an unsuccessful face graft in a shattered hand mirror. Roman Polanski's *Repulsion* also used reflections to suggest the schizophrenia of Catherine Deneuve's character Carol, who gazes at her distorted reflection in the polished surface of a kettle. We also see the distorted face of her boyfriend as she looks at him through the peephole in the front door, an image that eloquently expresses her psychopathic fear of sexuality. Mirrors as doorways to other parts of the psyche returned in *The Awakening* (dir. Mike Newell, 1980) when Stephanie Zimbalist's character Margaret Trelawny realizes she's being possessed by the spirit of an evil Egyptian queen. As she stares in the bathroom mirror she suddenly catches a glimpse of herself with her face half torn away as though she has already become a defaced statue. The horrible fear that we may be turning into someone else and have no control over the metamorphosis also affects the male psyche, as we are about to find out.

INTERLUDE

Werewolves

This chapter will begin with a little exercise in creative writing, inspired by what we've learned so far on our Grand tour of Gothic:

It must be hard for you to imagine, my dear friend, what it is like to be a guest in this castle, so far from the bustle of city life and surrounded by such dark and impenetrable forests. They rise all around one on the vertiginous slopes of this mountainous region. Sitting like an eagle in this splendid but somewhat overpowering isolation is, I must confess, both inspiring and terrifying. Let me describe my room to you. It is situated in one of the high turrets of the castle, so I have quite a climb to reach it every night. It is simply furnished, with only a single bed and an enormous cupboard, fit to house the wardrobe of an entire family, so my small possessions look very lost and comical inside its cavernous interior. From my window there is nothing but a sheer drop into the rocky chasm below, which plunges many hundreds of feet to the turgid waters of a winding river, overhung with ferns and other vegetation. Trees cling tenuously to the sides of the rocks, which are piled on top of each other as if they were toys in a giant's nursery. I wonder how it was ever possible to construct a castle such as this in a place so very inaccessible! But here it stands, notwithstanding, and I am to be a guest for several summer months within its walls.

The journey here was sublime in the true sense of the word, for we traveled along a narrow, winding road that hugged the contours of the mountainside like a piece of string. I was continually afraid that we would plunge into the abyss at any moment, but eventually we arrived and I was greeted by my uncle, a strange but quiet and very courteous man, whose initially rather alarming appearance I soon learnt was not matched by his gentle character. It is true, he does not look in any way how I imagined him to be. He is very tall and of a pale complexion, the pallor of which is emphasized by jet black hair that is both luxuriant and glossy. As I said, he is the very soul of courtesy, and yet his eyes, as black as his raven hair and the bushy brows above them, have an unnerving habit of staring at one like an owl, and he often lapses into silence in a quite unexpected manner in the midst of a lively conversation. At such times it appears that he is either thinking of or listening to something else, for his expression clouds over and it is as if he were completely oblivious of one's presence in the room until something distracts him from his reverie and he returns, sometimes with an apology, sometimes not, to the pleasantries of the evening. I do not have many opportunities during the day to converse with him. He is absent much of the time and we really only meet at meal times (during which he displays very little appetite).

Today has been intolerably hot: not a breath of wind and I have been in search of shade all day. I have had little with which to occupy myself other than my books and I have begun to wonder how I am to sustain a visit of so many weeks in such solitude, which is why I am writing to you. My uncle's express wish in his letter of invitation to me was for the companionship of a niece to alleviate his solitude after convalescing from an illness, the details of which he did not dilate at length, and yet he seems, in fact, to be quite the misanthrope.

There is a garden here, overlooking the gigantic panorama of the mountains, and there is a fountain too that refreshingly ripples the waters of an ornamental pool in which carp lie lazily under the broad lily pads. Towards five o'clock this afternoon, I heard distant rumbles of thunder from beyond the furthest peaks, which have continued into the evening; and now the summer night has added a melancholy chorus of wolves from the forests, as the storm advances.

You might ask if the girl's uncle in my pastiche of Gothic style is a werewolf or a vampire. Perhaps he is both, for vampires and werewolves are very closely related, but neither need live in a remote castle. They could just as effectively live next door. Like the vampire, a werewolf appears quite normal for most of the time, and would pass unremarked but for some strangeness about him. Perhaps the girl's uncle has hair on the palms of his hands? Perhaps his eyes are indeed bushier than those of her other relatives? Perhaps they meet over a hooded brow? Perhaps there is a flash of fire in the eyes and perhaps this uncle has a particular way of licking his lips after a meal?

Shape-shifting is as old as the hills. In Homer's *The Odyssey* we read of the soothsayer Proteus, who would never offer his prognostications unless forced to do so. Menelaus and his men trap him. They fling their arms around him and hold on tight, but Proteus turns into "a bearded lion and then into a snake, and after that a panther and a giant boar. He changed into running water too and a great tree in leaf."[1] One might also refer to the tenth book of *The Odyssey* which tells the story of Circe who transformed Odysseus and his men into swine. Shape-shifting also formed the subject of *The Golden Ass* of Lucius Apuleius (c. 123/125–180 B.C.), a book that has been called the world's first novel. In it we learn how a witch turns her husband into a beaver, because he loved someone else. The reason why she chose a beaver was "that it is his nature, when hee perceiveth the hunters and hounds to draw after him, to bite off his members, and lay them in the way, that the hounds may be at a stop when they finde then, and to the intent it might so happen unto him (because he fancied another woman) she turned him into that kinde of shape."[2] The story's narrator, fascinated by magic, later accidentally turns himself into the ass of the title, and is eventually bought by an unsympathetic master:

> And then he cryed that he was not able to rule me, and that hee would not drive mee any longer to the hill for wood, saying: Doe you not see this slow and dulle Asse, who besides all the mischiefes that he hath wrought already, inventeth daily more and more. For he espyeth any woman passing by the way, whether she he old or marryed, or if it be a young child, hee will throw his burthen from his backe, and runneth fiercely upon them. And after that he hath throwne them downe, he will stride over them to commit his buggery and beastly pleasure, moreover hee will faine as though hee would kisse them, but he will bite their faces cruelly[.][3]

The correlation between sexual desire, violence and transformation into a beast is clear. Shakespeare satirizes this connection in *A Midsummer Night's Dream*, when Titania falls passionately in love with the ass-headed Bottom. Bottom, however, isn't the only shape-shifter in the play. Puck also explains how he can transform himself into a variety of animals:

> I'll follow you, I'll lead you about a round,
> Through bog, through bush, through brake, through brier:
> Sometime a horse I'll be, sometime a hound,
> A hog, a headless bear, sometimes a fire;
> And neigh, and bark, and grunt, and roar, and burn,
> Like horse, hound, hog, bear, fire, at every turn.[4]

Shakespeare made a more specific reference to werewolf imagery in Act II, scene 1 of *Macbeth* in which Macbeth contemplates the imaginary dagger with which he fancies he will kill Duncan:

> There's no such thing:
> It is the bloody business which informs
> Thus to mine eyes. Now o'er the one half-world
> Nature seems dead, wicked dreams abuse
> The curtain'd sleep; witchcraft celebrates
> Pale Hecate's offerings; and wither'd murder,
> Alarum'd by his sentinel, the wolf,
> Whose howl's his watch, thus with his stealthy pace,
> With Tarquin's ravishing strides, towards his design
> Moves like a ghost.[5]

There is no werewolf imagery in Shakespeare's *King John*, though that unpopular king was once believed to have become a werewolf after his death. As Walter Keating Kelly explains, "An old Norman chronicle avers that the monks of Worcester were compelled by the frightful noises proceeding from his grave to dig up his body and cast it out of consecrated ground. 'Thus the ill presage of his surname Lackland was completely realized, for he lost in his lifetime almost all the domains under his suzerainity, and even after death he could not keep peaceful possession of his tomb.'"[6] Montague Summers disagreed, however, believing quite literally that King John became a vampire.[7]

The "were-" in werewolf derives from the Old English "wer," meaning man, and the resulting "man-wolf" has a long folklore history. The idea that a man in wolf's clothing would have more successes on the battlefield was commonplace. By wearing an animal skin, or a headpiece in the shape of an animal's head, the warrior was imbued with the power of the animal. Mythical werewolves, however, generally prefer solitude. Not only does hair on the palms of a man's hands indicate a werewolf nature, it is also a well-established sign of a masturbator. Leonard Wolf in his *Annotated Dracula* wondered "whether Stoker knew the American boys' entrapment game in which one boy says 'If you masturbate, you'll grow hair on your palms,' and watches to see which of his listeners looks guiltily down at his hands."[8] It's certainly not without significance that the count displays this peculiarity, because later in the novel he will turn into a wolf when the ship that brings him to England is washed up at Whitby. Dracula has cold hands "more like the hand of a dead than a living man,"[9] and he gives the general impression of "extraordinary pallor."[10] "Strange to say," Harker writes in his journal, "there were hairs in the centre of the palm."[11] Wolf adds a quotation from William Acton's *Functions and Disorders of the Reproductive Organs* (1857):

> However young the children may be, they become thin, pale and irritable, and their features assume a haggard appearance. We notice the sunken eye, the long, cadaverous-looking countenance, the downcast look which seems to arise from a consciousness in the boy that his habits are suspected, and at a later period, from the ascertained fact that his virility is lost... Habitual masturbators have a dank, moist, cold hand, very characteristic of vital exhaustion; their sleep is short, and most complete marasmus [wasting of the body] comes on; they may waste away if the evil passion is not got the better of, nervous exhaustion sets in, such as spasmodic contraction, or partial or entire convulsive movements, together with epilepsy, enclampsy, and a species of paralysis accompanied with contraction of the limbs.[12]

As Wolf points out, such symptoms have a great deal in common with Dracula's torpid state during the daylight hours spent in his coffin. Indeed, the eighteenth-century professor of pathology at the University of Berlin, Christoph Wilhelm Hufeland, went even further than Acton, stating, "Nature has a terrible prospect in store for such a sinner. He is like a faded rose, a withered tree, a walking corpse. All the fire of his life will be extinguished by this silent vice, which leads to enervation, listlessness, anaemia, decay of the body and depression of the mind."[13] The following passage from Stoker's text could have been written as a direct response to Hufeland's prognosis:

> There, in one of the great boxes, of which there were fifty in all, on a pile of newly dug earth, lay the Count! He was either dead or asleep, I could not say which—for the eyes were open and stony, but without the glassiness of death—and the cheeks had the warmth of life through all their pallor, and the lips were as red as ever. But there was no sign of movement, no pulse, no breath, no beating of the heart.[14]

One might say that this subsequent description of the blood-gorged vampire is a metaphor of the onanist's penile tumescence:

> There lay the Count.... Even the deep, burning eyes seemed set amongst swollen flesh, for the lips and pouches underneath were bloated. It seemed as if the whole awful creature were simply gorged with blood; he lay like a filthy leech, exhausted with his repletion.[15]

In this respect, there is a vampire in all of us, and a werewolf too, but because the inner werewolf is more integrated in the majority than in the character of the man who, in folklore, turns literally into something else. It does not force itself to the surface of our quieter lives. Normal sexual relations and social conformity see to that. It is, perhaps, the more refined amongst us, the aesthetes, the loners, and the psychological outsiders, whose sexual energies do not flow through established channels, who are more likely to become werewolves.

The werewolf's popular association with the pentagram is of more recent date, being the invention of Curt Siodmak (1902–2000), the screenwriter of *The Wolf Man* (dir. George Waggner, 1941). This is ironic as the pentagram itself is primarily a benign symbol. Like the swastika, its positive or negative associations depend upon its orientation. For Pythagoras it represented mathematical perfection, and consequently the perfection of the natural world. With one point at the top, two below, and the remaining two points at each side, it is a symbol of the four elements, with the spirit (or what the Qabalah calls the "heiron," or divine idea) at the top, all bound together by the circle that surrounds them. This is why the pentagram is used in magical conjurations (as we shall see in chapter ten). The influential nineteenth-century occultist Éliphas Lévi explains,

> The empire of will over the Astral Light, which is the physical soul of the four elements, is represented in Magic by the Pentagram.... The elementary spirits are subservient to this sign when

Left: Lon Chaney Jr. as the Wolf Man. **Right:** The Pentagram. Illustration by Éliphas Lévi in *Transcendental Magic—Its Doctrine and Ritual*.

employed with understanding, and, by placing it in the circle or on the table of evocations, they can be rendered tractable, which is magically called their imprisonment.... Thus, by means of the Pentagram, spirits can be forced to appear in vision[.][16]

Lévi goes on to suggest that the pentagram is also known as the Sign of the Microcosm and that it is the same to which Faust refers in Goethe's play in the following monologue (although Goethe calls it the Sign of the Macrocosm):

> Did not some god write these mysterious
> Signs, by whose might my soul is filled
> With peace again, my poor heart healed,
> And by whose secret impetus
> The powers of Nature all about me are revealed?
> Am I a god? Light fills my mind;
> In these pure lines and forms appear
> All Nature's workings, to my inner sense made clear.
> That sage's words at last I understand:
> "The spirit-world is open wide,
> Only your heart has closed and died[.]"[17]

This benign form of the pentagram was also said to represent the five wounds of Christ on the cross, but it is a symbol of humanity as well. As Lévi explains,

> [A]ccording to the direction of its points, this absolute magical symbol represents order or confusion, the Divine Lamb of Ormuz and St. John, or the accursed goat of Mendes.... The Pentagram with two points in the ascendent represents Satan as the goat of the Sabbath; when one point is in the ascendent, it is the sign of the Saviour. The Pentagram is the figure of the human body, having the four limbs and a single point representing the head. A human figure head downwards naturally represents a demon — that is, intellectual subversion, disorder or madness.[18]

The upper points of the star now represent the horns of the Devil, the lower two points the ears, and the bottom point the goat's chin and beard. What was once at the top of the star, the "heiron," is now at the bottom, which Richard Cavendish describes as "a symbol of spirit mastered by matter, man at the mercy of his flesh."[19]

A werewolf is certainly "at the mercy of his flesh," but is not in himself inherently evil. As Curt Siodmak, the founder of so much modern werewolf lore, wrote in his screenplay for *The Wolf Man*: "The way you walk is thorny through no fault of your own," the implication being that the sexual forces that make men act in the way they do are beyond their control. Werewolves are usually represented in films as sensitive fellows. They have problematic relations with girls (if they have any relations at all) and more often than not they end up attacking them: killing the person they think they love but about whom their feelings are in truth rather more ambivalent. The werewolf portrayed by Lon Chaney, Jr. for Universal's Wolf Man series, Oliver Reed in Hammer's *The Curse of the Werewolf* (dir. Terence Fisher, 1961) and David Rintoul in *Legend of the Werewolf* (dir. Freddie Francis, 1975) all conform to this sensitive type. In the literary source of *The Curse of the Werewolf*, Guy Endore's *The Werewolf of Paris* (1934), Endore is keen to suggest an Oedipal element in the makeup of his werewolf, Bertrand:

> Late at night, as he was lying asleep, he felt someone kiss him. He had been dreaming of Thérèse and for a moment did not fully understand that it was his mother, in her nightgown, who had opened his room and was now saying, between her kisses, "My darling boy. Get up and leave quickly before your uncle discovers that I stole the key."
>
> Sleepily he returned her kisses. "Wake up, child. I've got a bag packed with everything you

need. Money too. Quick! You must put a safe distance between you and this prison. Oh, my darling baby. How long will it be before I see you again? I have a mind to go with you."

She had sat down on the bed beside him, had lifted him up and held him embraced against her bosom. And he, too, put his arms around her and hugged her tightly. He was trying desperately to fight off the fog of his dream. But it had his faculties enmeshed as if in a mist of spiderwebs. He was holding Thérèse and she was taunting him to take off her shift.

"Darling baby... Why, Bertrand! What are you doing?"

"Stop it Bertrand!" she whispered as loud as she dared. "Bertrand, I tell you!" She struggled against his youthful muscular body, then she ceased and made no further resistance. A strange glow of satisfaction emanated from her sacrifice and caused her features to relax into an ecstatic smile....

When Bertrand awoke several hours later, he noted with his dismay his mother lying naked beside him, her limbs flung apart in complete relaxation.[20]

Oliver Reed as Leon in *The Curse of the Werewolf* (dir. Terence Fisher, 1960).

Hammer based its later television werewolf tale "Children of the Full Moon" (dir. Tom Clegg, 1980) around a mother figure; Diana Dors played the worryingly devoted parent of an entire werewolf brood. The cosseted, well-dressed, self-contained and artistic children on whom she lavishes her affection follow firmly in the Oedipal tradition of the werewolf child, but "Children of the Full Moon" also serves to question the preconception we have of children's innocence. The children here aren't concealing anything: they take their werewolf natures for granted. In that respect they are genuinely innocent. The horror of their true nature is reserved entirely for the adults who encounter them. The children themselves have no difficulties accepting what they are.

Gilles de Laval, the Maréchal de Retz (1404–1440), who slaughtered hundreds of children and erotically luxuriated in their blood, certainly exhibited all the psychological characteristics of a werewolf, even though he didn't transform physically into one. The way his beard caught the light gave it a bluish tinge, which was why he was known as Bluebeard. Gilles was an intelligent youth; as Sabine Baring-Gould describes him in his *Book of Werewolves*, he was on the surface at least, a devout and charitable individual:

> [It] was observed that the chapel of the castle was gorgeously decked with tapestries of silk and cloth of gold, that the sacred vessels were encrusted with gems, and that the vestments of the priests were of the most sumptuous character. The excessive devotion of the marshal was also noticed; he was said to hear mass thrice daily, and to be passionately fond of ecclesiastical music. He was said to have asked permission of the pope, that a crucifer should precede him in processions. But when the dusk settled down over the forest, and one by one the windows of the castle became illuminated, peasants would point to one casement high up in an isolated tower, from which a clear light streamed through the gloom of night; they spoke of a fierce red glare

Diana Dors as the mother of a family of werewolves in "Children of the Full Moon" (dir. Tom Clegg, 1980).

which irradiated the chamber at times, and of sharp cries ringing out of it, through the hushed woods, to be answered only by the howl of the wolf as it rose from its lair to begin its nocturnal rambles.

On certain days, at fixed hours, the drawbridge sank, and the servants of De Retz stood in the gateway distributing clothes, money, and food to the mendicants who crowded round them soliciting alms. It often happened that children were among the beggars: as often one of the servants would promise them some dainty if they would go to the kitchen for it. Those children who accepted the offer were never seen again.[21]

Countess Dracula, Hammer's version of the equally bloodthirsty story of Countess Elizabeth Báthory, presents a similar scene. Captain Dobi (Nigel Green) has been sent to find a virgin so that the correct kind of blood may be used to rejuvenate the countess. For sale in the marketplace there are various young women whose impressive strength is much puffed by the huckster promoting them: "She could pull the weight of any carriage," he says, drawing attention to her "thighs of solid teak," but none of them are pure enough for the purposes Dobi has in mind. Instead he settles on a young girl whom the huckster is willing to sell if Dobi is willing to take her goat as well. A bargain is struck and that's the last we see of the girl as she forlornly leads her goat towards the castle gate.[22]

The emphasis on Gilles de Retz's double standard, his love of music and luxury on the one hand and his depraved tastes on the other, is a crucial part of many werewolf tales. Right up to the 1990s' Hannibal Lecter films, starring Anthony Hopkins as a highly cultured psychopath, such stories suggest that the cultivation of excessive refinement can lead one into in danger of ignoring the bestial basis of the human personality. Unintegrated, it can easily grow out of control. Robespierre was another lace-cuffed and fashionable aesthete, an excellent example of an intellectual who threw his inner beast only the scraps left over from the unnourishing table of idealism. Not surprisingly, his beast grew ravenous indeed on such an excessively refined diet.

Adolf Hitler's favorite pet dog was, perhaps not surprisingly, called Wolf, and it's surely not a coincidence that his secret headquarters during the Second World War was known as "The Wolf's Lair." Hitler also called himself "Wolf" when staying with the family descendants of his idol, Richard Wagner. A frustrated (though talented) artist, a solitary frequenter of the opera, a devoted son with an Oedipal fixation, which precluded satisfactory sexual relationships with other women — Hitler possessed all those qualities that in myth make a man prone to lycanthropy. Circumstantial evidence suggests that Hitler conformed to many of the attributes of a repressed homosexual. Could this explain why the wolf in "Red Riding Hood" wears *women's* clothing, and why the Big Bad Wolf of "The Three Little Pigs" spends so much time attempting to gain entry into the respective homes of three *male* pigs?

Look into the mirror and stare, like Alice, at that other person who lives behind the glass. He does everything that you do, even when you cannot see him. His existence takes place in another world, a world in reverse, an existence that is parallel to, but separate from your own. This is the alternative you, the one who copies your every movement but who turns right into left. This is your twin, your *Doppelgänger*; or is it that *you* copy *him*? Perhaps you both only truly live when you meet each night and every morning, when your eye-beams join, making whole what the conventions of the day have severed. We all like to think we are the people others take us for. We hide those aspects of ourselves which we would rather not have anyone else know about. Sometimes we hide them from ourselves.

Werewolves articulate our own duality, for a werewolf is anyone who *expresses* his contradictions: the opera singer who joins the army, the artist who plays football, the bank manager who gambles. The werewolf is our secret double, the Mr. Hyde who dwells within, the skeleton in the cupboard, *The Beast in the Cellar*, the Mrs. Rochester we keep locked in the attic. Such creatures live in mirrors, they haunt the shadows and only come out when the moon is full. Werewolves are our own atavisms, our oppressed alternatives, the obverse of the coins of everyday exchange.

Those who refuse to acknowledge their violent twin will surely be destroyed by it. All doubles are deadly for they wish to devour the opposite that would cancel them out, deny them their existence. This is why legend has it that the moment we see our double is also the moment in which we will die. The task of integrating the two is a dangerous affair, and if left too late it is usually catastrophic. It forms the basis of Poe's "William Wilson" (1839), whose title character is pursued by his double throughout his life. Eventually he challenges the double to a duel, killing himself in the process. *The Student of Prague* (dir. Stellan Rye, 1913) and its remake (dir. Henrik Galeen, 1926) were both loosely based on this story.

However, some individuals who share lycanthropic tendencies have no difficulty with their condition. Dennis, in E.F. Benson's novel *Raven's Brood* (1934), is pulled out into the spring night to go running. He takes off his shirt and spread-eagles himself on the ground; his ecstasy in this union with the earth is extreme:

> He threw himself face-downward, bare-chested, on a bed of sprouting bracken, and lay there panting, while the arteries throbbed in his throat and temples. He flung wide his arms and legs, as if to wrestle with the earth his mother, or hold her in strong embrace, and with his spread fingers he dug into the soft soil, and with his teeth he bit the sappy fern stems. Then, as the ecstasy subsided into content and quietness, he lay there with eyes shut. God! what a good running it had been, what a spell, what a magic of springtime and night![23]

This is a reworking of what D.H. Lawrence had written in *Women in Love* (1921), when Birkin similarly communes with the earth-mother:

> He was happy in the wet hill-side, that was overgrown and obscure with bushes and flowers. He wanted to touch them all, to saturate himself with the touch of them. He took off his clothes, and sat down naked among the primroses, moving his feet softly among the primroses, his legs, his knees, his arms right up to his arm-pits, lying down and letting them touch his belly, his breasts. It was such a fine, cool, subtle touch all over him, he seemed to saturate himself with their contact.
>
> But they were too soft. He went through the long grass to a clump of young firs, that were no higher than a man. The soft sharp bough beat upon him, as he moved in keen pangs against them, threw little cold showers of drops on his belly, and beat his loins with their clusters of soft-sharp needles.... How fortunate he was, that there was this lovely, subtle, responsive vegetation, waiting for him, as he waited for it; how fulfilled he was, how happy![24]

How appropriate that in Ken Russell's film of *Women in Love* (1969), Alan Bates' Birkin eventually engages Hammer's one-time werewolf, Oliver Reed as Gerald Crich, in the infamous nude wrestling scene. There is no need for yak hair, pentagrams and silver bullets in either novel, for neither Dennis nor Birkin repress their instincts. The werewolves of the cinema are less fortunate. Leon in *The Curse of the Werewolf* is an orphan, the product of a rape, born on Christmas Day, which is an offense to God; but somehow he is also Christlike in his sufferings. Terence Fisher spends a great deal of time describing Leon's youth, his attachment to his foster mother (though never in such suggestive detail as in the above-quoted passage [see pages 138–39] from the original novel), his obsession with moonlight and his sensitivity to the pain and suffering of animals (he hates to see animals shot and is both repelled and attracted by their blood). He runs out into the moonlit night killing sheep without realizing what he's doing and wakes up the following morning with all the guilt and confusion of a boy after a wet dream. When he grows up, he's uninterested in the prostitutes he comes across, but the full moon makes him kill one of them. He's fonder of the young man with whom he works in the vineyard, and is of too humble an origin to marry the girl he thinks he really loves.

David Rintoul's Etoile in *Legend of the Werewolf* is similarly an orphan, while Lon Chaney's Larry Talbot in *The Wolf Man* is an American abroad when he's bitten by the wolf form of Bela Lugosi, and he remains in a constant state of exile throughout the subsequent Wolf Man sequels. Werewolves and their victims (before the victims themselves become werewolves) are often lost. The two American tourists of *An American Werewolf in London* (dir. John Landis, 1981) find themselves, like Larry Talbot, far from home when they are attacked on a desolate moor in the north of England. The British soldiers in *Dog Soldiers* (dir. Neil Marshall, 2002) are on exercise in the wilds of Scotland when the werewolf of that film strikes.

To be a werewolf is to be psychologically disoriented, lost to oneself, alienated from one's surroundings. Stevenson's *Dr. Jekyll and Mr. Hyde* merely stripped werewolf folklore of its occult trappings and substituted science as the method of transformation. Wally Westmore's makeup for Fredric March's Mr. Hyde in Rouben Mamoulian's adaptation of the story is more ape than wolf, emphasizing the Darwinian, *scientific* surface of the tale, but differing in few other psychological essentials from any other shape-shifter. Hyde terrifies us with his psychological cruelty, whereas the werewolf horrifies us with his physical violence. Hammer's attempt to ring the changes in *The Two Faces of Dr. Jekyll* (dir. Terence Fisher, 1960) by making Hyde young and attractive and Jekyll old and haggard wasn't so much of a twist after all, as Paul Massie's youthful incarnation is just as much motivated by desire and cruelty as any other manifestation of the Hyde character, and he's just as much of a wolf.

If the destiny of the repressed individual is to become a werewolf, one might also add particular kinds of artist to the list of candidates. A perhaps unexpected example is Gustav von Aschenbach, the hero of Thomas Mann's novella "Der Tod in Venedig" ("Death in Venice," 1912). There are ways in which one could look upon this story as a sublimated werewolf tale. Aschenbach is torn between his repressed homosexual desire (which Mann defines in Nietzchean terms as "Dionysian") and the contrary "Apollonian" restraint necessary for his art. Taking a leaf out of John Landis' screenplay, one could even re-title Visconti's 1971 film adaptation of "Death in Venice" as "An Austrian Werewolf in Venice." Instead of being transformed into a hairy beast, Aschenbach becomes an equally grotesque fop, his face painted white, his hair dyed black, his lips rouged in a ghastly attempt to regain his lost youth, and his death is just as inevitable as any werewolf's. His silver bullet is the beauty of the young boy Tadzio. It pierces a heart unable to contend with the full force of its passion. Aschenbach has spent too long worshipping at the shrine of Apollo. When (inspired by forbidden thoughts of Tadzio) he dreams of Dionysus, it is as a nightmare:

> From the wooded heights, from among the tree-trunks and crumbling moss-covered rocks, a troop came tumbling and raging down, a whirling rout of men and animals, and overflowed the hillside with flames and human forms, with clamour and the reeling dance. The females stumbled over the long, hairy pelts that dangled from their girdles; with heads flung back they uttered loud hoarse cries and shook their tambourines high in air; brandished naked daggers or torches vomiting trails of sparks. They shrieked, holding their breasts in both hands; coiling snakes with quivering tongues they clutched about their waists. Horned and hairy males, girt about the loins with hides, drooped heads and lifted arms and thighs in unison, as they beat on brazen vessels that gave out droning thunder, or thumped madly on drums. There were troops of beardless youths armed with garlanded staves; these ran after goats and thrust their staves against the creatures' flanks, then clung to the plunging horns and let themselves be borne off with triumphant shouts.... His senses reeled in the steam of panting bodies, the acrid stench from the goats, the odour as of stagnant waters—and another, too familiar smell—of wounds, uncleanliness, and disease.... They laughed, they howled, they thrust their pointed staves into each other's flesh and licked the blood as it ran down.[25]

Unfortunately, Visconti left all this out in his film, unsuccessfully implying this Dionysian nightmare in the short scene in which Aschenbach is booed after the performance of one of his symphonies. Visconti felt that anything more extreme "would have broken the tone, [violated] the taste in the film.... For the nightmare which, in the book, is the point of deepest depression and foretells [Aschenbach's] death, I substituted the concert fiasco, which fulfills the same function in the film and represents the despair that heralds the end."[26] Unfortunately, Visconti's substitution fails to convey the true sexual horror of Aschenbach's dream and severely undermines his desire to recreate the story exactly as Mann wrote it. As Gary Schmidgall observed, "[T]he film scarcely touched upon the keenly cerebrated terror Aschenbach experiences in his own mind. It simply could not explore the great interior monologues of the novella. The level upon which Visconti approached *Der Tod in Venedig* was, in short, its least important."[27] Schmidgall also points out, "The crux of the story is not sublimation of homosexual instincts, but more generally the sublimation of vital instincts—the instincts of life—which is a danger courted by the superior intellect—an intellect like Mann's own."[28] Having said that, there's no denying that Mann's "Death in Venice" is without doubt a masterpiece of "gay" fiction, and it was hardly sur-

Dirk Bogarde as Gustav von Aschenbach in *Death in Venice* (dir. Luchino Visconti, 1971).

prising that it should have been filmed by the homosexual Visconti, who always felt guilty about his own sexual orientation. It was no less surprising that it starred Dirk Bogarde, who was in terminal denial about the fact that he was gay as well. All of them, Aschenbach included, were *repressed*. The monstrously violent manifestations of Larry Talbot, Leon and Etoile, like those of Hitler and de Retz, all indicate desire denied and bottled up, reality resisted and reinvented. As the similarly repressed homosexual Friedrich Nietzsche (1844–1900) so accurately expressed it: "The degree and kind of a man's sexuality reaches up into the topmost summit of his spirit,"[29] but such a sexuality, if denied, reaches down to the very depths of his being as well.

Nietzsche's analysis of the relationship between ancient Greek society and its dramatic art in *The Birth of Tragedy* (1872), the book on which so much of "Death in Venice" is based, can also be interpreted as a study of *cultural* lycanthropy. Nietzsche's thesis attempts to explain how the society of ancient Greece, subjected to the violence of life's unavoidable horrors, faced up to them and bravely turned them into art. (There is an equivalent werewolf analogy from later in the history of the ancient world: Romulus, the son of Numitor, was suckled by a she-wolf before becoming the legendary founder of Rome.) Aschenbach, who has spent a lifetime creating art while ignoring life and what he regards as the horror of his own desires, dies; but death in such tales is always a transformation, never a mere termination. Aschenbach's death can also be read as a metaphor of integration. Thus, when werewolves die, they change back not merely into the men they were but into the men they have *become*. Such moments in films are far more than merely an opportunity for special effects. They demonstrate the regenerative effect of self-awareness. Silver bullets, usually fired by the person who most loves the lycanthropic one, are the soothing arrows of Apollo. The whole process should be seen as a symbol of how civilization and loving relationships within it are possible only through an acknowledgment, rather than a restraint, of the beast within. It is a very necessary, and in many ways an admirable beast, for without it there would be nothing from which to build a world in the first place; but, of course, it is also a beast that left to itself as an energy unchecked, would destroy that world.

Werewolves inspire not only horror but also our compassion. How desperately Larry Talbot longs for a cure, his sole motivation in all the Universal films. A cure for lycanthropy? Isn't that as hopeless as a cure for being different? All monsters are outsiders, persecuted by the norm, terrified most of all by themselves. These are adolescent fears: the fear of a breaking voice, of descending testicles, of hairs sprouting from smooth flesh, of desires unknown in "innocent" childhood. And how often it is that the *parent* kills the werewolf in the end. Claude Rains' Sir John Talbot destroys his son, Larry, while Oliver Reed's Leon is shot by his adopted father (played by Clifford Evans); and this is right and proper, for all parents have a duty to correct and balance the destructive impulses of their offspring. The werewolf within is controlled by love after it has been unleashed by lust. Of all his horror films, Terence Fisher was most fond of *The Curse of the Werewolf*, which he rightly regarded as a Gothic love story. He believed, as did Jean Cocteau in his version of Beauty and the Beast, that only love can redeem us from our bestiality: Apollo running to the rescue of Dionysus and learning how to dance in step with him.

A werewolf is much more frightening than any wolf (an animal that never attacks man if left to its own devices), for men are more frightening than any wild beast. What we fear when faced with a monster in the shape of an animal is not the animal but the man behind it. Such myths are the way in which we negotiate the horror we have of ourselves.

Seven

Ornate Coffins

Coppola's symbolist approach to *Bram Stoker's Dracula*, lavish and self-conscious though it is, wasn't breaking new ground. *Isle of the Dead*, as we have seen, has more of a claim to that distinction, but many Gothic horror films, particularly those of Hammer, have just as much (if not more) in common with the aesthetic of symbolism and decadence as with Gothic romance. Indeed, symbolist literature employed the trappings of Gothic after the example of Edgar Allan Poe (who simultaneously anticipated many of the symbolists' other obsessions). Symbolist writers such as Maurice Maeterlinck and Villiers de l'Isle Adam (1838–1889) used Gothic imagery to suggest the alienation and introversion with which they were concerned. Gothic romance and symbolist literature are also both very concerned with *décor*, and here again, Poe, who even wrote an essay titled "The Philosophy of Furniture" (1840), unites both perspectives. This was particularly the case after the baroque elaboration of his style was so influentially translated into French by Charles Baudelaire (1821–1867), the father of late nineteenth-century Parisian *décadence*. Some even claimed that Baudelaire's demonically elegant French even improved upon the studied prose of the Bard of Baltimore, opening Poe's world of aesthetic terrors not only to Villiers de l'Isle Adam but also to the composer Claude Debussy (1862–1918), who was one of Poe's most ardent musical admirers.

Debussy's unfinished opera on Poe's *The Fall of the House of Usher* would probably have been his masterpiece if he had been able to resolve the problem of the original story's dramatic stasis, which has so often plagued those who have tried to adapt Poe's works for the screen. Poe wasn't much interested in character and plot, being far more concerned with individual psychology, mood, philosophical enquiry and elaborate description. Consequently, several of the famous films purporting to be adaptations of his original stories and poems have little in common with the texts themselves. Roger Corman's *The Haunted Palace* (1963), for example, takes its title from Poe's poem but was really an adaptation of H.P. Lovecraft's *The Case of Charles Dexter Ward* (1941), which offers many more dramatic possibilities than Poe's symbolic disquisition on insanity. Even the horrors of Poe's "The Pit and the Pendulum" (1842) fail to furnish an entire screenplay, for how many times can one show the machinery of torture in action without anything else to keep the audience engaged? Corman had to invent an entirely new story in his 1961 adaptation of the story to build up to the climax in Daniel Haller's splendidly Gothic torture chamber, which is only revealed in its full majesty in the final scenes. Corman made a rather more successful attempt than Debussy at dramatizing "The Fall of the House of Usher," but despite the presence of Vincent Price, and some very impressive *matte* shots of the fatal mansion itself and its stagnant setting, the overall result is nowhere near as poetically dreamlike in its atmosphere as

Jean Epstein's 1928 silent version of the story. Corman's shots of the exterior of the Usher residence may be more compelling, but Epstein's interiors are not only more spacious than Corman's, they are also far more symbolist in their general atmosphere. A vast hall, billowing curtains, candles and shadows all contribute to the whole point of the story: that the house is a metaphor of Roderick Usher's madness. In spirit, Epstein attains the closest visualization of the tale yet achieved; and though there are references to Poe's other tales in this film, these aren't there to fill out the action (as one could argue was the case with Corman's 1964 adaptation of "The Masque of the Red Death," which conflates the main story with Poe's tale of a vengeful dwarf, "Hop-Frog"). Epstein's additions are more in the nature of asides. He calls one of Usher's dead ancestors Ligeia, and photographs the pendulum of Usher's tall case clock in a manner that at first resembles the clock in "The Masque of the Red Death" and later in a way that suggests Poe's dreaded pendulum.)

The whole point of Poe is psychological anxiety, which he explores, as often as not, in surroundings of eclectic, D'Annunzian excess. D'Annunzio outdid the interiors of Poe's "The Assignation" (1834) and "Ligeia" (1838) in the extravagant *décors* of his own home, the Vittoriale, overlooking Lake Garda in Lombardy. As Anthony Rhodes, his biographer, put it, D'Annunzio combined "cushions, velvets, damasks, brocades and the scents of Des Esseintes in the intense burners.... [A] crucifix by Giotto [hangs] next to an aeroplane propeller. In the garden is a sizable portion of the battleship *Puglie*, on which one of D'Annunzio's lieutenants, Tomaso Gulli, was killed in July 1920, in a raid on Split. Its radio-masts stick up in the sky, in curious company with the cypresses and poplars above the Lake of Garda."[1]

Admittedly, none of Poe's heroes were quite the men of action that D'Annunzio prided himself on being, along with his once preeminent status as Italy's leading poet. But D'Annunzio's habit of piling one thing on top of another thing, and mixing together objects from far-flung periods and times into a bewilderingly decadent, *fin de siècle* whole, was entirely in the manner of Poe's neurasthenic, intellectual outsiders, obsessed by their *surroundings* and symbolic *décors*. The (anti-)heroes of the Poe stories mentioned so far all remove themselves from the here and now and retreat into ivory towers, surrounded by a multitude of precious objects which they contemplate in an attempt to distract themselves from their intellectual despair, their fears of madness and death, or merely their *ennui*.

It's helpful to trace the famous synaesthetic stanzas of Baudelaire's poem "Correspondances" from his 1857 collection *Les Fleurs du mal*, with its highly influential line about sounds, colors and perfumes mingling in the evening air ("*Les parfums, les couleurs et les sons se répondent*"), back to Poe's equally synaesthetic setting for "The Assignation." Poe's tale, set against the broodingly voluptuous background of Gothic Venice, is a blueprint for all the decadent literature that followed (and many of the so-called "horror" films such literature inspired). The narrator of the tale is invited to the extravagant *palazzo* of a mysterious stranger whom he has seen previously by the Bridge of Sighs. On that occasion the narrator observed this stranger rescue the child of the Marchese di Mentoni, which had fallen from a window into the waters of the canal. The marchesa's name is surely a significant echo of one of the most famous of all Gothic villains, Count Montoni in Radcliffe's *The Mysteries of Udolpho*. So much for the Gothic credentials of the tale. More interesting are the interiors of the stranger's *palazzo*, which point the way towards the decadent interiors of the symbolists. The *palazzo* is filled with curios and magnificent antiquities, paintings, sculpture and music, which latter appears from no clearly defined source, suggesting the effect of the recorded music that we now take for granted. "In the architecture and embellishments of the chamber," Poe writes,

> the evident design had been to dazzle and astound. Little attention had been paid to the *decora* of what is technically called *keeping*, or to the proprieties of nationality. The eye wandered from object to object and rested upon none — neither the *grotesques* of the Greek painters, nor the sculptures of the best Italian days, nor the huge carvings of untutored Egypt.... The senses were oppressed by mingled and conflicting perfumes, reeking up from strange convolute censers, together with multitudinous flaring and flickering tongues of emerald and violet fire. The rays of the newly risen sun poured in upon the whole, through windows formed each of a single pane of crimson-tinted glass. Glancing to and fro, in a thousand reflections, from curtains which rolled from their cornices like cataracts of molten silver, the beams of natural glory mingled at length fitfully with the artificial light, and lay weltering in subdued masses upon a carpet of rich, liquid-looking cloth of Chili gold.[2]

Amidst this overwhelming luxury, the mysterious stranger eventually commits suicide by drinking poison at the exact moment when the unattainable (because already married) marchesa also kills herself. Hence the title of the tale: an assignation with Death. At one point, Poe specifically points out the synaesthetic effect of these tumultuous assaults on the senses. The "overpowering sense of splendor and perfume and music"[3] must surely have made as great an impression on Baudelaire as the experience of listening to Wagner's *Tannhäuser*. In his essay on Wagner, written as a direct response to that shattering experience, Baudelaire equated the effect of Wagner's music with a sensation of great light, and he claimed that he had the same feeling of familiarity with it as he had when translating Poe. Baudelaire tried to demonstrate that the effect of Wagner's music was the same as his own poetry, claiming that it was based, as Robert L. Delevoy puts it, "on the emotional ambiguity of images, on a sensorial topology, on the *deep and shadowy unity* of correspondences."[4]

The narrator of Poe's "Ligeia," "crushed into the very dust with sorrow"[5] after the death of his preternaturally beautiful and frighteningly intellectual wife, purchases and puts in some repair an abbey, situated, significantly, in "one of the wildest and least frequented portions of fair England."[6] Here is the traditional Gothic element, but Gothic meets decadence when we enter the interior of the building, which the unnamed narrator confesses to having decorated with "more than regal magnificence."[7] Egyptian sarcophagi vie with gorgeous draperies, carpets of tufted gold, ottomans and tapestries, as was the case with the mysterious stranger's Venetian but equally decadent interiors in "The Assignation," which predates "Ligeia" by four years.

The most famous study of decadent decor is to be found in Joris-Karl Huysmans' novel (more of a Bible for its devotees) *À Rebours* (1884). Appropriately, the hero of this work, Jean Des Esseintes, possesses a copy, bound in sea-green leather, of Poe's only novel, *The Narrative of Arthur Gordon Pym* (1838), "specially printed for his behoof on pure linen-laid paper, hand-picked, bearing a sea-gull for water mark."[8] Though influenced by the neurasthenics of Poe's fiction, Des Esseintes is not so ostentatious in his own interior design. He indulges in crushed morocco leather paneling on his walls, paints his moldings and plinths deep indigo and arranges silver angels to be embroidered onto a blue ground on his ceiling. Books and flowers punctuate the ensemble, while the floor is carpeted in tiger skins and blue-fox pelts. Deeply indebted to Poe, however, are the bluish-tinged windows whose curtains are made from old priestly stoles.

Oscar Wilde (1854–1900) was fascinated by *À Rebours* and lent that fascination to his own version of Des Esseintes in *The Picture of Dorian Gray* (1890). Wilde even went so far as to say that Dorian Gray had been poisoned by Huysmans' book:

For years, Dorian Gray could not free himself from the influence of this book. Or perhaps it would be more accurate to say that he never sought to free himself from it. He procured from Paris no less than nine large paper copies of the first edition, and had them bound in different colours, so that they might suit his various moods and the changing fancies of a nature over which he seemed, at times, to have almost entirely lost control.[9]

However, Wilde employs the spirit of symbolism and decadence for rather more moral reasons than Huysmans. *Dorian Gray* is a book more about sin than aesthetics, and the idea of becoming a complete recluse would have been anathema to one of the world's greatest conversationalists. The sin that is continually referred to by Wilde was, of course, homosexuality, the love that, in 1890, dared not speak its name in anything more precise than metaphors and suggestions. No wonder so many young Victorian ladies kept asking, "What exactly did Oscar Wilde *do*?" Wilde himself was no less coy in his novel, referring only obliquely to Dorian Gray's "mysterious and prolonged absences that gave rise to such strange conjecture among those who were his friends."[10] Only Dorian's portrait knows the truth, that the sum of his "crimes" amounts merely to the fact that he is homosexual. The novel, of course, only permits us to watch Dorian seducing and degrading a virtuous working-class girl. Wilde's own taste for rough trade had necessarily to be kept secret. It shows the level of self-destruction at work in Wilde's psyche, not to mention the oppressive power of Victorian society's dominant ideology, that the gay reality of Dorian's personality takes the

Donna Reed as Gladys Hallward and Hurd Hatfield as Dorian in *The Picture of Dorian Gray* (dir. Albert Lewin, 1945).

form of his portrait's hideous corruption. Wilde obviously felt that "Feasting with Panthers,"[11] as he termed his own sexual exploits, was not only dangerous from the point of view of its possible consequences in blackmail but also that it was positively sinful.

In the celebrated film version of *The Picture of Dorian Gray*, released in 1945, Hurd Hatfield's Dorian is even more oblique than he is in Wilde's text. Hatfield's blank expression and almost surgically manufactured looks suggest not only a sinister kind of androgyny, but also that his crime has been to consign his entire humanity, not merely his "sins," to the portrait. In his quest for eternal youth, Dorian has become a kind of vampire, in much the same way that Anton Diffring's Dr. Bonnet in Hammer's *The Man Who Could Cheat Death* (dir. Terence Fisher, 1959) could be said to be one of the undead in all but name. Apart from their obviously shared theme of immortality, what also unites these two stories are their decadent, *fin-de-siècle* settings. It's no accident, surely, that screenwriter Jimmy Sangster chose to relocate *The Man Who Could Cheat Death* to turn-of-the-century Paris (the original play by Barré Lyndon was set in the very English "Half Moon Street"). That Bonnet is also a sculptor brings him even closer to the artistic, contemplative world of Huysmans and Villiers, to say nothing of Oscar Wilde (one of Sangster's acknowledged inspirational sources).[12]

Sangster felt that because his screenplay was based on a stage play, the film suffered from being too static. He complained that the movie "really takes place on two sets, Bonnet's house and the cellar where the climax takes place,"[13] but there is a case for arguing that this very insular, almost claustrophobic quality is the best way to suggest the highly introverted world of a typical decadent aesthete. After all, Des Esseintes, with whom Bonnet has so much in common, is the ultimate armchair traveler. He has so arranged things that he can enjoy "the advantages of confinement in a cloister, while he escaped its inconveniences— the quasi-military discipline, the lack of comfort, the dirt and herding together and the monotonous idleness."[14] He rarely goes out but can travel anywhere in his imagination without the inconveniences and ultimate disappointments of reality. Aided by a few inspirational props, he has everything to hand to enable him to travel to the most exotic locations in his head. He makes only one attempt at a journey in the entire book when, inspired by a reading of Dickens, he plans an excursion to London; but by the time he arrives at the railway station, having eaten at an English restaurant and read Baedeker's Guide to London, his actual journey seems redundant and so he promptly returns to Fontenay, his hermetically sealed home. He has imagined England far more convincingly than any experience of it could provide. Villiers de l'Isle Adam put similar sentiments into the mouth of his symbolist hero, Axel:

> Oh! the external world! Let's not be dupes of that old slave, whom real light shows chained at our feet, and who promises us the keys to a palace of enchantment, when what his black hand hides is a fistful of ashes! A little while ago you spoke of Bagdad, Palmyra, where else? Jerusalem. If you knew what a heap of uninhabitable stones, what a sterile burning soil, what lairs of unclean beasts make up in *reality* these poor wretched towns which appear resplendent with associations in the depths of that Orient you carry within![15]

The static self-imprisonment of all these decadent heroes became the inheritance of Hammer films' most decadent anti-hero, Dr. Ravna, as played by Noel Willman in *The Kiss of the Vampire*. Admittedly, Ravna is a rather more sociable fellow than Des Esseintes or Axel, as he regularly holds parties at his elegant chateau and presides over the considerable membership of his own vampire cult, but the important point is that he never leaves the chateau itself. It's also important that his home is a chateau rather than a castle; though

Gothic enough on the outside, it is full of well-appointed comfort inside. Production designer Bernard Robinson's trademark Solomonic columns enjoy gilded decorations here, bringing with them the decadent perfume of Catholic Europe, as discussed in chapter three, and despite the griffons left over from *The Brides of Dracula*, a stained glass window, a few judiciously placed quatrefoils and some elaborate wrought iron candle sconces, there's nothing particularly Gothic about the architectural style of Ravna's living rooms.

As we've already seen, Robinson had also played down the traditional Gothic architectural elements in his castle interiors for Hammer's first *Dracula*. He included a screen of "depressed" arches in the castle's vestibule, and by so doing he was able to distance his designs further from those of Universal's *Dracula*. The doorway through which Christopher Lee's Dracula makes his first, full-fanged entrance in the library of the castle is contained by a Tudor arch, which form appears again in Dracula's crypt. (Typical of early 16th-century English architecture, the Tudor arch lends the ambience of a British stately home to Dracula's castle, which certainly matches the patrician accents of the actors who inhabit it.) Robinson did include two rather more pronounced lancet arches in the back wall of the hall where Harker eats his dinner, along with a Gothic arch complete with tracery over the exterior wicket gate that leads to the castle, but none of these, even taking account of Robinson's trademark quatrefoils, is anywhere near as overtly Gothic as Charles D. Hall's extravaganza of lancet and equilateral arches, mouldering stairs and gigantic cobwebs for Tod Browning's *Dracula*. Indeed, Robinson seems to favor Romanesque arches for most of the door frames and windows in the Hammer version. By these means, he was able to *suggest* Gothic rather than trowel it on, an appropriate restraint for what was, in 1958, a streamlined, "aesthetic" approach to the story. Props and furniture were also used to suggest rather than impose a Gothic atmosphere. (Jonathan Harker, for example, sits on a chair with a Gothic arched backrest in the opening scenes.)

When Robinson's wife Margaret observed that Dracula's castle was so incredibly clean and tidy — not a cobweb in sight — she asked who did the cleaning, complaining that the tidiness

One of Horace Walpole's specially designed Gothic chairs in Strawberry Hill. Art director Bernard Robinson also used furniture to suggest the Gothic atmosphere of Hammer's first *Dracula* production (dir. Terence Fisher, 1958).

didn't seem very logical. "Of course it is," Robinson replied, pointing out that the castle was kept clean by magic.[16] In Stoker's novel, of course, Count Dracula himself rather touchingly does all the domestic chores; but the real justification for Robinson's spick-and-span elegance in *Dracula* and later for *The Kiss of the Vampire* was Hammer's emphasis on the more decadent elements of their approach to these stories. Hammer's vampires were always more sophisticated and aesthetic than Lugosi. Their artistic, ultra-refined environments suggest that they have a great deal more in common with the convenient aestheticism of Des Esseintes. Their homes may be well-appointed but they are the opposite of "bourgeois" in every other respect, fulfilling all the fantasies of Baudelaire, Villiers, Huysmans and Poe in their continual undermining of the truly bourgeois values of their victims. Villiers indeed, stated that his aim in writing the novella *Claire Lenoir* (1887) was what Brian Stableford calls "intellectual subversion."[17] Villiers hoped to achieve this by inviting his middle-class readers to identify with his narrow-minded bourgeois narrator Tribulat Bonhomet, help them to recognize many of their own ideas and opinions in him, and then make them realize what an unimaginative, repellent person Bonhomet actually is. "As soon as we have a few subscriptions," Villiers announced, *à propos* of his new literary magazine in which he aimed to publish his stories, "we must drive the reader mad."[18] Stoker's Jonathan Harker, the ultimate prude, would no doubt have been one of those readers. Even though Hammer transformed Harker from a hapless estate agent into a ruthless vampire slayer, he is just as censorious, if not more so. In Sangster's version he uses deception and hypocritical courtesy to worm his way into the count's lair. He pretends to be a librarian intending all along to dispatch his aristocratic employer at the earliest opportunity, like one of those guardians of moral rectitude who originally found Hammer films so objectionable and wanted them banned. Hammer undoubtedly saw their undead vampires as being far more alive and far more interesting than their vampire killers.

In *The Kiss of the Vampire*, Gerald Harcourt (played by Edward de Souza) is a sensible, middle-class professional, replete with a De Dion Bouton motor car and an obedient, if spirited wife. Neither of them have the faintest idea of what's going on until it's nearly too late. When Harcourt helps the misanthropic academic Professor Zimmer to destroy the vampires, we can't help feeling that something wonderful and exciting has been destroyed by the dead hand of respectability and social conformity. None of Hammer's vampires is more like the Poe narrators than Dr. Ravna, the hall of whose chateau suggests the exquisite interiors of "Ligeia" and "The Assignation," to say nothing of Des Esseintes' Fontenay in *À Rebours*. It contains a cage in which a mockingbird chirps with sinister insistency. A demonic statue immediately attracts Gerald's attention, as he takes in the unusual home of his hosts for the night. In the music room (how appropriate that such an artistic family should have one of those) the decor is influenced by Japanese-style latticework screens, reflecting the interest in such things that was shared by the British aesthetic movement at the turn of the century. That movement had passed its peak by 1910, the year in which the film is set, but it would have coincided with the earlier part of Dr. Ravna's career. The piano, on which Barry Warren's Carl Ravna plays James Bernard's celebrated "Vampire Rhapsody," is a riot of rococo decoration. Elegantly framed landscapes and portraits adorn the walls, the family dog sleeps on a rug before a warm fire in the hearth. Horror seems a long way from such comfortable surroundings.

Having shown Gerald and Marianne Harcourt around his gilded jewel box of a home and offered them dinner, Ravna now indulges in some decidedly decadent after-dinner small talk. An unspecified "accident," he explains, has resulted in his chateau-bound exile, and he now surrounds himself with beautiful things. "You expected the inside of my house to be as unattractive as the outside. Is that it?" he inquires. "If it were I couldn't live here." He goes so far as to call his home an "ornate coffin" and begins to inform Marianne that the most beautiful things in life often have the most unpromising of origins: "That wine we enjoyed at dinner, made from grapes trampled by the feet of a peasant. Dirty feet as like as not." His next unsavory observation (that the pheasant they have all just consumed must have been hanging for several weeks) is interrupted by the protestation of his more circumspect vampire daughter, Sabena (Jacquie Wallis).

The film's subsequent plot has often been described as Hitchcockian but, as we shall see, it has more in common with Terence Fisher's (non–Hammer) romance *So Long at the Fair* (1950), in which similar events unfold. At the beginning of *The Kiss of the Vampire*, Gerald and Marianne, their De Dion Bouton having broken down, take refuge in a deserted hotel, the proprietors of which, we later learn, are being held to ransom by the evil Ravnas. Dr. Ravna has corrupted and abducted the hotelier's daughter Tanya (played with marvelously malevolent relish by Isobel Black). The Ravnas appear to use the hotel as a clearing house for potential disciples of their undead cult, and Gerald and Marianne are merely the latest victims. They are invited to a masked ball at the chateau, halfway through which Gerald is drugged. When Gerald awakens the following morning, Carl Ravna (who previously attempted to hypnotize Marianne by playing the "Vampire Rhapsody") denies all knowledge of Marianne. She has disappeared, her clothes back at the hotel along with her. Only Professor Zimmer, who, as his name suggests, keeps to his room at the hotel, can help the distraught Gerald. Together they attempt to rescue Marianne, who is being held prisoner at the chateau. Gerald is eventually trapped there and subjected to particularly nasty treatment at the hands of Dr. Ravna, who instructs Marianne (now being initiated into the vampire cult) to spit on her husband's face and renounce him. After that, it's Tanya's turn to expose her fangs and prepare to bite the bewildered hero who is being held by Carl and the

Solomonic columns behind the elaborate grand piano on one of Bernard Robinson's sets for Chateau Ravna in *The Kiss of the Vampire* (dir. Don Sharp. 1964).

Ravnas' burly manservant. Gerald's shirt is ripped off and the full horror of the psychosexual situation is exposed to far more unnerving effect than anything a more contemporary film might try throwing at us. However, religious symbolism comes to the rescue. Gerald smears the blood on his chest into a cross and makes his escape. The rest of the film describes how Zimmer destroys the vampires by raising occult forces to work against them.

So Long at the Fair concerns a young man who, much to the dismay of his bewildered sister, is spirited away while staying at a hotel in Paris. The reason for this is that the hotel manager believes the illness the young man has contracted might put off the other guests staying at his hotel. In terms of general mood, however, *The Kiss of the Vampire*, with its sophisticated, exquisitely mannered and highly cultured vampires, has much more in common with the decadent, psychosexual novel *Traumnovelle* (Dream Story), by the Viennese writer Arthur Schnitzler (1862–1931). First published in 1926, Schnitzler's novel is an exposé of the depravity that lurks beneath the surface of civilized society, and it is a direct descendent of symbolist literature's interest in the world of dreams and fantasy; but whereas the symbolists so often used dream imagery to articulate their spiritual idealism in an aesthetically mystical, frequently crypto–Catholic manner, Schnitzler was more interested in dreams as the arena of sexual fantasy. Indeed, the German word for dream, "Traum," bears a resemblance to the word "Trauma," and both Schnitzler's *Traumnovelle* and *The Kiss of the Vampire* deal with sexual trauma by similar means. The fantasy environment of both the film and the novel articulate the subconscious drives of their characters with far more immediacy and intensity than a more realistic approach could have achieved.

In Schnitzler's novel, the hero, Fridolin, is a doctor, married to Albertine; but in his subconscious, Fridolin isn't as faithful to his wife as his bourgeois exterior might suggest. The daughter of one of his patients confesses that she is in love with him. Coincidentally, she, like Gerald Harcourt's wife, is also called Marianne. She prostrates herself before Fridolin beside her father's deathbed, flinging her arms around the bewildered doctor's knees. Fridolin wonders if the court councillor, her father, really is dead. "Suppose he's in a cataleptic trance," he wonders, "and can hear everything."[19] Fridolin recalls having read about a young man who was raped beside his mother's deathbed, and he can't help thinking about his own wife due to the feelings of sexual guilt these thoughts arouse in him; but he isn't aroused by Marianne, even though the idea of extramarital relations lingers with him when he later encounters a prostitute after having become lost on his way home. Schnitzler describes the prostitutes, "on their nightly man-hunt,"[20] as being like ghosts, and they also resemble the female bloodsuckers of *The Kiss of the Vampire*.

Later in the novella, Fridolin meets his old student friend Nachtigall, who has become a Bohemian pianist. Nachtigall's latest engagement is to play the piano for a ball at a secret gathering somewhere in the city. Fridolin is intrigued and persuades Nachtigall to let him accompany him. He purchases a fancy-dress costume (a monk's habit), and now the parallels with *The Kiss of the Vampire* become explicit. All the guests at the ball are wearing masks, as in the film. Fridolin is taken to the ball's venue in a closed carriage, which resembles a hearse. Similarly, Gerald and Marianne are taken to Chateau Ravna in the same coach in which Carl and Sabena arrived at the hotel to invite them to the ball. It will be remembered that when the sun begins to emerge from the clouds halfway through their visit, the vampire siblings make a dash for their carriage and pull down the blinds, instructing the coachman to "drive like the devil."

At the *Traumnovelle* ball, Fridolin meets a woman with a "red mouth glistening behind a lace veil,"[21] an emphasis that not only suggests the vampire's kiss but also the lace finishings inside a coffin. The women at this strange ball are all at first dressed in nuns' habits, but they eventually disappear only to return naked, while the men exchange their monks' robes for brightly colored courtiers' costumes. The atmosphere grows increasingly macabre and menacing in a manner comparable to the equally colorful ball scene in *The Kiss of the Vampire* with its masks, costumes and Chinese lanterns. In the film, however, this gaiety is undercut by James Bernard's unnerving score when Carl puts on a mask that is identical to the one Gerald is wearing, and thus sets about his abduction of Marianne.

In Schnitzler's novel, Fridolin grows increasingly fascinated by the woman with the blood-red mouth and asks if there are any discrete apartments "where couples who have discovered one another can retire?"[22] It is just this kind of apartment to which Marianne in *The Kiss of the Vampire* is lured by Carl, who then locks her in, while downstairs Gerald is drugged by a "special glass of champagne" and taken to another room. In *Traumnovelle*, things also take a dangerous turn when the woman with the blood-red mouth tells Fridolin that he has been spotted as an intruder and that he must flee to escape the penalty.

"Come with me," she says, explaining that if she were to flee with him she would be forfeiting not only her own life but his as well. Fridolin is described as being "at once thirsty and delirious."[23] He reaches out to remove the woman's veil but she prevents him, explaining that when someone tried that with another girl, the man was driven out with a whip and the girl was forced to kill herself.

When one of the courtiers asks Fridolin for a second password, he is exposed as an intruder, but whatever ghastly punishment is planned for him, the woman saves him. The price for this act of generosity, we later discover, is her own life. Fridolin is released with the warning to "beware of delving more deeply into secrets you've merely sneaked across the threshold of."[24] Fridolin is then taken on a wild ride in a coach, which rivals those we experience in so much Gothic cinema:

> He knocked at the glass pane, shouted, screamed, but the coach rolled on. He tried to open first the door on the left-hand side and then on the right, but they simply would not yield, and his redoubled cries were lost amid the rumbling wheels and the whistling of the wind. The coach began to jolt as it drove downhill at an ever faster pace, and Fridolin, seized by anxiety and fear, was on the point of smashing one of the opaque windows when the carriage suddenly came to a halt.[25]

When Fridolin eventually returns home, he isn't sure if the whole experience of the night was real or imaginary (which is precisely Gerald Harcourt's dilemma after his unceremonious eviction from Chateau Ravna). Fridolin is also unnerved to learn that his wife has had a similar psychosexual dream in which Fridolin was being punished for having dallied with a princess. In Augustine's dream, Fridolin's hands are tied behind his back. In *The Kiss of the Vampire*, Gerald, when he is brought before Dr. Ravna after his failed attempt to rescue Marianne, is also held by Carl and the Ravnas' manservant. Fridolin is naked; Gerald has his shirt ripped open. The parallels are quite vivid. Augustine's dream came to an end when Fridolin was about to be executed for his "crime" in a castle courtyard. He is saved, however, by the princess, who says that his death sentence will be remitted if he is prepared to become her paramour. Fridolin resists and remains faithful to his wife, at which the princess shrugs her shoulders while Fridolin is whipped. As Albertine remembers:

> The blood flowed from you in streams, and, seeing it flow, I was aware of my own horror without being surprised by it.[26]

Gerald's bloody encounter with Isobel Black's sexy Tanya in *The Kiss of the Vampire* is along the same lines: if he accepts the vampire's kiss he will escape a more conventional death, but, like Fridolin, he resists.

Traumnovelle draws to a close with Fridolin's visit to a morgue. Having read about the suicide of a baroness in the newspapers, he's convinced that this suicide is the woman with the blood-red mouth whom he met at the ball. A decidedly necrophiliac encounter with her corpse in the morgue has much in common with Marianne's encounter with Dr. Ravna just before her presentation to the cult as a new disciple.

> Almost as if driven by some unseen power, Fridolin touched the woman's brow, cheeks, arms and shoulders with both hands; then he intertwined his fingers with the dead woman's as if to fondle them, and, stiff as they were, they seemed to be attempting to move and to take hold of his; instead, he thought he could detect a faint and distant gleam in the eyes beneath those half-closed lids, trying to make contact with his own; and, as if drawn by some enchantment, he bent down over her.[27]

The final line here strongly resembles the shot of Ravna looming down over Marianne, his fangs bared, as she lies in her initiate's robes.

If it is the spirit of decadence, surrealism and Freudian psychodrama that suffuses *The Kiss of the Vampire*, it is the ghost of symbolist literature that haunts Hammer's most metaphysically intriguing Frankenstein film, *Frankenstein Created Woman*. The title of this film originated as a joke at the expense of Roger Vadim's *And God Created Woman* (1957),[28] but the film itself has, as we shall see, much in common with the novella *L'Eve future* (1886) by Villiers de l'Isle Adam. Like Poe, the impecunious Villiers consoled himself by describing exotic *décors* and ivory tower heroes in his fiction. His masterpiece, *Axel* (1890), about which Villiers received advice from no less a master than Richard Wagner, whom he much admired, abounds in typically symbolist disdain for the real world in favor of the ideal world of dreams. "As for living?" his hero famously asks at the end of this gigantic idealist drama, "our servants will do that for us."[29] Those who have glimpsed the ideal have little time or need for prosaic reality, and so, inevitably, Axel and his beloved, having discovered untold wealth (that alchemical symbol of true wisdom) in the House of Usher that is Axel's castle, enter a suicide pact.

Villiers' *L'Eve future*, which has so much in common with *Frankenstein Created Woman*, concerns a scientist, based on Thomas Alva Edison (1847–1931), who creates a female android for his lovesick, aristocratic friend Lord Ewald. Ewald loves Alicia, a completely empty-headed beauty. He is obsessed by her beauty to such an extent that for him to consider taking up another woman is impossible, but he is in such despair over her intellectual and artistic vacuity that he determines to resolve his dilemma by blowing his brains out. The professor persuades him to postpone this drastic action until he has seen the android he's been working on, a perfect reproduction of Alicia in every respect except for a much more acceptable personality than the one the real Alicia had been given by nature. The professor has imbued the soul of another woman into his android by telepathic means, and when introducing his new Eve, the professor compares her to Poe's Ligeia, E.T.A. Hoffmann's Coppélia and Wagner's Venus. The android herself, whose mechanical joints are lubricated with rose oil, is called Hadaly, and she is the embodiment of Ewald's ideal. Indeed, Villiers' distinctly misogynistic tale is not far from the basic idea of *The Stepford Wives* (dir. Bryan Forbes, 1974); a similar idea formed the basis of Jules Verne's novel *Le Château des carpathes* (1892). This not only has a Transylvanian setting with a Gothic castle but also an eccentric scientist who, infatuated with an opera singer called La Stilla (since deceased), has arranged

Noel Willman as Dr. Ravna and Jennifer Daniel as Marianne Harcourt stand before Bernard Robinson's combination of solomonic columns and Japanese-style screen in *The Kiss of the Vampire* (dir. Don Sharp, 1964).

to have recordings of her voice played alongside a portrait of her that is projected onto a sheet of glass with lifelike verisimilitude:

> By means of glasses inclined at a certain angle calculated by Orfanik, when a light was thrown on the portrait placed in front of a glass, La Stilla appeared by reflection as real as if she were alive, and in all the splendour of her beauty.[30]

Peter Cushing as Baron Frankenstein lifts Susan Denberg's newly transformed Christina in *Frankenstein Created Woman* (dir. Terence Fisher, 1967).

Villiers, however, was also making a deeper, more philosophical point related to the philosophy of Georg Wilhelm Friedrich Hegel (1770–1831), to which we will be returning in the next chapter. Hegel's basic idea, however, pertains to the idea that the world is our own creation and therefore can only be said to exist in our own minds. As the professor explains, Ewald's love for Alicia does not exist in her human form. It exists only in Ewald's own desires. Alicia "is this vision conjured up by your desires, which you have called forth, which you have created in your living being, and this vision is nothing more than a double of your own soul, which you have transplanted into her."[31] The advantage of Hadaly is that she will be able to reciprocate Ewald's desires, respond sensitively to his intellectual and emotional needs and fully reflect his soul back at himself. The professor continues:

> Why should you not endeavour by means of your living faith to project some of your ideals into Hadaly in the same manner in which you strive to project them into your living friend?
> Try it. Breathe upon this ideal forehead of Hadaly and suggest to her your idealized being, and you will see how the Alicia of your dreams will be realized, unified, and animated in this phantom.[32]

Hadaly, like all "must-have" male accessories, even has her own "carrying case," not merely the metaphorical "ornate coffin" of Dr. Ravna but her own actual coffin, made of ebony and upholstered in black silk. Ewald eventually packs her up in this and ships her off to England, but unfortunately the ship sinks and both Ewald and Hadaly are drowned.

The philosophical point of Villiers' tale seems to be that the only thing that matters in life is the Idea, that as our emotions exist only inside the mind, so too does the rest of reality. Such a world-view was central to the outlook of the symbolist generation. The spokesman for French symbolism in England was the poet and critic Arthur Symons (1865–1945) who expressed the self-sufficient, introverted aesthetic of the movement in his poem "Laus Virginitatis":

> The mirror of men's eyes delights me less,
> O mirror, than the friend I find in thee;
> Thou lovest, as I love, my loveliness,
> Thou givest my beauty back to me.
>
> I to myself suffice; why should I tire
> The heart with roaming that would rest at home?
> Myself the limit of my own desire,
> I have no desire to roam.[33]

The Belgian symbolist artist Fernand Khnopff (1858–1921) summed up this attitude in his own personal motto "On n'a que soi" ("One has only oneself"). Khnopff's home in Brussels, which has been demolished, was really a temple to his own imagination. According to one of his earliest biographers, "His goal is to raise up the ivory tower of pessimism."[34] Khnopff himself said, "Sleep is the most perfect thing in our existence,"[35] because in sleep we are not even responding to exterior stimuli. (Ever since Kant, philosophers have argued what exactly constitutes "The Thing in Itself," that which is independent of our own response to it.) In dreams we can truly say that we create the world in which we live, or, as Wagner (the godfather of the symbolist movement) put it in *Tristan und Isolde*, "selbst dann bin ich die Welt" ("I myself am the world").[36] According to this view of reality, we can know nothing beyond our own imagination, our own cognition of the phenomenal world. As the professor in *L'Eve future* puts it, it is far better to "say farewell to the pretended reality, the everlasting deceiver and accept the artificial and its novel incitements."[37] At another stage, the professor explains to Sowana, the somnambulist who projects her own soul into Hadaly, that Hadaly "is imbued with our two wills; they are united in her; it is a dualism."[38]

So, Hadaly has three souls at work within her body, which is a similar predicament to that suffered by Christina, the unfortunate heroine of *Frankenstein Created Woman*. We are first introduced to Christina when she is a disfigured hunchback in love with Hans, the son of a guillotined murderer. This boy is later guillotined for a crime he didn't commit, and in her despair over the injustice, Christina kills herself. This tragedy gives Peter Cushing's baron his long-awaited opportunity to experiment with the transference of souls. He puts Christina's body back together again, cures her deformities, and pops Hans' soul into it. With the added influence of Frankenstein's Godlike will controlling her destiny, Christina is just as much a tri-souled automaton as Hadaly.

In filming this fascinating variation on the theme of Frankenstein, director Terence Fisher would not have forgotten his previous attempt in the field of identity swapping. This was for *Stolen Face* (1952), produced by Hammer's parent company, Exclusive, and starring Paul Henreid. In it, Henreid plays a plastic surgeon who grafts the face of the dead concert pianist he had been in love with onto a disfigured female convict, with predictably disastrous results. Georges Franju's *Les Yeux sans visage* (1960) explored the same idea a few years later, though rather more gorily; but grafting on a different face isn't anywhere near as metaphysically challenging (or fascinating) as transplanting the soul of one body into another. Fisher would reprise the experiment of *Frankenstein Created Woman*, but rather more materialistically, in *Frankenstein Must Be Destroyed*, where the baron has regressed in his line of research by merely transplanting brains rather than souls.

Without a doubt, what the baron achieved in *Frankenstein Created Woman* remains his most noble experiment. It is also perhaps Hammer's most symbolist film, as it is far more interested in metaphysics, love and identity than anything particularly Gothic or even horrific. Indeed, Frankenstein's lab in this film is the most modest of his various scientific workshops, being no more than a large room at the back of an ordinary house. The Gothic castle to which Frankenstein returned in the previous episode in Hammer's saga, *The Evil of Frankenstein*, only to discover that it had been vandalized and pillaged, has been completely forgotten in *Frankenstein Created Woman*. There isn't a Gothic arch in sight, and no doubt because the baron can't afford even a bottle of champagne without pawning his assistant's coat for the privilege, neither are there any exotic interiors to match Villiers' sumptuously decadent *décors* in *L'Eve future*. This is a shame on one level, as it would have been fun to see an equivalent of the "clear blue light" that illuminates what Villiers describes as "a vast hall" in the professor's under-

Anonymous illustration for Jules Verne's **The Castle of the Carpathians**, London, Sampson, Low, Marston & Company, 1893.

ground lair, where tremendous pillars support "a dome of basalt," the whole being "gorgeously decorated in Syrian fashion." The description continues:

> Large sheaves and garlands of silver were entwined on a bluish background. In the centre of the vault, suspended from a long golden chain, was a cluster of powerful electric lights shaded with blue globes.... Picturesque waterfalls flowed and cascades bubbled, and under the caress of an imaginary breeze wonderful flowers of the Orient grew in profusion. Birds from southern climates warbled gaily in this garden of artificial flora.[39]

By contrast, Cushing and his two assistants, played by Thorley Walters and Robert Morris, have only a large deep freeze, the energy harnessed from deep within a cliff face exposed in their basement, and a couple of wire-mesh, umbrella-like dishes at their disposal to capture Hans' soul. But more spectacular settings might have detracted from the film's intimate, almost theological atmosphere.

Because Cushing's baron is far more interested in ethereal than medical things in this film, his personality is consequently considerably less ruthless and more humane than in any other of his other Hammer incarnations. In this respect he again resembles the professor in Villiers' novel, who is described as having "more the appearance of a distinguished artist than a plodding scientist."[40] With an almost uncanny prescience, Villiers seems to be describing Cushing's own physiognomy in his description of the professor's face:

> Although the inventor's hair was greying on the temples, his face was boyish, his smile was frank and winning. Around his mouth were little lines which told of the struggles and hardships which he had encountered in the early days of his career. It had been bitter uphill work, but he now stood on the pinnacle of fame[.][41]

It's tempting to think that it is due to the failure of his female experiment that the baron turns into the sadistic misogynist he becomes in *Frankenstein Must Be Destroyed*, but if Frankenstein is a latent misogynist in *Frankenstein Created Woman*, Christina becomes a real man-hater, killing the opposite sex with furious intensity; and lest we should think that Villiers' Hadaly was merely a passive android, we shouldn't forget that, like Christina, she carries a dagger in her stocking to defend herself against male attack. (So too does Mrs. Hyde in *Dr. Jekyll and Sister Hyde* for that matter.) However, in the end Christina is horrified by the revenge killings her alter-ego has made her commit, and she throws herself off a cliff, suffering a similar fate (death by drowning) to that of Hadaly.

Villiers' novel was never an acknowledged inspiration for *Frankenstein Created Woman*, and there's no evidence to suggest that screenwriter Anthony Hinds had even read it. The parallels between the two are intriguing, however, especially as Jimmy Sangster, for one, was well aware of the symbolist and decadent elements in many of the Hammer films with which he was involved. He described the plot of *The Man Who Could Cheat Death*[42] as "a 'Dorian Gray' situation," and Wilde's mixture of elegance, wit and horror was the role model for many of Hammer's films. This is especially the case in *The Curse of Frankenstein* (dir. Terence Fisher, 1957) when Cushing asks Hazel Court to "pass the marmalade" immediately after the Creature has murdered his housemaid. "It brought the house down," Sangster recalled.[43] The Wildean elements are even more to the fore in Bert Batt's screenplay for *Frankenstein Must Be Destroyed*, when Cushing's baron demolishes his ill-informed fellow guests (led by actor Frank Middlemass) in the rooming house of Anna Spengler (played by Veronica Carlson):

FRANKENSTEIN: Excuse me, I didn't know that you were doctors.
GUEST: Doctors? We're not doctors!
FRANKENSTEIN: I beg your pardon. I thought you knew what you were talking about.

GUEST: You're damn rude, sir!
FRANKENSTEIN: I'm afraid that stupidity always brings out the worst in me.
GUEST: Stupidity!
FRANKENSTEIN: Stupidity. It is fools like you who have blocked progress throughout the ages. You make pronouncements on half-facts that you don't understand anyway.
GUEST: I find your tone and manner highly objectionable, sir, but if you wish to involve yourself in an argument about it, pray explain the word "progress" in this context.
FRANKENSTEIN: You wouldn't understand it; but I will give you a parallel that you may just appreciate. Had not man been given to invention and experiment, then tonight, sir, you would have eaten your dinner in a cave; you would have strewn the bones about the floor and then wiped your fingers on a coat of animal skin. In fact, your lapels do look somewhat greasy. Goodnight.

One has only to compare Wilde's description of the horrors of the dissecting room in *Dorian Gray* alongside Hammer's gory way with Frankenstein, to cement the connection. In blackmailing a former friend to help him dispose of the body of the artist who painted Dorian's portrait, and whom Dorian has just killed, Wilde writes:

Only listen, Alan. All I ask of you is to perform a certain scientific experiment. You go to hospitals and dead-houses, and the horrors that you do there don't affect you. If in some hideous dissecting-room or fetid laboratory you found this man lying on a leaden table with red gutters scooped out in it for the blood to flow through, you would simply look upon him as an admirable subject. You would not turn a hair.[44]

We can go further by comparing Villiers' collection of sardonic *symboliste* fantasies, *Contes cruels* (1883), with the portmanteau horror films of Amicus, Hammer's greatest English competitor.[45] Amicus worked on even tighter budgets than Hammer, and in this fact one might draw further comparisons with the impecunious Villiers who was himself working on a virtually nonexistent budget of his own. Written on scraps of paper in the corners of the cafes he frequented, his tales, like Hammer and Amicus at their best, belie their humble origins. An excellent example of how the general atmosphere of a Villiers tale was taken up by Amicus occurs in *Vault of Horror*. It's revealing to compare one episode in this film, "Midnight Mess," with certain aspects of a concise tale from *Contes cruels*, "The Very Image." The latter is a satire on the bankers Villiers hated. They have murdered their souls to gain comfort from wealth, and Villiers compares them to the suicides in a morgue who have murdered their bodies to attain comfort in death. Though it tells a different story, "Midnight Mess" exudes a similar hallucinatory mood. Daniel Massey's character pays a visit to his sister in a small town (the sister is played by Massey's real-life sister Anna). The town is always deserted at dusk, an occurrence that creates an atmosphere reminiscent of the brooding surrealist townscapes of Paul Delvaux and Georgio de Chirico. (Surrealism grew out of the symbolist aesthetic.) Roy Ward Baker's shot of the street is simplicity itself. It consists of a restaurant's fluorescent sign in the center background of the shot, the damp cobblestones of the street leading up to it in the foreground, and on the left a Victorian street lamp, which nods in the direction of the same kind of lamp in René Magritte's painting *Empire of Lights* (1953–54). Both lamps cast unsettling shadows over the walls of the buildings they illuminate. Indeed, this is the kind of street scene we have all dreamed about: at once familiar and unsettling.

After dark, however, figures do appear and make their way to the restaurant. The sense of desolation created by Baker's atmospheric direction is similar to the kind of thing that Villiers captured so succinctly in "The Very Image," when the narrator describes the morgue as a "stone apparition," which "reared up in the mist." Villiers adds that despite the dismal, eerie vapour in which it was enveloped, I recognised a certain cordial air of hospitality about it which reassured me.

"The people who live here," I said to myself, "must surely be sedentary folk. The threshold has an inviting look: isn't the door open?"[46]

Of course, Villiers is being highly ironic here to emphasize his scathingly mordant point, but Baker (and his DC comic source) are similarly able to be both facetious and unsettling. There is no mist in the street scene of "Midnight Mess," though the shadows cast by the lamp create an equivalent sense of ambiguity. The inviting morgue of "The Very Image" with its suicide corpses is again comparable to the inviting restaurant with its undead diners. Massey enters the restaurant and the vampires eventually hang him from the ceiling, fix a tap to his jugular vein, and refill their glasses of fresh blood, Massey's undead sister among them.

It's a very simple story, as lightweight as many of Villiers' plots, but what lingers in the memory is the symbolist mood created by the brief street scenes. These present reality as something not to be trusted, as a symbol, indeed, of a reality we might prefer not to know. As Oscar Wilde put it in the famous Preface to *The Picture of Dorian Gray*:

> All art is at once surface and symbol.
> Those who go beneath the surface do so at their peril.[47]

Though not "horror" stories in the popular sense of the term, Villiers' *Contes cruels* are nonetheless full of horrors: the leper who is the title character of "The Duke of Portland," for example, who throws lavish parties in his "massive crenellated mansion"[48] on Portland Bill, while keeping himself locked away from sight in the keep. Villiers chose Portland Bill because of its desolate landscape, an atmosphere which was not lost on Joseph Losey when he went there to film *The Damned* for Hammer in 1961.[49] The Duke of Portland, who has obviously been reading his Poe, has "the walls and ceilings of the vast underground rooms of the castle covered with huge Venetian mirrors."[50] He lays mosaics on the floors and hangs rich draperies and golden chandeliers, and fills the spaces with Oriental furniture, scented fountains, flowers and exquisite statues, for the entertainment of his guests. In this respect he resembles Prince Prospero in Poe's "The Masque of the Red Death," but while Prospero is trying to escape the plague, the Duke of Portland is already suffering from leprosy. He never appears at his own revels, his armchair downstairs always remaining empty.

Harry Alan Towers' trashy production of *The Masque of the Red Death* (dir. Alan Birkinshaw, 1990) seems to be an unwitting conflation of Poe's original and Villiers' "The Duke of Portland," a tale that Poe undoubtedly inspired. Unlike Poe's Prospero, the Prospero in Birkinshaw's film, played by Herbert Lom, keeps himself to himself, more like the Duke of Portland, and watches events unfold at his castle on CCTV. As a setting for the power-crazed recluse, Towers chose King Ludwig II of Bavaria's *Neuschwanstein* castle, but this spectacular location was hardly used to its best effect in this unfortunate film. "The Duke of Portland" has none of the grisly murders of Birkinshaw's film and, even more mercifully, none of the 1980s Euro-pop music that accompanies a great deal of the party sequences, but the parallels between the two stories can help us to chart the literary ancestry of this kind of entertainment. One could continue the process with other comparisons. Villiers' "Occult Memories," the penultimate tale in *Contes cruels*, could even claim to be an anticipation of Steven Spielberg's *Indiana Jones* adventure movies. Villiers' tale describes, in lush detail, the exploits of an explorer who amasses treasures from exotic temples set amidst "horrible forests." "Creepers, grass, and dry boughs litter and obstruct paths which were once crowded avenues, from which the sound of chariots, arms, and singing has faded."⁵¹ There is even a premonition of Indiana Jones' well-known fear of snakes a little later in the story:

> Here and there are stones, broken arches, and shapeless statues, bearing inscriptions more worn than those of Sardis, Palmyra, or Khorsabad.... The silence is disturbed only by the sound of the snakes sliding among the fallen shafts of the columns or hissing as they coil up under the reddish mosses.⁵²

In "The Desire to Be a Man," Villiers anticipated Gaston Leroux's *The Phantom of the Opera* (1909). It is the deeply ironic tale of an aging actor who, having imitated emotions for so many years on the stage, realizes to his distress that he has never felt a genuine emotion. Consequently, he becomes an arsonist and hopes to enjoy the feelings of remorse his crimes will induce. The tragedy is that, after causing terrible mayhem, he feels nothing at all. In Leroux's much more sensationalist novel, Eric the Opera Phantom similarly commits atrocities to revenge himself upon an unfeeling public, a theme which went on to inspire several cinematic adaptations.

Villiers also wrote a kind of vampire tale called *Claire Lenoir* (published in 1887), which has been translated by Brian Stableford as *The Vampire's Kiss*, though its relation to traditional vampires is really rather tenuous. The plot of *Claire Lenoir* pivots upon the scientific speculation of the optogram. This idea suggests that the last thing animals (and humans) see before the moment of death is recorded on the retinas of their eyes just like a photograph:

Peter Cushing and Christopher Lee examine the eye of the monster in *Horror Express* (dir. Eugenio Martin, 1972).

It is henceforth established that animals destined for our nourishment, such as sheep, cattle, lambs, horses and cats, retain in their eyes, after the fatal stroke of the butcher's sledgehammer, the imprint of the objects of their last gaze. It is a veritable photograph *of paving-stones, stalls, gutters and vague figures, among whom can nearly always be distinguished that of the man who strikes them down. The phenomenon lasts until decomposition sets in.*[53]

Villiers takes the idea one step further by insisting that one's last *spiritual vision* can also be recorded in the eye. Claire Lenoir herself has such a vision in which she sees her husband's vengeful soul, now reincarnated as a savage cannibal, decapitating her guilty lover on a remote desert island.

There have been several other stories based on the idea of optograms, notably Jules Verne's *Les Frères Kip* (1902), in which a murder is solved by means of them. H. P. Lovecraft, once again, provides another example in a tale on which he collaborated with Hazel Heald, "Out of the Aeons." It combines various motifs mentioned in earlier chapters of his book, concerning, as it does, a curious mummy which finds its way to a Boston museum. The story is set in 1932 which, coincidentally, was the year in which Universal's *The Mummy* was released. However, Lovecraft's mummy differs from the ancient Egyptian variety, in that its skin is half-leathery, half-stony, and is the product of a kind of Gorgonic petrification. Beneath the petrified-leathery skin, however, its brain and internal organs are fully intact and horribly alive. Lovecraft uses the idea of the optogram to allow his academic narrator, Dr. Richard H. Johnson, to see, by means of autopsy, the last thing the mummy itself saw, and which transformed it into its mummified state. The mummy turns out to have been a human being who lived millions of years ago on the mythical land of Hyperborea (the same that was mentioned by Madame Blavatsky in her *Secret Doctrine*). This unfortunate individual once looked upon the full horror of a demon–God called Ghatanotha and, like the Gorgon, this demon was so abhorrent that the Hyperborean was turned into its eccentric mummified, yet still hideously alive state, merely by catching a glimpse of it. Odd though Lovecraft's superb tale is, it's still not quite so bizarre as Villiers' *Claire Lenoir*, the tale by which Villiers hoped to bamboozle empiricist science and "prove" that the universe was a far more mysterious and spiritual place than the likes of Tribulat Bonhomet, his bourgeois narrator, would have us believe.

Claire Lenoir also has certain things common with the Anglo-Spanish horror film *Horror Express* (dir. Eugenio Martin, 1972), in which Christopher Lee plays an explorer who has unearthed a Neanderthal embodiment of evil. This creature, of course, goes on the rampage, disturbing the peace of the passengers of the Trans-Siberian express. Eventually, Peter Cushing, who is also traveling on the train, gets the opportunity to examine one of the creature's eyes under a microscope and discovers floating in the retinal fluid an image of its last victim. The big idea behind all Villiers' stories was, however, borrowed, as already briefly mentioned, from Hegel, and in the next chapter we'll be exploring the perhaps unlikely effect of that obscurest of German philosophers on popular Gothic horror.

Eight

Hegelian Horrors

It's reassuring to know that even the *Oxford Companion the Philosophy* admits that the works of Hegel have a reputation for being amongst the most impenetrable of all philosophical texts, adding that "at first glance most readers will find his sentences simply incomprehensible."[1] This is perhaps how Villiers de l'Isle Adam felt as, according to his biographer A.W. Raitt, Villiers relied heavily on Augusto Véra's *Introduction to the Philosophy of Hegel*, first published in Paris in 1864, for his erudition on the subject.[2] One of Villiers' Hegelian stories in *Contes Cruels* is actually named after the Italian writer he found so indispensable, though Villiers turned Véra's surname into a female forename. In its original form, Villiers' tale "Véra" was also inspired by the example of Poe's "Ligeia" in that it concerns the spirit of a woman (Véra) who haunts her distraught husband, Comte d'Athol. The comte finds life so intolerable without her, he literally imagines her back to life. As Villiers puts it:

> Ideas are living creatures; and since the count had hollowed out in the air the shape of his love, that space had to be filled by the only creature which was homogeneous with it, or else the Universe would have collapsed. The impression was created at that moment, final, simple and absolute, that She must be there in the room. He was as calmly certain of this as of his own existence, and all the objects around him were saturated with this conviction.[3]

The original version of the story ended with these words: "And they realized then that they were in fact *one and the same being*."[4] Villiers later expanded the ending and, as Raitt puts it, made the story "less an affirmation of faith in the power of the mind, and more of an expression of trust in life after death."[5] It is, however, the former version that interests us here, as it is an expression of one of Hegel's principal ideas. Hegel belongs to a tradition of German philosophy that followed in the wake of Immanuel Kant (1724–1804), whose particular concern was with the division between our *perception* of the world and what he called the "Ding an sich." This "thing in itself" is the actuality of the world which we can know only through our unreliable senses, and can, therefore, *never* know. Hegel went further than Kant, however, by suggesting that the *only* thing we can know is the mind, as there is nothing *beyond* the mind. In fact, earlier philosophers who had inspired Kant had put forward this proposition. George Berkeley (1685–1753), for one, denied the existence of matter, arguing that everything is the product of mind. Berkeley argued that if our understanding of the world depends on our mental image of it, there's no logical reason for believing that the world has any reality beyond our *idea* of it. David Hume (1711–1776) proposed that we can only know *our perceptions* of the world. What we take on trust to be "real" is unprovable. Kant arrived at his own conclusions having read Hume, and thus laid the foundation stone of German metaphysics. Arthur Schopenhauer (1788–1860) similarly divided the world into Will and Representation (respectively what Kant called "the thing in itself" and "the world of phenomena"), and was thus able to say that the world is created by the mind, or, in his famous phrase, that "the world is my idea." Hegel's view of the world, inspired by Kant, was rejected by Schopenhauer, who liked to claim that he was the only person to have fully understood Kant's theory, but, as we shall see, Hegel's idea came from the same source. The most famous artistic follower of Schopenhauer was Richard Wagner, but he was equally, if not more influenced by Hegel. For egoists like Villiers and Wagner (who also absorbed Hegel's ideas at second hand—from his Uncle Adolf, and his uncle's friend, Christian Hermann Weisse, as a matter of fact), Hegel's idea that everything (and everybody else) are really one's own creation, was a godsend. As Wagner's biographer Joachim Köhler explains, thanks to Hegel, "Man was able to see himself not only as the centre of all creation but at the same time as its creator, a creator who simultaneously raised it to its highest pitch of perfection."[6] When Wagner understood this, it was only a matter of time before his Tristan would sing: "selbst dann bin ich die Welt" ("I myself am the world"). This idea, as we have seen, became one of the basic building blocks of the symbolist and later decadent movements. Mind (or, as Hegel would have put it, *Geist*) is all we have. The whole purpose of history is so that *Geist* can understand itself. As Brünnhilde sings in her immolation scene at the end of Wagner's *Götterdämmerung*: "mich mußte der Reinste verraten, daß wissend würde ein Weib!" ("this innocent had to betray me so that I should become a woman of wisdom!").[7] In other words, Siegfried, the great hero she loves, who represents all human history, had to go through all his (and the world's) suffering in order that *Geist*, represented by Brünnhilde, might understand itself. This is why the world ends shortly after Brünnhilde sings these words, for *Geist*'s mission has been achieved. It is the same idea that Oscar Wilde refers to in his essay *De Profundis*:

> I said in *Dorian Gray* that the great sins of the world take place in the brain, but it is in the brain that everything takes place. We know now that we do not see with the eye or hear with the ear. They are merely channels for the transmission, adequate or inadequate, of sense impressions. It is in the brain that the poppy is red, that the apple is odourous, that the skylark sings.[8]

Bernard Shaw was also indebted to Hegel's *Geist* for his concept of "Creative Evolutionism," which he discussed in plays such as *Man and Superman* (1903) and *Back to Methuselah* (1918–1920), the former of which explains that "Life was driving at brains—at its darling object: an organ by which it can attain not only self-consciousness but self-understanding."[9]

The idea that Mind is everything, that it *creates* reality and is not merely a part of reality has also had several intriguing expressions in popular horror films. One of the reasons why horror films are so compelling (and have been so persistent throughout film history) is that they often grapple with philosophical issues, albeit in a simplified manner, that are overlooked by more realistic genres. The seductive theory that one can control everything by means of Mind has naturally appealed to many right-wing occultists. As the ultimate secret weapon, no wonder some Nazi theorists were so fascinated by the possibility of Mind over Matter. Chief amongst the popular writers who were intrigued by the power of Mind, and one who believed that fascination had been shared by Hitler was Dennis Wheatley (1897–1977). His novel *They Used Dark Forces* (1964) attempted to suggest exactly that. It would have made the basis for an exciting Hammer film, no doubt, but was unfortunately never turned into one. However, Hammer did film Wheatley's classic occult novel *The Devil Rides Out* (1934) and I'll be discussing that in more detail in chapter eleven.

While it would be unreasonable to claim that anyone at Hammer (let alone Dennis Wheatley) consciously had Hegel in mind when making these popular entertainments, it is possible to connect them to Hegel's idea of *Geist*, via the symbolist writers whom Hegel influenced. Certainly, Villiers' interest in the transference of souls, which we have already explored with regard to *L'Eve future*, is a central aspect of *The Devil Rides Out*. In Terence Fisher's film version of the latter, Mocata refers to "the transference of souls" when explaining that he intends to sacrifice the Eatons' daughter, Peggy, and exchange her soul for that of Tanith (who has already died by this point). Souls are more important than bodies in Mocata's view of the world. It doesn't matter whose body is being used. The soul is the thing; indeed, it is the only *real* thing. If the Will can effect material change, the material is weaker, less substantial than the spiritual. As Poe, quoting Joseph Glanville, reiterates in "Ligeia":

> And the will therein lieth which dieth not. Who knoweth the mysteries of the will, with its vigor? For God is but a great will, pervading all things by nature of its intentness. Man doth not yield himself to the angels, nor unto death utterly, save only through the weakness of his feeble will.[10]

Roger Corman's film version of this story, retitled *The Tomb of Ligea* (1964), personifies Ligeia's defiant Will with the traditional image of a black cat. Verden Fell, the name Corman gives to Poe's unnamed narrator (played by Vincent Price), is another typical neurasthenic like Roderick Usher. Though little is revealed about the physical characteristics of this character in Poe's original story, Corman is keen to point out Fell's sensitivity to light (he wears wraparound sunglasses) and to noise (he cannot endure anyone raising their voice). Fell is also studiously attired in mourning and eloquently demonstrates his ability to hypnotize Lady Rowena (Elizabeth Shepherd), who becomes his second wife. He has just regressed her back to childhood when, unexpectedly, the will of his first wife, Ligeia, takes command of Rowena's voice with the terrifying words, "I will always be your wife." Ligeia's will is also capable of causing physical change (she defaces her own tomb, removing the date of her death). Poe's original story, however, is rather more successful in Hegelian terms than Corman's adaptation, as it suggests that this "hideous drama of revivication"[11] is all in the mind of the narrator. Poe's unnamed narrator is unreliable to say the least (he is an opium addict), and he is apparently unaware that he has poisoned Rowena, even in the moment of administering the drug. But Poe also leaves room for this crime to have been committed by the vengeful spirit of Ligeia. The narrator recalls:

> I became distinctly aware of a gentle footfall upon the carpet, and near the couch; and in a second thereafter, as Rowena was in the act of raising the wine to her lips, I saw, or may have dreamed that I saw, fall within the goblet, as if from some invisible spring in the atmosphere of the room, three or four large drops of a brilliant and ruby colored fluid. If this I saw—not so Rowena. She swallowed the wine unhesitatingly, and I forbore to speak to her of a circumstance which must, after all, I considered, have been but a suggestion of a vivid imagination, rendered morbidly active by the terror of the lady, by the opium, and by the hour.[12]

Nothing Poe's narrator says can be trusted, and perhaps the whole story is a figment of his imagination. Hegel, of course, would have said that *everything* is a figment of the imagination, that Poe's narrator, like Wagner's Tristan, is himself the world and that the world is him. (Corman's film, by contrast, leaves us in no doubt that Ligeia has come back to life.)

Poe went even further in his vast essay *Eureka* (1848), written in a style that itself approaches the turgid complexities of Hegel's prose. Though Hegel isn't mentioned in it, the basic idea of this essay is highly Hegelian. Poe's basic argument is that everything in the Universe is part of everything else. Originating in Oneness, the "primordial Particle" was atomized by the Creator into all matter. All matter is consequently attempting to coa-

Publicity poster for *The Tomb of Ligeia* (dir. Roger Corman, 1964).

lesce back into its original Oneness, and the human soul is part of that process. For Poe, there is, therefore, nothing greater than his own soul, as that soul is part of the primordial Particle of Oneness. (One might compare this idea with Aleister Crowley's famous dictum "Every Man and Woman Is a Star" in *The Book of the Law* of 1904.[13]) The dual concept that there is nothing greater than one's own soul, that it somehow contains everything within it, and that each individual is a part of the diffused and atomized Oneness of the Creator was particularly important to subsequent symbolists. In Poe's mystical conviction that we are all "infinite individualizations of Himself"[14] we have Poe's version of the Hegelian dialectic between the Infinite Mind (*Geist*) and the finite minds of individual humans, the ultimate mission of which is to be united with *Geist*.

A particularly Hegelian tale occurs in one of the stories of Amicus' portmanteau horror film *The House That Dripped Blood*. In the first story of this four-part collection, a writer (played by Denholm Elliott) takes up residence in the house of the film's title and is impressed not only by its macabre atmosphere but also by the large collection of books on occult and horror subjects on the shelves of its library. (These include works by Montague Summers, Robert Bloch, who wrote the screenplay, and even Lotte H. Eisner's classic study of German cinema, *The Haunted Screen*.) As we later learn from the estate agent (knowingly called Mr. Stoker), the secret of the house is that it reflects the personalities of its owners. The writer in the first tale specializes in horror stories and has created a fictional murderer called Dominick. The author is so carried away by his own creation that he begins to believe Dominick is real and in the house with him, and true to form, Dominick eventually kills his creator. So far, we have a classic example, in popular terms, of Hegelian metaphysics. Even death seems to be the creation of Mind. Indeed, the story follows the same basic lines as Villiers' "Véra"; but, unfortunately for fans of Hegelian horror, we soon find out that Dominick has been a hoax all along. The writer's wife has arranged for her lover to dress up as Dominick and terrify her husband to death so that they can both inherit the money which his fictional character has generated.

The idea of a creation killing its creator is a central aspect of all the films based on Mary Shelley's *Frankenstein,* but *Frankenstein* is predominantly a physical affair (excepting Hammer's foray into metaphysics in *Frankenstein Created Woman*). The concept of pure Mind existing beyond a physical vehicle for its expression understandably concerns occult cinema more than any other subgenre. As I mentioned earlier, I'll be dealing with occultism in more detail in chapter eleven, but I will briefly mention here Hammer's Dennis Wheatley adaptation *To the Devil a Daughter* as it contains several examples of the power of Mind at least over our perception of reality if not over reality itself. In this film, Christopher Lee's devil worshipper, Father Michael Rayner, telephones Denholm Elliott's Henry Beddows and manages to make him think that the telephone cord has turned into a serpent, entwined around his wrist. Like Mocata, Father Michael is also able to influence Nastassja Kinski's Catherine Beddows, the innocent (though indoctrinated) nun who is eventually to be baptized in the service of the demon Astaroth. Under Father Michael's influence, she drives a metal comb handle into Honor Blackman's neck and then, like Ayesha in *The Vengeance of She* (dir. Cliff Owen, 1968), finds herself compelled to seek out the source of Father Michael's telepathic command. She's prevented from doing this by the writer John Verney (played by Richard Widmark), causing Father Michael some psychic discomfort when the link between them is interrupted. Father Michael is also able to manifest himself in a flash of lightning after Verney has watched Anthony Valentine (or rather stuntman Eddie Powell) spontaneously combust in a deserted church.

The Innocents, Jack Clayton's 1961 adaptation of Henry James' story "The Turn of the Screw," also wonders if hallucinations are merely aberrations in our perception of reality or if *everything* we perceive is a hallucination. Clayton's film cast Deborah Kerr as a Victorian governess who is increasingly convinced that the young charges under her care in a remote country mansion have been morally corrupted and are still haunted by the spirits of previous servants, now dead. Is Kerr's governess making it all up, thanks to her sexually frustrated imagina-

Christopher Lee as Father Michael Rayner in *To the Devil a Daughter* (dir. Peter Sykes, 1976).

tion, or do the ghosts actually exist? The film, like James' story, leaves the question unanswered, providing ample evidence to support both arguments. The governess hectors Miles, the boy in her care, to such an extent that he runs out into the moonlit garden. "Say his name!" she insists. Miles, terrified, shouts "Peter Quint! Where? You Devil!" and we see Quint (played by Peter Wyngarde) standing above both figures in the formal garden in which they now find themselves. Quint raises his hand, but Miles seems confused. Has he really see this apparition? The governess seems not to have seen Quint either, and Miles dies in her arms (presumably of a heart attack). The film draws to a close with only the sound of a bird singing in the darkness as the governess plants a troubled, passionate and politically incorrect kiss on the boy's lips.

Hegel's insistence that Mind creates reality, and that each finite mind is part of *Geist* is hardly the philosophy of an atheist. Indeed, for Hegel, *Geist* is God, the eternal essence that existed before the creation of nature and the finite mind of humanity. We can, however, find a secular version of this concept at work in the unlikely place of a British exploitation horror film made in 1967. Admittedly, *The Sorcerers,* directed by Michael Reeves for Tony Tenser's Tigon production company, is not about pure Mind, divorced from the brain, but it does rather nicely set up the dialectic between Godlike *Geist* and the individual finite mind of which Hegel speaks. *The Sorcerers* is indeed concerned with the power of Mind to create a universe of sensations. In the film these are experienced vicariously by the two characters played by its superannuated stars, Boris Karloff and Catherine Lacey. Karloff plays a disgraced, retired hypnotist called Marcus Monserrat. Lacey plays his wife, Estelle. Together, they experiment with their own version of the transference of souls, though in their case the transference is not literal but rather "scientific." Monserrat has created a machine that will allow him and his wife to indulge in some psychic eavesdropping. He programs the brain of a young man called Mike (played by Ian Ogilvy) and this allows him to "tune in" to what Mike is doing at any given moment. Thus, the elderly couple are now able to experience the physical sensations of a youthful body at second hand, but so vividly that it seems as if the sensations are their own. After indulging in vicarious sex, Estelle soon realizes that not only can she experience Mike's feelings, she can also influence his actions. She henceforth sets about releasing all her pent-up frustrations by commanding Mike to commit increasingly nasty crimes so that she can experience the thrill of violence for herself. Monserrat is appalled but unable to prevent his wife from indulging in these psychic trips, which culminate in Mike's death in a car crash. So complete is Mike's hypnotic relationship with the Monserrats by this time, his death triggers their own. Mike's car bursts into flames and in the final shots of the film we are shown the charred faces of Monserrat and Estelle lying in a room far from the place of the accident itself. It's more a case of symbiotic rather than spontaneous combustion. Verdict: death by voyeurism.

Karloff had tried much the same experiment earlier in his career in *The Man Who Changed His Mind* (dir. Robert Stevenson, 1936). Also made in England, this film concerns Dr. Laurience, who, like Monserrat, once had a respectable reputation but who is now investigating the origins of the mind and the soul. He is assisted in his work by a young surgeon and a disabled, wheelchair-bound fellow-traveler called Clayton. Laurience transfers Clayton's mind into the body of the wealthy Lord Haslewood, and so gains control of Haslewood's fortune. Laurience then attempts to put his own mind in the body of Lord Haslewood's son Dick, in a Faustian attempt to attract the attentions of his (Laurience's) female assistant. Things now grow complicated, especially so when it's discovered that Laurience had killed Clayton's body when Clayton's mind was in Lord Haslewood's body. Dick's mind is now trapped in Laurience's body, and so it's really Dick who will be hanged for the murder of the person everyone thinks is his father. A plot like that indeed makes the confused and disguised identities of comic opera seem quite prosaic.

Admittedly, neither of these films contains quite the same thing as the "genuine" transference of souls we find in *Frankenstein Created Woman* and *The Devil Rides Out*. *The Sorcerers* is more a case of extreme hypnotic suggestion, while *The Man Who Changed His Mind* takes a similar, though less surgical approach to the fifth experiment of Cushing's baron in *Frankenstein Must Be Destroyed*. Karloff's Laurience merely had a more sophisticated means of transplanting minds than Frankenstein. The implication of all these films, however, is the same: that Mind is more significant and more lasting than matter. Even though Estelle depends upon her youthful host for her vicarious experiences, she still experiences these by means of what we would now term virtual reality, the aim of which is to replace reality by means of an imaginatively constructed world with the help of a computer rather than a human being as host.

Hegel's ideas influenced other dramas outside the horror genre. Luigi Pirandello's play *Six Characters in Search of an Author* (1921) contrasts six fictional characters with a group of actors in a theater, and asks who is the more real. Are fictions as real as so-called reality? After all, when we are watching a play or a film we suspend our disbelief and "believe" in the characters whose story we become involved with. Many people still believe that the characters in a television soap

Boris Karloff as Dr. Laurience and Anna Lee as Dr. Clare Wyatt in *The Man Who Changed His Mind* (dir. Robert Stevenson, 1936).

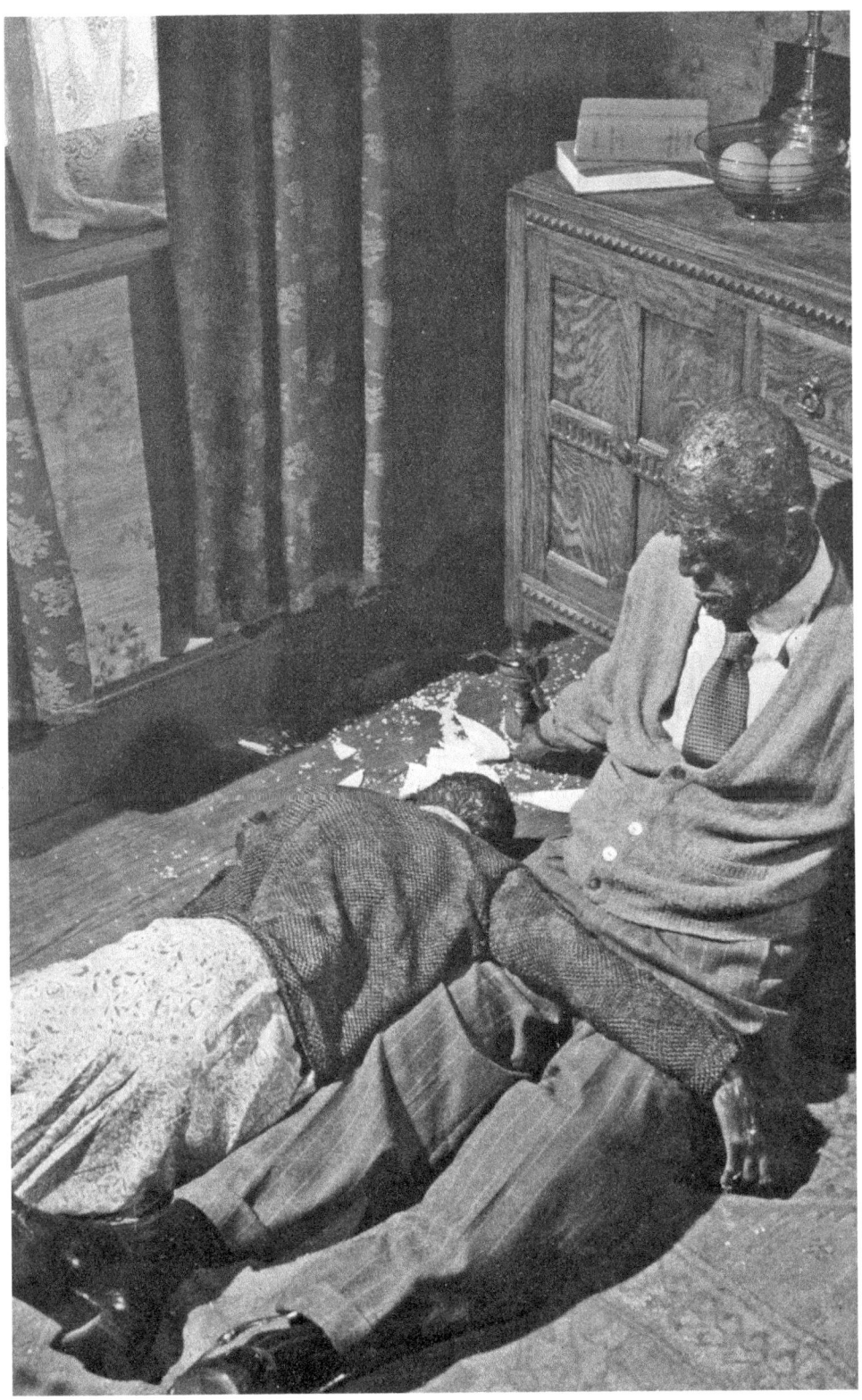

Boris Karloff and Catherine Lacey as Marcus and Estelle Monserrat, telepathically incinerated at the end of *The Sorcerers* (dir. Michael Reeves, 1967).

opera are real, and not actors. One of Pirandello's six characters, who wander into a theater rehearsal, explains that he and his five fellow fictional characters have been abandoned by their author:

> THE FATHER: [T]he author who created us alive no longer wished, or was no longer able, materially to put us into a work of art. And this was a real crime, sir; because he who has had the luck to be born a character can laugh even at death. He cannot die. The man, the writer, the instrument of the creation will die, but his creation does not die. And to live for ever, it does not need to have extraordinary gifts or to be able to work wonders. Who was Sancho Panza? Who was Don Abbondio? Yet they live eternally because — live germs as they were — they had the fortune to find a fecundating matrix, a fantasy which could raise and nourish them: make them live for ever![15]

Pirandello here seems to be suggesting that fictional characters are rather like vampires: they are immortal but they need to be nourished by the life blood of a plot or narrative. As The Father puts it to the Theatre Manager, "We want to live … in you."[16]

The Father goes on to argue that he and his five fellow fictional characters are more "real" than the actors as fictional characters cannot change or evolve like living people:

> THE FATHER: Our reality doesn't change: it can't change! It can't be other than what it is, because it is already fixed for ever. It's terrible.[17]

The fact that living people are subject to change might make them seem more chimerical, more of an illusion than a character in a book or a play who is always there. One can depend on a book in a way one can never depend on a real person. Many people, after all, find much comfort in reading the Bible or a favorite poem. However, The Father goes on to explain:

> When the characters are really alive before their author, the latter does nothing but follow them in their action, in their words, in the situations which they suggest to him; and he has to will them the way they will themselves—for there's trouble if he doesn't. When a character is born, he acquires at once such an independence, even of his own author, that he can be imagined by everybody even in many other situations where the author never dreamed of placing him; and so he acquires for himself a meaning which the author never thought of giving him.[18]

Pirandello's idea that the product of an author's consciousness attains a life of its own, is a strong echo of Hegel's belief that we all create our own idea of reality. As Anthony Thorlby puts it:

> With Hegel, the mind's role becomes creative in an absolute sense: its activity generates reality. Needless to say, reality has a singular meaning for Hegel; it means nothing less than the whole; that is, something more than either the empirical world of things or the ideal world of thought. Hegel imagined these two worlds as two aspects of the same reality, the external and internal aspect of being. Individual things or thoughts are real only in relationship to one another, and they achieve this relationship in the cumulative consciousness of mankind. The wholeness of reality is thus itself in process of becoming.[19]

As, for Hegel, everything is the product of *Geist*, there is no substantial difference between so-called fiction and so-called fact. The two are equally products of the only significant and knowable thing, which can only be *Geist*:

> The goal of all history is that mind should come to understand itself as the only ultimate reality. When is that understanding first achieved? By Hegel himself in the *Phenomenology* [*of Mind*]! If Hegel is to be believed, the closing pages of his masterpiece are no mere description of the culmination of everything that has happened since finite minds were first created: they *are* that culmination.[20]

One of the most interesting cinematic parallels of Pirandello, which also incorporates traditional horror film imagery into its narrative, is Alain Resnais' *Providence* (1977). Whereas Pirandello's drama features six characters in search of an author, Resnais described *Providence* as a chamber quintet "with Ellen Burstyn as the violinist, Elaine Stritch the double-bassist, David Warner as the viola player, [John] Gielgud the cellist, and Dirk [Bogarde] at the piano."[21] Bogarde predicted that the film "will either be a load of pretentious crap or else Resnais' masterpiece."[22] The film concerns a writer called Clive Langham (played by Gielgud) who uses members of his own family (his two sons, one of them illegitimate, his dead wife, his daughter-in-law) as the basis of the characters in his last novel. Langham is dying and his imaginings take place during a painful night, through which he eventually drinks himself into oblivion. Screenwriter David Mercer has explained that Langham's nocturnal ordeal comprises nightmare, literary creation and imagination.[23] The nightmare aspect is generated by fear of death, the collapse of past certainties (as represented by the demolition of architecture and various acts of terrorism) and the memory of past suffering (non-specific images of war). The literary creation revolves around Langham's attempt to construct a novel from the "raw" material of his own family (or, at least, his own impression of that family). The imaginary aspect concerns how he transforms "reality" into a fantasy that seems more real to him than the surface world of appearances.

The following morning, Langham wakes up to his seventy-eighth birthday. His pain-ridden, creatively imaginative night is now replaced by a warm sunny afternoon filled with familial bliss. (One is reminded of Amfortas' line in the first act of Wagner's *Parsifal*: "Nach wilder Schmerzensnacht, nun Waldesmorgenpracht!" ("An anguished painful night now yields to morning's light!").[24] The dysfunctional family we were introduced to as part of Langham's fantasy are now all shown to be quite different from his idea of them. Bogarde's waspish, cynical and supercilious lawyer, Claud, turns out to be a loving, decent son, whom his self-indulgent, reprobate father has always thought too good to be true and therefore imagines to be the prig whom Bogarde has so extravagantly portrayed him to be until now. The two sons are not the rivals they were shown to be, and Claud, far from hating his wife, is discovered to be devoted to her. The lover whom Langham thought up for the fictional Claud turns out to be Langham's own wife who had committed suicide because she couldn't endure her husband's selfish behavior. Oedipal attraction between mother and son is therefore implied (Claud has never forgiven his father for his mother's death), and this suggests that the paradise presented at the end of the film is not quite as it seems. Was the nightmare vision of Langham's imagination perhaps telling us the truth after all? Is the sweetness and light portrayed in the film's final section less real than Langham's nightmare vision? Could the sibling rivalry of the first part of the film have been more psychologically truthful than the studied brotherly love with which we are ultimately presented? Was Claud's apparently imaginary resentment of his father and his wish that he would hurry up and die, in fact the subconscious truth? Resnais asks his audience to weigh up which version is the more truthful: the surreal, vicious, subconscious world dreamed up by Langham or the naturalistic, benevolent, conscious world of the last section? Hegel, of course, would have argued that both realities were equally real, but the fact that Langham imagines most of the film, and is heard dictating what the characters should do throughout the proceedings, provides us with a wonderfully fluid cinematic metaphor of Hegel's dictum that Mind is the only reality, and that we are the sum of everyone else's interpretation of us.

But how does *Providence* fit into the scheme of Gothic horror? There are several parallels. Stephen Jones, who described David Mercer's screenplay as "pretentious nonsense,"[25] nonetheless included the film in his *Illustrated Werewolf Movie Guide,* because of two examples of werewolf imagery. David Warner at first plays Langham's imagined idea of his illegitimate son, Kevin. At this stage in the proceedings he is presented as a soldier who inflicts a mercy killing on an old man who is turning into a werewolf. The werewolf represents Langham's own sense of physical transformation as his body succumbs to cancer. Langham then imagines his own autopsy in a scene far more gruesome than anything Hammer ever revealed on camera. We see the werewolf's body cut open; but this is not the only horror that Langham imagines. The country in which his "novel" is set is overrun by terrorists and ruthless developers. Bombs explode in the distance, drawing only casual comments from the characters, by which Resnais seems to be saying that we have learned to live with the perpetual anxiety of modern life, its conflicts, its social disintegration, its self-consuming obsession with "progress." Equally troubling are the dreamlike suggestions of Nazi atrocities, which are no doubt versions of Langham's own wartime memories, as well as anxieties of conflicts yet to come. By coincidence, while filming *Providence,* Bogarde visited the nearby French village of Oradour-sur-Glane, the entire population of which was killed by the Waffen SS on June 10, 1944. He was so moved by the experience that he returned in the company of the younger members of the cast and crew:

> Dirk felt that in an environment on-set where they were hearing "of 'progressiveness and the moral language of Man' and all that crap," it would "do them good to see just what man can do to man...and only thirty years ago."[26]

Later, Kevin begins to transform into a werewolf, as though he is relieving Langham of the burden of his illness, and thus echoes the Christlike symbolism of Leon in *The Curse of the Werewolf,* who is not only born on Christmas Day but is also ultimately sacrificed in the bell-tower of a church.

Langham's huge mansion is revealed in the last section of the film during the "idyllic" birthday party scene, but the building's towering Gothic gloom rather undermines the tranquility. Originally built in the late nineteenth century for the wealthy American porcelain maker Theodore Haviland, the Château de Mont-Méry, nine miles from Limoges, is a French equivalent of Hammer's Oakley Court. It certainly gives the impression of a foreboding nursing home rather than the comfortable domestic retreat of a wealthy writer, especially with its two excessively attentive servants. The interiors of the château were also used for earlier scenes, further emphasizing that the whole film until this point has been the product of Langham's housebound imagination, not that one should take every image in Resnais' film as being of deep significance. When Bogarde and Warner had to pick up a hedgehog, which the camera them zoomed in upon, Bogarde asked the director if it *meant* anything. "No," Resnais replied, "it is just to give the intellectuals of *Cahiers du Cinéma* something to discuss."[27]

Resnais' use of Château de Mont-Mèry follows in the venerable tradition of the Gothic castle. It not only represents patriarchal oppression (a classic Gothic theme) but also the oppression of the unconscious, which is another of the Gothic threads that was picked up by surrealism. (André Pieyre de Mandiargues, for example, combines the erotic violence of de Sade with surrealist nightmare in a similarly Gothic environment in his 1953 novel *L'Anglais décrit dans le château fermé,* translated by J. Fletcher as *Portrait of an Englishman in His Chateau.*) The street scenes in *Providence,* which had earlier shown Claud driving to the assignation he has planned with his lover/mother, have a distinctly surrealist quality, again suggesting the foreboding desolation of paintings by de Chirico and Magritte. They also echo the static aesthetic of the Belgian symbolist Fernard Khnopff in paintings such as *À Bruges (Le Lac d'amour)* and *Une Ville abandonnée*, both of which date from 1904. Such echoes help us to trace the cultural lineage of *Providence*, which is now revealed as an amalgam of the surrealist and symbolist imagery that evolved from Gothic, coupled with the Hegelian idea of *Geist* that unites them all.

While *Providence* at first seems quite the opposite of a Gothic horror film, we can now see that it shares many of the same concerns. We might also extend the argument to a discussion of Resnais' most famous film, *L'Année dernière à Marienbad*. Though in architectural terms, this film is anything *but* Gothic (the buildings and formal gardens, which form the principal characters, are all Rococo or Baroque), the way in which these architectural spaces are used strongly suggests an approach to architecture that is shared by Gothic romance. The fact that the architecture plays so central a role in this film is Gothic in itself. After all, Mrs. Radcliffe didn't call her most famous novel after its unfortunate heroine, Emily Saint Aubert but, rather, after the castle of Udolpho itself. Resnais also emphasizes the importance of architecture in *L'Année dernière à Marienbad* by combining the languorously drifting images of corridors and ceilings which open the film with a poetic voice-over:

> [T]hrough the corridors, salons, galleries, the structure of this mournful mansion from another age ... this huge and luxurious mansion, baroque, lugubrious...silent rooms where footsteps are absorbed by carpets, so heavy, so thick ... transverse corridors leading to deserted salons, encrusted with the ornamentation of another age....

That Resnais overlays the soundtrack with Francis Seyrig's threateningly Baroque organ music also orientates our response to these images, adding an ecclesiastic (and hence Gothic) symbolism of foreboding and significance, in much the same way that Bach's famous *Toccata and Fugue* in D minor is often employed for "horror" atmosphere, as in the main title sequence of *Tales from the Crypt* (dir. Freddie Francis, 1971). Terence Fisher's *The Phantom of the Opera*, which was released the year after *L'Année dernière à Marienbad*, starts out in a manner that's similar to the opening of Resnais' film. Like Resnais, Fisher begins with a shot of a ceiling and the sound of an organ (composed in this instance by Edwin Astley). The camera stares up at the chandelier of the Wimbledon Theatre, which somewhat unconvincingly stands in for the Paris Opera House, and then pans around the deserted auditorium before a dissolve takes us to the cellars below. We now learn the origin of this strange music and observe Herbert Lom's Phantom sitting at his instrument, watched impassively by his servant (played by Ian Wilson). There, perhaps, the comparisons between the two films come to an end, but the similarity is worth pointing out to help identify the signifying role of the organ music along with some of Resnais' connections with Gothic tradition.

L'Année dernière à Marienbad is very much a study of space, both physical and metaphorical: the space of memory, which, of course, comes from the past but lives only in the present, while simultaneously propelling us into the future. (Stanley Kubrick's 1980 horror film *The Shining* similarly exploits the threatening menace of empty architectural space as a way of evoking the past. It is in the deserted hotel corridors of that film that the two ghostly girls appear to such terrifying effect.) Resnais and his screenwriter Alain Robbe-Grillet attempt to compress past, present and future into a single temporal unity: we are no longer sure of time, still less of place (the film was deliberately shot in various locations to emphasize such "placelessness"). Did "X" (played by Giorgio Albertazzi) actually meet the woman "A" (played by Delphine Seyrig) last year at Marienbad? She doesn't remember.

L'Année dernière à Marienbad (dir. Alain Resnais, 1961).

Again Resnais asks if we can be certain of anything. Not only does memory distort what may have happened, but what we think may have happened may not have happened at all from someone else's perspective. Again, to use Hegel's argument, we can be certain of nothing in a world that is not merely interpreted by Mind but *created* by Mind. Resnais presents us with a world in which we are not even sure that we exist. The people we are first shown in the film appear like statues, but we are then shown that they have been watching a play performed in equally statuesque fashion. The voice-over refers to "these long-dead people" who inhabit the "deserted salons … of another age." Later, we overhear two of the immaculately dressed guests who are reflected in a mirror. One of them says: "These days worse than death, we live through side by side, like two coffins buried together in a petrified garden." The vampire imagery is again implicit here, even though we see the guests' reflections. (Perhaps the use of reflections here is nonetheless an inverted reference in that Gothic direction.) These people feed off their memories, which justify the pointless activities of the present. They play games with matches and walk up and down an impressive staircase (another contender for inclusion in chapter one). They contemplate statues in a formal garden that are hardly different from their own statuesque poses. Their virtually undead lives are so aimless that there is hardly any point in their considering the future, though "X"'s desire for "A" will no doubt propel him into that future. (The sinister countenance of "M" [Sacha Pitoëff], who is "A"'s current paramour, suggests that there is trouble to come.) When the voice-over tells us that "everything was deserted in this immense hotel," we are reminded of the deserted hotel not only in *The Kiss of the Vampire* but also of the empty Belgian hotel in Harry Kümel's "contemporary" version of the story of Countess Elizabeth Báthory, *Les Lèvres rouges* (*Daughters of Darkness*, 1971). The connection between this latter and *L'Année dernière à Marienbad* is strengthened by the fact that Delphine Seyrig (who played "A" in Resnais' film) appears as the vampire Countess in Kümel's film. Like the Ravnas, she too infiltrates her way into the lives of another honeymoon couple in an empty public space. The laws of society seem to have vanished in all three films. There can be no safety in numbers here, no shared values, no certainties…

Comparing such an art-house classic to popular horror films is less surprising than it might at first appear when one realizes that *L'Année dernière à Marienbad* may well have been based on the 1940 science fiction–horror novel *The Invention of Morel* by Adolfo Bioy Casares. Having some things in common with H.G. Wells' *The Island of Doctor Moreau* (another source of several other horror films), Casares' story concerns an inventor, Morel, who lives on an island where he has created a kind of holographic camera that films in three dimensions but which also has the unfortunate side-effect of destroying what it holographs. The flesh literally rots on the bones of the holographed tourists on the island, but their well-dressed holographs continue to "dance, stroll up and down, and swim in the pool, as if this were a summer resort like Los Teques or Marienbad."[28] Morel's invention is therefore able to create an alternative reality. The island has two suns, but this is because the holographed sun, captured when it was in a different position in the sky, has been projected against the "real" sun. Morel's machine also captures souls and projects them back again into the world. Morel will therefore be able to live forever with Faustine, the girl he loves, like a vampire who has no need of blood to nourish him, and like the statuesque, obsessive figures in Resnais' timeless film. The holographic camera is also a rather Hegelian device: It *projects* reality onto the world, just as Mind (according to Hegel, anyway) projects itself onto the world, and thus creates it. Similarly, "X" in *L'Année dernière à Marienbad* projects his own desires and memories onto "A," whose perspective and memories are very different. Each of us creates his or her own reality.

Perhaps the ultimate cinematic expression of Hegel's concept of *Geist* is Larry and Andy Wachowski's 1999 science-fiction film *The Matrix*, in which reality is discovered to be entirely simulated by machines that wish to control humanity. Each human in this film really could be said to be an example of Hegel's "finite mind," with the Matrix itself as the Godlike *Geist* presiding over all. One might even be tempted to connect it with Pirandello's *Six Characters in Search of an Author*, considering what the Father in that play says about fictional characters, who are nourished by "a fecundating matrix"; but such a film moves us rather too far away from the Gothic parameters of this book towards the field of technological science fiction. Fortunately, such parameters will not prevent us from visiting Egypt, the exotic location of our next chapter.

Nine

Ancient Egypt

Ancient Egypt has fascinated filmmakers since the beginning of cinema history. Even before the cinema was invented, Verdi's ancient Egyptian opera *Aida* (1871), with its epic settings and melodramatic plot, pointed towards future cinematic developments. With *Aida*, Verdi also invented the idea of the split screen, for in the opera's final scene, when Radames and Aida find themselves imprisoned in an underground vault, we see the priests and priestesses in the temple simultaneously going about their business directly over their heads. The original stage directions are:

> The Scene is divided into two floors. The upper floor represents the Interior of the Temple of Vulcan, resplendent with light and gold; the lower floor a subterranean hall; long rows of arcades which are lost in the darkness; colossal statue of Osiris, with the hands crossed, sustains the pillars of the vault.
> Radames is in the subterranean hall, on the steps of the staircase by which he has descended; above, the two PRIESTS, engaged in closing the stone over the subterranean entrance.[1]

For much of the time, Verdi's music for this opera remained characteristically Italian in style but from time to time, such as in the temple scene in Act 1, scene 2, he included the local color of an "Egyptian" manner, using musical techniques which composers of mummy films would imitate some decades later. Composed towards the end of his long career, *Aida* was Verdi's only Egyptian opera, though its Egyptian setting had been and would continue to be very popular in nineteenth-century Europe, particularly in France. Indeed, the original libretto of *Aida* had been by a French writer, Camille du Locle. Berlioz had helped start the fashion for musical Egyptiana in 1829 with an operatic *scena* with which he hoped he might win the coveted *Prix de Rome*. (It didn't, though he eventually did win on his fifth attempt.) The *scena* in question was called *La Mort de Cléopâtre*. "I did my best," Berlioz complained to one of the judges after the disappointing verdict. "That is exactly what we have against you," the judge replied. "You should not have done your best. Your best is the enemy of the good. How can I be expected to approve of such things when you know that what I like most is soothing music?" As Berlioz pointed out, it is rather hard to write soothing music for an Egyptian queen "who has been bitten by a poisonous snake and is dying a painful death in an agony of remorse."[2]

As the nineteenth century progressed, Cleopatra became an increasingly popular subject, particularly for academic painters. Alexandre Cabanel (1823–89) showed Cleopatra testing poisons on condemned men, Henri Dejussieu (1857–1900) had her being served by a slave, Gustave Lassalle-Bordes (1814–68) showed her dying, as did Jean André Rixens (1846–1924), while German von Bohn (1812–99) had beaten both Lassalle-Bordes and Rixens to it in 1841. It wasn't surprising that so many painters rushed to paint the dying Cleopatra as it gave them ample opportunities to show a naked woman in a position that was about as close to a representation of orgasm (or what the French have always called *la petite mort*) as was deemed respectable at the time. The English Victorian artist Val Prinsep (1838–1904) was, as one might expect, a little more discrete. His dying Cleopatra is fully clothed and looks as though she's falling asleep in her chair rather than dying (or succumbing to sexual ecstasy), and she also holds a decorous rose in her exhausted grasp. Indeed, anticipating the Hollywood epics that were to come, Prinsep was more concerned with the Egyptian architecture that occupies the upper half of the canvas.

The most dedicated champion of the Egyptian picture in England was probably Edwin Longsden Long (1829–91) whose immense canvas from 1877, *An Egyptian Feast,* is, even more than Prinsep's picture, a taste of the things that were to come from Hollywood in the twentieth century. As Long's biographer Mark Bills puts it, the painting is "overtly theatrical" and demonstrates Long's desire "to present a well-researched reconstruction of ancient history."[3] The painting is a riot of archaeological detail, Egyptian objects, musical instruments and sculpture, all of which demonstrate Long's desire for "authenticity." As we shall see, this combination of theatricality and research went on to inform all the mummy movies that grew out of this particular style of art. Many of the grandest Victorian painters, those artists whom the critic William Gaunt called "Olympians,"[4] also experimented with ancient Egypt. Sir Lawrence Alma Tadema (1836–1912) tried his hand at Egyptian scenes in the earlier stage of his career before transferring his allegiance to ancient Rome; and both Frederic, Lord Leighton (1830–96) and Sir Edward John Poynter (1836–1919) also had their Egyptian moments. At a time of empire-building, it was natural that the British (and the French for that matter) should have modeled themselves on the great empires of the past. The novelist H. Rider Haggard followed suit in his 1889 adventure *Cleopatra,* which charts the power struggle between the priest Harmachis and the Egyptian queen. Haggard presents us with a literary equivalent of the Egyptian fantasies of Victorian painting: sumptuous banquets, magnificent architecture and occasional supernatural elements, as in the chapter in which Harmachis experiences a series of visions from the past, culminating in a visitation from the spirit of Isis:

> Behold! the dark cloud came down and rested on the Altar, the Serpent of fire stretched itself towards me, touched me on the forehead with its forky tongue and was gone. From within the cloud a Voice sweet and low and clear spoke in heavenly accents:
> "Depart, ye Ministers, leave Me with my son whom I summoned...."
> "O Harmachis," said the Voice, "be not afraid, I am she whom thou dost know as Isis of the Egyptians; but what else I am strive not thou to learn, it is beyond thy strength. For I am all things, Life is my spirit, and Nature is my raiment."[5]

Though no mummies come to life in *Cleopatra,* there is one scene in which Cleopatra and Harmachis unwrap a mummy in their search for hidden treasure:

> Now Cleopatra took my dagger, and with it cut loose the bandages which held the wrappings in their place, and the lotus-flowers that had been set in them by loving hands, three thousand years before, fell down upon the pavement. Then we searched and found the end of the outer bandage, which was fixed in at the hinder part of the neck. This we cut loose, for it was glued fast. This done, we began to unroll the wrappings of the holy corpse. Setting my shoulders against the sarcophagus, I sat upon the rocky floor, the body resting on my knees, and, as I turned it, Cleopatra unwound the cloths; and awesome was the task. Presently something fell out; it was the sceptre of the Pharoah, fashioned of gold, and at its end was a pomegranate cut from a single emerald....
> Cleopatra plunged her hand into the dead breast and drew forth somewhat. She held it to the

"I saw the world as it had been before man was." Illustration by R. Caton Woodville for H. Rider Haggard's *Cleopatra*, London, Longmans, Green, and Co., 1914, facing p. 85.

light, and gave a little cry, for from the darkness of Pharoah's heart there flashed into light and life the most beauteous emerald that ever man beheld.... Again, again, and yet again, she plunged in her hand and drew great emeralds from Pharoah's breast bedded there in spices.[6]

In France, especially as the nineteenth century drew to a close, Egyptiana found equal favor at the Paris Opera House, a development that failed to materialize in the less operatically inclined United Kingdom, despite the paintings of Alma Tadema and the novels of Rider Haggard. Jules Massenet's 1894 adaptation of Anatole France's novel *Thaïs* (1890) brought an Egyptian courtesan on stage and proceeded to convert her to Christianity by means of the only section of the score to have entered the popular repertoire (the famous "Méditation" for violin harp and string orchestra). Massenet followed this up with a Cleopatra opera in 1912, just before his own death, and only a couple of years before the First World War put an end to such theatrical extravagances; but there had been Cleopatra operas since 1653 (not long after Shakespeare's *Antony and Cleopatra* play, in fact), while the cult of Isis and Osiris, via its adoption by the Masonic movement, had found its way into Mozart's *Die Zauberflöte* (1791). Diaghilev's Ballets Russes had also exploited Cleopatra in a ballet of that name which was a huge success with Parisian audiences in 1909 when it was premiered. The musical score was an assemblage of pieces by six different pieces, but it was really the exotic setting that made the impact. The great Pavlova danced Ta-Hor, a temple attendant, while the equally great choreographer Fokine interpreted the role of Amoun, an Egyptian nobleman. Cleopatra herself was introduced in a spectacular manner, as Richard Buckle described in his biography of Diaghilev:

> First the attendants opened a big sarcophagus to reveal a mummy-case, from which they lifted the bandaged body of the Queen. Her many-coloured veils were ritually unwound, then [Ida] Rubinstein, with an imperious gesture, threw off the last veil to reveal her pale features, framed by a pale wig, bound with gold and jewels.[7]

Cleopatra then agrees that Amoun may spend the night with her providing he agrees to commit suicide afterwards. Such a mixture of jewels, Egyptian decor, sex, suicide and music was perhaps bound to be a success, especially as it boasted the presence of three of the world's most famous dancers, but part of that success was due to the prevailing fashion for Egyptiana, which *Cléopâtre* ruthlessly exploited. The Russian composer Anton Arensky (perhaps better known as Rachmaninoff's teacher) had also tried his hand at this sort of subject a few years earlier in 1900, called *Egyptian Nights*, so it was hardly surprising that Debussy was eventually approached by the English ballerina Maud Allan to compose an Egyptian ballet of his own in 1913. The result, *Khamma*, paralleled Stravinsky's *Rite of Spring* in that the title role, a priestess, dances herself to death to save her city from invasion. Debussy regarded the plot as "childishly simple and, rightly, presents no interest in itself,"[8] but its Egyptian atmosphere contributed considerably to its effect. In the temple of Amon-Ra, the sun god, Khamma dances three times before a statue of the god and "perceives that the head and shoulders of the statue begin to move. The hands of the stone god rise from the knees, the palms turned upwards."[9] This *deus ex machina* anticipates the moment at the climax of Universal's *The Mummy* when the statue of Isis raises her arm to save Helen from the machinations of Karloff's Imhotep:

> [T]he goddess moves slowly, holding out to her suppliant priestess of old the crux ansata or symbol of eternal life—this is fashioned in the form of the heiroglyph meaning of "millions of millions of years"—There is a blinding flash of light.[10]

Isis and Osiris had also been given a prominent position on the facade of the once well-known, but long-since demolished Egyptian Hall in London's Piccadilly. First opened in 1812, this exhibition show hall was the chosen venue of famous midget Tom Thumb, who used to pull huge crowds there. There was also a panorama of Mont Blanc, along with a natural history collection, a bazaar, and a grand hall, which eventually housed Giovanni Batista Belzoni's Egyptian exhibition of 1821. An explorer, one-time strongman and impresario, Belzoni had spent many years and considerable energy in Egypt locating ancient sites and unearthing antiquities. As John Romer explains, Belzoni's London exhibition consisted principally of plaster casts made by his own hands from the tomb of Seti I, "as well as a model of the tomb itself and some assorted mummies and other antiquities." He also created Egyptian-style settings for his exhibits and recreated Seti's tomb, which Romer records as being "over two hundred feet long and more than eight feet high. Part of the show was lit by gaslight, still very much a showman's novelty in those days."[11] At the grand opening, Belzoni even unwrapped a mummy. So successful was the entire extravaganza, the publisher, John Murray published a folio of engravings and an equally lavish commemorative volume to go with it.

So, mummy movies didn't come from nowhere, not that all films with *Mummy* in the title offer what they seem to promise. Ernst Lubisch's *Die Augen der Mumie Ma* (*The Eyes of the Mummy*, 1918) doesn't actually feature a mummy at all. Starring Pola Negri as a young girl called Mara, the story tells how she was abducted and imprisoned in the tomb of Queen Ma. (The eyes peering from behind the stone relief of a mummy mask on a wall of the tomb turn out to be hers.) She's rescued by a young man called Albert Wendland (played by Harry Liedtke), who takes her to London and launches her, rather prosaically (given the exciting title of the film), on a theatrical career. For "*Mummy* movie" fans, *The Eyes of the Mummy* is bound to disappoint. A similar response might await the expectant twenty-first century reader of Theophile Gautier's tale "The Mummy's Foot" (1840), for this turns out to be nothing more dangerous than a whimsical dream. The narrator visits a D'Annunzian antique shop, and Gautier spends a great deal of time describing its unusual and exotic curiosities, following the example of Poe stories where *décor* and props play such a crucial part in the creation of *mood*. The narrator decides to purchase the mummy's foot of the title, which he takes home, only to fall asleep while contemplating it. His subsequent dream, heightened by the perfume of ancient gums and embalming fluids that linger in the antiquity, involves the Egyptian princess to whom the foot once belonged. She seems to appear in his room and offers to take him back to ancient Egypt, delighted to have found her foot again. Gautier doesn't explain that all this is a dream until the end of his story, but we hardly need telling. There's no curse, no threat, nothing sinister at all, not even any magic, unless we count the hallucination of the dream as such; but things were about to change…

One thing both *The Eyes of the Mummy* and "The Mummy's Foot" do have in common with the later conventions of the mummy movie is the contrast they make between Egypt and the West. It is a Westerner who rescues the Egyptian girl in *The Eyes of the Mummy*, and it's presumably a nineteenth-century Parisian who buys the mummy's foot in Gautier's tale. This contrast of civilizations was to become a positive clash of cultures in the classic mummy movies. Indeed, it's one of the two fundamental *raisons d'être* of this particular genre, for mummy movies are largely about the intrusion of the obviously alien into the apparently normal. We'll be dealing with that aspect after considering the first essential element, which is what marks the mummy movie out from so many science fiction or vampire movies, and this once more raises the question of *décor*.

We have the eighteenth-century architect and engraver Giovanni Battista Piranesi to thank for what eventually developed into a host of mummy movie sets, for Piranesi was designing Egyptian etchings and pharaonic fireplace surrounds a good thirty years before Napoleon's conquest of Egypt in 1797. It's often assumed that it was entirely due to Napoleon that Westerners first began to appreciate Egyptian art but, as a study of Piranesi's fertile imagination proves, Egyptian motifs had been all the rage long before. All manner of things were affected by the craze for Egyptiana, even musical instruments. The Victoria and Albert Museum in London, for example, possesses a splendid pedal harp by the celebrated Jean Henri Naderman, made in Paris in 1785, the pillar of which is adorned with an Egyptian bust.

The main difference between Piranesi's mid–eighteenth-century approach and Napoleon's late eighteenth-century one has a direct bearing on the aesthetic of later mummy movies. Piranesi's Egyptian designs are entirely whimsical, whereas Napoleon and his impressive team of experts who travelled with him to the Land of the Pharaohs (there were over 150 of them) were keen to approach the subject of Egyptology seriously and with appropriate academic rigor. All this is not to deny that there had also been emotional, far less rational reasons for Napoleon's expedition to Egypt than those he used to justify the endeavor. True, it had been inspired by a thirst for knowledge, and a desire to spread modern "civilization." There were military reasons too: a triumph in Egypt would have overthrown English power in India, but, as Napoleon's biographer Frank McLynn points out, the emotional impulse behind the expedition, had been just as romantic and irrational as Piranesi's Egyptian fireplaces.[12] "I don't want to stay here [in Europe]," Napoleon said to his secretary Louis Bourienne, "there's nothing to do... Everything's finished here but I haven't had enough glory. This tiny Europe doesn't provide enough, so I must go east."[13] So in reality, Napoleon's expedition to Egypt was born from the same kind of boredom that still leads us into a cinema on a wet Sunday afternoon to watch a mummy movie, though nowadays, of course, we're more likely to stay at home and watch a DVD.

With nothing left to conquer in Europe (apart from England), Egypt offered the bored Napoleon an excellent opportunity for exotic adventure, and exotic adventure was what everyone was looking for at the time. It still is. Exotic adventure is a preeminently Romantic obsession. Napoleon originally had the idea for the expedition in 1797, only three years after the first publication of *The Mysteries of Udolpho*. Admittedly, Mrs. Radcliffe went to Italy rather than Egypt for her inspiration in this novel, but the same Romantic impulse was at work in both the emperor and the novelist. Radcliffe's follow-up to *Udolpho*, *The Italian*, appeared in the same year that things Egyptian began to tantalize Napoleon. So, if we can trace the traditional gothic horror film back to Radcliffe (and thence back to Horace Walpole), we can trace the mummy movie back to around the same time, long before the 1922 discovery of Tutankhamun's tomb by Howard Carter, which certainly revived interest in the subject but didn't entirely *create* it.

It's true that ancient Egypt formed no part of Ann Radcliffe's novels, nor Matthew Lewis' infamous *The Monk*. Neither did Horace Walpole inject the mystery of Egypt into his *Castle of Otranto*. The literary seed of later mummy tales and subsequent movies based upon them was instead planted by the fabulously wealthy William Beckford, whose fascination with all things oriental led him to include references to the Land of the Pharaohs in his Arabian romance *Vathek* (1786). *Vathek* is one of the earliest of Gothic novels, though its oriental setting marks it out as an exception to the general rules of the genre. There are no Gothic ruins in *Vathek*, despite the fact that Beckford went on to create the grandest of all Gothic follies in Fonthill Abbey. The Caliph Vathek does, however, enjoy building towers as high as the one that eventually collapsed over Beckford's ill-fated abbey; and Vathek himself is the first Gothic villain in Western literature, anticipating not only the villains of Radcliffe's novels but also the whole cult of the brooding Byronic hero. Mummy movies as a genre within a genre (Egyptian Gothic horror, so to speak) inhabit a space originally put aside for them by Beckford's curious oriental romance. In the dungeons beneath Vathek's tower, Vathek's mother Carathis has created the kind of "deep vaulted cell" in which the witches of Henry Purcell's opera *Dido and Aeneas* (1689) prepare their evil charms:

> First she descended, by small steps cut into the thickness of the walls, and known only to her and to Vathek, into mysterious pits which formed the repositories for a number of mummies of the ancient Pharaohs, filched from their tombs. Of these she took a goodly quantity, and then made her way to a gallery where, under the guardianship of fifty dumb negresses, blind in the right eyes, were kept the oil from the most venomous serpents, the tusks of rhinoceroses, and logs cut by magicians in the interior of the Indies, which emitted a suffocating odour; not to mention a thousand other horrible rarities.[14]

Carathis orders the mutes to take the mummies and the other "horrible rarities" onto the balconies of the tower where she sets fire to them. This causes such a huge black cloud that Vathek's subjects rush up the tower to extinguish the flames; but so thick is the smoke, they do not realize the trap into which they have stumbled. The mutes fall upon them and hang them as a sacrifice to the demonic Giaour whom Vathek wishes to appease. This is *Vathek*'s only specific reference to mummies, but it is significant, grafting, as it does, the Egyptian element (within *Vathek*'s overall Arabian context) onto mainstream Gothic.

Piranesi was more of a combination of ancient Rome and Egyptian fantasy, but he approached Roman antiquities with rather more architectural rigor than he did his Egyptian designs for murals and fireplaces. While he believed that the ancient Romans had been influenced more by ancient Egypt than by ancient Greece (Hadrian's villa at Tivoli, for example, contains some of the earliest examples of Egyptian revival art), Piranesi nonetheless used Egyptian motifs playfully and irreverently. His Egyptian designs were true *capriccios*. He had no understanding of the actual meaning of hieroglyphs (the Rosetta Stone wasn't discovered until 1799), and he had little interest in the meaning of the other symbols and motifs he employed. His approach was, on the contrary, entirely decorative and *suggestive of* the Land of the Pharaohs, but there was nothing in the least *correct* about them, and in this approach lay the beginnings of so many mummy movie set designs. Piranesi's eleven astonishing designs for fireplace surrounds, along with the two wall decorations he provided for the Caffé degli Inglesi on the Piazza di Spagna in Rome, are the basis of every mummy movie ever made, for his bizarre amalgams incorporate every Egyptian motif one can imagine, purely *for effect*: pyramids, pharaonic headdresses, obelisks, hieroglyphics, lotus leaves, canopic jars, winged figures, sacred bulls, sphinxes and various Egyptian caryatids which hold either the mantelpieces of the fireplaces in their hands or sit down and support them on their suitably attired Egyptian heads.

It's revealing to compare Piranesi's fireplaces with the sets of *The Mummy's Hand* (dir. Christy Cabanne, 1940) which were left over from a non–Egyptian adventure, *Green Hell* (1940). *Green Hell* was set in the Amazonian jungle, and turned out to be one of the worst films ever made, despite the presence of Douglas Fairbanks Jr., George Sanders and Vincent Price, not to mention the illustrious James Whale who directed the proceedings from behind Karl Freund's camera. *Green Hell* may have failed, but *The Mummy's Hand*, for all its vulgarities, was an immensely popular follow-up to Boris Karloff's original *The Mummy* of eight years before. The main tomb set of *The Mummy's Hand* consists of what look like two gigantic Peruvian llama heads (which stand in here for more appropriately Egyptian jackals). These hover over a sacrificial altar, while the walls are a riot of rather crudely executed hieroglyphs. The jackal/llama heads and hieroglyphs are even more whimsical than the outsize locusts, alligators and Egyptian symbols that adorn Piranesi's fabulous fireplaces. What's important in *The Mummy's Hand* is not, after all, archaeological *authenticity* but exotically Egyptian *effect*.

The sets for Universal's original, and much superior, *The Mummy* had been executed with rather more care than those for *The Mummy's Hand*, no doubt because they were especially created by the distinguished illustrator Willy Pogany, who referred to *The Book of the Dead* and the artifacts from Tukankhamen's tomb when working on his designs. Even so, Piranesi's spirit was behind them. Pogany's designs are far removed from the concerns of Egyptology. The same could be said of Bernard Robinson, who took up Pogany's approach for the sets of Hammer's first Egyptian horror *The Mummy* (1959). Oddly, despite Robinson's following of Pogany's lead with regard to the sets and props, screenwriter Jimmy Sangster looked rather more in the direction of *The Mummy's Hand* for the plot. Hammer didn't revive Karloff's Imhotep but Tom Tyler's Kharis. Unlike Imhotep, Christopher Lee's Kharis, like Tyler's, never got out of his bandages; but like Tyler, Lee's mummy was still in love with Princess Ananka, who is reincarnated this time in the lovely form of Yvonne Furneaux. Both Kharises also suffer the indignity of having their tongues cut out and both are discovered by an archaeologist called Banning.

Design for a chimneypiece in Egyptian style from Giovanni Battista Piranesi's *Diverse Ways of ornamenting chimney pieces and all other parts of houses taken from Egyptian, Etruscan, and Grecian architecture with an Apologia in defense of Egyptian and Tuscan architecture*, 1769 (photograph reproduced with permission from the Ministero per i Beni e le Attività Culturali).

Tom Tyler as Kharis with Peggy Moran as Marta in *The Mummy's Hand* (dir. Christy Cabanne, 1940).

Egyptian decoration of the Caffè degli Inglesi, Rome, from Giovanni Battista Piranesi's *Diverse Ways of ornamenting chinmeypieces and all other parts of houses taken from Egyptian, Etruscan, and Grecian architecture with an Apologia in defense of Egyptian and Tuscan architecture,* 1769 (photograph reproduced with permission from the Ministero per i Beni e le Attività Culturali).

Hammer had color, of course, as well as the expert advice of Andrew Low, the son of the distinguished Egyptologist Professor A.D. Low, who pressed for positively Napoleonic rigor in the designs, writing extensive memos and expressing concern that Hammer didn't confuse mummification with embalming.[15] However, despite Low's professional advice, no Egyptian tomb has ever been suffused with pea-green light, as is the case with Ananka's, and though the details attempt correctitude, Piranesi might have been of more use to Bernard Robinson than Low, not that he really needed either of them. The settings, props and costumes didn't quite reach the heights of Hollywood Biblical epics, but *The Mummy* is certainly one of Hammer's most elegantly dressed productions, and Franz Reizenstein's inventive score, replete with a wordless chorus, also added an epic element that was more atmospheric than many a bigger-budgeted Biblical blockbuster.

Not until the remake of Universal's *The Mummy* (dir. Stephen Sommers, 1999) was the splendor of a film like *Cleopatra* (Joseph L. Mankiewicz, 1963) or *The Egyptian* (dir. Michael Curtiz, 1954) showered on the humble mummy movie, but large budgets don't necessarily bring with them the narrative conviction of Universal and Hammer at their best, and big-budget mummy movies often demonstrate that the recreation of Egypt's mighty majesty isn't enough to meet the more complex demands of this subgenre. We can put up with the obvious fact that Hammer's Valley of the Kings in *The Mummy's Shroud*

Elizabeth Taylor in *Cleopatra* (dir. Joseph L. Mankiewicz, 1963).

(dir. John Gilling, 1966) is just a (rather damp) sandpit near Gerrards Cross in Buckinghamshire, and we can tolerate the need for tight camera angles and the somewhat underpopulated ranks of supers in the temple scenes of *The Curse of the Mummy's Tomb* because it's really the conflict between an ancient mummy and contemporary reality that motivates these films.

A mummy film set entirely in Egypt is in danger of becoming a mere adventure story of the Indiana Jones variety. It's essential to set up a tension between the cultures of East and West and the easiest way to achieve that is to transplant elements of ancient Egypt to England or America. The exceptions that proved the rule were Universal's first two mummy films, which were entirely set in Egypt, but as we shall see, Karloff's *The Mummy* was an exception in other ways as well. The principal difference was that the mummy concerned wasn't interested in exacting revenge, but was rather in pursuit of love. *The Mummy's Hand* also notched up the conflict between its trustworthy American heroes and the sinister forces of old Egypt, which aimed to put American values at risk. To emphasize the evil of the film's heavy, Professor Andoheb, Universal cast the British character actor George Zucco, whose clipped patrician accent and gimlet gaze provided a role model for all future mummy movie villains.

If Piranesi was the source of all inspiration for the production designers and set dressers of mummy movies, the literary sources most favored by screenwriters were Sir Arthur Conan Doyle's two short stories "Lot 249" and "The Ring of Thoth." Both were written in the 1890s and both were products of the British Empire. In the former, an Oxford undergraduate manages to bring a mummy back to life, while in the second, Doyle introduced the idea of an elixir that has kept an ancient Egyptian priest called Sosra alive over the centuries. All that time, Sosra has been seeking the antidote to this elixir, the only remaining dose of which is concealed in the ring of Thoth that is worn by his rival in love, Parmes. Parmes, who had also drunk of the elixir, took the antidote after the princess both men loved died of the plague, but Parmes took his secret with him and Sosra has spent four centuries trying to track down the location of Parmes' mummy. Parmes was buried with the princess and Sosra eventually locates them in the Louvre museum of antiquities in Paris.

It's therefore fairly obvious where the makers of the classic 1932 Karloff mummy film found their inspiration, though in many respects the film is also a Egyptianized reworking of Universal's *Dracula* released in the previous year. Having said that, H. P. Lovecraft seems to have anticipated Karloff's Imhotep in his story "The Last Test," written in collaboration with Adolphe de Castro and first published in 1928. A sinister Tibetan called Surama features in this tale; one of the other characters says that "a Pharoah's mummy, if miraculously brought to life, would form an apt twin for this sardonic skeleton."[16] Lovecraft's Egyptian fantasy "Imprisoned with the Pharaoh's" (1924) was also far more grotesque than anything in Universal's *The Mummy* released eight years later. Ghost-written for the great escapologist Harry Houdini, "Imprisoned with the Pharaohs" describes how Houdini escapes from an Egyptian tomb, but not before he encounters a gathering of reanimated composite mummies:

> [T]he mummies without souls ... the meeting-place of the wandering ... the hoards of the devil-cursed pharaonic dead of forty centuries ... the *composite mummies* led through the uttermost onyx voids of King Khephren and the ghoul-queen Nitocris ... I heard their creaking joints and nitrous wheezing above the dead music and the dead tramping.[17]

The idea that there can be soulless mummies (Imhotep and Kharis clearly are not soulless) was shared by August Strindberg in his curious chamber play *The Ghost Sonata* (1907), where he uses the image of an Egyptian mummy to represent the withered wife of a bankrupt colonel. Strindberg's Mummy lives in a cupboard and squawks only inanities such as "Pretty Poll" until she addresses the real villain of the piece, the corrupt usurer Jacob Hummel, whom she accuses him of being "a robber of souls, for you robbed me of mine with your false promises; you murdered the consul they buried today, you strangled him with your notes of hand; and now you have stolen the student's soul for a feined debt of his father, who never owed you a penny."[18]

The refreshing thing about the first Universal mummy film is that Imhotep isn't at all interested in revenging himself on those who have desecrated his tomb. In fact, he must have been rather grateful to Bramwell Fletcher's archaeologist inadvertently reading aloud the Scroll of Thoth and bringing him back to life. When we next encounter the mummy he has removed his bandages, Karloff's face instead having been covered in layers of beauty clay to create the required effect of fragile antiquity. As photographed by Charles J. Stumar, this visage of death reanimated has never been bettered. Jack Pierce's makeup made Karloff's already cadaverous features even more sunken, pinched and shriveled. Like two stagnant pools in the desert moonlight, a pair of eyes stare out at us across the centuries. Imhotep also dislikes being touched, giving the impression that if he was, he would collapse into a heap of dust.

No, it is not revenge he seeks, nor mere sexual conquest like Dracula. Imhotep seeks, rather, the reincarnation of his long lost love. Unlike Christopher Lee's Kharis, he does not discover his princess by accident while he's stomping over the living room carpet. Imhotep sets out deliberately to find her. He lures her to the Museum of Antiquities and hopes ultimately to embalm her, like himself, for all time. In this respect he strongly resembles Dracula who also seeks an immortal consort, but here the affection is genuine and moving. Dracula's interest in women more closely resembles that of James Bond: Bond and the vampire may gratify their desires, but they're really far more interested in overpowering their male competitors. Women are only really useful to Dracula if they help him achieve domination over other men. As Stoker has Dracula put it in the original novel: "Your girls that you all love are mine already; and through them you and others shall yet be mine—my creatures, to do my bidding and to be my jackals when I want to feed."[19] (Christopher Lee perceptively included an amended version of this line in *The Satanic Rites of Dracula*.) How different is Karloff's mummy, surely the most Romantic of all movie monsters, even though the heroine is understandably rather reluctant to become his Bride of Death:

> IMHOTEP: It was not only this body I loved—it was thy soul, O Princess—I destroy this lifeless thing—for but a few moments *thou shalt take its place*—and then rise again as I have risen.... For thy love I was buried alive—I ask of thee only a moment of agony—only *so* can we be united—[20]

Mummy movies are also very much tales of empire, and they eloquently express the imperialist desire to dominate and exploit the exotic, along with the repressed guilt that accompanies such a desire. That's probably why stories with an Egyptian theme that were written earlier in the nineteenth century lack that important element of threat: The guilt simply hadn't had time to ferment into the heady brew it became by the late Victorian period. Mummy tales by writers who came from outside the British Empire, such Poe's "Some Words with a Mummy," are often entirely lacking in menace or even Egyptian *mood*. There is no real sense of mystery in Poe's tale either, and what tension Poe does build up prior to the reanimation of his mummy is undermined by the comic dénouement of the story. Poe uses his mummy as a means of satirizing then-contemporary American society and culture, but he does not threaten it. Alemistakeo, Poe's typically punning name for his ancient Egyptian, expresses nothing but amused, sometimes bad-tempered contempt for the modern world, but he doesn't wreak vengeance on anyone. Alemistakeo does, however, complain about having been desecrated, and that connects this tale to the horrors that were to follow:

> What am I to think of your standing quietly by and seeing me thus unhandsomely used? What am I to suppose by your permitting Tom, Dick, and Harry to strip me of my coffins, and my clothes, in this wretchedly cold climate?[21]

Poe's satirical words here were made far more menacing in Hammer's version of *The Mummy*, in which there is a conversation between George Pastell's Mehemet Bey (the *eminence gris* behind the nefarious activities of the murderous Mummy) and Peter Cushing's very British Egyptologist, Stephen Banning. Their atmospheric and elegantly performed duel of words is one of the best scenes in the film, although it's perhaps in the wrong place, as by the time it occurs we already know that Bey keeps a reanimated mummy in his living room. Dramatically the whole scene, from the point of view of plot development, is consequently rather redundant.

BANNING: I made an extensive study of this so-called religion. It's based on artificial creeds and beliefs, some of them ludicrous in the extreme.
BEY: Did it ever occur to you that beneath the superficial you've learned about, there could be a great and passionate devotion to this god?
BANNING: It occurred to me but I dismissed it.
BEY: You're intolerant, Mr. Banning.
BANNING: Not intolerant, just practical.
BEY: Intolerant. Because you are unable to experience the greatness of a deity, you dismiss it as of no consequence; but believe me, to those who worship and serve Karnak, he is all-powerful.
BANNING: Surely there can't be people who still have such beliefs?
BEY: Now you talk about something of which you know nothing. You've scratched only the surface and you know nothing. You assume the right to disturb the everlasting peace of the gods. You pry and meddle with unclean hands and eyes. Profanity, blasphemy, religious desecration — all these you are guilty of, but the powers with which you have meddled do not rest easy. I think you will not go unpunished.
BANNING: Punished? By whom?
BEY: There are certain things for which civilization has no answer, but if you choose to meddle thus, then you must be prepared to face the consequences, whatever they are.
BANNING: Consequences? That sounds like a threat.

This scene is the crux of the entire film, if we are to take Terence Fisher's film more seriously than a mere sequence of murders. *The Mummy* was released on September 25, 1959. Just three years before (on October 29, 1956, to be precise), the Suez crisis had begun when British troops invaded Egypt to help prevent President Nasser's plan of nationalizing the Suez Canal. That trigger was the culmination of a series of frictions between Egypt and Britain, and it was a symptom, of course, of the disintegration of the British Empire: in fact, its last gasp. The affair would still have been fresh in the minds of *The Mummy*'s original audience, and it's hard not to see Sangster's script favoring Mehemet Bey over the arrogant, interfering and intolerant emissary of the British Empire, Stephen Banning. Like Kharis in *The Mummy's Hand*, Banning is crippled, a lame dog, still trying to rule the world. Banning, though played with great charm by Cushing, proves to be an insensitive scientist and, despite appearances, the real villain of the piece. That he emerges triumphant at the end only reinforces his dominant position, especially as his wife turns out to be a reincarnation of the princess for whom Kharis committed sacrilege, had his tongue cut out and was buried alive. Not only has Banning desecrated Ananka's tomb, he's also stolen the woman for whom Kharis sacrificed everything. By comparison with all that, Banning's single, very well-staged combat with the bandaged horror pales into insignificance. He doesn't even have to leave the comfort of his own living room as Kharis obliges him with a visit.

The conversation between Bey and Banning has even more relevance today, with the continued anxieties of the West over Eastern cultures it often regards as bent on its destruction. Mummy movies are a powerful embodiment of the West's misunderstanding and fear of the East. As Andrew Low was so keen to point out, mummification isn't the same thing as embalming, but we don't really care. Our popular misunderstanding of Egyptian culture is the result of having imposed Western ideas upon it. After all, the ancient Egyptians didn't envisage death in the way the West does. It would never have occurred to them that a mummy could come back to life. The Victorian painter Edward Poynter implied that the pyramids were build by slaves in his painting *Israel in Egypt* (1867). He was wrong. We now know that though there were indeed slaves in ancient Egypt, the individuals who built the pyramids were well-treated workers. But the myth of slaves toiling for the pharaoh was strengthened by Cecil B. DeMille's *The Ten Commandments* (1923 and 1956), films largely informed by paintings like Poynter's.

Such facts, obviously, are hardly the point of mummy movies. No matter how accurate the artifacts and sets of such films, the important thing is to arrange to have your mummy smash, literally and metaphorically, through the French windows of an elegantly appointed study or drawing room. Christopher Lee dislocated his shoulder doing that for Hammer's first mummy film. Dickie Owen then took over in *The Curse of the Mummy's Tomb*, another late–Victorian tale, this time concerning the troubled relationship between two immortal ancient Egyptian brothers. The mummy of the title is one, while the other masquerades as a wealthy playboy called Adam Beauchamp (Terence Morgan), who can only find eternal rest by being slain by his bandaged brother. This is why Adam summons the mummy back to life and keeps him in the cellar of his London residence. Significantly, like Terence Fisher before him, Michael Carreras went to just as much trouble to recreate the atmosphere of Victorian England as that of ancient Egypt in this film. He lingers on details, such as a sumptuous cut glass decanter stopper, just as much as he does on the impressive array of Egyptian relics on display. (Carreras' penchant for the spectacular might have been limited for budgetary reasons in the Egyptian scenes, but he did manage some very lavish camerawork on board the ship that brings the artifacts back to England: we move from the porthole of Professor Dalrymple's cabin right up to the top of the ship's deck in a single take.) The film's key scene occurs when the mummy appears at the top of a flight of dockland steps before dispatching the philistine entrepreneur (Fred Clark) who plans to exhibit the contents of the tomb for mere profit. What better way of epitomizing Imperialist exploitation? The sound of foghorns before the mummy's threatening appearance adds immeasurably to the sinister effect of the swirling yellow fog here. It's a perfect expression of Egyptian Gothic. Yellow, incidentally, is the film's primary color. Adam Beauchamp's underground lair is decorated with yellow-gold wallpaper, and the heroine wears a yellow dress, all of which suggest something of the decadent "yellow" '90s of late–Victorian England with its *Yellow Book* and yellow-bound French novels. (The action is set in 1900.)

The cellar in *The Curse of the Mummy's Tomb* is only *accessorized* with Egyptian decor, but in *Blood from the Mummy's Tomb*, Hammer's most interesting mummy movie, an entire tomb has been reconstructed in a British suburban cellar, and the mummy is there with it.

Unlike all the others, this mummy is the perfectly preserved body of an evil Egyptian queen called Tera, who plans to return to life in the body of Valerie Leon, who plays Margaret Fuchs, the daughter of the Egyptologist who originally discovered Tera's tomb. One might ask why, if the mummy is perfectly preserved, the spirit of Queen Tera needs to enter Margaret's body at all. The answer is that *Blood from the Mummy's Tomb*, like the Bram Stoker novel on which it's based, is a study of incestuous desire, and that makes it rather a different kettle of embalming fluid to all the other mummy movies we've been exploring so far.

The underlying evil in the film is really Fuchs' love of his own daughter, and it's tempting to speculate that this was why Hammer changed his name from Trelawny, which was Stoker's name for him in *The Jewel of Seven Stars* (1903), to Fuchs. Trelawny is a good Cornish name, which gives Stoker the opportunity to set his final chapters on the Cornish seacoast, where Trelawny has a suitably remote retreat. Fuchs, on the other hand, is a name that lends itself to being mispronounced ("h" is, after all, only three letters away from "k") and as a result it might suggest what the professor has had in mind all along regarding his feelings for Queen Tera and his daughter. Andrew Keir, who plays Fuchs, manages to convey all his pent-up desire in a single expression when, as he leans over Tera's Mummy midway through the film, he almost licks his lips in anticipation of the delights to come. He's then struck down by the spirit of the Egyptian queen, who represents his own *psychological* guilt, just as Corbeck, played with ruthless charm by James Villiers, represents Fuchs' alter ego and its desire for power.

Incest has a venerable ancestry in Gothic fiction. In Ann Radcliffe's *The Italian*, the corrupt priest of the title unwittingly attempts to stab his own daughter, a symbolic way of suggesting a sexual violation if ever there was one. Radcliffe's earlier *Romance of the Forest* has the villain of the piece attempting to seduce the heroine, whom we later learn is similarly his own offspring. Incest is an introverted, secretive passion, so it's appropriate that *Blood from the Mummy's Tomb* dwells so often on the padded cells and corridors of a lunatic asylum in which one of Fuchs' expedition party is incarcerated. Everywhere we look there are confined or secretive places: Fuchs' underground study; the deserted suburban streets with their clipped hedges and furtive windows; the dusty museum room filled with packing cases where Geoffrey Dandridge (another member of Fuchs' original archaeological team, played by Hugh Burden) works as a curator of Egyptian artifacts. Even the empty house occupied by Corbeck is locked, boarded up and for sale (courtesy of "Neame and Skeggs"—the names of the film's two producers, masquerading as otherwise unseen estate agents). Together, these creepy spaces create an appropriately claustrophobic atmosphere that's a perfect metaphor for incest.[22]

Fuchs is obsessed by his secret passion. Only Corbeck is brave enough to contemplate the sexual forces he's unleashed. Corbeck says that Fuchs is too frightened to face up to his true feelings, fascinated by the source and nature of Tera's power while trying to keep the evil bottled up. "All you've done is sit in here and play games," he says. "'Wouldn't it be fun if it were all true?' Well, it is true, undeniably so, and you are scared. Every waking moment you are scared; but she's made you see, hasn't she? Tera has given you a warning: 'Don't let me down. Don't try and back out or you are dead.'"

Only when it's too late does Fuchs face up to the truth: that Margaret, under the influence of Tera, was responsible for the death of her own boyfriend. The unfortunate Tod Browning (Mark Edwards) finds himself intruding on the love between father and daughter and has to pay the price. Neither Margaret nor Fuchs want to accept the truth about their incestuous feelings for one another. When Tera comes to life at the end of the film, Margaret tries to kill her, but she's really killing herself; and then Tera kills Fuchs. Significantly, Margaret's mother died in childbirth. Fuchs never mentions his wife. Her only function, it seems, was to give birth to his daughter. Although she survives childbirth in *The Awakening* (1980), Mike Newell's very underrated version of the same novel, her redundancy is again made clear. When Margaret is born in Newell's film, her mother (played by Jill Townsend) realizes all too clearly how little she counts in the scheme of things. "You weren't there," she recalls in hospital when the professor comes to visit her after a difficult childbirth. He was too busy with his Queen Tera to bother much about a mere mortal woman. He has his daughter and that's all that matters.

As if to clarify Hammer's suggestion that Fuchs and Corbeck are two sides of the same coin, Newell's film combines both roles in one. The Egyptologist played by Charlton Heston in *The Awakening*, is called Professor Corbeck (and anyway, by 1980, the name Fuchs would probably have raised knowing titters). Queen Tera also becomes Queen Kara, for less apparent reasons. When Heston's professor enters Kara's womblike tomb, Newell suggests that he is guilty of a kind of rape, especially when he intercuts this scene with shots of Corbeck's wife suffering her first birth pangs.

The Awakening had various problems to solve for a 1980s audience that was light years away from the Edwardian twilight world that still lingered in *Blood from the Mummy's Tomb* for all its then-contemporary setting. In Stoker's 1903 novel, Professor Trelawny has shipped the entire tomb, walls and all, to the cellar of his palatial residence in Kensington Palace Road. That was believable in 1903, when an English Egyptologist had a great deal more self-determination than he would have today. It was always a little difficult to accept that such a thing would have been possible in 1971, as by then the Egyptian authorities would never have permitted it; but there's a certain timelessness about Seth Holt's direction of *Blood from the Mummy's Tomb*, despite Mark Edwards' sports car and Valerie Leon's kinky boots. Andrew Kier's Professor Fuchs wears traditional tweed three-piece suits, replete with watch chain, and the suburban house in which much of the action takes place is sufficiently Edwardian for us to overlook the impossibility of Fuchs ever having been allowed out of Egypt with an entire tomb in his suitcase.

The problem is only amplified by the ruthlessly up-to-date 1980s setting of *The Awakening*. To accommodate this with the needs of the story, various changes had to be made. Fuchs is given an ankh-shaped mirror from the tomb he has discovered, as a gesture of appreciation from the Egyptian government, but he *steals* the canopic jars that he needs for the magical ceremony he plans. The ceremony itself takes place neither on the Cornish coast nor in the cellar of a suburban villa but in the British Museum itself where the mummy has more believably been brought for safekeeping. Such tweakings may seem superficial, but they are, in fact, vital, as it is essential that Egypt is brought to England in order for the story to work.

The only one of Hammer's four mummy films to stay in Egypt for the duration of its running time, *The Mummy's Shroud* made sure that there was a strong flavor of English life and culture represented by the characters who act out the story mostly in the ex-pat confines of the Cairo hotel at which they're all staying. André Morell plays an English version of Howard Carter called Sir Basil Walden; John Phillips plays his egoistic financier Stanley Preston; Michael Ripper, as his put-upon secretary talks nostalgically of home, while Preston's wife, played by Elizabeth Sellars, can afford to be cool and unflappable as she is the only one who survives the rampages of the mummy.

Eddie Powell taking a break during the filming of *The Mummy's Shroud* (dir. John Gilling, 1967) to advertise the Milk Marketing Board.

Catherine Lacey's old crone, Haiti, in *The Mummy's Shroud,* and Rosalie Crutchley's fortune teller, Helen Dickerson, in *Blood from the Mummy's Tomb* gaze into crystal balls, and to a greater or lesser extent mummy movies refer, in their confused way, to the tradition of Egyptian magic that also formed the basis of the nineteenth-century magical revival. Madame Blavatsky, for example, launched herself on the international scene in 1877 with her book *Isis Unveiled,* and this brings us to the occult aspects of Gothic horror, which will form the subject of our penultimate chapter.

Ten

The Occult

Whatever else Mummy films may be, they are all concerned with that branch of magic known as necromancy: the raising of the dead. One of the first Gothic novels and one which was mentioned in the famous list of seven "horrid novels" in Jane Austen's *Northanger Abbey*, was called *The Necromancer, or the Tale of the Black Forest*. Originally written in German by Lorenz Flammenberg, the pseudonym of Karl Friedrich Kahlert (1765–1813), it was translated into English by Peter Teuthold, the pseudonym of Peter Will, and it contains some powerful descriptions of occult magic, such as the following scene set in "the gothic remains of a half-decayed castle" in the middle of the Black Forest:

> [The] Necromancer did not move a limb, still staring at the coffin with a haggard look. Now the noise was on the staircase of the cellar and still he was motionless, his eyes being immoveably directed towards the coffin: But now the noise was in the cellar; he brandished his wand, and all around was buried in awful silence. He pronounced again three times an unintelligible word with a horrible thundering voice. A flash of lightning hissed suddenly through the dreary vault, licking the damp walls, and a hollow clap of thunder roared through the subterraneous abode of chilly horror. The light in the lamp was now extinguished, silence and darkness swayed all around; soon after we heard a gentle rustling just before us, and a faint glimmering was spreading through the gloomy vault. It grew lighter and lighter, and we soon perceived rays of dazzling light shooting from the marble coffin, the lid of which began to rise higher and higher — at once the whole vault was illuminated, and a grisly human figure rose slow and awful from the coffin. The phantom, which was wrapped up in a shroud, bore a dying aspect, it trembled violently as it rose, and emitted an hollow groan, looking around with chilly horror. Now the spectre descended from the pedestal, and moved with trembling steps and haggard looks towards the circle where we were standing.[1]

Jane Austen obviously had little time for this kind of thing, and the mistress of Gothic romance herself, Ann Radcliffe, might also have disapproved had not Flammenberg/Kahlert's overt supernaturalism been proved to be a hoax by the time we arrive at the end of this somewhat densely plotted novel. Matthew Lewis had no such rational qualms, however, and *The Necromancer* no doubt made a powerful impression on his fevered adolescent imagination. It may even have contributed, in part, to the supernatural scenes in his famous novel *The Monk* (published in 1796 but written in 1794, the same year that *The Necromancer* appeared in Teuthold's translation). In *The Monk*, Lewis affronts Radcliffe's aesthetics by plunging headlong into Satanism, which he combined with traditional elements of Gothic fiction in a manner then unprecedented in the English novel. As he languishes in prison for his crimes, the Monk, Ambrosio, summons the Devil himself to effect his escape:

> He pronounced the last word, when the effects of the charm were evident. A loud burst of Thunder was heard; The prison shook to its very foundations; A blaze of lightning flashed through the Cell; and in the next moment, borne upon sulphurous whirl-winds, Lucifer stood

before him a second time. But He came not, as when at Matilda's summons He borrowed the Seraph's form to deceive Ambrosio. He appeared in all that ugliness, which since his fall from heaven had been his portion: His blasted limbs still bore marks of the Almighty's thunder: A swarthy darkness spread itself over his gigantic form: His hands and feet were armed with long Talons: Fury glared in his eyes, which might have struck the bravest heart with terror: Over his huge shoulders waved two enormous sable wings; and his hair was supplied by living snakes, which twined themselves round his brows with frightful hissings.[2]

The new element of occultism in *The Monk*, which we are asked to take on face value with no rational explanation, formed the foundation of all the occult literature and films of a later age. There was nothing new about occultism, of course, and it had appeared in literature long before *The Monk*. Shakespeare included many references to magical practices and phenomena in his plays, but these were fully integrated in the Elizabethan *Zeitgeist*. Lewis popularized the occult for an audience that mainly no longer believed in it. In a word, he *sensationalized* it by combining it with the period's most fashionable form of fiction: the Gothic novel.

The word "occult" merely means hidden, though, of course, there is nothing insignificant about what is supposedly to be discovered beyond the veil. The modern way of attempting to explain occultism from a psychological point of view may be said to begin with Spinoza, who, as we saw in chapter four, was the first modern to promote the idea of pantheism, which proposes that God dwells *in* nature itself and that consequently God can be found within ourselves. It was a deeply shocking idea for the time, as it implied that God has a physical, not wholly spiritual dimension. In his *Ethics* (published in 1677), Spinoza argued,

> As God is a being absolutely infinite, to whom no attribute expressing the essence of substance can be denied ..., and as he necessarily exists ..., if any other substance than God be given, it must be explained by means of some attribute of God, and thus two substances would exist possessing the same attribute, which ... is absurd; and so no other substance than God can be granted, and consequently no not even conceived. For if it can be conceived it must necessarily be conceived as existing, and this by the first part of this proof is absurd. Therefore except God no substance can be granted or conceived. Q. e. d.[3]

Spinoza also proposed that there are many aspects of God/Nature that are "occult." As T.L.S. Sprigge puts it in his article on Spinoza,

> [T]he physical world is God's body, God in his physical aspect, rather than the totality of what God is. Humans, as it happens, only know of one other of these attributes, namely thought. God or the universe is thus both an infinite physical thing and an infinite thinking thing (as well as an infinite number of other infinite things the nature of which is hidden from us).[4]

Spinoza's emphasis on thought here links us, via our earlier discussion of Hegel's idea of *Geist*, to the concise definition of occult magic explained by Charles Gray's Mocata in Hammer's *The Devil Rides Out*. While in the process of hypnotizing Marie Eaton (Sarah Lawson), he points out that magic is "the science of causing change to occur by means of one's will." He very nearly succeeds in completely draining Marie's will when Marie's manservant interrupts the proceedings and Mocata's spell is broken. "I shall not be back," he explains, icily, as he is being shown out, "but something will. Something will come for Simon and the girl," the girl being Tanith, who, like Simon Aron, is under Marie's protection. When that "something" does appear later in the film, it manifests itself in various guises, providing an excellent metaphor of Hegel's conviction that Mind creates the world, rather than the other way around. Mocata's will is responsible for these illusions, but might it not also be the case that every mind is responsible for the illusions we take for reality?

Spinoza also argued that thought (or will) is the only aspect of God beyond the physical world that is known to humans, and much of occultism concerns itself with developing the power of the mind as the key to unlocking the infinite things of Nature. Such views have always been anathema to organized religion, the aims of which are to control individual freedom, as Spinoza was very well aware.

> And hence it comes about that those who wish to seek out the causes of miracles, and who wish to understand the things of nature as learned men, and not stare at them in amazement like fools, are soon deemed heretical and impious, and proclaimed such by those whom the mob adore as the interpreters of nature and the Gods. For these know that once ignorance is laid aside, that wonderment which is the only means of preserving their authority would be taken away from them.[5]

Spinoza's commitment to individual freedom and the development of what he called each finite thing's *conatus* (or striving) to become what it is in its fullest sense indeed anticipates Nietzsche's anti–Christian concept of the Superman. Spinoza also thought that much of organized religion was merely life-denying superstition. As Nietzsche would emphasize two centuries later, Spinoza believed that we should seek to become God ourselves through intuitive understanding of Nature and our place in it. A Jungian psychologist would say that we should aim to become individuated, that our primary aim in life should be to fulfill the potential within us and become truly who we are.

We will be returning to these ideas throughout this chapter, which seeks to chart the rise and fall of occult cinema and the ways in which it is connected with the occult revival in the late nineteenth and twentieth centuries. One of the earliest of occult films was Rex Ingram's silent classic *The Magician* (1927), starring Paul Wegener as Satanist Oliver Haddo, in an adaptation of Somerset Maugham's novel of the same name. Haddo was based on the infamous real-life magician, Aleister Crowley, whom Maugham had met (and disliked) in Paris in 1897. In Maugham's opinion, Crowley "was a fake, but not entirely a fake."

> He was a liar and unbecomingly boastful, but the odd thing was that he had actually done some of the things he boasted of....
> At the time I knew him he was dabbling in Satanism, magic and the occult. There was just then something of a vogue in Paris for that sort of thing, occasioned, I surmise, by the interest that was still taken in a book of Huysmans's, *Là Bas*. Crowley told fantastic stories of his experiences but it was hard to say whether he was telling the truth or merely pulling your leg.[6]

Whatever Crowley may have been, Haddo is not a fake. He attempts to create a homunculus for which he requires virgin's blood. Thus is Maugham's seduction plot justified. Notably, in the novel, Haddo employs the aesthetic/decadent prose of Walter Pater to achieve this end. He seduces heroine Margaret with the passage about Leonardo's *Mona Lisa* which we encountered in chapter five.

> His voice, poignant and musical, blended with the suave music of the words so that Margaret felt she had never before known their divine significance. She was intoxicated with their beauty. She wished him to continue, but had not the strength to speak. As if he guessed her thought, he went on, and now his voice had a richness in it as of an organ heard afar off. It was like an overwhelming fragrance and she could hardly bear it.[7]

Obviously Crowley wasn't the only person to have been inspired by the example of Huysmans' *Là Bas*. Once a disciple of Zola, Huysmans was quite specific in his thoroughly researched descriptions of Parisian Black Masses:

> A choir boy, clad in red, advanced to the end of the chapel and lighted a stand of candles. Then the altar became visible. It was an ordinary church altar on a tabernacle above which stood an

infamous, derisive Christ. The head had been raised and the neck lengthened, and wrinkles painted in the cheeks, transformed the grieving face to a bestial one twisted into a mean laugh. He was naked, and where the loincloth should have been, there was a viril member projecting from a bush of horsehair.[8]

No film in the 1920s or '30s could have presented that kind of imagery, but Ingram's *The Magician* went as far as it could, employing one of the dancers of the Folies Bergère to impersonate Pan during the orgy scene, which derives from this hallucinatory passage in the novel:

> And in a moment she grew sick with fear, for a change came into the tree, and the tremulousness of life was in it; the rough bark was changed into brutish flesh and the twisted branches into human arms. It became a monstrous, goat-legged thing, more vast than the creatures of nightmare. She saw the horns and the long beard, the great hairy legs with their hoofs, and the man's rapacious hands. The face was horrible, with lust and cruelty, and yet it was divine. It was Pan, playing on his pipes, and the lecherous eyes caressed her with a hideous tenderness. But even while she looked, as the mist of the early day, rising, discloses a fair country, the animal part of that ghoulish creature seemed to fall away, and she saw a lovely youth, titanic but sublime, leaning against a massive rock. He was more beautiful than the Adam of Michael Angelo who wakes into life at the call of the Almighty; and, like him freshly created, he had the adorable langour of one who feels still in his limbs the soft rain on the loose brown earth. Naked and full of majesty he lay, the outcast son of the morning.[9]

If one were looking for proof of Maugham's own homosexuality, one need surely look no further than this passage. Paul Wegener's Haddo and Alice Terry (as his supplier of virginal

Bela Lugosi as "Murder" and Robert Frazer (carrying Madge Bellamy) are flanked by the undead in *White Zombie* (dir. Victor Halperin, 1932).

blood) certainly look suitably impressed by Stowitts (the American dancer of Pan) as he poses angularly before them in the cinematic adaptation of this scene. Ingram also exploited the dramatic spectacle of Gothic imagery in this film which, combined with impressive laboratory sets, unsurprisingly went on to influence James Whale's *Frankenstein*.

The most extreme example of Gothic occultism from the early days of macabre cinema must surely be the strange Bela Lugosi vehicle called *White Zombie* (dir. Victor Halperin, 1932). It's a genuinely unnerving experience, in which Lugosi plays "Murder" Legendre, a voodoo necromancer who creates Negro zombies to work the sugar mills in Haiti. This is frightening enough, but what was felt to be truly horrific when the film was made is that he attempts to turn a white girl (played by the soulful-eyed Madge Bellamy) into a zombie as well, hence the title. This act is originally on behalf of a wealthy plantation owner who has fallen in love with her and wants to steal her from her fiancé, so he invites the happy couple to his estate on Haiti, obtains a poisoned rose from Legendre to drug her at her wedding breakfast and waits for the voodoo master to burn a wax effigy of the unfortunate bride who accordingly faints, seemingly lifeless. Legendre then sets about resurrecting her as a kind of zombie (though surely not quite the real thing as she hasn't actually died).

The sets for this film were rearranged and redressed relics from Charles D. Hall's creations for *Dracula* and *Frankenstein*, on loan from Universal Studios. *White Zombie*, however, uses them far more imaginatively than had Tod Browning. While not a masterpiece like Whale's *Frankenstein*, *White Zombie* is certainly a classic of its kind. Lugosi never acted under more impressive Gothic arches. There's also a splendid Gothic balcony on which the zombified Madge Bellamy appears like Juliet, and beneath the towering columns of this Gothic castle that has somehow found its way to Haiti, she also plays Liszt's *Liebestraum* on a grand piano. She is indeed a kind of Hadaly, but far less intellectually stimulating. Even the plantation owner who is responsible for this outrage is frustrated and longs for a little more life in his Stepford Wife, but as Lugosi points out: "How do you suppose those eyes will regard you when the brain is able to understand?"

Until the end, Legendre is able to defend himself simply by staring at his assailants (somewhat in the manner of the alien children in John Wyndham's *The Midwich Cuckoos*). Shots of his famously intense gaze frequently punctuate the action, often superimposed over long shots. His face even stares at the heroine as she looks into her wedding goblet. Rarely has the occult power of the will been better suggested by any other actor, though the ocular intensity of Christopher Lee and Charles Gray is surely no less effective. Alternatively, Legendre can always set his zombie bodyguard onto whoever it is that needs to be silenced, but in the end, of course, he is defeated and hurled over the castle ramparts. Carlos Clarens aptly described this peculiar film as "a Gothic fairy tale filled with traditional symbols, dreamlike imagery, echoes of Romanticism, and (probably unintentional) psychosexual overtones,"[10] and it's as good a description as any.

Hammer attempted the same basic narrative in John Gilling's *The Plague of the Zombies* (1965), but they dispensed with the Gothic trappings, substituting Cornish tin mines for Haitian sugar mills. The film's Victorian setting with its carefully delineated class structure of upper class landowners, middle class doctors and working class village folk emphasized an underlying (though presumably unwitting) Marxist allegory: a ruthless mine owner (played by John Carson) exploits the downtrodden subterranean zombies under his command to increase his wealth. It's Hammer's version of Wagner's *Das Rheingold* in which Nibelung dwarves toil for Black Alberich. (As Bernard Shaw put it in his analysis of that opera, "This gloomy place need not be a mine: it might just as well be a match-factory, with yellow phosphorus, phossy jaw, a large dividend, and plenty of clergymen shareholders."[11]) *White Zombie* is more unnerving than *The Plague of the Zombies* in its much heavier Gothic atmosphere, and it also demonstrates the occult element of will power in a rather more effective manner than the waxen voodoo dolls and African drumming of the Hammer version, hugely enjoyable and visually impressive though Gilling's film is in its own way. Unfortunately, during the ritual scenes of *The Plague of the Zombies*, Carson's face is covered by a tribal mask, so we don't see his eyes, those windows of the soul (though there is one powerful scene in which he appears without his robes and mask to hypnotize Jacqueline Pearce's unfortunate character, Alice).

The only other particularly occult film from the first wave of Hollywood horrors was Edgar G. Ulmer's *The Black Cat* which, as we have seen, updated the trappings of Gothic to Bauhaus modernity. Occultism thrives, nonetheless, in the basement of this chromium-plated mausoleum. Inverted crosses, a fleeting appearance by the black cat itself, and cowled devil worshippers all do as much as the Hays Code allowed at the time (though the original script wanted them to do much more). More interesting was Val Lewton's subdued essay in Satanism, *The Seventh Victim* (dir. Mark Robson, 1943). As with all Lewton's horror films, suggestion proves more powerful than anything more explicit. We are shown the Satanists of this film assembled in conventional domestic settings, wearing everyday dress (frighteningly padded shoulders for the ladies and even more intimidating forties headgear). They even listen to a Brahms waltz being played on the piano, but we're never shown what they get up to, or how they achieve their ends. *I Walked with a Zombie*, directed for Lewton by Jacques Tourneur in the same year, similarly lacks an overriding focus on will power, *à la* Lugosi, though the zombies themselves (if, indeed, that is really what they are) are more frightening than any others on offer in this drama set in the West Indies. Particularly atmospheric is the famous scene set in a moonlit field of corn, which rustles in the breeze while the sound of distant drumming announces the appearance of Darby Jones' expressionless zombie, Carrefour. Carrefour leads the way to the island's witch doctor whom a nurse (played by Frances Dee) has decided to approach in the hope that he might be able to cure the catatonic condition to which her patient (played by Christine Gordon) has fallen victim. But as ever with Lewton, ambiguity is the key word in this very loose reworking of Charlotte Brontë's *Jane Eyre*.

John Carson as Squire Hamilton in *The Plague of the Zombies* (dir. John Gilling, 1965).

The Seventh Victim is particularly important, not only for its own qualities but also because it initiated the classic occult films that appeared between the late 1950s and 1970s. Its importance lies in the fact that it stripped away the Gothic surroundings that connected films like *White Zombie* to Lewis' *The Monk*, and placed the occult activity in the midst of apparent normality instead. Such an approach created a powerful visual metaphor of what Professor Sprigge, in his analysis of Spinoza's ideas, identified as the "infinite number of other infinite things the nature of which is hidden from us." According to this world view, apparent normality is exactly that. It is only *apparent*, and that complete but hidden reality (whatever such a reality might be) is what the occultist aims to reveal.

The ghost story writer M.R. James (1862–1936) was a master at conveying this particular quality of the unnerving supernatural erupting into the prosaically normal, and *Night of the Demon* (dir. Jacques Tourneur, 1957), based on James' story "Casting the Runes" (1911), is the first British film successfully to explore the occult in this manner. There is, however, nothing new in its basic idea, which can be traced at least as far back as the *Faust* legend. Just as Faust sells his soul to the Devil for material gain, so too does Julian Karswell, the Satanist of *Night of the Demon*. The story has even more in common with Maturin's *Melmoth the Wanderer*. When a slip of paper with magical runes is passed to one's enemy, it proves to be as good as a death warrant, but when one is passed back to Karswell he is unable to escape his doom, just as Melmoth, unable to pass on his curse of immortal life to anyone else, must ultimately pay the price of his bargain with Satan. In *Night of the Demon*, Karswell was played by the Irish actor Niall MacGinnis (who, as we've seen, had previously appeared in Olivier's *Hamlet*), and he perfectly captured the avuncular, balding

Satanism as *film noir*: Jean Brooks and unidentified player in a scene from ***The Seventh Victim*** (dir. Mark Robson, 1943).

malevolence of a character whom James describes simply as "a stout gentleman." Disguised as a clown while entertaining local children on his commodious estate, MacGinnis' Karswell becomes the very devil himself, summoning a thunderstorm to prove his powers to the disbelieving Dana Andrews. He's certainly much more frightening than the atrociously absurd demon that was foisted on the despairing Tourneur by the film's producers; it spoils but fortunately doesn't ruin this film's compelling atmosphere of pervasive evil.

Karswell, like Oliver Haddo, was also based on Crowley. Maugham's story was published in 1908, three years before "Casting the Runes," and as Maugham mentioned in his introduction to *The Magician*, Crowley was part of what had originally been a mid–nineteenth-century occult revival, stimulated by the fallout over Darwin's theories of evolution in his *Origin of Species* (1859). Reacting to the doubt such theories cast over humanity's previously assumed supremacy in the natural scheme of things, along with the advancing materialism of the Victorian industrial age, spiritualism and a variety of other occult "sciences" were revived as a way of filling the perceived spiritual void. *Là Bas* (1890), in which Huysmans applied Zola-esque naturalist methods to the occult underworld of turn-of-the-century Paris, was merely one manifestation of occultism that had been flourishing for several decades.

Evolving out of the interest in spiritualism, while simultaneously negotiating the scientific spirit of the age, Madame Blavatsky put forward an alternative evolutionary theory of her own. According to her, humanity is in the process of evolving through seven "Root Races." The first was a kind of invisible jellyfish, the second lived in Hyperborea, the third (giant ape-like beings with eyes in the backs of their heads) lived in Lemuria. When Lemuria sank, the fourth Root Race developed in Atlantis. We are currently of the fifth Root Race. The sixth will appear in North America, the seventh in South America. One need look no further for evidence of Darwin's unsettling cultural effect than the fact that Blavatsky's ideas were taken up so passionately by so many intelligent and creative people who felt spiritually bereaved by the idea of natural selection and other spiritually challenging advances in the empirical sciences. Behind her bizarre evolutionary theories lay an exercise in comparative religion similar to that of Sir James Frazer's *The Golden Bough* (1890). However, in her magnum opus *The Secret Doctrine* (1888), Blavatsky went further than Frazer by suggesting that the reason why so many religions have so much in common with each other is due to a secret doctrine, communicated telepathically across the ages by Tibetan spiritual masters, with whom Blavatsky claimed to be in regular telepathic contact.

Theosophy eventually exerted a limited but fascinating influence on the arts. It was a brief efflorescence, but it inspired geniuses such as the poet W. B. Yeats (1865–1939) and the Russian composer Alexander Scriabin (1872–1915), whose tone poem *Prometheus, the Poem of Fire* appeared in 1910, neatly between Maugham's *The Magician* and James' "Casting the Runes." *Prometheus* has been described as the most theosophical piece of music ever written, concerned, as it is, to transcribe Blavatsky's ideas of spiritual evolution into music. Scriabin was a devout theosophist, and *Prometheus* describes the development of the human spirit from Original Chaos, leading to the birth of the ultimate human, disembodied and ethereal. A choir announces the arrival of this new Child of the Universe with vowel sounds, an idea which predated the conclusion of Stanley Kubrick's *2001— A Space Odyssey* by fifty-eight years. *Prometheus* uses the orchestra to represent the macrocosm of the universe and the piano to encapsulate the microcosm of humanity. Scriabin's biographer Faubion Bowers described *Prometheus* as "the most densely Theosophical piece of music ever written"[12] but this musical process of human evolution takes only about twenty minutes to perform. Ideally, it should be performed with an instrument that didn't exist when Scriabin composed his masterpiece. This was the keyboard of light, which he envisaged would bathe the concert hall with colored lights throughout the performance. Scriabin, who enjoyed the psychological condition of synaesthesia, created a complex system of key-color symbolism, which he incorporated into the very structure of *Prometheus'* harmonic structure. As Scriabin himself explained to the conductor Serge Koussevitsky:

> "What plans I have, what plans! You know I have lights in *Prometheus*. [He whispered the word "lights."] I will play it for you. Lights. It's a poem of fire. Here the hall has changing colors. Now they glow; now they turn into tongues of flame. Listen how all this music is really fire."[13]

Ken Russell's radio play *The Death of Alexander Scriabin*, first broadcast on BBC Radio Radio 3 on June 18, 1995, brought Crowley and Scriabin together in a satirical romp starring Oliver Reed as Crowley, who comes across Scriabin playing his "Black Mass" piano sonata while sacrificing a goat in St. Basil's Cathedral in Moscow at midnight on Walpurgis Night. Both men were present in the Russian capital in 1914, the time in which the play is set, so Russell's unlikely proposition could have happened. If it didn't, it really *should* have.

Theosophy also influenced several artists who later became champions of modernism, such as Paul Klee (1879–1940) and Piet Mondrian (1872–1944), but theosophy has had little influence on popular cinema. Perhaps the closest commercial cinema has came to touching theosophical concerns is with adventure films such as *Atlantis — the Lost Continent* (dir. George Pal, 1961) in which the Atlanteans are portrayed in Blavatskian manner as super-scientists, planning to rule the world with an atomic ray gun. Such ambitions all go predictably wrong (a dénouement which Blavatsky would have claimed to be nothing short of historical truth), and Atlantis sinks, in equally Blavatskian manner, beneath the sea. *Warlords of Atlantis* (dir. Kevin Connor, 1978) developed this idea, making the Atlanteans aliens from Mars who are stranded under the Atlantic Ocean. They telepathically influence human history, encouraging the development of atomic physics, which they hope to exploit in order eventually to propel themselves back out into space. Both these films exploit similar Atlantean eschatologies to those espoused by Blavatsky and her followers, such as Rudolf Steiner, the founder of the Anthroposophical Society, but they are the last link in a chain of influence that no longer seems to carry much weight in popular culture of this kind.

The connection between theosophy and the particularly unpleasant racial occultism which influenced (and to some extent helped perpetuate) Nazi ideology in the Germany of the 1930s is both fascinating and disturbing. Both theosophy and Nazism were influenced by the ideas of the Victorian novelist Edward Bulwer-Lytton, later Lord Lytton (1803–73), who was rumored to have been the president of a secret Rosicrucian order in England. There's some uncertainty about that claim but it's certainly true that he was profoundly interested in occult matters and he did meet the grand magus of the nineteenth-century occult revival, Éliphas Lévi (real name: Alphonse Louis Constant) (1810–75) when Lévi visited England in 1854. Lytton apparently encouraged Lévi to write what became one of the foundation stones of the modern occult revival, a book which Levi published in 1855 under the title *Dogma et Rituel de la Haute Magie*. In this work, he elaborates an occult perspective of Hegel's theory of *Geist*:

> As a fact, the word, or speech, is the veil of being and the characteristic sign of life. Every form is the veil of a word, because the idea which is the mother of the word is the sole reason for the existence of forms. Every figure is a character, every character derives from and returns to a word.[14]

Levi's subsequent influence on the Order of the Golden Dawn and especially on Aleister Crowley (who thought himself to be a reincarnation of Lévi) demonstrates not only his own importance but also the significance of the now rather neglected Bulwer-Lytton in the history of ideas. Despite this, none of Bulwer-Lytton's fascinating occult novels have ever been filmed. The three most overtly occult of these, *Zanoni* (1842), *A Strange Story* (1862) and *The Coming Race* (1871), had also had a direct influence on the formation of Madame Blavatsky's ideas. So too did *The Last Days of Pompeii* (1834), which describes the Isis cult in Rome during the first century A.D. It was this book which first inspired Blavatsky's interest in the magical tradition of ancient Egypt.[15] Bulwer-Lytton's novels were also extremely popular in Germany at the turn of the century. *The Coming Race*, concerning a subterranean race of supermen who command a powerful natural force called "Vril," interested Willy Ley, the rocket engineer who worked for the Third Reich before defecting to America. As Nicholas Goodrick-Clarke confirms in *The Occult Roots of Nazism*, belief in "Vril" was shared by some high-ranking Nazis,[16] though it was not quite so significant a factor in Nazi policy as some more sensationalist historians (and novelists) have suggested. More significant were those occultists who grasped and manipulated the racist potential of theosophy for their own nationalist aims. Men such as Jörg Lanz von Liebenfels, who developed what he called Theozoology in books such as *Die Theosophie und die assyrischen "Menschentiere"* ("Theosophy and the Assyrian 'Man-Beasts'"), did indeed have an influence on the young Adolf Hitler, fueling the future Führer's own, less metaphysical ideas of racial purity. This is not the place for a full discussion of the influence of occultism on Nazi philosophy (Goodrick-Clarke's study is by far the most balanced and well-researched account of that particular subject), but it is of relevance to us in that Nazism emerged around the same time that one of England's most prolific popular novelists, Dennis Wheatley, was first making his impact in the field of occult adventure stories.

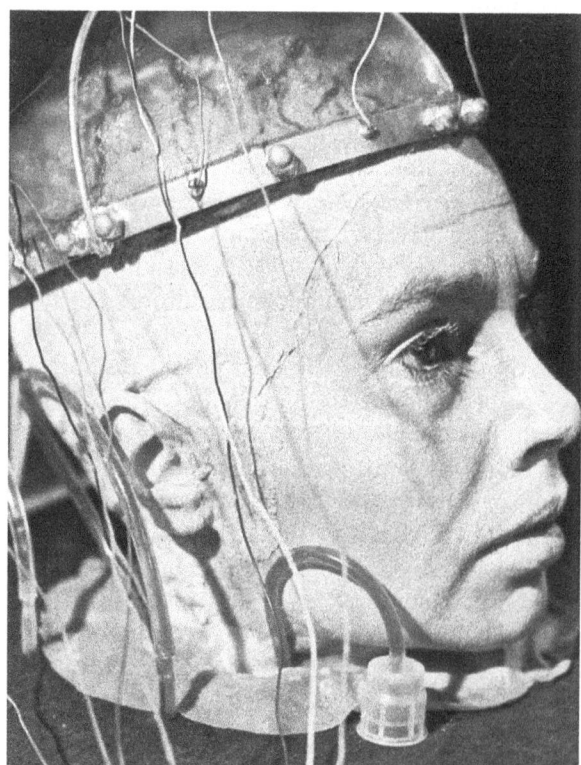

Baphomet. Kathleen Breck plays a severed head kept alive in Dana Andrews' laboratory in **The Frozen Dead** (dir. Herbert J. Leder, 1967).

The general mood of what was happening in Germany was also reflected in the series of "mad scientist" movies that Hollywood produced in the 1930s and '40s, in particular *Island of Lost Souls* (dir. Erle C. Kenton, 1932) in which Charles Laughton played H.G. Wells' Dr. Moreau. His performance is uncannily like the Nazi, Dr. Mengele. One of the operation scenes in which he creates one of his hideous man-beasts is unnervingly reminiscent of Nazi medical atrocities. The atrocity is made especially horrible by Laughton's furious expression as he spins around to face the camera when caught in the act. (Laurence Olivier would echo this kind of thing in 1976's *Marathon Man* [dir. John Schlesinger].) Mad scientist films, such as *The Raven* (dir. Lew Landers, 1935) in which Bela Lugosi plays a deranged plastic surgeon who disfigures Boris Karloff's wanted criminal Edmond Bateman, were also part of this general sense that something was rotten in the state of Deutschland. As David J. Skal observed, in the 1930s "medicine was becoming demonized along lines very much like those depicted in horror films, in the very country that had first introduced cinematic ghosts and goblins."[17]

Only later, in the 1960s, did the more occult preoccupations of the Nazis find a place in the cinema. *The Frozen Dead* (dir. Herbert J. Leder, 1966) gave Dana Andrews another opportunity to explore the demonic as a scientist who keeps Nazis in cryogenic suspended animation. The severed head of another of his experiments (played by Kathleen Breck) is kept alive by means of various tubes and electrodes and provides an interesting modern echo of the severed head of the demon Baphomet that was said, in some accounts, to have been worshipped by the Knights Templars.[18] The theme of keeping Nazis alive, like King Arthur, until the right time for their return, was later developed by Ira Levin's novel *The Boys from Brazil*, filmed in 1978 (dir. Franklin Schaffner). This time, Laurence Olivier was cast on the side of the angels, as a Nazi hunter in pursuit of Gregory Peck's Dr. Mengele, who has created clones of Hitler.

Whereas theosophy had originally been a reaction against religious doubt in the wake of Darwin, Nazism's interest in the occult was driven by fears of modernity and democracy. Occultism offered a way out of an increasingly globalized, multicultural and industrialized society. Wheatley himself was a rather more casual but no less instinctive racist, and his interpretation of democracy was hardly of the socialist variety, so in that respect he could be said to have had certain things in common with the Nazi ideology he professed to despise. His own interest in the occult, apart from the realization that stories featuring it would bring considerable commercial benefits, was tempered with caution, at least for his readers. His Author's Note at the beginning of *The Devil Rides Out* was a carefully constructed titillation:

> Should any of my readers incline to a serious study of the subject, and thus come into contact with a man or woman of Power, I feel that it is only right to urge them, most strongly, to refrain from being drawn into the practice of the Secret Art in any way. My own observations have led me to an absolute conviction that to do so would bring them into dangers of a very real and concrete nature.

Like the newspapers, which took so much horrified interest in Crowley, Wheatley always associated occultism with "the enemy." Sometimes that enemy was the Third Reich, as in 1964's *They Used Dark Forces*, in which Hitler is given such lines as, "Predictions made to me have not been fulfilled, so I have dismissed their authors. The Reichsführer's man, Herr Wolf, has been the most reliable occultist I have consulted, but his master can spare him only occasionally. This man of yours sounds promising and I badly need guidance."[19] On other occasions the occultists are more generalized foreigners who, in Wheatley's racist right-wing universe, could never become decent chaps like his very British heroes. Mocata in *The Devil Rides Out* (1934), for example, is a very different character, visually at least, from the suave man-about-town presented by Charles Gray in Hammer's 1968 film. In the novel he is described as a fleshy, bald, moonfaced man with a lisp, confirming Wheatley's admission that he based Mocata on Crowley, whom he wined and dined as part of his considerable research for the book.[20] This research did indeed give considerable authenticity to the proceedings. The film version brought more research to bear. A great deal of the magical iconography of Fisher's *The Devil Rides Out* is indebted to Éliphas Lévi's *Transcendental Magic — Its Dogma and Ritual*. The main title sequence (which almost attains the arty sophistication of a James Bond film) features an inverted pentagram, with the various parts of a goat's head occupying the five points of the star, as discussed earlier. The title of the film is then superimposed over a reproduction of Lévi's illustration of "The Satanic Goat." However, Levi did not regard this image as wholly evil. He connected it to the two goats,

> one pure and one impure, [which] were consecrated in Judea; the first was sacrificed in expiation for sins; the other, loaded with those sins by imprecation, was set at liberty in the desert.... We must recognise therefore a Magic of the Sanctuary and that of the wilderness, the White and the Black Church, the priesthood of public assemblies and the Sanhedrim of the Sabbath. The goat which is represented in our frontispiece bears upon its forehead the Sign of the Pentagram with one point in the ascendant, which is sufficient to distinguish it as a symbol of light. Moreover, the sign of occultism is made with both hands, pointing upward to the white moon of CHESED, and downwards to the black moon of GEBURAH. This sign expresses the perfect concord between mercy and justice.... The torch of intelligence burning between the horn is the magical light of equilibrium.... The monstrous head of the animal expresses horror of sin, for which the material agent, alone responsible, must alone and for ever bear the penalty, because the soul is impassible its nature and can suffer only by materialising.[21]

"The Satanic Goat" illustration by Éliphas Lévi in *Transcendental Magic—Its Doctrine and Ritual*.

Hammer's use of this image in *The Devil Rides Out* is, therefore, rather more simplistic than Lévi's interpretation.

The main title card for Rosalyn Landor and Russell Waters is superimposed over another Lévi illustration, which appears on page 389 in the A.E. Waite translation of *Transcendental Magic*, which Lévi called the "Goetic Circle of Black Evocations and Pacts." This is perfectly appropriate, but other images are more problematic. Behind the musical credits for James Bernard, Philip Martell and choreographer, David Toguri, the main title sequence presents us with Lévi's design on page 200, symbolizing "The Cherub of Ezekiel," a magical image certainly, but quite the opposite of a demonic one. Lévi's design here also forms the basis of the insignia of the purple robes worn by Charles Gray's Mocata and his fellow Satanists, though the face of the cherub has been replaced by an inverted pentagram in that instance. Perhaps even more inappropriately, Bernard Robinson included Lévi's design for the Apocalyptic Key of the Seven Seals of St. John as one of the murals in Simon Aron's "observatory." We can see it quite clearly behind Patrick Mower, who plays Simon, in one particular shot. Lévi believed that these seals "are explained by the analogies of the numbers, characters and figures of the Tarot.... The explanation of the book of St. John by the characters of the Kabalah will be an entirely new revelation, though foreseen by several distinguished Magi."[22] This isn't the place for Lévi's subsequent analysis, but it is important to make clear that Lévi's approach to magic was not the simplistic Manichean division between good and evil that Hammer would have us believe by their somewhat casual use of such occult iconography.

There are, however, more appropriate uses of the rituals of transcendental magic in *The Devil Rides Out*. Tanya Krzywinska points out that the ritual in which de Richleau summons the spirit of Tanith to help him find where Mocata has taken the girl, Peggy, is based on the kind of Babylonian/Egyptian ritual magic that Crowley would have imbibed from his time as a member of the Order of the Golden Dawn.[23] Christopher Lee's de Richleau performs the sign of Osiris slain and the sign of Osiris risen, summoning the spirit of Tanith with salt, hair and blood, but it should be emphasized that these specifics are not described in Wheatley's novel. Lee, a friend of Wheatley and instrumental in suggesting that Hammer film *The Devil Rides Out*, also did his own research for the movie, discovering an authentic invocation to stand in for Wheatley's unspecified Sussamma ritual which alters time and space but "*which shall never be done except in the direst emergency when the very soul is in peril of destruction.*"[24] However, that de Richleau should deign to practice magic at all exposes the central weakness in Wheatley's overall view, as expressed in his Author's Note. Despite his research, Wheatley, like the popular press (and Hammer films later), misunderstood Crowley's magickal philosophy. Mocata's definition of magick as "the science of causing change to occur by means of will" in which "there is neither good nor evil"[25] is indeed fully in accord with Crowley's will-based "Thelematic Magick," but Wheatley then makes Mocata contradict himself by

Left: "The Cherub of Ezekiel" illustration by Éliphas Lévi in *Transcendental Magic—Its Doctrine and Ritual*. *Right:* "Goëtic Circle of Black Evocations and Pacts" illustration by Éliphas Lévi in *Transcendental Magic—Its Doctrine and Ritual*.

APOCALYPTIC KEY

The Seven Seals of St John

"Apocalyptic Key—The Seven Seals of St. John" illustration by Éliphas Lévi in *Transcendental Magic—Its Doctrine and Ritual*.

turning him into an embodiment of pure evil, dragging occultism into the mud with him. Krzywinska correctly argues, "Wheatley's rather simplistic interpretation of Crowley's magickal system is painted very negatively as black magic; something with which Crowley would not have agreed,"[26] and in support of this, she adds a quotation from Kenneth Grant, one of Crowley's adherents: "To anyone familiar with the ways of genius, particularly in occult and religious spheres, the veil of illusion which produced the mirage of 'the demon Crowley' could and did have a single aim: that of weeding out the magically competent from the inept."[27] Wheatley did, however, attempt to free the swastika from its Nazi connotations. In the novel, de Richleau places a small golden swastika around Simon's neck while hypnotizing him. Rex van Ryn is horrified. "Fancy hanging a Nazi swastika round the neck of a professing Jew," he complains.

"My dear Rex!" de Richleau replies. "Do try and broaden your outlook a little. The swastika is the oldest symbol of wisdom and right thinking in the world. It has been used by every race and in every country at some time or other."[28]

Unsurprisingly, though disappointingly, Hammer replaced the swastika with a simple crucifix.

It's deeply ironic that the arch-conservative, almost lunatic-fringe right-winger Wheatley should have helped fuel 1960s hippie counterculture by popularizing such a distorted image of Crowley. (The Beatles, hardly in the same universe as Wheatley, took a more enlightened view of Crowley when they included a picture of him on Peter Blake's sleeve cover for *Sgt. Pepper's Lonely Hearts Club Band* in 1967 as one of the "People We Like.") Robert Irwin's novel *Satan Wants Me* (1999) amusingly explores this apparent contradiction in a story set during the Summer of Love, in which a sociology student and apprentice sorcerer joins an occult brotherhood run by a pedantic, middle-aged occultist who believes the student to be a reincarnation of Crowley himself. At one point the hero writes to Wheatley and receives a pompous reply in the terms of the Author's Note at the beginning of *The Devil Rides Out*. Regarding the Author's Note itself, the student aptly remarks, "What a wonderful come-on…"[29]

Crowley's appeal to the hippie generation lay not only in his advocacy of drugs, sex and alternative Eastern religions, but also, and more significantly, in the belief enshrined in his own *Book of the Law*: "There is no law beyond do what thou wilt," which, of course, can be interpreted in a variety of ways. Spinoza's concept of *conatus* is probably closer to the spirit of Crowley's dictum than the total anarchy it implies to some, but anyway the idea wasn't Crowley's own. The phrase in fact derives from the *Gargantua and Pantragruel* of François Rabelais (c. 1494–1553) in which the gigantic hero, Gargantua, founds an abbey called Theleme dedicated to freedom, free thought and licentiousness. Rabelais describes the Thelemites who dwell there as the ultimate freedom-seeking hedonists:

> All their life was spent not in laws, statutes, or rules, but according to their own free will and pleasure. They rose out of their beds when they thought good; they did eat, drink, labour, sleep, when they had a mind to it, and were disposed for it. None did awake them, none did offer to constrain them to eat, drink, nor do any other thing; for so had Gargantua established it. In all their rule and strictest tie of their order, there was but this one clause to be observed:
> DO WHAT THOU WILT[30]

It was hardly surprising that Crowley, the highly repressed son of devout Plymouth Brethren, should have found such a creed immensely appealing. What better name for his own religion than Rabelais' name for Gargantua's abbey of Thelema? On the gates of Rabelais' Theleme is an immense inscription barring conventional moralists from its precincts but welcoming the truly virtuous:

Here enter not, religious boobies, sots,/Imposters, sniveling hypocrites, bigots…/attorneys, barraters,…/pinching usurers …/Gold-graspers, coin-grippers, gulpers of mists/… Here enter you, and welcome from our hearts,/All noble sparks, endow'd with gallant parts…./Here enter you, pure, honest, faithful, true,/Expounders of the *Scriptures*, old and new.[31]

Crowley would no doubt have liked to think of himself as one of the noble sparks, though his behavior rather disqualified him from that role in the eyes of many. He agreed with much of Blavatsky's teaching[32] but he was not a theosophist. For a time he was involved with the Magical Order of the Golden Dawn, another offshoot of the *fin de siècle* occult revival, where he met Yeats, whom he described as a "lank, dishevelled demonologist."[33] Yeats, like Somerset Maugham, loathed him, but no institution seemed big enough to contain Crowley's self-confidence nor the breadth of his ideas, so he had no alternative but to found his own "religion." For all his pranks, practical jokes and outrageousness, Crowley was sincere in his belief in the efficacy of Magick:

> I further resolved to uphold the dignity of Magick by pressing into its service science and philosophy, as well as the noblest English that I could command, and to present it in such a form as would of itself command respect and attention. I would do nothing cheap: I would be content with nothing second-rate.[34]

While Crowley's activities commanded attention, they failed to command an equal respect during his lifetime. Despite his belief that "every man and every woman has each definite attributes whose tendency, considered in due relation to environment, indicate a proper course of action in each case" and that to pursue this course of action "is to do one's true will"[35] (ideals with which both Spinoza and Nietzsche would surely have agreed), Crowley was popularly known merely as "the wickedest man in England," and it took until the 1960s for his reputation and ideas to be reassessed. By that time, he had become enshrined as Mocata and Karswell, among numerous other fictional Satanists.

Christopher Lee recalled, "Hammer had always worried about the Church's reaction to the screening of the Black Mass. But we thought the charge of blasphemy would not stick if we did the thing with due attention to scholarship."[36] However, such qualms hadn't stopped the company from including an occult ritual at the end of *The Kiss of the Vampire*, in which Professor Zimmer draws an encircled pentagram in chalk on the floor of his hotel bedroom. It serves the same function as the admittedly much bigger pentagram that Lee's Duc de Richleau draws on the floor of Richard and Marie Eaton's sitting room in *The Devil Rides Out*. Zimmer uses his pentagram to protect him during a compact little ceremony called *Corpus diabolo levitum* (literally "raising the body of the devil"). It must be performed at the time of the full moon when Capricorn is in conjunction with Saturn; and with the use of some traditional (though in the case of the third, rather unspecific) occult props (the Ring, the Sword, the Liquid and the Horn), Zimmer forces evil to destroy itself. "I conjure thee in the name of the mighty Beelzebub!" he shouts at the climax of his invocation. "Appear!" After a dramatic silence, the spell proves very efficacious, causing a flock of bats to attack Dr. Ravna and his vampire cult in a scene that anticipated Hitchcock's *The Birds* (1963).

Hammer continued their interest in the occult experimentation in both the modern manner instigated by *The Seventh Victim* and the more Gothic approach of *The Monk*. *The Witches* (dir. Cyril Frankel, 1966) was an essay in the former style, set in a bucolic village where everything seems quite normal but, of course, isn't, as all the villagers are devil worshippers under the leadership of (probably lesbian) journalist Stephanie Box (played by Kay Walsh). The film is in the mode of *So Long at the Fair* and *The Kiss of the Vampire*, with conspiracy and abduction generating much of the plot, but the finale shows us (absurdly, in the opinion of its screenwriter, Nigel Kneale[37]) the demonic truth behind the veneer. Stephanie gets togged up as a pagan priestess and attempts to provide herself with a new "skin for dancing in," by transferring her own soul into the body of a young girl. It's just the same sort of thing that Mocata attempts at the end of *The Devil Rides Out*.

Hammer's sequel to *She*, under the title *The Venegeance of She*, contains some visually impressive black magic scenes in the somewhat Atlantean-style palace of Kuma, ruled by the immortal Kallikrates (John Richardson). A gigantic pentagram, surrounded by flaming *torcheres*, provides the sorcerer, Men-Hari (played by Derek Godfrey), with magical protection as he raises demonic forces to destroy André Morell's Kassim. Kassim, in his own, much more humble pentagram, fails to ward off these demonic forces, and Carol/Ayesha (played by Olinka Berova), whom he has been trying to protect, can now no longer withstand the psychic summons from Kuma, where Kallikrates awaits her. Noel Willman plays Za-Tor, the elderly white magician of Kuma who has presided over a community of somewhat Qabalistic magi. "For fifty centuries," he mutters, "we have held ourselves apart from the world to seek the growth of mind and spirit. We have traveled far along that path. Soon we shall be ready to go out into the world bearing all the fruits of our wisdom, solving all problems, teaching the world to live in peace and happiness." However, now that Men-Hari has

Kay Walsh as Stephanie Bax presides over the occult ceremony at the climax of **The Witches** (dir. Cyril Frankel, 1966).

taken over the reins of power, Za-Tor can "hear the beat of dark wings" and knows that his "great and starry order has fallen at last."

The name Za-Tor sounds suitably Hebraic for such a Qabalistic ceremony (echoing, perhaps, the *Zohar,* the name of the principal scripture of the Qabalah), and Men-Hari's name similarly echoes Hebraic models (even, on a profane level, that of Ben-Hur). Men-Hari's subsequent summoning of demonic forces also employs somewhat Crowleyian, Quabalistic vocabulary, which wouldn't have been out of place in a ceremony of the Order of the Golden Dawn: "Hark ye! Ye timeless ones! Ye elementals of the earth and of the air and of fire and of water, take heed of my commands, I whom am Ipsissimus and to whom is given the power of authority." The hieratic, pseudo–Egyptian poses of the officiating maidens might also have found favor with Crowley, but Men-Hari's subsequent sacrifice of a woman belongs more to the pages of a tabloid newspaper like *The Sun* than the grimoires of the Golden Dawn. As human sacrifices go, however, it's very dramatic: the unfortunate virgin is pierced through the heart by a sword of Damocles.

Hammer's most memorable example of Satanic human sacrifice in full Gothic mode occurs in *Twins of Evil* in which Damien Thomas' Count Karnstein loses patience with the fake Satanists provided for him by his obsequious servant Dietrich (played by Dennis Price). "Your Excellency is pleased with the entertainment?" asks Dietrich. "He's calling up the Devil!"

KARNSTEIN: Well, so can I—or you—but will the Devil come?
DIETRICH: Fresh blood!
KARNSTEIN: The guts of a chicken or a suckling pig. The Devil won't be cheated as easily as that, Dietrich.
DIETRICH: Your Excellency is pleased with the girl?
KARNSTEIN: A peasant bought for a few gold coins. Can you never find anything new? Different?

Just as the cowled high priest is about to sacrifice the obligingly writhing maiden on the slab before him, Karnstein knocks the blade from his grasp and throws everyone out of his quite splendid castle. He then points to the portraits of his illustriously diabolical ancestors. "They knew!" he shouts at Dietrich. "They didn't play at being wicked. They worshipped the Devil and he taught them delights you will never know. Of punishment. Inflicting and receiving it. Of torture and death. Yes, of death and of pleasure beyond the grave, something you could not even comprehend! But I know...." He then sets about raising the Devil himself, this time successfully, if raising the ghost of the vampire Mircalla Karnstein is quite the same as the Devil.

There is another strand of occult cinema which is more pagan or anthropological than Gothic or Crowleyian. It was pioneered in *Eye of the Devil* (dir. J. Lee-Thompson, 1967) and it followed the approach of *The Seventh Victim* by placing its occult goings-on in an apparently everyday setting (even though that setting is a very affluent, upper-class one). The casting of David Niven, as the Marquis Phillippe Montfaucon, in a genre with which he was not normally associated, also helped to "normalize" the opening scenes of the film. However, despite its many visual virtues and imaginatively executed set pieces, this film might have been more successful had it carefully followed Lewton's example and opted for

Opposite, top: "It begins": Christopher Lee as Duc de Richleau in *The Devil Rides Out* (dir. Terence Fisher, 1968). Paul Eddington, Patrick Mower and Sarah Lawson observe the proceedings from behind. *Opposite, bottom:* Filming the ritual invocation scenes of *The Vengeance of She* (dir. Cliff Owen, 1968).

Poster for *Eye of the Devil* (dir. J. Lee Thompson, 1967).

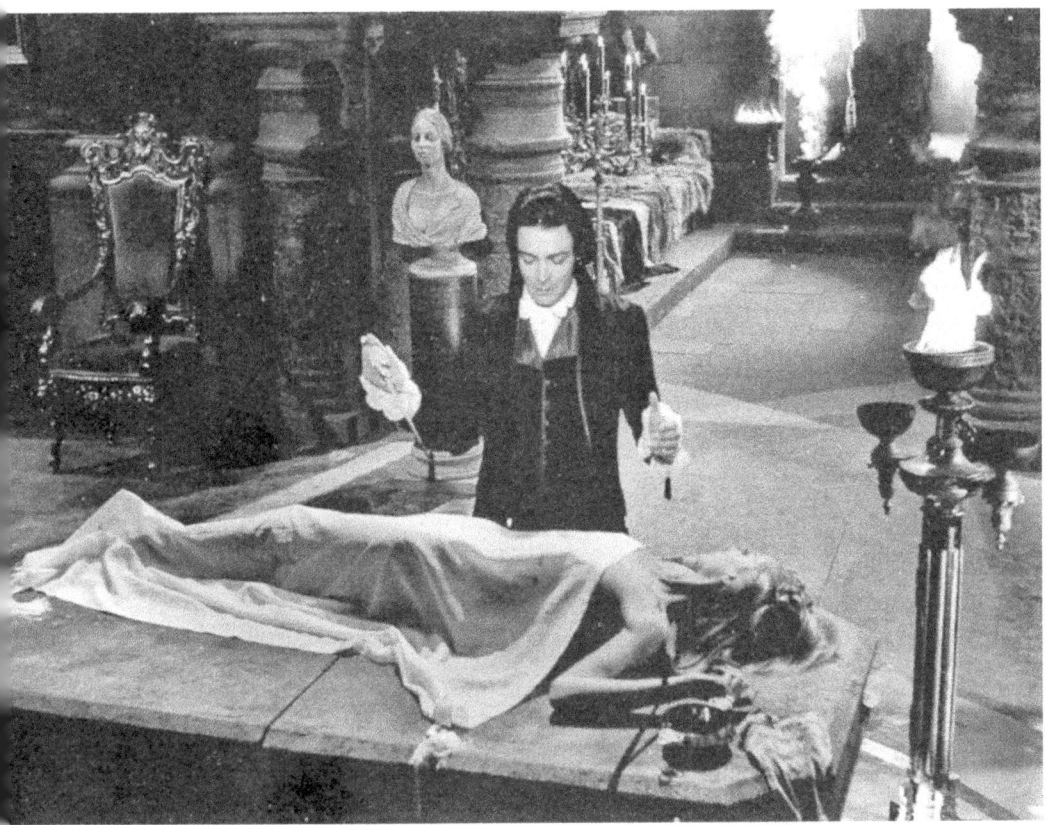

Damien Thomas as Count Karnstein performs his own Black Mass in *Twins of Evil* (dir. John Hough, 1971).

ambiguity rather than the explicit approach it ultimately takes to the subject. Its tale of a vineyard that fails and the sacrifice of its owner (Montfaucon) to ensure a successful harvest the following year, derives from the chapters on "The Corn Spirit" in Frazer's *The Golden Bough*, that vast investigation into why the Priests of Nemi had to defend themselves from those who would slay them and take over their position as King of the Wood. Frazer's exploration of harvest rituals concerned with this myth reveal that

> the identification of the victim with the corn, in other words, the view that he is an embodiment of the spirit of the corn, is brought out in the pains which seem to be taken to secure a physical correspondence between him and the natural object which he embodies or represents. Thus the Mexicans killed young victims for the young corn and old ones for the ripe corn.... Thus the fertilising virtue ascribed to the corn-spirit is shown equally in the savage custom of mixing the victim's blood or ashes with the seed-corn and the European custom of mixing the grain from the last sheaf with the young corn in spring.[38]

The Marquis Montfaucon is similarly sacrificed, and, like a Priest of Nemi, immediately replaced by his successor (in this case, his son). Unlike a Priest of Nemi, however, Montfaucon is a willing victim. He goes to his doom as a thing inevitable and even desirable, and makes no attempt to defend himself.

The problems of making such a story entirely convincing in a modern setting were brilliantly solved by the makers of *The Wicker Man* (dir. Robin Hardy, 1973), which has much the same story of sacrifice to ensure crops (apples rather than grapes in this instance). But the film avoids all explicit magical phenomena, being much more a study of religious belief than a demonstration of magical power. Stephen King's novel *Children of the Corn* unfortunately ignored this lesson, as did its 1984 film adaptation (dir. Fritz Kiersch), opting again for overt supernaturalism in the form of a demonic force called "He Who Walks Behind the Rows [of corn]." However, the cultish children who sacrifice adults to this unspecified, somewhat Lovecraftian corn demon are considerably more frightening than the corn demon itself and could easily have carried the film alone, without supernatural intervention.

While each of these sacrificial films are more *pagan* than Satanic, *Eye of the Devil*, with its imposing French chateau, shadowy goings-on, cowled priests and explicit magic is the most Gothic of the three. By contrast, *Night of the Eagle*, which we mentioned in chapter two, manages to bridge the two approaches by displaying what Frazer defined as "sympathetic magic" rather than truly miraculous magic. For Frazer, sympathetic magic can be either "homeopathic" or "contagious":

> Homeopathic magic is founded on the association of ideas by similarity: contagious magic is founded on the association of ideas by contiguity. Homeopathic magic commits the mistake of assuming that things which resemble each other are the same: contagious magic commits the mistake of assuming that things which have once been in contact with each other are always in contact.... Perhaps the most familiar application of the [homeopathic] principle that like produces like is the attempt which has been made by many peoples in many ages to injure or destroy an enemy by injuring or destroying an image of him, in the belief that, just as the image suffers, so does the man, and that when it perishes he must die.... The most familiar example of Contagious Magic is the magical sympathy which is supposed to exist between a man and any severed portion of his person, as his hair or nails; so that whoever gets possession of human hair or nails may work his will, at any distance, upon the person from whom they were cut.[39]

These are precisely the kinds of magic (or witchcraft) that we encounter in *Night of the Eagle*. In this film, the jealous academic (played by Margaret Johnston) who runs the medical school at which Peter Wyngarde's character has just begun work as a lecturer in anthropology, is everyone's idea of a malevolent anima figure ("an old witch" indeed; she even has a limp, that archetypal sign of the Devil). By means of sympathetic magic she aims to rid herself of this academic competition, but the very means by which she does this (mind over mind) gives the audience the option of interpreting the magical events that do seem to occur (such as the transformation of a stone eagle into a giant living bird) as merely the result of suggestion, hypnosis or induced hallucination. Even the final scene in which Wyngarde's house is burned down "sympathetically" by means of setting a house of cards on fire, could be a coincidence, in much the same way that the storm "summoned" by Karswell in *Night of the Demon* might also be coincidental (though unfortunately the obvious demon that was forced on that film drastically undermines the overall effect of this ambiguity). A similar example of such sympathetic magic occurs in Hammer's *To the Devil a Daughter*, when Beddows' telephone cord is "transformed" into a snake by means of Father Michael's suggestion; but *Eye of the Devil*, like *Night of the Demon*, leaves no room for such ambiguity when it so easily could, as for instance in Odette's transformation of a frog into a dove. This becomes a miracle rather than a possible example of hypnotic suggestion. Ironically, ambiguity would have made the magic more believable.

Frogs, or more specifically toads, also appear in *Psychomania* (dir. Don Sharp, 1972), one of the strangest of British occult films, and consequently one of the most interesting.

The film concerns a group of motorbike Hell's Angels who discover that the secret of eternal life depends upon the strength of one's belief that it is possible to come back from the dead. If you really believe that this is possible, all you have to do is commit suicide, and eternal life is yours for the taking. Consequently, the members of the biker gang (appropriately called "The Living Dead") cheerfully do away with themselves in a variety of ways and subsequently return to cause as much havoc as they can. Only one girl (something of a goody two-shoes, who doesn't take a strong enough overdose) survives to help the police with their inquiries.

This really *is* a Hell's Angels film, a kind of biker's *Paradise Lost* in which Nicky Henson's gang leader, Tom Latham, is a leather-clad version of Milton's Satan and the other bikers play the lesser angels under his command. There are other comparisons one could make with Milton's epic analysis of evil, for Tom discovers the secret of eternal life after spending an afternoon in the strangely deserted room in which his father died. Armed with a strange frog amulet to protect him, he enters this odd occult space where there are unlit candles in sconces on the black walls. The floorboards are black too, and a mirror hangs opposite a window screened by a venetian blind. The effect reminds one of how Milton described Hell as "darkness visible."[40] This room, indeed, appears to be an anteroom of Hell itself. Tom's father, we are told, died in it attempting immortality for himself but he failed due to a few remaining doubts which surfaced just before he died. His spectacles remain on the floor. Tom picks these up, puts them on and sees a vision in the mirror of his mother entering into a pact with the Devil. This pact somehow involves him as well, for his mother holds up his infant self as if in sacrifice.

Having gained the secret, Tom sets out on his Satanic mission. First he kills several people in a pub, and when the other gang members are fully undead they go on to ram-raid a 1970s supermarket. As if that's not enough, they run over a baby in a pram, bring mayhem to a brutalist '70s shopping center (making it even more unpleasant than it already was in purely architectural terms), drive through brick walls and go around "teaching people a lesson" by causing as many road accidents as they can. When some of them are locked up by the police, Tom and his female sidekick liberate them by ram-raiding the police cells. The film is astonishingly antisocial, and even more remarkable in the glee it takes in so being. Director Sharp, like Milton before him, manages to make us sympathize with the Hell's Angels rather than with the forces of law and order.

Indeed, it's revealing to compare Milton's own lines about Satan's mission on earth with what Tom says to his devil-worshipping mother:

Tom: There's lot's to be done. For starters, do you know how many policemen there are? And judges, teachers, preachers, do-gooders?
Shadwell: Do you mean the entire establishment?

He surely does. Milton's Satan, though he expresses himself in somewhat more elevated language, has, as we can see, a very similar agenda:

> [H]ere perhaps
> Some advantageous act may be achieved
> By sudden onset, either with hell fire
> To waste His whole creation, or possess
> All as our own, and drive as we were driven
> The puny habitants; or if not drive,
> Seduce them to our party, that their God

Members of the motorbike gang "The Living Dead" in *Psychomania* (dir. Don Sharp, 1972).

> May prove their foe, and with repenting hand
> Abolish His own works. This would surpass
> Common revenge, and interrupt His joy
> In our confusion, and our joy upraise
> In His disturbance; when His darling sons,
> Hurled headlong to partake with us, shall curse
> Their frail original, and faded bliss,
> Faded so soon.[41]

Beryl Reid realizes that her wayward son has gone too far. (This mother/son relationship intriguingly has certain things in common with the Oedipal one of Baron and Baroness Meinster in *The Brides of Dracula*.) Mrs. Latham may have entered into a pact with the Devil (in the shape of George Sanders' demonic butler, Shadwell) but she now decides that enough is enough and in a curious occult ceremony, played out against the eccentric post-swinging '60s decor of her living room, she allows herself to be turned into a toad so that her mad, bad and motorbiking son will be turned into a standing stone and his reign of terror ended, which is exactly what happens.

The film's last shot of George Sanders being driven away in his sinister Bentley is made rather more poignant by hindsight as it was immediately after making this truly strange but weirdly compelling film that Sanders committed suicide on April 23, 1972, in a hotel in Castelldefels, near Barcelona in Spain. His suicide note read:

> Dear World, I am leaving because I am bored. I feel I have lived long enough. I am leaving you with your worries in this sweet cesspool. Good luck.[42]

Meanwhile, there was still life left in Hammer, and the company's last two Dracula films were far more Satanic than any of their earlier ones. Again, no detail was ignored. As mentioned in chapter three, the elegantly curved bookshelves of Professor Van Helsing's study in *Dracula A.D. 1972* were carefully filled with appropriate volumes. They include Arthur Edward Waite's *The Brotherhood of the Rosy Cross* (1928), *The Occult Arts of Ancient Egypt* by Bernard Brommage (1960), Rollo Ahmed's *The Black Art* (published, with an introduction by Dennis Wheatley, by Jarrolds in 1967), the 1968 Richard Wilhelm–C.G. Jung edition of the *I Ching* and Colin Wilson's then only recently published *The Occult* (1971). Van Helsing also owns Marius Malchus' translation of *The Secret Grimoire of Turiel*, in an edition equally hot off the press at the time, published by S. Weiser in 1971. One year previously, Weiser had also published an edition of Moses Gaster's 1896 classic *The Sword of Moses — An Ancient Book of Magic* and that's on the shelves as well, along with A.E. Wallis Budge's translation of *The Book of the Dead*, C. L'Estrange Ewen's *Witchcraft and Demonianism* (1933), Paul Huson's *Mastering Witchcraft* (1970), the *Treatise on the Black Mass* that Jessica takes down for her "quiet bit of mind-blowing" and the equally well-made fake of *Legend of Dracula the Vampire* by Lawrence Van Helsing.

Johnny Alucard's invocation to bring Dracula back from the grave also contains an impressive list of theologically correct demons, many of whom, naturally enough, feature in Milton's *Paradise Lost*. Johnny first calls upon Andras, grand marquis of Hell, who is said to have thirty legions of demons under his command. His angelic body has the head of an owl or a raven, and he rides upon the back of a black wolf, stirring up discord and rebellion in his wake. Behemoth, whom Johnny calls "arch-devil of the black delights," is also summoned. Medieval demonologists associated Behemoth with gluttony because he is described in the Book of Job as eating grass like an ox. He also has immense strength. Milton described Behemoth as similarly gargantuan:

> Behemoth, biggest born of earth, upheav'd
> His vastness: fleeced the flocks and bleating rose,
> As plants: ambiguous between sea and land
> The river horse and scaly crocodile.[43]

Next, Johnny calls on "Asmodeus, the destroyer," who was originally a Persian demon. In his Hebraic manifestation he is among the highest order of the Seraphim, and he helped to build Solomon's Temple after King Solomon was given a magic ring (by the archangel Michael) which enabled him to summon various demons to assist with the work. Consequently, Johnny's appellation of "destroyer" is perhaps a little unfair, but nonetheless Asmodeus was a high-ranking member of Hell with three heads (a bull, a man and a ram) and who also breathed fire (so perhaps Johnny wasn't so far off after all). Asmodeus was also referred to as one of the seven princes of Hell, each prince equating to one of the seven deadly sins. It was Asmodeus' privilege to preside over Lust.

Johnny describes the next demon, Astaroth, as "friend of all the great lords of Hell." According to the *Pseudomonarchia Daemonum*, the great "Hierarchy of Demons" which formed the appendix of Johann Weyer's *De praestigiis daemonum* of 1577, Astaroth appears in the shape of a foul angel sitting upon an infernal dragon, carrying a viper in his right hand. He also emits a strong stench, from which the magician who summons him must protect himself by holding a magic ring under his nose. Like Professor Zimmer before him, Johnny also calls upon Beelzebub, called "the prince of demons" by St. Matthew. "Bel" or "Baal" means "Lord" and Beelzebub consequently means "Lord of the Flies," the same infernal demon to whom William Golding was referring in his novel of that name. The Jews regarded Beelzebub as the greatest of the demons, and Milton described him as next to Satan in power "and next in crime."[44] Johnny is therefore almost right in saying that Beelzebub is one of the "many names of Satan." Next on his list is Lucifer, a devil of particular importance to theosophists such as Scriabin, because Lucifer, being the bringer of light (he is also the morning star), was a symbol of wisdom and insight. Along with Prometheus, Lucifer became a heroic figure for the composer, as he was for Rudolf Steiner and Madame Blavatsky, who founded a theosophical journal called *Lucifer* in 1887.

Other demons in Johnny's lengthy peroration include Balberith, Hell's secretary and archivist, and Leviathan, the gigantic whale which is impervious to weapons, and which Milton called "the Arch-Fiend." Belpheggor was worshipped in the form of a phallus, and according to medieval legend, after having been sent to earth to investigate human marriage, Belpheggor fled back to Hell grateful that such an institution didn't exist there. As a misogynist, he is an appropriate demon for Johnny to summon just before the sacrifice of the beautiful Caroline Munro to the arch-vampire, but after such a diabolical roll call, Dracula's eventual appearance might be regarded as something of an anticlimax.

The *A.D. 1972* sequel, *The Satanic Rites of Dracula*, also does its very best with the occult *bric-a-brac* of the opening (and recurring) scene of devil worship. This is nothing short of necromancy: a young girl is ritually slain and then brought back to life. Later on, Van Helsing unfurls an impressive chart showing how Satanic activity over the centuries has influenced world history. He also places a great deal of significance on the date of November 23, claiming that it is the Sabbath of the Undead, when the Devil marshals his forces. It is on this date that Dracula intends to unleash the plague bacillus that will destroy humanity. One possible explanation of why November 23 was chosen is that this was on that day in 1963 that the very first *Doctor Who* episode ("Unearthly Child") was seen on BBC television, exactly ten years before the supposed date of the events in *The Satanic Rites of Dracula*. As an established *Doctor Who* scriptwriter, screenwriter Don Houghton may well have been having a private joke here, as, indeed might his entire script, as much of it is derived from ideas he had for *Doctor Who*'s Time Lord villain, The Master. Indeed, at one point in the script of *Dracula A.D. 1972*, Dracula himself is referred to as "The Master." By the time of *Satanic Rites*, Dracula had evolved from a Byronic vampire in the 1958 *Dracula*, through an inverted Christ figure in *Dracula Has Risen from the Grave* and *Taste the Blood of Dracula*, to a version of Milton's Satan, truly living up to the original Rumanian meaning of Vlad Dracul's name, Vlad the Devil, as he sends out the four horsemen of his own created apocalypse to destroy mankind.

Hammer's second attempt at Wheatley occultism, *To the Devil a Daughter* was very different from *The Devil Rides Out*, but no less successful, even though its relation to the book on which it was based became increasingly remote as the script evolved. Wheatley was understandably furious. Christopher Lee's Satanist, Father Michael, proved to be one of his most demonic roles and the film as a whole creates a tangible sense of the demonic, concerned, as it is, with Father Michael's attempt to turn a young nun into the embodiment of Astaroth, one of the demons in Johnny Alucard's demonic roll call. As Richard Verney (played by Richard Widmark) puts it, "Ninety-eight percent of Satanists are nothing but pathetic freaks who get their kicks out of dancing naked in freezing churchyards and use the Devil for getting some sex, but then there's that other two percent. I'm not so sure about them." It's not long before Verney realizes that he's dealing with that other two percent, and so does the audience of this extremely well made film. Its unnervingly subdued and cerebral ending is nowhere near as much of a disaster as many people (including Lee) have insisted. Lee, following very much in the footsteps of his friend Wheatley, was also keen to point out what he regarded as the underlying reality of the story:

> It is not a horror film in the sense that the term is normally used. It is terrifying, but not fantasy. Behind the story lies a dreadful truth. The cinema is a reflection of life and the perfect medium to show what lies beneath the surface attraction of dabbling in witchcraft. As an actor, what better reason could I have for appearing in a film that will, I hope, shock people by showing them how much of this does go on and how terrible it is.[45]

To the Devil a Daughter successfully attempts a blend of modern, *Seventh Victim*–style occultism with more Gothic elements derived from Matthew Lewis: there is a scene filmed in St. Botolph's Church in the village of Shenley, Hertfordshire, replete with Gothic arches, in which Anthony Valentine spontaneously combusts, and which also serves as the backdrop for the demonic birth of Catherine (Nastassja Kinski). The finale is set in the flint, neo-classical Dashwood Mausoleum just outside West Wycombe, which nicely contrasts with the trendy London settings in which much of the other action takes place. In this respect alone, Peter Sykes' stylish conclusion to Hammer's final horror film production tidily sums up the cinematic development of Gothic occultism.

A somewhat different approach to the occult had also emerged at this time, however. *The Exorcist* (dir. William Friedkin, 1973) brought larger budgets and mainstream marketing to the previously less respectable subject of demonic possession. Its style was certainly graphic but definitely not Gothic. Neither did its then contemporary setting enjoy the ambiguity of *The Seventh Victim*. Demonic power is far more corporeally manifest here than at any other time in cinematic history and this formed the basic novelty and consequent box office success of this film. The emphasis of *The Exorcist* is also very strongly Christian (and Catholic at that) rather than Crowlean. Having said that, it's very different from the Gothic Catholicism of a film like Hammer's *Dracula Has Risen from the Grave*. With the important exception of Father Shandor in *Dracula, Prince of Darkness,* the clerics in Hammer films are mere bystanders: think of the priest in *The Kiss of the Vampire* (played by Noel Howlett) who does nothing at all. It's Professor Zimmer inside his pentagram who defeats the forces of evil in that film, not the priest. The same can be said of Christopher Lee's Duc de Richleau in *The Devil Rides Out* in which there are no ecclesiastical figures at all. Father Michael in *To the Devil a Daughter* is, of course, on quite the other side. The Duc de Richleau figure in that film is Widmark's very secular author; but in *The Exorcist* it is Max von Sydow's priest who is in charge. Suburbia also replaces stately homes or Gothic castles as a setting. Indeed, the real setting of *The Exorcist* is the body of the possessed girl Regan (played by Linda Blair), in which the evil spirit takes up residence. The film is consequently more about body horror than anything else. The host of slasher flicks that emerged in the 1980s can be traced back to the ordeals undergone by Blair in this film.

Richard Donner's *The Omen*, which followed in 1976, took a slightly more Gothic line. For a start the film is mostly set in England, which brings a Gothic resonance to the proceedings. There is also a creepy Italian graveyard, cowled monks and dark corridors from which Billie Whitelaw's apostate of Hell can emerge. The grand finale even takes place in a church, on the altar of which Gregory Peck attempts to kill his demonic son; but like *The Exorcist*, *The Omen* is technically a series of physical horrors strung together by an occult premise. In this respect, *The Omen* resembles Hammer's *Hands of the Ripper* (dir. Peter Sasdy, 1971) in which the Ripper's daughter Anna (played by Angharad Rees) executes a variety of nasty killings while supposedly under the influence of her dead father's spirit. As with *The Exorcist,* the Catholic rather than Crowlean emphasis of *The Omen* is central. Patrick Troughton's Irish priest, who knows what's afoot, is eventually done away with, but the strongly Christian drive of the film remains. It's true that it's left to Peck's American senator rather than a freelance occultist to try (and fail) to stop the Devil, but one might almost go so far as to claim that both *The Exorcist* and *The Omen* are responses to the evangelical Christianity which appeared at a time when, in reaction to the hippie/Crowley/Hammer–orientated '60s, neo-conservative politics in America were just beginning to emerge.[46]

In contrast to the new wave of occult horror from the States, Hammer nonetheless had one more old-fashioned occult thriller up its sleeve. In "Guardian of the Abyss," the episode from Hammer's *Hammer House of Horror* television series already mentioned in chapter six, John Carson reprised his hypnosis scene from *The Plague of the Zombies,* this time even more successfully conveying the power of mind over mind. Carson's Charles Randolph is a black magician intent on working the Choronzon ritual. Randolph claims that no magician or occultist has ever succeeded in raising this demon before, but Aleister Crowley (on whom Randolph, inevitably, was partly based) claimed that he had. In his *Confessions,* Crowley described Choronzon as "The Dweller in the Abyss,"

> but he is not really an individual. The Abyss is empty of being; it is filled with all possible forms, each equally inane, each therefore evil in the only true sense of the word — that is, meaningless but malignant, in so far as it craves to become real. These forms swirl senselessly into haphazard heaps like dust devils, and each such chance aggregation asserts itself to be an individual and shrieks, "I am I!" though aware all the time that its elements have no true bond; so

Choronzon appears in "The Guardian of the Abyss" (dir. Don Sharp, 1980).

Simon Callow as Aleister Crowley in the poster for *Chemical Wedding* (dir. Julian Doyle, 2008).

that the slightest disturbance dissipates the delusions just as a horseman, meeting a dust-devil, brings it in showers of sand to the earth.[47]

Crowley goes on to describe the several ways in which Choronzon appeared to him and even managed to attack his companion in the form of a naked savage through a gap in magic circle that protected them.

In "Guardian of the Abyss," Choronzon appears in only one form, as a horned, hideous demon; but before that, Randolph must reclaim the young woman, Allison, who is to be sacrificed to it. The latter was played by Rosalind Landor, who had played Peggy in *The Devil Rides Out*. Having escaped from Randolph's clutches, she takes refuge with Michael Roberts, an antiques dealer (played by Ray Lonnen), but Randolph discovers where she's hiding and, having spent the night trying to make her kill the antiques dealer by telepathic means, he pays a visit the following morning.

Dressed in the same suave manner as Charles Gray's Mocata, in a three-piece suit with a crisp white handkerchief in his jacket pocket and a neatly knotted gray silk tie, Randolph sits down and crosses his legs (again like Mocata). The camera then zooms towards his face as he begins to hypnotize Roberts. He tilts his head in sinister fashion as he asks for a glass of wine. Then he requests a little dry bread, and finally a little salt to go with the bread; but just as he's about to consume this humble feast, Allison rushes in and hurls the tray to the floor: "Don't you know you must never give a black magician bread or wine or salt in your own home?" she shrieks. Obviously a cup of tea would have been much safer. Occultism, however, has never attracted cinematic satirists in the way that pure Gothic has.

An uneasy balance between satire and straightforward Satanism occurred in 2008 with *Chemical Wedding* (dir. Julian Doyle), in which the personality of Crowley is transferred into contemporary university academic Oliver Haddo (played by Simon Callow), who then causes mayhem on the university campus. Screenwriter Bruce Dickinson originally planned an adaptation of Maugham's *The Magician* (hence the use of Haddo's name) but was forced to abandon a period setting for budgetary reasons. Neither could he afford a biopic of Crowley's life, but by bringing Crowley up to date in 2008, the project did at last become financially viable. Dickinson's professed aim was to make a film about Crowley, but whatever else it is (and there is much to enjoy here despite considerable narrative incoherence), *Chemical Wedding* is no more a film about Crowley than was Maugham's *The Magician*. Despite a truly disturbing performance by Callow as the reincarnated Beast, the film falls into the trap of all the other fictionalized versions of Crowley's persona, presenting a sensationalized tabloid newspaper impression of what Crowley stood for, rather than the more interesting ideas and magickal systems he developed. Simply repeating "Do What Thou Wilt" and "Love Is the Law. Love Under Will" doesn't, unfortunately, get us very far. The film's string of Satanic murders also betrays the screenplay's Dennis Wheatley origins, and the introduction of quantum physics into the equation takes *Chemical Wedding* into the realm of science fiction, a genre that isn't strictly relevant to this study of Gothic. There is, however, a deal of knowing Gothic satire in *Chemical Wedding*. Jud Charlton plays Victor Newman, a character based on the real-life Victor Neuberg, as a parody of Ygor in the Universal Frankenstein films, and Callow's immensely impressive Crowley recites Crowley's satire on Hamlet ("To pee or not pee") before taking out his penis and urinating over the undergraduates in the front row of a lecture hall, in the film's most striking moment. Our next and final chapter is in similar satirical mood.

Eleven

Satire

The fact that fang-in-neck can so easily become tongue-in-cheek was a danger of which both Peter Cushing and Christopher Lee were well aware when embarking on their serious approach to fantasy roles for Hammer. So too were Boris Karloff and Bela Lugosi for their Universal horrors. There are others who find it impossible to suspend their disbelief, and it's true that to engage with the Romantic, mythical and fairy tale subjects of the genre, one does need to have sufficiently escaped the "Shades of the prison-house" mentioned by Wordsworth in his ode "Intimations of Immortality from Recollections of Early Childhood." So many adults, corrupted by what Wordsworth terms "the light of common day," remain childish for all their cynicism but it's perhaps only the childlike who can really respond to Gothic romance. The suspension of disbelief can lead one to some very nourishing psychological places, which are denied to social realism and comedies of manners; but if one's life seems irredeemably prosaic, a Gothic horror film will inevitably seem to be a complete waste of time. The same could be said of any non-naturalistic genre. The improbabilities of opera and Wagnerian music-drama, their often mythical narratives and emotional rather than realistic landscapes, attract similar incomprehension from the uninitiated. When I watch Gothic horror on my own, I am so absorbed in the conventions of its emotional landscape that nothing seems absurd, but if I watch the same film in the company of someone less sympathetic, its absurdities are exposed and its nourishment is poisoned. The same thing happens in dreams. When we are locked in the dream as we dream it, everything seems perfectly logical and psychologically rewarding, if also possibly unnerving; but a conscious analysis of it destroys it completely. What those who have no time for low-budget horror films forget is that a large part of the unconscious mind operates on similar lines to such films.

Having said that, there are some even more unfortunate individuals who are so attuned to their alternative worlds that they cannot tolerate any kind of lampoon. For them, Anna Russell's satire on Wagner's *Der Ring des Nibelung* is forbidden territory. Russell's description of Wotan as "a crashing bore" applies equally well to them. Disciples of Gothic can also be rather too devoted, but sensitively done, there's nothing better than a send-up, and the best satires are always the affectionate ones. Vincent Price's straight performances always had a tendency to totter on the brink of self-parody, so when he lets himself go in films that send up his Gothic image, such as *The Raven* (dir. Roger Corman, 1963) and *Madhouse* (dir. Jim Clark, 1974), he is perhaps even more successful than in his mastery of such neurasthenic characters such as Roderick Usher and Verden Fell. The grotesquely comic (and very bloody) story of an unfashionable actor manager who murders his unsympathetic critics along Shakespearean lines in *Theater of Death* (dir. Douglas Hickox, 1973) gave Price the perfect opportunity to display his full performance range, along with a perfectly legitimate reason for overacting.

The outlook of Gothic romance and the symbolist aesthetic into which it evolved was, as we have seen, primarily antisocial. Such an outlook interpreted the world from the point of view of the isolated individual, the anti-hero, the monster, the outcast, the aesthete. Thrust into the hurly-burly of a day-to-day social context, such characters inevitably run the risk of appearing absurd, a process that was duly noted by D.H. Lawrence, who championed the realistic novel over all other literary forms:

> In a novel, everything is relative to everything else…. You can fool nearly every other medium. You can make a poem pietistic, and still it will be a poem. You can write *Hamlet* in drama: if you wrote him in a novel, he'd be half comic, or a trifle suspicious: a suspicious character, like Dostoevsky's Idiot. Somehow you sweep the ground a bit too clear in the poem or the drama, and you let the human Word fly a bit too freely. Now in a novel there's always a tom-cat, a black tom-cat that pounces on the white dove of the Word, if the dove doesn't watch it: and there's a banana-skin to trip on: and you know there's a water-closet on the premises. All these things help to keep the balance.[1]

Gothic romance never shows one the water closet, and though there are plenty of banana skins on the floor, good actors do their best to avoid them. Satirists, on the other hand, try to tread on as many as possible, and throw down even more, opening the water closet for all to see. In a satire, all forms of narcissism, neurasthenia, power complexes, and other antisocial characteristics become, like Hamlet in a novel of *Hamlet*, deeply suspicious, for satire has a relentless urge to *socialize* such behavior. The American comic writer Thornton Wilder immediately took this approach with the "sensitive" Elbert Hughes in his novel *Theophilus North* (1974). The eponymous hero of this novel describes Elbert as

> a reedy youth, barely twenty-five, belonging to that often wearisome category of human beings known as "sensitive." This adjective once meant intensely aware of aesthetic and spiritual values; then it took on a sense of someone quick to resent slights; recently it has become a euphemism for someone incapable of coping with even the smaller demands of our daily practical life. Elbert chiefly fulfilled the third description.[2]

Elbert is also a great fan of Edgar Allan Poe. "There's a lot about graves and tombs in Poe's writings. He's my favorite writer that ever lived," he says.[3] Wilder's approach here could be said to be a direct satire on the narrator of H.P. Lovecraft–C.M. Eddy's once notorious necrophiliac tale "The Loved Dead" (1924), who describes himself thusly: "Strictly ascetic, wan, pallid, undersized, and subject to protracted spells of morbid moroseness, I was ostracized by the healthy, normal youngsters of my own age. They dubbed me a spoilsport, an 'old maid,' because I had no interest in the rough, childish games they played, or any stamina to participate in them, had I so desired."[4] Wilder's jovial impatience with this type of character had been embedded in Gothic satire virtually since the inception of the Gothic romance. One of the most affectionate satires of the Gothic Romantic individual can be found in Thomas Love Peacock's *Nightmare Abbey* (1818), in which Peacock sent up, among others, his friend Shelley, a caricature of whom appears in the book as Scythrop Glowry. Scythrop inhabits a tower on the estate of Nightmare Abbey, a conceit that so delighted Shelley that he often referred to himself as Scythrop, and when in Valsovano in Italy he was delighted to find that the little country house he rented there also had a tower not unlike like Scythrop's, which he immediately decided to use as a study.[5] Scythrop's father has a butler called Raven, a steward called Crow and a valet called Skellet. His grooms are called Mattocks and Graves, and Mr. Glowly himself is horrified by round ruddy faces and laughing eyes, for he has a "very fine sense of the grim and the tearful."

> No one could relate a dismal story with so many minutiae of supererogatory wretchedness. No one could call up a *raw-head and bloody-bones* with so many adjuncts and circumstances of ghastliness. Mystery was his mental element. He lived in the midst of that visionary world in which nothing is but what is not. He dreamed with his eyes open, and saw ghosts dancing round him at noontide.[6]

Rather like Vincent Price's Verden Fell in *The Tomb of Ligeia*, Mr. Glowry has "plunged into the central opacity of Kantian metaphysics, and lay *perdu* several years in transcendental darkness, till the common daylight of common sense became intolerable to his eyes."[7]

Common sense was also the watchword of one of Gothic romance's most influential satirists, Jane Austen. It's important to remember, however, that the target of Austen's satire in *Northanger Abbey* (1803) wasn't so much the genre of Gothic romance as its obsessively fanatical and often ill-informed readers, the ones, indeed, who had no sense of humor. Obsessive film fans today (not to mention humorless Wagnerians) are no different from Catherine Morland's fanatical insistence that the novels her friend Isabella has lined up for them both to read "are all horrid." The gossip between them about the suspenseful happenings in *The Mysteries of Udolpho* is just the same as that of horror fans at a convention nearly two hundred years later. Austen isn't just annoyed by this kind of thing, as a similar kind of writer today might express annoyance at TV audiences thinking the characters in a soap opera are real people; she also sees such behavior as socially dangerous. Her point is emphasized in the scene in which Catherine deeply offends the sympathetic Mr. Tilney by visiting his dead mother's room, in the ridiculous belief that the elder Mrs. Tilney had met a "Gothic" rather than perfectly natural end. Mr. Tilney is given Austen's own personal feelings to speak at this point:

> Dear Miss Morland, consider the dreadful nature of the suspicions you have entertained. What have you been judging from? Remember the country and the age in which you live. Remember that we are English, that we are Christians. Consult your own understanding, your own sense of the probable, your own observation of what is passing around you. Does our education prepare us for such atrocities? Do our laws connive at them? Could they be perpetrated without being known, in a country like this, where social and literary intercourse is on such a footing; where every man is surrounded by a neighbourhood of voluntary spies, and where roads and newspapers lay everything open? Dearest Miss Morland, what ideas have you been admitting?[8]

By this time, Austen has already debunked the absurdities of Catherine's obsession, most famously with the celebrated discovery of what turns out to be a laundry list in an old chest in her bedroom at Northanger Abbey. But even before that scene, Austen has provided an argument *in favor* of Gothic romance if experienced as part of a balanced program of reading. Again, Mr. Tilney and his sensible sister are Austen's spokespeople here:

> The person, be it gentleman or lady, who has not pleasure in a good novel, must be intolerably stupid. I have read all Mrs. Radcliffe's works, and most of them with great pleasure. The Mysteries of Udolpho, when I had once begun it, I could not lay down again; — I remember finishing it in two days — my hair standing on end the whole time.[9]

But when Mr. Tilney's sister adds that she also enjoys reading history, Catherine is somewhat dismayed. It has never occurred to her to broaden her literary horizons.

Of course, one needs to be conversant with a thing before being able to satirize it successfully. Ineffective satire comes from misunderstanding, or (worse) lack of affection, which is why Mel Brooks' *Young Frankenstein* (1974) is a hilarious *homage*, while *Abbott and Costello Meet Frankenstein* (dir. Charles Barton, 1948), despite the fact that the latter was made by the same studio who created the first great wave of Hollywood horror classics, was more of a commercially speculative spoof. Having said that, *Young Frankenstein* has its less effective moments, while there are some really good lines in the Abbott and Costello film:

> TALBOT: You don't understand. Every night when the moon is full, I turn into a wolf.
> COSTELLO: You and fifty million other guys.

In Abbott and Costello's later encounter with the Mummy, Bud Abbott asks, "How stupid can you get?" to which Lou Costello replies, "How stupid do you want me to be?" Well, satires can indeed be very stupid, but so can the kind of films they are lampooning. The Abbott and Costello series worked because all the horror stars who appeared in them played their monsters straight, but sometimes the cruelest satire is when a straight performance is unintentionally comedic in its effect. Whether that happens or not largely depends on one's personal tolerance for such things. Bela Lugosi's first entrance as Dracula has been sent up a thousand times, and it *is* dangerously close to self-parody if looked at from the wrong point of view. Christopher Lee was nervous about appearing in *The Satanic Rites of Dracula*, which was originally to be called *Dracula Is Dead and Well and Living in London*, a comic title for a straight-faced film in which the count has become a property developer with a phony Russian accent; but he had more to worry about in the earlier *Scars of Dracula*, which he rightly described as "truly feeble":

> Even the Hammer makeup for once was tepid. It's one thing to look like death warmed up, quite another to look unhealthy. I was a pantomime figure. Everything was over the top, especially the giant bat whose electrically motored wings flapped with slow deliberation as if it were doing morning exercises.[10]

Hammer didn't intentionally send itself up until *The Horror of Frankenstein* (dir. Jimmy Sangster, 1970) in which Dave Prowse's Creature makes a rude V sign, and "Carry On"–style jokes about Kate O'Mara's cleavage abound. Lee himself made only two intentionally satirical vampire films and neither were for British companies. The first, *Tempi duri per i vampiri* (dir. Stefano Vanzina, 1959), was made shortly after Hammer's inaugural *Dracula*, and cast Lee as a Dracula substitute called Baron Roderigo de Braumfürten. The film itself wasn't very funny and neither was Lee, but that was intentional on Lee's part at least, as he played Braumfürten completely straight, following the approach of the old Abbott and Costello monster comedies. Lee was unhappy about the title of his other vampire comedy *Dracula père et fils* (dir. Edouard Molinaro, 1976):

> It's totally misleading. I do not play the part of Dracula in the picture.... The reason I did it was not to parody myself, which I do not do, but because by doing this I can close the door very firmly on the vampire. Let's put it that way. And I feel this is my last word on the subject, if I may say so.[11]

"I refuse to feed you out of a bottle," Lee's vampire insists to his vampire son. "You're 116 years old and without your first victim!"

The other difficulty with sending up Gothic horror is that in attempting to do so, one can make an unintentionally serious movie. This was a trapdoor which Roman Polanski tried to avoid falling through in *The Fearless Vampire Killers* (1967), otherwise known as *Dance of the Vampires*. It was an obvious *homage* to Hammer's *The Kiss of the Vampire*; no

Gothic vampire film, in color at least, had ever before enjoyed such spectacular sets as the ones that grace Polanski's lavish production. The salon of Castle Krolock stretches back in a faded Baroque splendor that would have been the envy of Terence Fisher and Bernard Robinson; and the snowy fairy tale landscapes of the exteriors are truly sublime, creating a haunting, magical atmosphere, amidst which many of the jokes seem to get in the way. Classic one-liners (such as Alfie Bass's Jewish vampire laughing, "Have you got the wrong vampire!" when shown a crucifix) survive, and the encounter with Count von Krolock's gay vampire son is a positive gem. But the comedy is often very heavy-handed and the high production values make one rather wish that everything had been Hammered home with a straight face all the way through.

Comedy, however, was always an integral part of Gothic romance. The garrulous servants we meet in Walpole's *The Castle of Otranto* and Radcliffe's *The Mysteries of Udolpho* formed a necessary series of breathers amidst the tension and were ultimately derived from the example of Shakespeare, in particular the scene in the third act of *Macbeth* when the Porter takes an inordinate amount of time to answer the knocking on the castle gate:

> Here's a knocking indeed! If a man were porter of hell-gate he should have old turning the key [*Knocking within.*] Knock, knock, knock! Who's there, i' the name of Beelzebub? Here's a farmer that hanged himself on the expectation of plenty: come in time; have napkins enough about you; here you'll sweat for't [*Knocking within.*] Knock, knock! Who's there i' the other devil's name![12]

Even more Gothic is the celebrated gravediggers' scene in *Hamlet*, the black humor of which leads to Hamlet's famous "Alas, poor Yorick" soliloquy. Two pedantic and loquacious clowns perform this scene; Ann Radcliffe must have had them in mind when writing the dialogue for the equally loquacious and pedantic servants in her Gothic novels. The clowns are preparing the grave of Ophelia, who has drowned herself.

"Is she to be buried in Christian burial that willfully seeks her own salvation?" asks the first clown.

> SECOND CLOWN: I tell thee she is; and therefore make her grave straight: the crowner hath sat on her, and finds it Christian burial.
> FIRST CLOWN: How can that be, unless she drowned herself in her own defence?
> SECOND CLOWN: Why, 'tis found so.
> SECOND CLOWN : It must be *se offendendo*; it cannot be else. For here lies the point: if I drown myself wittingly it argues an act; and an act hath three branches; it is, to act, to do, and to perform: argal, she drowned herself wittingly.
> SECOND CLOWN : Nay, but hear you, goodman delver —
> FIRST CLOWN: Give me leave. Here lies water; good; here stands the man; good; if the man go to this water, and drown himself, it is, will he, nill he, he goes; mark you that? but if the water come to him, and drown him, he drowns not himself: argal, he that is not guilty of his own death shortens not his own life.[13]

Horace Walpole was also indebted to Shakespeare for his talkative servants who lose the thread of their arguments through multiple asides. In *The Castle of Otranto*, the servant Bianca infuriates Manfred with her interminable tale of a supernatural happening:

> I believe I look very pale; I shall be better when I have recovered myself.—I was going to my lady Isabella's chamber by his highness's order—We do not want the circumstances, interrupted Manfred: since his highness will have it so, proceed; but be brief.—Lord, your highness thwarts one so! replied Bianca—I fear my hair—I am sure I never in my life—Well! as I was telling your greatness, I was going by his highness's order to my lady Isabella's chamber: she lies in the watchet-coloured chamber, on the right hand, one pair of stairs: so when I came to the great

stairs—I was looking on his highness's present here. Grant me patience! said Manfred, will this wench never come to the point?[14]

The following extract from Radcliffe's *Romance of the Forest* demonstrates a similar kind of servant:

> "As I was saying, Ma'mselle, Monday night, when the Marquis slept here, you know he sat up very late, and I can guess, perhaps, the reason of that. Strange things came out, but it is not my business to tell all I think."
> "Pray do speak to the purpose," said Adeline impatiently, "what is this danger which you say threatens me? Be quick, or we shall be observed."
> "Danger enough, Ma'mselle," replied Peter, "if you knew all, and when you do, what will it signify, for you can't help yourself. But that's neither here nor there: I was resolved to tell you, though I may repent it."
> "Or rather you are resolved not to tell me," said Adeline; "for you have made no progress towards it. But what did you mean? You were speaking of the Marquis."[15]

The early Universal horrors trod this path very cautiously. *Dracula*, indeed, has no comic asides. Neither does *The Mummy*, though James Whale's way with *Frankenstein* is nothing if not a black joke all the way through. Whale was very much aware, when making *Bride of Frankenstein*, that the trick with this kind of approach was, as his biographer Mark Gatiss puts it, "to satisfy those eager for genuine horror, while at the same time getting away with as much tongue-in-cheek campery as he could."[16] The film does encounter the danger of going off in a completely different direction during the scene in which Dr. Pretorius (Ernest Thesiger) displays his miniature human creatures, but for the most part Whale achieves exactly what he aimed for. Indeed, Thesiger's waspish Dr. Pretorius is first introduced to us in a manner that reminds us of the knocking at the gate in *Macbeth*. As he stands outside in a lashing gale, the sound of his insistent hammering at the door of Castle Frankenstein reverberates through Charles D. Hall's spectacularly Gothic sets. The epitome of a camp queen before such terminology was coined, Pretorius' subsequent delivery of the line that explains how he was "booted out" of university ("booted, my dear baron, is the word, for knowing too much") is delivered in a manner that leaves us in no doubt as to the nature of his sexual orientation.

Whale also made sure that all the characters' weaknesses are exposed. Only Karloff's tragic Monster is treated with respect. He is the ultimate outsider, with whom the homosexual, ex-pat and upwardly mobile Whale could so readily identify. Taunted by terrified and incomprehending villagers, the Monster is an example of what would nowadays be called a gay icon, but with none of the sniggering innuendo of the gay vampire in Polanski's *The Fearless Vampire Killers*. Whale's irreverent use of Christian imagery adds further weight to the Monster's Christ-like suffering. (At one point in *Bride of Frankenstein*, Karloff is virtually crucified.)

Hammer was also well aware of the importance of the Shakespearean comic interlude. In a scene midway through *The Curse of Frankenstein* we are treated to a party thrown by Frankenstein to celebrate his marriage to Elizabeth (Hazel Court). The camera pans over to the burgomeister, played by Andrew Leigh, who can't resist refilling his glass with punch while making imaginary toasts. He is eventually interrupted by Ann Blake, who plays his wife:

BURGOMEISTER: To the bride and groom ... to the happy couple ... to the bridesmaids...
WIFE: What are you jibbering about?
BURGOMEISTER: I was just rehearsing my speech, my dear.

WIFE: Fool. That's not until tomorrow, after the wedding.
BURGOMEISTER: Yes, I know, my dear, but these things take time.
WIFE: Come along, we're going.
BURGOMEISTER: So soon?
WIFE: [*Making him put down the glass*] Come on!

Hammer's comic interludes were frequently performed by Miles Malleson and Michael Ripper, the company's two resident comedians. In the 1958 *Dracula*, Malleson temporarily lightens the mood as an absent-minded undertaker who shows Van Helsing and Arthur Holmwood around his establishment in search of Dracula's coffin:

Perhaps you better lead the way. I know these steps—they can be dangerous...yes...we don't want to have an accident. No, we don't! But, do you know, an old man came here once to see his dear departed and he fell down these stairs. [*Laughs*] It was quite amusing, yes! He came to pay his last respects and he remained to share them. [*Laughs again*] Quite amusing it was, really. [*Drums on the lid of a coffin*] Now, where are, where are we, where are we?

George Benson provided additional humor in the same film as a permanently half-dressed and easily bribable frontier official:

FRONTIER OFFICIAL: You've got to have permission from the ministry in writing. I have my orders and I must obey them. It is laid down in the government regulations that under no circumstances...
[*Holmwood produces a banknote and pushes it onto the receipt spike on the desk, but the official ignores it.*]
FRONTIER OFFICIAL: ...under no circumstances can an unauthorized person be permitted to examine...
[*Holmwood lays down another banknote, and the official begins to change his mind.*]
FRONTIER OFFICIAL: Of course, in the case of an emergency, we do sometimes make an exception...

In *The Mummy*, we are treated to two drunken carters who have been hired to transport the Mummy to its new home.

"A man's best friend is a horse," says one, as he gets ready for the journey.

"It's a dog," says his mate.

"It's a horse. I'm not *that* drunk."

Michael Ripper supplied another comic cameo in this film. He's just seen the bandaged horror on his way to the pub: "Hey, Bill, give me a whiskey," he gasps as he staggers up to the bar. "Make it a large one.... I've seen the like tonight that mortal eyes shouldn't look at."

"You've been around to Molly O'Grady's again," smirks the barman.

Ripper repeated this type (though rather more of an old soak this time) in *The Curse of the Werewolf*, for which he donned a white powdered wig and a green caped coat. "It was no ordinary wolf, gentlemen," he boasts, swaying around the bar. "No ordinary wolf would tear out the throat and drain blood. Every last drop."

Ripper also joined forces with Malleson in *The Brides of Dracula*. Ripper opens the film as the boggle-eyed coachman who drives Yvonne Monlaur's Marianne to the ladies' finishing school where she's to take up her new post. Ripper doesn't have much dialogue in these scenes, but his comic appearance nicely counterpoints the Gothic dankness of the scene in question. Later, Malleson appears as the hypochondriac Dr. Tobler, who's preparing to take an inhalation and has grafted the assistance of Vera Cook, who plays the landlord's wife. "Now, my good woman, the towel!" he begins. "That's right! Right over my head, and don't you pay any attention to anything I may say."

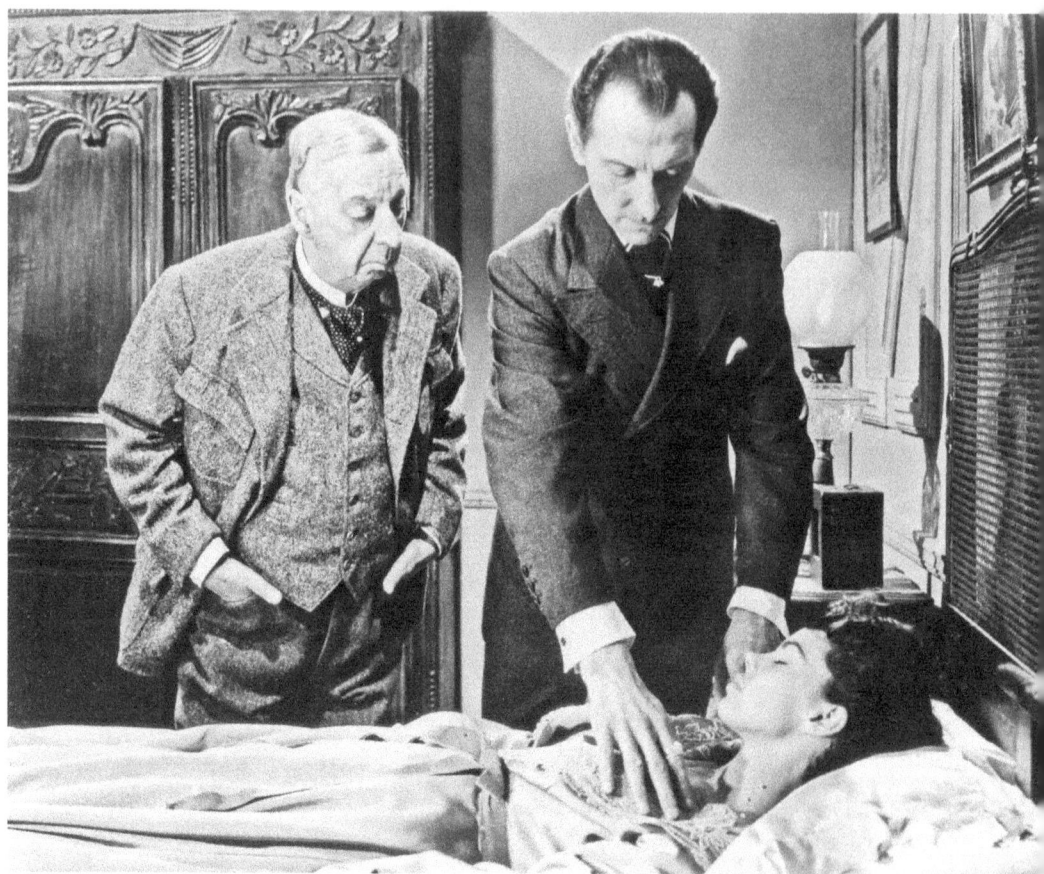

Miles Malleson peers over Peter Cushings's shoulder as he attends to Andrée Melly in *The Brides of Dracula* (dir. Terence Fisher, 1960).

Tobler then goes on to make a dreadful fuss, complaining that he can't breathe, and so the landlord's wife lifts off the towel. Annoyed, Tobler insists on having another try, but the landlady loses patience: "You see after yourself. I've got my living to earn." Tobler is dumbfounded for a moment, then walks over to the priest who's eating at another table.

> TOBLER: What doctors have to put up with. First it's you clericals, Father, with your monolithic superstitions—peasants like her with her troglodyte indifference. [*Thinks about the dead girl he's been called in to inspect.*] Of course, she may have died of heart failure. I mean, the heart may have just slowed down and stopped. Well, that's clearly a case for *nux vomica*. [*He swallows some of this medication.*] Or perhaps it galloped itself to a standstill? Well, in that case: *digitalis*. [*He swallows some of this.*] And, of course, always and all the time, *valerian* to quieten the nerves. [*Swallows some valerian and washes it down with a large drink. Looks at the empty glass.*] Oh, I say, I haven't drunk you out of house and home?
> PRIEST: But if the patient is dead, what's the use of all these concoctions?
> TOBLER: Precautions are better than cure, Father. By doing this, I've survived a *vast* number of other people's deaths, and I mean to survive a great many more.

When Van Helsing appears, Tobler asks if he might put his specialist fees "on my own little account." They set off to their next case together, Tobler in a "comic" blue check caped coat, that makes an amusing contrast with Van Helsing's sober dark blue overcoat with its elegant fur-trimmed collar. "I'll leave everything to you," Tobler adds later. "Except the fee, of course!" Like the burgomaster in *The Curse of Frankenstein*, Tobler is also fond of a tipple and sips sherry at every opportunity.

Hammer continued to pepper their films with such comic cameos. One of their most garrulous servants appears in *Hands of the Ripper*, in which Marjorie Rhodes plays Mrs. Bryant, the housekeeper of Eric Porter's Dr. Pritchard. In the best Radcliffe tradition she fusses to such an extent that Pritchard gets visibly annoyed with her. "I'm only a singular person," she complains, when asked to be in two places at one time.

There are many more Hammer chuckles along the way: the grotesque rat-catcher of Patrick Troughton in *The Phantom of the Opera*; Thorley Walters' snuff-sniffing, irascible police inspector in *Frankenstein Must Be Destroyed* (not to mention Walters' much more sympathetic "muddle-headed" Dr. Hertz in *Frankenstein Created Woman*); the frustrated fabric salesman in *The Curse of the Mummy's Tomb* who despairs of ever gaining the attention of Fred Clark's impresario during the preparation of the Mummy's unveiling; Bernard Cribbins' comic valet Job in *She*; Michael Ripper's worried, fussy, shortsighted and lonely Longbarrow in *The Mummy's Shroud*. Sometimes the comedy was reduced to single lines in otherwise steadfastly serious epics such as *The Devil Rides Out* in which Rosalyn Landor plays Peggy, the daughter of Richard and Marie Eaton. She's terribly excited about the arrival of Uncle Rex at their home in the country. Rex is bringing Tanith to stay with the family to put her out of the clutches of the Satanist Mocata, but Tanith is still under Mocata's control and as soon as Rex arrives and gets out of the car to say, "Hello," Tanith slides over into the driving seat and speeds away. Rex borrows Richard Eaton's car and hurtles after her. "He didn't stay long, did he?" says a crestfallen Peggy in the film's only intentionally comic moment. (Christopher Lee did, however, confess to rather enjoying his line, "Yes, take any of them," when Rex asks if he can borrow one of his cars a few scenes earlier on.)

In 1968, just before filming *The Devil Rides Out*, Hammer made *The Anniversary* (dir. Roy Ward Baker), starring Bette Davis in her most gruesomely comic mode as a vicious widow who enjoys humiliating the various members of her dysfunctional family. Hammer went on to make low-comedy spinoffs of TV sitcoms, such as *On the Buses* (dir. Harry Booth, 1971), but *The Anniversary* had higher ambitions than those. Though it wasn't a horror film, it was nonetheless derived from the Gothic

Michael Ripper in ***Dracula Has Risen from the Grave*** (dir. Freddie Francis, 1968).

Bette Davis as her most glamorously grotesque in *The Anniversary* (dir. Roy Ward Baker, 1968).

grotesqueries of films such as *Sunset Blvd.* and *What Ever Happened to Baby Jane?* (dir. Robert Aldrich, 1962), and it initiated the new kind of Hammer horror film that appeared when *The Avengers* creator, Brian Clemens became one of the company's producers. *Dr. Jekyll and Sister Hyde* was his idea, and it took a similar approach to James Whale in its blend of ironic humor and genuine thrills, as well as subtly injecting the knowing satire of *The Avengers* into the proceedings. The idea of Jekyll turning into a woman gave ample opportunity for sexual comedy beneath the apparently straight-faced nature of Roy Ward Baker's direction, even though Baker knew very well that what he was in charge of was a black farce. Originally the character of Howard, played by Lewis Fiander, was to have been called Mark Spencer, but that suggestion of one of Britain's most famous high street retailers was fortunately changed. Other innovations remained, as we have already seen regarding Howard's confusion when he meets Dr. Jekyll outside a dress shop, unaware that the good doctor is also the sexy *femme fatale* with whom he's started to have a relationship.

Clemens followed up the Dr. Jekyll film with the comic-strip campery of *Captain Kronos — Vampire Hunter*, which he directed in 1972. But ironically, Hammer's more traditional Gothic fare in the early 1970s cut out the Shakespearean comedy asides altogether. There was no comedy in any of their Dracula sequels, unless one counts the rather lame "Carry On" routine brought to *The Scars of Dracula* by Bob Todd as a boggle-eyed burgomeister who really belongs in a Benny Hill skit. There are a few lines of modish wit in the two modern-dress Draculas but the rest remained entirely straight-faced. *The Horror of Frankenstein*, which had none of the wit of *Dr. Jekyll and Sister Hyde*, attempted to send the whole thing up but only did so with very heavy-handed material.

Hammer's great English rival at the time, Amicus, continued the tradition of Gothic satire in many of their anthology horror films, which usually contained one comedy item. *The House That Dripped Blood* had Jon Pertwee as a horror star at the mercy of a vampire's cloak, which turned him into a genuine bloodsucker whenever he put it on. Due to the comic book origin of many of Amicus' other films, there are facetious lines scattered throughout even ostensibly "serious" material. "This town isn't big enough for two doctors — or two vampires," says Max Adrian to his colleague, having persuaded him to stake his own wife in *Dr. Terror's House of Horrors*. Comedy star Terry-Thomas even appeared in *Vault of Horror* as the obsessively neat husband of very untidy Glynis Johns, whose character is so terrorized by her husband's insistent demands for order that she eventually chops him up and packs the freezer with his various body parts, all labeled and neatly tied up in brown wrapping paper. Later in the same film, two actors famous at the time for their roles on British television as comedy doctors (Robin Nedwell and Geoffrey Davis) appeared in the story concerning Michael Craig, who arranges to have himself temporarily buried alive in order to defraud his life insurance company. It all goes horribly wrong, of course, but it's mostly played for laughs.

The year after Hammer's last vampire film *The Legend of the Seven Golden Vampires* (dir. Roy Ward Baker, 1975), maverick film director Ken Russell (who hated Hammer horror films) sent up much of their imagery in what might seem to be a rather unlikely place. Chapter two touched on the vampire imagery of Russell's *Lisztomania*, but there was a deal more Gothic satire going on in that film. Liszt's son-in-law Richard Wagner is also represented in it as a Frankenstein figure, imbuing life into the monster of a belching Aryan Superman (Rick Wakeman) by playing it the music of other composers; and Russell summons memories of the laboratories in James Whale's and Hammer's *Frankenstein* films in these scenes. No other film has managed to combine Dracula and Frankenstein in a single character as Russell does here. After Wagner's defeat by Liszt's flame-throwing piano, Russell emphasizes the point he has been making all along concerning the uncomfortable influence of Wagner's ideas on Adolf Hitler, by having the composer resurrected as a cross between the great dictator and Boris Karloff's Monster, who opens fire on Jews with a machine-gun in the shape of an electric guitar. Liszt puts Wagner out of his misery by blowing him to pieces from his jet-powered organ while singing an updated version of "Liebestraum," reassuring us that love has won. Rarely have politics, satire, horror films, high art, and high camp been so successfully blended to make a serious point about the history of ideas in a popular entertainment.

Russell continued to flirt with Gothic, his most overt experiments in that direction being *Gothic* (1986) and *The Lair of the White Worm* (1988). The latter was a fairly loose adaptation of Bram Stoker's 1911 novel of the same name in which Amanda Richardson plays a snake woman by the name of Lady Sylvia Marsh. Midway through the film she takes a stranded boy scout called Kevin (played by Chris Pitt) to her palatial home, and this gives Russell an opportunity to echo the scene in Hammer's *The Reptile* when Jacqueline Pearce's Anna Franklin infuriates her father by playing the sitar. Instead of a sitar, Kevin performs an extract from Rimsky-Korsakov's *Scheherazade* on the mouth-organ. The music brings out the snake in Lady Sylvia, who starts to dance like an enchanted cobra, and it's only when Kevin pauses for breath at the end of a phrase that she is able to snatch the instrument from his lips. "That's enough of that, Kevin," she says. "That sort of music freaks me out." But it's now Kevin's turn to be freaked out. He thinks he's been invited just for a game of snakes and ladders and a change of clothes but Lady Sylvia has something much more interesting in mind. She seduces him in a bubble bath and then buries her venomous fangs in his penis, in a heterosexual take on the vampiric breast-biting in Hammer's lesbian vampire films.

There's plenty more vampire imagery in Russell's film, Richardson sporting fangs that make Hammer's dentistry look positively parsimonious. The succession of snakes also provides endless phallic *frissons* in the manner of the German symbolist painter Franz von Stuck, whose most famous painting *Die Sünde* ("Sin") features a green-faced *femme fatale* draped with a distinctly penile python. The pit in which Russell's D'Ampton worm slimily resides is suitably vaginal too, but for those who thought all this just another example of typical Russell extravagance, a reading of Stoker's original novel is instructive. Stoker's description of the worm's lair suggests a horror of sex that might help to explain the horrors of his other novels. In chapter eighteen, Lady Arabella March (on whom Richardson's character in Russell's adaptation is based) throws a Negro servant, called Oolanga, into the worm's foul-smelling pit:

> The gloom which surrounded that horrible charnel pit, which seemed to go down to the very bowels of the earth, conveyed from far down the sights and sounds of the nethermost hell. The ghastly fate of the African as he sank down to his terrible doom, his black face growing grey with terror, his white eyeballs, now like veined bloodstones, rolling in the helpless extremity of fear. The mysterious green light was in itself a *milieu* of horror. And through it all the awful cry came up from that fathomless pit, whose entrance was flooded with spots of fresh blood.[17]

Stoker then describes how the hero, Adam Salter, who witnesses this horror, "made a wild rush forward — slipped on the steps in some sticky, acrid-smelling mass and, falling forward, felt his way into the inner room, where the well-shaft was not."[18] These suggestions of semen, blood and foul-smelling holes are more than enough to suggest what Stoker really had in mind here. It seems to confirm all the rumors about his marriage to Florence Balcombe, the one-time flame of Oscar Wilde. Was Florence frigid? Was Stoker sexually frustrated? Or, was he fundamentally a misogynist? Could it be that Stoker was homosexual? Did he have a horror of all forms of penetrative sex? Whatever the answers to all those questions, what's important is the power of image itself and it puts all of Russell's frequently derided excesses in perspective. All his dildos and kinky boots, all the black PVC and leather, Catholic guilt, vampiric fellatio and vaginal symbolism (which includes the cave mouth that opens the film) derive from Stoker's troubled symbolism. Russell's job was to respond to his source material, and he certainly did that, amplifying but not distorting Stoker's weirdest of visions.

Oolanga, the mute Negro servant, is another of Stoker's sexual nightmares, for he has a habit of staring at people, particularly young women. "Monsters such as he is belong to an earlier and more rudimentary stage of barbarism," says Stoker's Van Helsing lookalike, Sir Nathaniel de Salis. "This being has enough evil in his face to frighten even a strong man. It is little wonder that the sight of it put that poor girl into a dead faint!"[19] Russell transformed Oolanga into Hugh Grant's equally unnerving butler Peters (played by Stratford Johns), who, instead of blacking up, transforms himself into a florid old roué. Grant's character, Lord James D'Ampton, was Russell's version of Stoker's Edgar Caswall, a very peculiar eccentric with an interest in mesmerism, who runs a succession of weird objects up the string of a huge kite which he flies from the turret of his mansion. The point of this is to scare away the flocks of birds, which sense something larger than a tasty garden worm is in the vicinity, but the kite begins to obsess Caswall as he gradually descends into madness. Stoker's description of the eerie avian invasion anticipates Daphne du Maurier's "The Birds" and, of course, Hitchcock's adaptation of it:

The air was full of a muttered throb. No window or barrier could shut out the sound, till the ears of any listener became dulled by the ceaseless murmur. So monotonous it was, so cheerless, so disheartening, so melancholy, that all longed, but in vain, for any variety, no matter how terrible it might be.[20]

Russell replaced Caswall's kite with a series of loudspeakers, which Lord James has rigged up on the roof of his ancestral home; through them he plays snake-charmer music, with the intention of luring Lady Sylvia away from her lair. The ruse works, and we watch her appear from a wicker laundry basket, writhing snakily in her black PVC skin-suit. Russell may have cut out the image of sending up runners to a kite, but he is obviously sending other things up here. Even so, the effect is both amusing and rather unnerving. Russell's entire approach to Stoker's story is a similarly uneasy mixture of sexual horror and cinematic satire. Hugh Grant plays Lord James D'Ampton as a parody of David Niven taking on the Nazis, even wearing an RAF uniform at one stage. Lady Sylvia is also knowingly ironic about what she is. Being a snake woman is nowhere near as troubling for her as it was for Anna Franklin in *The Reptile*. She's quite happy about it, and full of smiles and innuendo, though she presides over the ritual sacrifice at the end of the film with a completely straight face, absurd though it is. Its absurdity is so extreme that it also becomes rather frightening, just as a truly bad film often has the compelling fascination of kitsch; and it is this balancing act that Russell achieves so expertly. Innuendo, irony, cliché and campery all combine with truly disturbing scenes of sexual horror. When Jimmy Sangster tried the same approach in *Lust for a Vampire*, the film fell flat. Russell, by contrast, uses shock tactics to punctuate the irony. Just when we think he's not taking things seriously, he inserts a dream sequence of nuns being raped by Roman soldiers, or a shot of Lady Sylvia in a head scarf, spitting poison through her fangs at a crucifix, or a close-up of a snake-bitten policeman (played by Paul Brooke) skewered through one of his eyeballs; and the aforementioned fellatio scene is one of the film's most precocious combinations of comedy and death. "Watch out for your asp," as the tag line of the film's publicity put it.

Russell was the last major British film director to explore Gothic in commercial terms. Tim Burton has kept the flag flying in Hollywood, though inevitably through a post-modern lens that can never quite recapture the essential naivety of the genre. On the whole, the spirit of Gothic romance at the beginning of the twenty-first century seems unlikely to become as mainstream a genre as it was throughout the twentieth. That's not to say it never will, but as we've seen, the whole point of Gothic was its interest in the past and a literary tradition which post-modernism has now fractured. It was also inherently antisocial, individualistic and pantheistic. Christianity may currently be enjoying a revival of its more evangelical wing, but this has little to do with an interest in the Gothic past and it seems highly unlikely that it will initiate another Gothic revival in architectural or any other terms. Neither does the past hold so much appeal for a culture as obsessed with the future and as uninterested in history as our own. In a world of immediate gratification, which somewhat smugly sees itself as the end product of history, the past offers few comforts and has little relevance. While the Green movement and global warming have made us aware as never before of the vital importance of the natural world for the survival of the planet itself, contemporary film culture (with the possible exception of *The Lord of the Rings*) isn't anywhere near as interested as it once was in viewing nature from a Romantic perspective of the sublime or the picturesque. Our approach to nature is now primarily scientific and recreational, not poetic and spiritually redemptive. Whatever fears we have are really technological. We approach global warming as a problem caused by technology. Nature itself doesn't seem to be a suitable reflection of our emotional fears any more. Increasingly urbanized, international and interconnected as we have become, outsiders (gays, racial minorities, the disabled, "foreigners," etc.) have been officially "included" as never before in our history, with the consequence that their mythological counterparts seem to have less relevance as well. There can be no monsters in a world of political correctitude. "Difference," which was once something to be proud of and celebrated, has now been superficially grafted onto the mainstream. No one is officially "different" any more, even though racial, sexual and economic prejudice is just as strong as it always has been under the neat surface of our so-called "equal opportunities" and inclusiveness. As there are no official outsiders any more, "difference" is no longer regarded as something worth discussing.

In the "real" world, monsters of tyranny and terrorism abound, however, and at a time when atrocities have become commonplace, Gothic horror has come to seem old-fashioned. Also, Gothic was the product of a rigidly structured, admittedly repressive and rather uncomfortable society, in which sexuality, individuality and power structures were strongly codified by manners and particular modes of behavior. These have largely been eroded, and the safety valve of Gothic horror has become redundant. Sex and violence are now so ubiquitous in popular culture that they no longer have a powerful effect. If an actor fails to shoot someone and follow it up with a sex scene, his Hollywood career will be very short-lived indeed. Virginity, if it still exists, is something most people want to lose, not protect. Gothic horrors are now served up for children's entertainment. Beginning with the *Addams Family* cartoons and the TV sitcom *The Munsters*, the old monsters have been transformed into cartoon characters: Count Duckula, Mona the Vampire, even the arithmetical Count of *The Muppets*. When Hollywood dusts down its old monsters, as it did with *The Mummy* in 1996, narrative conviction inevitably gives way to digital verisimilitude. There was plenty of post-modern irony in the remake of *The Mummy* and its sequels, but very little emotional depth, a problem which began with *Star Wars* in 1977. Tom Shone, in his study of the Hollywood blockbuster, observed, "For a generation of fans, 1977 would forever be a sort of cinematic year zero: the year movies proper began,"[21] but for Gothic cinema it was an unmitigated disaster. As Roy Skeggs wistfully explained when discussing the demise of Hammer, "no one wanted us any more."[22]

But one day, when we're a little more uncomfortable, the dead will rise again. Who knows ... perhaps—tonight!

Chapter Notes

Introduction

1. August Strindberg, *Plays: One* (trans. Michael Meyer) (London: Methuen, 1982), pp. 149–50 (Meyer's introduction to *The Ghost Sonata*).
2. Peter Cushing, *Past Forgetting—Memoirs of the Hammer Years* (London: Weidenfeld and Nicolson, 1988), p. 27.
3. Wagner didn't, in the end, set these lines to music, but did have them printed as a variant in his collected writings (see Barry Millington, *Wagner*, The Master Musicians series [London: Dent, 1994], p. 226). The original German text is:

>   des ew'gen Werdens
>   off'ne Thore
>   schliess' ich hinter mir zu:
>   nach dem wunsch—und wahnlos
>   heiligstem Wahlland,
>   der Welt-Wanderung Ziel,
>   von Wiedergeburt erlös't,
>   zieht nun die Wissende hin.

4. Sigmund Freud, *The Interpretation of Dreams* (trans. James Strachey) (Harmondsworth: Penguin, 1983), pp. 119–20.
5. Alan Frank, "Christopher Lee Speaks Out," *Hammer's Halls of Horror*, no. 21, June 1978, p. 6.
6. *The Evening Standard*, London, August 1, 1996.
7. *The Guardian*, London, August 1, 1996.
8. Christopher Lee, *Tall, Dark and Gruesome* (London: Victor Gollancz, 1997), p. 163.
9. Campbell Dixon's review of Hammer's *The Curse of Frankenstein* (dir. Terence Fisher, 1957) in *The Daily Telegraph*, London, May 4, 1957.

Chapter One

1. Alan Frank, *Horror Films* (London: Hamlyn, 1977), p. 75.
2. Kenneth Clarke, *The Gothic Revival* (London: John Murray, 1974), p. 58.
3. Adolphe Appia, *Adolphe Appia: Texts on Theatre* (ed. Richard C. Beacham) (London: Routledge, 1993), pp. 1–12.
4. Richard C. Beacham, "Adolphe Appia and Wagnerian Opera," *The Opera Quarterly*, vol. 1, no. 3, Autumn 1983, pp. 135–38.
5. Lotte H. Eisner, *The Haunted Screen* (trans. Roger Greaves) (London: Secker & Warburg, 1983), pp. 119–20.
6. Dennis Gifford, *A Pictorial History of Horror Movies* (London: Hamlyn, 1979), p. 126.
7. Lotte H. Eisner, *The Haunted Screen* (note 5), p. 121.
8. *Loc. cit.*

9. Sigmund Freud, *The Interpretation of Dreams* (trans. James Strachey) (Harmondsworth: Penguin, 1983), p. 472 (footnote).
10. Kevin Brownlow, *David Lean—A Biography* (London: Richard Cohen, 1996), p. 209–10.
11. Charles Dickens, *Oliver Twist/Great Expectations* (London: Hazel, Watson & Viney, c. 1933), p. 394 (*Great Expectations*).
12. Eric Csapo, *Theory of Mythology* (Oxford: Wiley-Blackwell, 2005), pp. 97–98 (Freud quoted).
13. Peter Cushing, *Past Forgetting—Memoirs of the Hammer Years* (London: Weidenfeld and Nicolson, 1988), p. 25.
14. Christopher Lee, *Tall Dark and Gruesome* (London: Victor Gollancz, 1997), p. 121.
15. William Shakespeare, *Shakespeare Complete Works* (ed. W.J. Craig) (Oxford: Oxford University Press, 1978), p. 891 (*Hamlet*, Act III, scene 2, lines 413–17).
16. Anthony Holden, *Olivier* (London: Sphere, 1989), p. 268.
17. William Shakespeare, *Shakespeare's Complete Works* (note 15), p. 888 (*Hamlet*, Act III, scene 2, line 124).
18. *Op. cit.*, p. 876 (*Hamlet*, Act I, scene 4, lines 40–43).
19. Daphne du Maurier, *Rebecca* (London: Heron Books, 1971), p. 189.
20. Jonathan Rigby, *American Gothic* (Richmond: Reynolds & Hearn, 2007), p. 275.
21. Horace Walpole, *The Castle of Otranto* (ed. W.S. Lewis) (London: Oxford University Press, 1969), p. ix.
22. As Frederick Garber points out in his introduction to Radcliffe's *The Italian* (London: Oxford University Press, 1970, pp. xii–xiii), the anti-hero of that novel, Schedoni, "was the one who captured the Romantic imagination with his blend of pride, melancholy, mystery and dignity. In many ways he represents the final stage before Byron in the whole complicated genealogy of the Romantic hero."
23. William Hughes Mearns, "Antigonish," *Psycho-ed*, 1899, first published in *New York World*, March 27, 1927.

Chapter Two

1. Ann Radcliffe, *The Mysteries of Udolpho* (ed. Bonamy Dobrée) (London: Oxford University Press, 1970), p. 339.
2. William Shakespeare, *Shakespeare Complete Works* (ed. W.J. Craig) (Oxford: Oxford University Press, 1974), p. 876 (*Hamlet*, Act I, scene 4, lines 8–12).

3. Rictor Norton, *Mistress of Udolpho* (London: Leicester University Press, 1999), p. 89.
4. Thomas De Quincey, *Collected Writings of Thomas De Quincey* (ed. David Masson) (Edinburgh: Adam & Charles Black, 1889–90), vol. 3, p. 282.
5. John Keats, *The Letters of John Keats* (ed. H. Buxton Forman) (Whitefish MT: Kessinger, 2004), p. 100 (letter of March 14, 1818).
6. Lord Byron, *Childe Harold's Pilgrimage*, Canto IV, stanza 18.
7. William Shakespeare, *Shakespeare Complete Works* (note 2), p. 924 (*King Lear*, Act III, scene 2, lines 1–7).
8. Ann Radcliffe, *The Romance of the Forest* (ed. Chloe Chard) (Oxford: Oxford University Press, 1986), p. 4.
9. *Op. cit.*, p. 265.
10. *Op. cit.*, p. 266.
11. Oliver Strunk (ed.), *Source Readings in Music History*, vol. 5, "The Romantic Era" (London: Faber and Faber, 1981), pp. 70–71 (Hector Berlioz: "Rossini's 'William Tell,'" 1834).
12. William Mann, CD notes for Herbert von Karajan's recording of *Eine Alpensinfonie*, Deutsche Grammophon, 439017-2.
13. Kurt Wilhelm, *Richard Strauss—An Intimate Portrait* (London: Thames and Hudson, 1989), p. 106.
14. Charles Maturin, *Melmoth the Wanderer* (ed. Douglas Grant) (Oxford: Oxford University Press, 1989), p. 61.
15. Bram Stoker, *Dracula* (Westminster: Archibald Constable, 1904), p. 79.
16. Percy Bysshe Shelley, *The Complete Poetical Works of Percy Bysshe Shelley* (ed. Thomas Hutchinson) (London: Oxford University Press, 1956), p. 597 ("A Vision of the Sea," lines 11–34).
17. *Op. cit.*, p. 531 ("Hymn to Intellectual Beauty," lines 49–52).
18. Percy Bysshe Shelley, *Zastrozzi and St. Irvyne* (ed. Stephen C. Behrendt) (Oxford: Oxford University Press, 1986), p. 109.
19. Percy Bysshe Shelley, *The Complete Poetical Works of Percy Bysshe Shelley* (note 16), p. 382 (*The Witch of Atlas*, lns, 441–47).
20. *Op. cit.*, p. 41 (*The Revolt of Islam*, Canto I, stanza 3, lines 145–50).
21. Mary Shelley, *Frankenstein* (London: Dent, 1941), p. 51.
22. *Loc. cit.*
23. Percy Bysshe Shelley, *The Complete Poetical Works of Percy Bysshe Shelley* (note 16). pp. 578–79 ("Ode to the West Wind," lines 18–64).
24. *Op. cit.*, p. 579 ("Ode to the West Wind," lines 66–70).
25. Peter Cushing, *Past Forgetting—Memories of the Hammer Years* (London: Weidenfeld and Nicolson, 1988), p. 28. Cushing believed that the minds of Frankenstein and Dr. Robert Knox "were driven by a single desire: to enquire into the unknown. Ahead of their time, like most good scientists, their work and motives were misunderstood."
26. W. Somerset Maugham, *The World Over—The Collected Short Stories*, vol. 1 (London: Reprint Society, 1961), p. 18 ("Rain").
27. Edgar Allan Poe, *The Complete Illustrated Stories and Poems of Edgar Allan Poe* (London: Chancellor Press, 1988), p. 27 ("The Fall of the House of Usher").

Chapter Three

1. Ann Radcliffe, *The Romance of the Forest* (ed. Chloe Chard) (Oxford: Oxford University Press, 1986), pp. 15–16.
2. *Op. cit.*, p. 15.
3. *Op. cit.*, p. 16.
4. William Beckford, *Life at Fonthill* (trans. & ed. Boyd Alexander) (Stroud: Nonsuch, 2006), p. 71.
5. John Ruskin, *The Stones of Venice* (London: Folio Society, 2001), p. 142.
6. Kenneth Clarke, *The Gothic Revival* (London: John Murray, 1974), pp. 171–72.
7. Christopher Newall, *Frederick Leighton 1830–1896* (London: Royal Academy of Arts, 1996), p. 236.
8. David Huckvale, *Hammer Film Scores and the Musical Avant Garde* (Jefferson NC: McFarland, 2008), p. 155.
9. Éliphas Lévi, *Transcendental Magic—Its Dogma and Ritual* (trans. Arthur Edward Waite) (Twickenham: Senate, 1995), p. 48.
10. Éliphas Lévi, *Magic, A History of Its Rites, Rituals and Mysteries* (trans. Arthur Edward Waite) (New York: Dover, 2006), pp. 56–57. Lévi refers to the anonymous *Book of the Penitence of Adam*, which claims that the wood used to construct the two columns, Jachin and Boaz, derives from the Tree of Knowledge and the Tree of Life in the Garden of Eden. From these trees' seeds grew the Burning Bush, the branches of which became the wand of Moses. This was placed in the Ark of the Covenant and was later planted on Mount Zion. From the tree it grew into, Solomon made Jachin and Boaz; the wood from the threshold to the temple, which came from the same source, eventually formed the basis of Christ's crucifix. According to Lévi's anonymous source, Solomonic columns therefore carry with them a theological significance quite independent of their later associations with Catholicism.
11. Ann Radcliffe, *The Romance of the Forest* (ed. Chloe Chard) (note 1), p. 15.
12. *Horror of Dracula*, Silva Screen FilmCD 708. This is a digital transfer of the vinyl LP *Hammer Presents Dracula with Christopher Lee*, EMI, TWOA 5001, 1974.
13. Ann Radcliffe, *The Mysteries of Udolpho* (ed. Bonamy Dobrée) (London: Oxford University Press, 1970), pp. 226–27.
14. J. Sheridan Le Fanu, *In a Glass Darkly* (London: John Lehmann, 1947), p. 276 ("Carmilla").
15. *Op. cit.* p. 278 ("Carmilla").
16. Christopher Woodward, *In Ruins* (London: Chatto & Windus, 2001), pp. 177–204.
17. *The Complete Words of Percy Bysshe Shelley* (ed. Thomas Hutchinson) (London: Oxford University Press, 1956), p. 550 (*Ozymandias*).
18. Christopher Woodward, *In Ruins* (note 16), p. 153.
19. H. Rider Haggard, *She* (London: Collins, 1974), pp. 186–87.
20. *Op. cit.*, p. 187.
21. Christopher Woodward, *In Ruins* (note 16), p. 123.
22. Henry Pleasants (ed. & trans.), *The Musical World of Robert Schumann* (London: Victor Gollancz, 1965), p. 93.
23. Charles Rosen, *The Romantic Generation* (London: HarperCollins, 1996), p. 153.
24. Keith Hartley (ed.), *The Romantic Spirit in German Art 1790–1990* (London: Thames and Hudson, 1994), p. 292.
25. *Op. cit.*, p. 293.

26. *Loc. cit.*
27. H. Rider Haggard, *She* (note 19), p. 194.

Chapter Four

1. Jean-Jacques Rousseau, *Emile, or Education* (trans. Barbara Foxley) (London: J.M. Dent, 1930), p. 26.
2. Charles Rosen, *The Romantic Generation* (London: HarperCollins, 1996), p. 127.
3. *Op. cit.*, pp. 129–35.
4. Anthony and Pip Burton, *The Green Bag Travellers—Britain's First Tourists* (London: Andre Deutsch, 1978), pp. 32–33.
5. *Op. cit.*, p. 35.
6. *Op. cit.*, p. 36.
7. Kenneth Clarke, *The Romantic Rebellion—Romantic Versus Classic Art* (London: Futura, 1976), p. 45.
8. Anthony and Pip Burton, *The Green Bag Travellers* (note 4), p. 37.
9. Aristotle, Horace, Longinus, *Classical Literary Criticism* (trans. T.S. Dorsch) (Harmondsworth: Penguin, 1979), p. 100.
10. *Op. cit.*, p. 107.
11. Edmund Burke, *A Philosophical Enquiry into the Origin of Our Ideas of the Sublime and Beautiful* (ed. Adam Phillips) (Oxford: Oxford University Press, 1990), pp. 110–11.
12. *Op. cit.*, p. 36.
13. *Op. cit.*, p. 54.
14. *Op. cit.*, pp. 60–61.
15. *Op. cit.*, p. 66.
16. Peter Cushing, *Past Forgetting—Memories of the Hammer Years* (London: Weidenfeld and Nicolson, 1988), p. 27.
17. Edmund Burke, *A Philosophical Enquiry into the Origin of Our Ideas of the Sublime and Beautiful* (note 11), pp. 36–37.
18. John Milton, *The Poetical Works of John Milton* (London: Frederick Warne, 1896), p. 105 (*Paradise Lost*, Book I, lines 44–69).
19. *Op. cit.*, p. 149 (*Paradise Lost*, Book II, lines 876–83).
20. Rictor Norton, *Mistress of Udolpho* (London: Leicester University Press, 1999), pp. 97–98.
21. Ann Radcliffe, *The Mysteries of Udolpho* (ed. Bonamy Dobrée) (London: Oxford University Press, 1970), pp. 42–43.
22. Percy Bysshe Shelley, *The Complete Poetical Works of Percy Bysshe Shelley* (ed. Thomas Hutchinson) (London: Oxford University Press, 1956), p. 27 (*Alastor; or the Spirit of Solitude*, lines 577–78).
23. Rictor Norton (note 20), pp. 78–79.
24. Percy Bysshe Shelley, *The Complete Poetical Works of Percy Bysshe Shelley* (note 22), p. 532 ("Mont Blanc," lines 8–35).
25. Mary Shelley, *Frankenstein* (London: J.M. Dent, 1941), pp. 98–99.
26. CD booklet for Carl Maria von Weber's *Der Freischütz*, cond. Carlos Kleiber/Staastskapelle Dresden, Deutsche Grammophon, 289 457 736–2.
27. Richard Wagner, *My Life* (trans. Andrew Gray) (Cambridge: Cambridge University Press, 1987), p. 13.
28. Edward Seckerson, *Mahler—His Life and Times* (Tunbridge Wells: Midas Books, 1982), p. 62.
29. *Loc. cit.*
30. *Loc. cit.*
31. James Fenimore Cooper, *The Last of the Mohicans* (Oxford: Oxford University Press, 1994), p. 57.
32. Sir Walter Scott, *Waverley* (Edinburgh: Adam and Charles Black, 1860), p. 164.
33. *Loc. cit.*
34. Bram Stoker, *Dracula* (Westminster: Archibald Constable, 1904), pp. 7–9.
35. Keith Hartley (ed.), *The Romantic Spirit in German Art 1790–1990* (London: Thames and Hudson, 1994), p. 29.
36. Modris Eksteins, *Rites of Spring* (London: Papermac, 2000), p. 82.
37. Keith Hartley, *The Romantic Spirit in German Art 1790–1990*, (note 35), p. 193.
38. Percy Bysshe Shelley, *The Complete Poetical Works of Percy Bysshe Shelley* (note 22), pp. 26–27 (*Alastor; or the Spirit of Solitude*, lines 539–50).
39. *Bayreuth 1988—Rückblick und Vorschau* (Review and Preview) (Bayreuth: Bayreuth Festspiel, 1987), p. 29 (Alan Hollinghurst quoted).

Chapter Five

1. Mario Praz, *The Romantic Agony* (Oxford: Oxford University Press, 1970), p. 202.
2. *Loc. cit.*
3. See *The Hour of One—Six Gothic Melodramas* (ed. Stephen Wischhusen) (London: Gordon Fraser, 1975).
4. Raymond T. McNally, *In Search of Frankenstein* (Massachusetts: New York Graphic Society, 1975), pp. 165–66.
5. Matthew Lewis, *The Monk* (ed. Howard Anderson) (Oxford: Oxford University Press, 1977), pp. 379–81.
6. Tim Greaves, *Veronica Carlson—An Illustrated Memento* (Eastleigh: 1-Shot Publications, 1993), p. 12.
7. Oscar Wilde, *Complete Works of Oscar Wilde* (London: Collins, 1977), p. 575 (*Salome*).
8. Percy Bysche Shelley, *The Complete Works of Percy Bysshe Shelley* (ed. Thomas Hutchinson) (London: Oxford University Press, 1956), p. 582 ("On the Medusa of Leonardo da Vinci in the Florentine Gallery," lines 4–10).
9. Bruce Sachs and Russell Wall, *Greasepaint and Gore—The Hammer Monsters of Roy Ashton* (Sheffield: Tomahawk Press, 1991), p. 126.
10. Percy Bysshe Shelley, *The Complete Works of Percy Bysshe Shelley* (note 8), p. 583 ("On the Medusa of Leonardo da Vinci in the Florentine Gallery," lines 19–23).
11. H.P. Lovecraft, *The Loved Dead & Other Stories* (Ware: Wordsworth, 2007), p. 275 ("The Man of Stone").
12. Carl Gustav Jung, *On the Nature of the Psyche* (trans. R.F.C. Hull) (London: Routledge & Kegan Paul, 1982), p. 51 ("On Psychic Energy"): "Over against the polymorphism of the primitive's instinctual nature there stands the regulating principle of individuation. Multiplicity and inner division are opposed by an integrative unity whose power is as great as that of the instincts. Together they form a pair of opposites necessary for self-regulation, often spoken of as nature and spirit. These conceptions are rooted in psychic conditions between which human consciousness fluctuates like the pointer on the scales."
13. Mario Praz, *The Romantic Agony* (note 1), pp. 215–16.
14. *Op. cit.*, p. 263.
15. *Op. cit.*, 253–54.
16. David Huckvale, *James Bernard—Composer to Count Dracula* (Jefferson NC: McFarland, 2006), p. 146.

17. Mario Praz, *The Romantic Agony* (note 1), pp. 249–50.
18. *Op. cit.*, pp. 250–51.
19. *Op. cit.*, p. 251.
20. E.T.A. Hoffmann, *The Nutcracker and The Golden Pot* (New York: Dover, 1993), pp. 4–5 (*The Golden Pot*, trans. Thomas Carlyle).
21. *Op. cit.*, p. 67 (*The Golden Pot*, trans. Thomas Carlyle).
22. John Keats, *The Letters of John Keats* (ed. H. Buxton Forman) (Whitefish MT: Kessinger, 2004), p. 394 (letter of September 19, 1819).
23. John Keats, *Keats Poetical Works* (ed. H. W. Garrod) (London: Oxford University Press, 1973), p. 162 ("Lamia," Book I, lines 59–65).
24. *Op. cit.*, p. 165 ("Lamia," Book 1, lines 185–89).
25. Samuel Taylor Coleridge, *Coleridge Poetical Works* (ed. Ernest Hartley Coleridge) (London: Oxford University Press, 1974), pp. 215–16 ("Christabel," Part I, lines 1–23).
26. *Op. cit.*, p. 218 ("Christabel," Part 1, lines 71–74).
27. *Op. cit.*, p. 223 ("Christabel," Part 1, lines 237–38).
28. *Op. cit.*, p. 224 ("Christabel," Part I, lines 245–54).
29. Bruce Sachs and Russell Wall, *Greasepaint and Gore—The Hammer Monsters of Roy Ashton* (note 9), pp. 149–50. According to Ashton, "A lot of research went into the appearance of the Reptile. Again I consulted anatomical authorities.... To suggest the scales I took a discarded boa constrictor's skin and made a female caste of this in plaster. ... The extended fangs were a complete acrylic set.... I made the eye pieces with lenses built in. They were separate so that I could fit them just before each take so there wasn't too much discomfort for the artist while she was waiting about."
30. Samuel Taylor Coleridge, *Coleridge Poetical Works* (note 25), p. 233 ("Christabel," Part II, lines 583–87).
31. *Op. cit.*, p. 228 ("Christabel," Part II, lines 379–82).
32. Tim Greaves (ed.), *Ingrid Pitt—Queen of Horror* (Eastleigh: 1-Shot Publications, 1995), p. 14.
33. Rictor Norton, *Mistress of Udolpho* (London: Leicester University Press, 1999), p. 148.
34. *Loc. cit.*
35. *Op. cit.*, p. 150.

Chapter Six

1. Jane Austen, *Northanger Abbey* (Ware: Wordsworth, 1995), p. 25.
2. Ann Radcliffe, *The Mysteries of Udolpho* (ed. Bonamy Dobrée) (London: Oxford University Press, 1970), p. 233.
3. *Op. cit.*, p. 662.
4. Edmund Burke, *A Philosophical Enquiry Into the Origin of Our Ideas of the Sublime and Beautiful* (ed. Adam Phillips) (Oxford: Oxford University Press, 1990), pp. 36–37.
5. Morris Bright & Robert Ross, *Mr. Carry On—The Life and Work of Peter Rogers* (London: BBC, 2000), p. 140.
6. Horace Walpole, *The Castle of Otranto* (ed. W.S. Lewis) (London: Oxford University Press, 1969), pp. 23–24.
7. W.S. Gilbert, *The Savoy Operas* (London: Papermac, 1983), p. 416 (*Ruddigore*, Act II).
8. John Milton, *The Poetical Works of John Milton* (London: Frederick Warne, 1896), p. 80 (*Comus, a Mask*).
9. Miranda Seymour, *Mary Shelley* (London: John Murray, 2000), p. 157. (This is a quotation from the diary of Dr. J.W. Polidori, June 18, 1816.)
10. Derek Malcolm, "Scare tactics that ruin the horror show," *The Guardian*, London, February 7, 1987.
11. Leslie Halliwell, *Film and Video Guide 2000 Edition* (ed. John Walker) (London: HarperCollins, 1999), p. 201.
12. Maurice Maeterlinck, *The Treasure of the Humble* (trans. Alfred Sutro) (London: George Allen, 1897), p. 25: "Certain it is that there passes not a day but the soul adds to its ever-widening domain. It is very much nearer to our visible self, and takes a far greater part in all our actions, than was the case two or three centuries ago. A spiritual epoch is perhaps upon us."
13. Ingrid Ehrhardt and Simon Reynolds, *The Kingdom of the Soul—Symbolist Art in Germany 1870–1920* (Munich: Prestel, 2000), pp. 30–1.
14. Francis Ford Coppola and James V. Hart, *Bram Stoker's Dracula—The Film and the Legend* (London: Pan, 1992), p. 70.
15. Böcklin visited Wagner in 1871 and suggested he should paint his portrait. Wagner later returned the compliment and approached Böcklin to design the sets for the Ring cycles, but apparently Böcklin didn't much care for Wagner, the man or his music, and turned down the offer. This was a pity as Böcklin had a great deal in common with Wagner's synaesthetic ideals and might have provided more interesting sets than those of the Brückner brothers who eventually got the job. Böcklin did at least go on eventually to inspire the sets of Bayreuth's centenary production of the Ring cycle in 1976. For this groundbreaking production, Patrice Chéreau commissioned Richard Peduzzi sets which featured a ruined version of *The Isle of the Dead*. Stripped of its cypress trees, the outline of the rock is nonetheless unmistakable, with the doors leading to supposed catacombs on each side. It was onto this ruined Isle of the Dead that the Valkyries brought slain heroes collected during the famous "Walkürenrit." But the singular appropriateness of this image failed to impress audiences, who thought it resembled more an Aztec pyramid or the Matterhorn, and seemed not to get the point, while Chéreau received death threats for his audacity. Böcklin's ghost might well have been amused.
16. Modris Eksteins, *Rites of Spring* (London: Papermac, 2000), p. 93.
17. *Loc. cit.*
18. *Op. cit.*, p. 94.
19. *Op. cit.*, p. 92.
20. Sheridan Le Fanu, *Uncle Silas* (ed. W.J. McCormack) (Oxford: Oxford University Press, 1981), p. xii.
21. *Op. cit.*, p. 9.
22. *Op. cit.*, p. xii.
23. *Portrait from Life* was also the title of a 1948 Terence Fisher film. There's nothing supernatural or Gothic about it; starring Mai Zetterling and Herbert Lom, it concerns the portrait of a girl who has been lost in a German concentration camp.
24. Sir James Frazer, *The Golden Bough* (London: Macmillan, 1950), p. 12.
25. *Op. cit.*, p. 13.
26. Bram Stoker, *Dracula* (Westminster: Archibald Constable, 1904), p. 27.
27. Alfred Lord Tennyson, *Poetical Works of Alfred Lord Tennyson* (London: Macmillan, 1911), p. 28 ("The Lady of Shalott").

28. Tennyson was vehemently opposed to Art for Art's Sake. When accused of being an adherent of such a cause, he replied with an epigram that was quoted in *Alfred Lord Tennyson — A Memoir by His Son* (London: Macmillan, 1897), vol. II, p. 92:
> Art for Art's sake! Hail, truest Lord of Hell!
> Hail, Genius, Master of the Moral Will!
> "The filthiest of paintings painted well
> Is mightier than the purest painted ill!"
> Yes, mightier than the purest painted well,
> So prone are we toward the broad way to Hell.

29. Éliphas Lévi, *Magic — A History of Its Rites, Rituals and Mysteries* (trans. Arthur Edward Waite) (New York: Dover, 2006), p. 40.
30. Lewis Carroll, *The Complete Illustrated Works of Lewis Carroll* (London: Chancellor Press, 1985), p. 127 (*Through the Looking Glass*).
31. Hans Christian Andersen, *The Complete Illustrated Stories of Hans Christian Andersen* (London: Chancellor Press, 1985), p. 315 ("The Snow Queen").
32. Lewis Carroll, *The Complete Illustrated Works of Lewis Carroll* (note 30), pp. 127–28 (*Through the Looking Glass*).
33. Richard Wagner, *Parsifal — Opera Guide 34* (trans. Andrew Porter) (London: John Calder, 1986), p. 96.
34. Lewis Carroll, *The Complete Illustrated Stories of Lewis Carroll* (note 30), p. 127 (*Through the Looking Glass*).
35. Robert Louis Stevenson, *The Strange Case of Dr. Jekyll and Mr. Hyde and Other Stories* (New York: Peebles Classic Library, 1974), pp. 221–22 ("Markheim").
36. *Op. cit.*, p. 239 ("Markheim").
37. H. P. Lovecraft, *The Haunter of the Dark and Other Stories* (London: Panther, 1974), p. 16 ("The Outsider").

Interlude

1. Homer, *The Odyssey* (trans. E.V. Rieu) (London: Guild Publishing, 1991), p. 76 (Book 4).
2. Lucius Apuleius, *The Golden Asse of Lucius Apuleius* (trans. William Adlington) (London: The Abbey Library, 1923), p. 11.
3. *Op. cit.*, p. 164.
4. William Shakespeare, *William Shakespeare Complete Works* (ed. W.J. Craig) (Oxford: Oxford University Press, 1978), p. 179 (*A Midsummer Night's Dream*, Act III, scene 1, lines 112–17).
5. *Op. cit.*, p. 852 (*Macbeth*, Act II, scene 1, lines 47–56).
6. Walter Keating Kelly, *Curiosities of Indo-European Tradition and Folk-Lore* (Whitefish MT: Kessinger, 2004), p. 261.
7. Montague Summers, *The Werewolf* (Whitefish MT: Kessinger, 2003), p. 189.
8. Leonard Wolf, *The Annotated Dracula* (London: New English Library, 1976), p. 22.
9. Bram Stoker, *Dracula* (Westminster: Archibald Constable, 1904), p. 16.
10. *Op. cit.*, p. 18.
11. *Loc. cit.*
12. Leonard Wolf, *The Annotated Dracula* (note 8), p. 23.
13. Joachim Köhler, *Zarathustra's Secret* (trans. Ronald Taylor) (New Haven: Yale University Press, 2002), p. 42 (Hufeland's *Macrobiotics, or the Art of Prolonging Life*, 1796, quoted).
14. Bram Stoker, *Dracula* (note 9), p. 49.
15. *Op. cit.*, p. 52.
16. Éliphas Lévi (trans. Arthur Edward Waite), *Transcendental Magic — Its Dogma and Ritual* (Twickenham: Senate, 1995), p. 84.
17. Johann Wolfgang von Goethe, *Faust — Part One* (trans. David Luke) (Oxford: Oxford University Press, 1987), p. 17.
18. Éliphas Lévi, *Transcendental Magic — Its Doctrine and Ritual* (note 16), p. 291.
19. Richard Cavendish, *The Tarot* (London: Chancellor Press, 1986), p. 119.
20. Guy Endore, *The Werewolf of Paris* (London: Sphere, 1974) (Vol. 2 in the "Dennis Wheatley Library of the Occult"), pp. 114–15.
21. Sabine Baring-Gould, *The Book of Werewolves* (London: Senate, 1995), pp. 186–87.
22. Also set in Hungary (and featuring another countess) was a two-part 1976 werewolf story from the BBC's *Supernatural* TV series. A mixture of filmed location work in atmospherically misty forests and videotaped studio interiors, "The Werewolf Reunion" and "Countess Ilona" starred Billie Whitelaw as Countess Ilona, an ex-courtesan, now widow of a depraved aristocrat, who exacts her revenge on four heartless lovers from her days of penury. She invites them to her Gothic castle in Hungary, wines and dines them, and waits for her werewolf husband to tear them to pieces on consecutive nights. We never see the werewolf itself, only its ominous shadow; the strength of the episodes lies in Robert Muller's literate, sophisticated scripts, the always dependable acting of Ian Hendry, Edward Hardwicke and Charles Kay, et al., and director Simon Langton's sympathetic understanding of hallowed Gothic conventions.
23. E.F. Benson, *Ravens' Brood* (Brighton: Millivres Books, 1993), p. 117.
24. D.H. Lawrence, *Women in Love* (London: Book Club Associates, 1980), p. 85.
25. Thomas Mann, *Stories of Three Decades* (trans. H.T. Lowe-Porter) (London: Martin Secker & Warburg, 1936), pp. 430–31 ("Death in Venice").
26. Laurence Schifano, *Luchino Visconti — The Flames of Passion* (London: Collins, 1990), p. 379.
27. Gary Schmidgall, *Literature as Opera* (New York: Oxford University Press, 1977), p. 325.
28. *Op. cit.*, p. 330.
29. Friedrich Niezsche, *Beyond Good and Evil* (trans. R.J. Hollingdale) (Harmondsworth: Penguin, 1983), p. 73 (Aphorism 75).

Chapter Seven

1. Anthony Rhodes, *The Poet as Superman — A Life of Gabriele D'Annunzio* (London: Weidenfeld and Nicolson, 1959), p. 238.
2. Edgar Allan Poe, *The Complete Illustrated Stories and Poems of Edgar Allan Poe* (London: Chancellor Press, 1988), p. 281 ("The Assignation").
3. *Op. cit.*, p. 282.
4. Robert L. Delevoy, *Symbolists and Symbolism* (London: Skira/Macmillan, 1982), p. 18.
5. Edgar Allan Poe, *The Complete Illustrated Stories and Poems of Edgar Allan Poe* (note 2), p. 173 ("Ligeia").
6. *Loc. cit.*
7. *Loc. cit.*
8. Joris-Karl Huysmans, *À Rebours* (London: Fortune Press, 1946), p. 30.
9. Oscar Wilde, *Complete Works of Oscar Wilde* (London: Collins, 1977), p. 102 (*The Picture of Dorian Gray*).

10. *Loc. cit.*
11. *Op. cit.*, p. 938 (*De Profundis*).
12. Jimmy Sangster, *Inside Hammer* (London: Reynolds & Hearn, 2001), p. 54.
13. *Loc. cit.*
14. Joris-Karl Huysmans, *À Rebours* (note 8), p. 69.
15. Villiers de l'Isle Adam, *Axel* (trans. M. Gaddis Rose) (London: Soho Book, 1986), p. 171.
16. Wayne Kinsey (ed.), *The House That Hammer Built* (Barnby: Special Issue, May 1998), p. 16.
17. Villiers de l'Isle Adam, *The Vampire Soul and Other Sardonic Tales* (trans. Brian Stableford) (Encino, CA: Black Coat Press, 2004), p. 16.
18. *Loc. cit.*
19. Arthur Schnitzler, *Dream Story* (trans. J.M.Q. Davis) (Harmondsworth: Penguin, 1999), p. 18.
20. *Op. cit.*, p. 23.
21. *Op. cit.*, p. 45.
22. *Op. cit.*, p. 48.
23. *Op. cit.*, p. 49.
24. *Op. cit.*, p. 53.
25. *Op. cit.*, p. 56.
26. *Op. cit.*, p. 67.
27. *Op. cit.*, p. 94.
28. Jimmy Sangster, *Inside Hammer* (note 12), p. 110.
29. Villiers de l'Isle Adam, *Axel* (note 15), p. 170.
30. Jules Verne, *The Castle of the Carpathians* (London: Sampson Low, Marston, 1902), p. 209.
31. Peter Haining (ed.), *The Frankenstein Omnibus* (London: Orion, 1994), p. 118 (Villiers de l'Isle Adam, *The Future Eve* [trans. Florence Crewe-Jones]).
32. *Op. cit.*, pp. 118–19.
33. Thomas Caldwell (ed.), *The Golden Book of Modern English Poetry* (London: Dent, 1935), p. 173 (Arthur Symons, "Laus Virginatatis").
34. MaryAnne Stevens & Robert Hoozee, *Impressionism to Symbolism — The Belgian Avant-Garde 1880–1900* (London: Royal Academy of Arts, 1994), p. 154.
35. *Loc. cit.*
36. Richard Wagner, *Tristan and Isolde* (trans. Stewart Robb) (New York: E.P. Dutton, 1965), p. 83 (Act II, scene 2).
37. Peter Haining (ed.), *The Frankenstein Omnibus* (note 31), p. 121 (Villiers de l'Isle Adam, *The Future Eve* [trans. Florence Crewe-Jones]).
38. *Op. cit.*, p. 87.
39. *Op. cit.*, p. 135.
40. *Op. cit.*, p. 84.
41. *Op. cit.*, p. 85.
42. Jimmy Sangster, *Inside Hammer* (note 12), p. 54.
43. *Op. cit.*, p. 32.
44. Oscar Wilde, *Complete Works of Oscar Wilde* (note 9), p. 130 (*The Picture of Dorian Gray*).
45. Amicus had other tenuous connections with the world of symbolist decadence. For example, *Torture Garden* (dir. Freddie Francis, 1967) derives its title (though nothing else) from *Le Jardin des supplices* (1899), Ocatave Mirbeau's nihilistic novel of exotic torture set in a beautiful Chinese garden.
46. Villiers de l'Isle Adam, *Cruel Tales* (trans. Robert Baldick) (Oxford: Oxford University Press, 1985), p. 102 ("The Very Image").
47. Oscar Wilde, *Complete Works of Oscar Wilde* (note 9), p. 17 (*The Picture of Dorian Gray*).
48. Villiers de l'Isle Adam, *Cruel Tales* (note 46), p. 64 ("The Duke of Portland").
49. In *The Damned*, radioactive children are kept in quarantine to prepare them for "life" after a nuclear war.
50. Villiers de l'Isle Adam, *Cruel Tales* (note 46), p. 67 ("The Duke of Portland").
51. *Op. cit.*, p. 230 ("Occult Memories").
52. *Op. cit.*, p. 231 ("Occult Memories").
53. Villiers de l'Isle Adam, *The Vampire Soul and Other Sardonic Tales* (note 17), p. 48 ("The Vampire Soul").

Chapter Eight

1. Ted Honderich (ed.), *The Oxford Companion to Philosophy* (Oxford: Oxford University Press, 1995), p. 339.
2. Villiers de l'Isle Adam, *Cruel Tales* (trans. Robert Baldick) (Oxford: Oxford University Press, 1985), p. 260 (footnote by A.W. Raitt).
3. *Op. cit.*, p. 20 ("Véra").
4. *Loc. cit.*
5. *Op. cit.*, p. 259 (footnote by A.W. Raitt).
6. Joachim Köhler, *Richard Wagner — The Last of the Titans* (trans. Stewart Spencer) (New Haven: Yale University Press, 2004), p. 256.
7. Richard Wagner, *Götterdämmerung* (trans. Lionel Salter), Deutsche Grammophon CD booklet for Herbert von Karajan's recording, DG 457 795-2, p. 211 (Act III, scene 3).
8. Oscar Wilde, *Complete Works of Oscar Wilde* (London: Collins, 1977), p. 929 (*De Profundis*).
9. George Bernard Shaw, *Complete Plays of Bernard Shaw* (London: Odhams Press, 19XX), p. 379 (*Man and Superman*, Act III).
10. Edgar Allan Poe, *The Complete Illustrated Stories and Poems of Edgar Allan Poe* (London: Chancellor Press, 1988), p. 167 ("Ligeia").
11. *Op. cit.*, p. 179 ("Ligeia").
12. Colin Wilson, *Aleister Crowley — The Nature of the Beast* (Wellingborough: Aquarian Press, 1987), p. 71.
13. Edgar Allan Poe, *The Science Fiction of Edgar Allan Poe* (ed. Harold Beaver) (Harmondsworth: Penguin, 1982), p. 309 (*Eureka!*).
14. Luigi Pirandello, *Three Plays — Six Characters in Search of an Author — "Henry IV" — Right You Are! (If You Think So)* (London: J.M. Dent, 1936), pp. 9–10 (*Six Characters in Search of an Author*).
15. *Op. cit.*, p. 10.
16. *Op. cit.*, p. 10.
17. *Op. cit.*, p. 60.
18. *Op. cit.*, p. 62.
19. David Daiches and Anthony Thorlby, *The Modern World II — Realities* (London: Aldus Books, 1972), p. 120.
20. Ted Honderich (ed.), *The Oxford Companion to Philosophy* (note 1), p. 342.
21. John Coldstream, *Dirk Bogarde — The Authorised Biography* (London: Weidenfeld and Nicolson, 2004), p. 392.
22. *Loc. cit.*
23. Emma Wilson, *Alain Resnais* (Manchester: Manchester University Press, 2006), p. 133.
24. Richard Wagner, *Parsifal — Opera Guide 34* (trans. Andrew Porter) (London: John Calder, 1986), p. 86.
25. Stephen Jones, *The Illustrated Werewolf Movie Guide* (London: Titan Books, 1996), p. 87.
26. John Coldstream, *Dirk Bogarde — The Authorised Biography* (note 21), p. 393.
27. *Op. cit.*, p. 394.
28. Adolfo Bioy-Casares, *The Invention of Morel and Other Stories* (trans, Ruth L.C. Simms) (Austin: University of Texas Press, 1964), p.11.

Chapter Nine

1. *The Opera Libretto Library* (New York: Avenel Books, 1980), p. 251 ("Aida").
2. Hector Berlioz, *The Memoirs of Hector Berlioz* (trans. David Cairns) (London: Cardinal, 1990), p. 82.
3. Mark Bills, *Edwin Longsdon Long RA* (London: Cygnus Arts, 1998), p. 112.
4. William Gaunt, *Victorian Olympus* (London: Non-Fiction Book Club, 1953), p. 29
5. H. Rider Haggard, *Cleopatra* (London: Longmans, Green, 1914), p. 66.
6. *Op. cit.*, pp. 186–88.
7. Richard Buckle, *Diaghilev* (London: Weidenfeld, 1993), p. 150.
8. Edward Lockspeiser, *Debussy, His Life and Mind*, vol. 2, 1902–1918 (London: Cassell, 1965), p. 153.
9. *Op. cit.*, p. 155.
10. Philip J. Riley (ed.), *The Mummy* (Absecon NJ: MagicImage Filmbooks, 1989), scene L-61.
11. John Romer, *Valley of the Kings* (London: Michael Joseph, 1981), p. 85.
12. Frank McLynn, *Napoleon* (London: Jonathan Cape, 1997), p. 169.
13. *Op. cit.*, p. 169.
14. William Beckford, *Vathek* (trans. Herbert B. Grimsditch) (London: Bodley Head, 1953), p. 42.
15. Marcus Hearn & Alan Barnes, *The Hammer Story* (London: Titan Books, 2007), p. 42.
16. H.P. Lovecraft, *The Loved Dead & Other Stories* (Ware: Wordsworth, 2007), p. 70 ("The Last Test").
17. *Op. cit.*, pp. 61–62 ("Imprisoned with the Pharaohs").
18. August Strindberg, *Plays: One* (trans. Michael Meyer) (London: Methuen, 1982), p. 180 (*The Ghost Sonata*).
19. Bram Stoker, *Dracula* (Archibald Constable: Westminster, 1904), p. 315.
20. Philip J. Riley (ed.), *The Mummy* (note 10), scenes L-42.
21. Edgar Allan Poe, *The Complete Illustrated Stories and Poems of Edgar Allan Poe* (London: Chancellor Press, 1988), p. 527 ("Some Words with a Mummy").
22. When the film was remade by Jeffrey Obrow as *Bram Stoker's Legend of the Mummy* (1997), this claustrophobic atmosphere was sensibly maintained. Despite this and the presence of Aubrey Morris, who played the role of Dr. Putnam in the Hammer version, the film was rather less successful than *Blood from the Mummy's Tomb*.

Chapter Ten

1. Peter Teuthold, *The Necromancer, or The Tale of the Black Forest* (ed. Jeffrey Cass) (Chicago: Valancourt Books, 2007), pp. 40–41.
2. Matthew Lewis, *The Monk* (ed. Howard Anderson) (Oxford: Oxford University Press, 1973), pp. 432–33.
3. Benedictus de Spinoza, *Ethics* (trans. Andrew Boyle) (London: Heron Books, 1969), p. 11.
4. Ted Honderich (ed.), *The Oxford Companion to Philosophy* (Oxford: Oxford University Press, 1995), p. 847.
5. Benedictus de Spinoza, *Ethics* (note 3), pp. 33–34.
6. W. Somerset Maugham, *The Magician/The Gentleman in the Parlour* (London: Heron Books, 1968), pp. 6–7.
7. *Op. cit.*, p. 104.
8. Joris-Karl Huysmans, *La Bas (Lower Depths)*, London: Daedalus, 1986, p. 242.
9. W. Somerset Maugham, *The Magician/The Gentleman in the Parlour* (note 6), p. 114.
10. Carlos Clarens, *Horror Films—An Illustrated Survey* (London: Secker & Warburg, 1967), p. 114.
11. George Bernard Shaw, *Major Critical Essays: The Quintessence of Ibsenism. The Perfect Wagnerite. The Sanity of Art* (London: Constable, 1932), p. 179.
12. Faubion Bowers, *The New Scriabin—Enigma and Answers* (Newton Abbot/London: David & Charles, 1974), p. 192.
13. *Op. cit.*, p. 191.
14. Éliphas Lévi, *Transcendental Magic—Its Doctrine and Ritual* (trans. Arthur Edward Waite) (Twickenham: Senate, 1995), p. 41.
15. Nicholas Goodrick-Clarke, *The Occult Roots of Nazism—The Ariosophists of Austria and Germany 1890–1935* (Wellingborough: Aquarian Press, 1985), p. 19.
16. *Op. cit.*, p. 219.
17. David J. Skal, *The Monster Show—A Cultural History of Horror* (London: Plexus, 1993), p. 195.
18. As Goodrick-Clarke explains, the Knights Templars provided a degree of inspiration for the later Nazi SS organization, which he traces back to Jörg Lanz von Liebensfels' Templar-derived Racist/Nationalist New Templars (Ordo Novi Templi), the published organ of which, *Ostara*, was certainly read by Adolf Hitler. Intriguingly, Lanz's O.N.T. emerged around the same time that Crowley became involved with a different German occult group, Ordo Templi Orientis (O.T.O), for which Crowley took the magical name of Baphomet. By Christmas 1908, Lanz was hoisting a swastika flag over the castle he had bought in Austria especially to host meetings of the O.N.T. Crowley, who had nothing to do with Lanz's racist organization, was an active member of the O.T.O. by 1912. (See *The Occult Roots of Nazism* [note 13], pp. 108–09.)
19. Dennis Wheatley, *They Used Dark Forces* (London: Heron Books, 1973), p. 388.
20. Dennis Wheatley, Introduction to *The Dennis Wheatley Library of the Occult* edition of Aleister Crowley's *Moonchild* (London: Sphere, 1974), p. 9.
21. Éliphas Lévi, *Transcendental Magic, Its Dogma and Ritual* (note 14), pp. 376–78.
22. *Op. cit.*, p. 485
23. Tanya Krzywinska, *A Skin for Dancing In—Possession, Witchcraft and Voodoo in Film* (Trowbridge: Flicks Books, 2000), p. 93.
24. Dennis Wheatley, *The Devil Rides Out* (London: Heron Books, 1972), p. 235.
25. *Op. cit.*, p. 166.
26. Tanya Krzywinska, *A Skin for Dancing In—Possession, Witchcraft and Voodoo in Film* (note 23), p. 94.
27. *Op. cit.*, p. 95.
28. Dennis Wheatley, *The Devil Rides Out* (note 24), p. 19.
29. Robert Irwin, *Satan Wants Me* (Sawtry: Daedalus, 1999), p. 77.
30. François Rabelais, *The Works of Rabelais* (London: Chatto and Windus, 1875), p. 113.
31. *Op. cit.*, pp. 107–08.
32. Aleister Crowley, *The Confessions of Aleister Crowley, An Autohagiography* (ed., John Symonds and Kenneth Grant) (Harmondsworth: Arkana, 1989), p. 582.
33. *Op. cit.*, p. 177.
34. *Op. cit.*, p. 582.

35. *Op. cit.*, p. 400.
36. Christopher Lee, *Tall, Dark and Gruesome—An Autobiography* (London: Victor Gollancz, 1997), p. 235.
37. Marcus Hearn and Alan Barnes, *The Hammer Story* (London: Titan, 2007), p. 109.
38. Sir James Frazer, *The Golden Bough—A Study in Magic and Religion* (abridged edition) (London: Macmillan, 1950), p. 438.
39. *Op. cit.*, pp. 12–38.
40. John Milton, *Milton's Poetical Works* (London: Frederick Warne, 1896), p. 105 (*Paradise Lost*, Book 1, line 63).
41. *Op. cit.*, p. 135 (*Paradise Lost*, Book II, lines 362–76).
42. Sanders addressed the note to his sister Margaret.
43. John Milton, *Milton's Poetical Works* (note 40), p. 265 (*Paradise Lost*, Book VII, lines 471–74).
44. *Op. cit.*, p. 106 (*Paradise Lost*, Book I, line 76).
45. Marjorie Bilbow, *The Facts About a Feature Films, Featuring Hammer Films* (London: G. Whizzard/André Deutsch, 1978), p. 32.
46. The term "neoconservatism" applies to a political philosophy that attempts to demonstrate and take action against what it regards as the failure of liberalism. Significantly, the word was first used in this post-liberal sense by American democratic socialist Michael Harrington in an article for the magazine *Dissent* in 1973, the same year in which *The Exorcist* was released. Former neocon Michael Lind has explained, "For the neoconservatives, religion is an instrument of promoting morality. Religion becomes what Plato called a noble lie. It is a myth which is told to the majority of the society by the philosophical elite in order to ensure social order." (Michael Lind quoted in the BBC-TV documentary *The Power of Nightmares* by Adam Curtis, 2004).
47. Aleister Crowley, *The Confessions of Aleister Crowley—An Autohagiography* (note 32), p. 623.

Chapter Eleven

1. D.H. Lawrence, *Phoenix*, vol. II (London: Heinemann, 1968), pp. 417–18.
2. Thornton Wilder, *Theophilus North* (London: Allen Lane, 1974), p. 141.
3. *Op. cit.*, p. 143.
4. H.P. Lovecraft, *The Loved Dead & Other Stories* (Ware: Wordsworth, 2007), p. 25 ("The Loved Dead").
5. Edmund Blunden, *Shelley* (London: Collins, 1946), p. 202.
6. Thomas Love Peacock, *The Novels of Thomas Love Peacock* (ed. David Garnett) (London: Rupert Hart-Davis, 1948), p. 360 (*Nightmare Abbey*).
7. *Loc. cit.*
8. Jane Austen, *Northanger Abbey* (Ware: Wordsworth Classics, 1995), p. 140.
9. *Op. cit.*, p. 76.
10. Christopher Lee, *Lord of Misrule—The Autobiography of Christopher Lee* (London: Orion, 2003), p. 301.
11. Jonathan Rigby, *Christopher Lee—The Authorised Screen History* (London: Reynolds & Hearn, 2001), p. 170.
12. William Shakespeare, *Shakespeare Complete Works* (ed. W.J. Craig) (Oxford: Oxford University Press, 1974), p. 853 (*Macbeth*, Act II, scene 3, lines 1–9).
13. *Op. cit.*, p. 901 (*Hamlet*, Act V, scene 1, lines 1–21).
14. Horace Walpole, *The Castle of Otranto* (ed. W.S. Lewis) (London: Oxford University Press, 1969), p. 99.
15. Ann Radcliffe, *The Romance of the Forest* (ed. Chloe Chard) (Oxford: Oxford University Press, 1986), p. 138.
16. Mark Gatiss, *James Whale, or The Would-Be Gentleman* (London: Cassell, 1995), p. 111.
17. Bram Stoker, *The Lair of the White Worm* (London: Arrow, 1975), p. 118.
18. *Op. cit.*, p. 119.
19. *Op. cit.*, p. 53.
20. *Op. cit.*, p. 72.
21. Tom Shone, *Blockbuster* (London: Simon & Schuster, 2004), p. 52.
22. Roy Skeggs in the DVD documentary *To the Devil ... The Death of Hammer* (Optimum Releasing, 2006).

Select Bibliography

Andersen, Hans Christian. *The Complete Illustrated Stories of Hans Christian Andersen*. London: Chancellor Press, 1985.

Appia, Adolphe (ed. Ruchard C. Beacham). *Adolphe Appia: Texts on Theatre*. London: Routledge, 1993.

Apuleius, Lucius. *The Golden Asse of Lucius Apuleius* (trans. William Adlington). London: Abbey Library, 1923.

Aristotle, Horace, Longinus. *Classical Literary Criticism* (trans. T.S. Dorsch). Harmondsworth: Penguin, 1979.

Austen, Jane. *Northanger Abbey*. Ware: Wordsworth, 1995.

Baring-Gould, Sabine. *The Book of Werewolves*. London: Senate, 1995.

Beacham, Richard C. "Adolphe Appia and Wagnerian Opera" in *The Opera Quarterly*, vol. 1, no. 3, Autumn 1983.

Beckford, William. *Life at Fonthill* (trans. and ed. Boyd Alexander). Stroud: Nonesuch, 2006.

____. *Vathek* (trans. Herbert B. Grimsditch). London: Bodley Head, 1953.

Benson, E.F. *Raven's Brood*. Brighton: Millivres Books, 1993.

Berlioz, Hector. *The Memoirs of Hector Berlioz* (trans. David Cairns). London: Cardinal, 1990.

Bilbow, Marjorie. *The Facts About a Feature Film, Featuring Hammer Films*. London: G. Whizzard/André Deutsch, 1978.

Bills, Mark. *Edwin Longsdon Long RA*. London: Cygnus Arts, 1998.

Bioy-Casares, Adolfo. *The Invention of Morel and Other Stories* (trans. Ruth L. C. Simms). Austin: University of Texas Press, 1964.

Blunden, Edmund. *Shelley*. London: Collins, 1946.

Bowers, Faubion. *The New Scriabin: Enigma and Answers*. Newton Abbot/London: David & Charles, 1974.

Bright, Morris, and Robert Ross. *Mr. Carry On: The Life and Work of Peter Rogers*. London: BBC, 2000.

Brownlow, Kevin. *David Lean: A Biography*. London: Richard Cohen, 1996.

Buckle, Richard. *Diaghilev*. London: Weidenfeld, 1993.

Burke, Edmund (ed. Adam Phillips). *A Philosophical Enquiry into the Origin of Our Ideas of the Sublime and Beautiful*. Oxford: Oxford University Press, 1990.

Burton, Anthony and Pip. *The Green Bag Travellers— Britain's First Tourists*. London: Andre Deutsch, 1978.

Byron, Lord. *Poetical Works*. London: Virtue, 1855.

Caldwell, Thomas (ed.). *The Golden Book of Modern English Poetry*. London: Dent, 1935.

Carroll, Lewis. *The Complete Illustrated Works of Lewis Carroll*. London: Chancellor Press, 1985.

Cavendish, Richard. *The Tarot*. London: Chancellor Press, 1986.

Clarens, Carlos. *Horror Films: An Illustrated Survey*. London: Secker & Warburg, 1967.

Clarke, Kenneth. *The Gothic Revival*. London: John Murray, 1974.

____. *The Romantic Rebellion: Romantic Versus Classic Art*. London: Futura, 1976.

Coldstream, John. *Dirk Bogarde: The Authorised Biography*. London: Weidenfeld and Nicolson, 2004.

Coleridge, Samuel Taylor. *Coleridge Poetical Works* (ed. Ernest Hartley Coleridge). London: Oxford University Press, 1974.

Cooper, James Fenimore. *The Last of the Mohicans*. Oxford: Oxford University Press, 1994.

Coppola, Francis Ford, and James V. Hart. *Bram Stoker's Dracula: The Film and the Legend*. London: Pan, 1992.

Crowley, Aleister (ed. John Symonds and Kenneth Grant). *The Confessions of Aleister Crowley: An Autohagiography*. Harmondsworth: Arkana, 1989.

____. *Moonchild*. London: Sphere, 1974.

Csapo, Eric. *Theory of Mythology*. Oxford: Wiley-Blackwell, 2005.

Cushing, Peter. *Past Forgetting: Memoirs of the Hammer Years*. London: Wiedenfeld and Nicolson, 1988.

Daiches, David, and Anthony Thorlby. *The Modern World II: Realities*. London: Aldus Books, 1972.

Delevoy, Robert L. *Symbolists and Symbolism*. London: Skira/Macmillan, 1982.

De Quincey, Thomas (ed. David Masson). *Collected Writings of Thomas De Quincey*. Edinburgh: Adam & Charles Black, 1889–90.

Dickens, Charles. *Oliver Twist/Great Expectations*. London: Hazel, Watson & Viney, c.1933.

du Maurier, Daphne. *Rebecca*. London: Heron Books, 1971.

Ehrhardt, Ingrid, and Simon Reynolds. *The Kingdom of the Soul: Symbolist Art in Germany 1870–1920*. Munich: Prestel, 2000.

Eisner, Lotte H. *The Haunted Screen* (trans. Roger Greaves). London: Secker & Warburg, 1983.

Eksteins, Modris. *Rites of Spring*. London: Papermac, 2000.

Endore, Guy. *The Werewolf of Paris*. London: Sphere, 1974.

Florescu, Radu. *In Search of Frankenstein*. Boston: New York Graphic Society, 1975.

Frank, Alan. *Horror Films*. London: Hamlyn, 1977.

Frazer, James. *The Golden Bough*. London: Macmillan, 1950.

Freud, Sigmund. *The Interpretation of Dreams* (trans. James Strachey). Harmondsworth: Penguin, 1983.

Gatiss, Mark. *James Whale, or The Would-Be Gentleman*. London: Cassell, 1995.

Gaunt, William. *Victorian Olympus*. London: Non-Fiction Book Club, 1953.

Gifford, Denis. *A Pictorial History of Horror Movies*. London: Hamlyn, 1979.

Gilbert, W.S. *The Savoy Operas*. London: Papermac, 1983.

Goethe, Johann Wolfgang von. *Faust — Part One* (trans. David Luke). Oxford: Oxford University Press, 1987.

Goodrick-Clarke, Nicholas. *The Occult Roots of Nazism: The Ariosophists of Austria and Germany 1890–1935*. Wellingborough: Aquarian Press, 1985.

Greaves, Tim. *Veronica Carlson: An Illustrated Memento*. Eastleigh: 1-Shot Publications, 1993.

Haggard, H. Rider. *Cleopatra*. London: Longmans, Green, 1914.

_____. *She*. London: Collins, 1974 (originally published New York: Harper & Bros., 1886).

Haining, Peter (ed.). *The Frankenstein Omnibus*. London: Orion, 1994.

Halliwell, Leslie (ed. John Walker). *Film and Video Guide 2000 Edition*. London: HarperCollins, 2000.

Hartley, Keith (ed.). *The Romantic Spirit in German Art 1790–1990*. London: Thames and Hudson, 1994.

Hearn, Marcus, and Alan Barnes. *The Hammer Story*. London: Titan Books, 2007.

Hoffmann, E.T.A. *The Nutcracker and the Golden Pot* (trans. Thomas Carlyle). New York: Dover, 1993.

Holden, Anthony. *Olivier*. London: Sphere, 1989.

Homer. *The Odyssey* (trans. E.V. Rieu). London: Guild Publishing, 1991.

Honderich, Ted (ed.). *The Oxford Companion to Philosophy*. Oxford: Oxford University Press, 1995.

Huckvale, David. *Hammer Film Scores and the Musical Avant-Garde*. Jefferson, NC: McFarland, 2008.

_____. *James Bernard, Composer to Count Dracula*. Jefferson, NC: McFarland, 2006.

Huysmans, Joris Karl. *À Rebours*. London: Fortune Press, 1946.

_____. *La Bas* (*Lower Depths*). London: Daedalus, 1986.

Irwin, Robert. *Satan Wants Me*. Sawtry: Daedalus, 1999.

Jung, Carl Gustav. *On the Nature of the Psyche* (trans. R.F.C. Hull). London: Routledge & Kegan Paul, 1982.

Keats, John (ed. H.W. Garrod). *Keats Poetical Works*. London: Oxford University Press, 1973.

_____. *The Letters of John Keats* (ed. H. Buxton Forman). Whitefish, MT: Kessinger, 2004.

Kelly, Walter Keating. *Curiosities of Indo-European Tradition and Folk-Lore*. Whitefish, MT: Kessinger, 2004.

Köhler, Joachim. *Richard Wagner: The Last of the Tribunes* (trans. Stewart Spencer). New Haven: Yale University Press, 2004.

_____. *Zarathustra's Secret* (trans. Ronald Taylor). New Haven: Yale University Press, 2002.

Krzywinska, Tanya. *A Skin for Dancing In: Possession, Witchcraft and Voodoo in Film*. Trowbridge: Flicks Books, 2000.

Lawrence, D.H. *Phoenix*, vol. II. London: Heinemann, 1968.

Le Fanu, Sheridan. *In a Glass Darkly*. London: John Lehmann, 1947.

_____. *Uncle Silas* (ed. W.J. McCormack). Oxford: Oxford University Press, 1981.

Lee, Christopher. *Lord of Misrule: The Autobiography of Christopher Lee*. London: Orion, 2003.

_____. *Tall, Dark and Gruesome*. London: Victor Gollancz, 1997.

Lévi, Éliphas. *Magic — A History of Its Rites, Rituals, and Mysteries* (trans. Arthur Edward Waite). New York: Dover, 2006.

_____. *Transcendental Magic — Its Dogma and Ritual* (trans. Arthur Edward Waite). Twickenham: Senate, 1995.

Lewis, Matthew (ed. Howard Anderson). *The Monk*. Oxford: Oxford University Press, 1977.

Lockspeiser, Edward. *Debussy: His Life and Mind, vol. 2, 1902–1918*. London: Cassell, 1965.

Lovecraft, H.P. *The Haunter of the Dark and Other Stories*. London: Panther, 1974.

———. *The Loved Dead and Other Stories*. Ware: Wordsworth, 2007.

Maeterlinck, Maurice. *The Treasure of the Humble* (trans. Alfred Sutro). London: George Allen, 1897.

Mann, Thomas. *Stories of Three Decades* (trans. H.T. Lowe-Porter), London: Martin Secker & Warburg, 1936.

Maturin, Charles (ed. Douglas Grant). *Melmoth the Wanderer*. Oxford: Oxford University Press, 1989.

Maugham, W. Somerset. *The Magician/The Gentleman in the Parlour*. London: Heron Books, 1968.

———. *The World Over — The Collected Short Stories, vol. 1*. London: Reprint Society, 1961.

McLynn, Frank. *Napoleon*. London: Jonathan Cape, 1997.

Millington, Barry. *Wagner* (The Master Musicians series). London: Dent, 1994.

Milton, John. *The Poetical Works of John Milton*. London: Frederick Warne, 1896.

Newall, Christopher. *Frederick Leighton 1830–1896*. London: Royal Academy of Arts, 1996.

Nietzsche, Friedrich. *Beyond Good and Evil* (trans. R.J. Hollingdale). Harmondsworth: Penguin, 1983.

Norton, Rictor. *Mistress of Udolpho*. London: Leicester University Press, 1999.

The Opera Libretto Library. New York: Avenel Books, 1980.

Peacock, Thomas Love (ed. David Garnett). *The Novels of Thomas Love Peacock*. London: Rupert Hart-Davis, 1948.

Pirandello, Luigi. *Three Plays: Six Characters in Search of an Author — "Henry IV" — Right You Are! (If You Think So)*. London: J.M. Dent, 1922.

Poe, Edgar Allan. *The Complete Illustrated Stories and Poems of Edgar Allan Poe*. London: Chancellor Press, 1988.

———. *The Science Fiction of Edgar Allan Poe* (ed. Harold Beaver). Harmondsworth: Penguin, 1982.

Praz, Mario. *The Romantic Agony*. Oxford: Oxford University Press, 1970.

Radcliffe, Ann. *The Italian* (ed. Frederick Garber). London: Oxford University Press, 1970.

———. *The Mysteries of Udolpho* (ed. Bonamy Dobrée). London: Oxford University Press, 1970.

———. *The Romance of the Forest* (ed. Chloe Chard). Oxford: Oxford University Press, 1986.

Rhodes, Anthony. *The Poet as Superman: A Life of Gabriele D'Annunzio*. London: Weidenfeld and Nicolson, 1959.

Rigby, Jonathan. *American Gothic*. Richmond: Reynolds & Hearn, 2007.

———. *Christopher Lee: The Authorised Screen History*. London: Reynolds & Hearn, 2001.

Riley, Philip J. (ed.). *The Mummy*. Absecon, NJ: MagicImage Filmbooks, 1989.

Romer, John. *Valley of the Kings*. London: Michael Joseph, 1981.

Rosen, Charles. *The Romantic Generation*. London: HarperCollins, 1996.

Rousseau, Jean-Jacques. *Emile, or Education* (trans. Barbara Foxley). London: J.M. Dent, 1930.

Ruskin, John. *The Stones of Venice*. London: Folio Society, 2001.

Sachs, Bruce, and Russell Wall. *Greasepaint and Gore: The Hammer Monsters of Roy Ashton*. Sheffield: Tomahawk Press, 1991.

Sangster, Jimmy. *Inside Hammer*. London: Reynolds & Hearn, 2001.

Schifano, Laurence. *Luchino Visconti: The Flames of Passion*. London: Collins, 1990.

Schmidgall, Gary. *Literature as Opera*. New York: Oxford University Press, 1977.

Schnitzler, Arthur. *Dream Story* (trans. J.M.Q. Davis). Harmondsworth: Penguin, 1999.

Scott, Sir Walter. *Waverley*. Edinburgh: Adam and Charles Black, 1860.

Seckerson, Edward. *Mahler: His Life and Times*. Tunbridge Wells: Midas Books, 1982.

Seymour, Miranda. *Mary Shelley*. London: John Murray, 2000.

Shakespeare, William. *Shakespeare's Complete Works* (ed. W.J. Craig). Oxford: Oxford University Press, 1978.

Shaw, George Bernard. *Complete Plays of Bernard Shaw*. London: Odhams Press, 1937.

———. *Major Critical Essays: The Quintessence of Ibsenism, The Perfect Wagnerite, The Sanity of Art*. London: Constable, 1932.

Shelley, Mary. *Frankenstein*. London: Dent, 1941.

Shelley, Percy Bysshe. *The Complete Poetical Works of Percy Bysshe Shelley* (ed. Thomas Hutchinson). London: Oxford University Press, 1956.

———. *Zastrozzi and St. Irvyne* (ed. Stephen C. Behrendt). Oxford: Oxford University Press, 1986.

Shone, Tom. *Blockbuster*. London: Simon & Schuster, 2004.

Skal, David J. *The Monster Show: A Cultural History of Horror*. London: Plexus, 1993.

Spinoza, Benedictus de. *Ethics* (trans. Andrew Boyle). London: Heron Books, 1969.

Stevens, MaryAnne, and Robert Hoozee, *Impressionism to Symbolism: The Belgian Avant-Garde 1880–1900*. London: Royal Academy of Arts, 1994.

Stevenson, Robert Louis. *The Strange Case of Dr. Jekyll and Mr. Hyde and Other Stories*. New York: Peebles Classic Library, 1974.

Stoker, Bram. *Dracula*. Westminster: Archibald Constable, 1904.

Strindberg, August. *Plays: One* (trans. Michael Meyer). London: Methuen, 1982.

Strunk, Oliver (ed.). *Source Readings in Music His-*

tory, vol. 5: "The Romantic Era." London: Faber and Faber, 1981.

Summers, Montague. *The Werewolf.* Whitefish MT: Kessinger, 2003.

Tennyson, Hallam. *Alfred Lord Tennyson: A Memoir by His Son.* London: Macmillan, 1897.

Teuthold, Peter (ed. Jeffrey Cass). *The Necromancer, or The Tale of the Black Forest.* Chicago: Valentine Books, 2007.

Verne, Jules. *The Castle of the Carpathians.* London: Sampson Low, Marston, 1902.

Villiers de l'Isle Adam, Auguste. *Axel* (trans. M. Gaddis Rose). London: Soho Book, 1986.

____. *Cruel Tales* (trans. Robert Baldick). Oxford: Oxford University Press, 1985.

____. *The Vampire Soul and Other Stories* (trans. Brian Stableford). Encino, CA: Black Coat Press, 2004.

Wagner, Richard. *My Life* (trans. Andrew Gray). Cambridge: Cambridge University Press, 1987.

____. *Parsifal — Opera Guide 34* (trans. Andrew Porter). London: John Calder, 1986.

____. *Tristan and Isolde* (trans. Stewart Robb). New York: E.P. Dutton, 1965.

Walpole, Horace. *The Castle of Otranto* (ed. W.S. Lewis). London: Oxford University Press, 1969.

Wheatley, Dennis. *The Devil Rides Out.* London: Heron Books, 1972.

____. *They Used Dark Forces.* London: Heron Books, 1973.

Wilde, Oscar. *Complete Works of Oscar Wilde.* London: Collins, 1977.

Wilder, Thornton. *Theophilus North.* London: Allen Lane, 1974.

Wilhelm, Kurt. *Richard Strauss: An Intimate Portrait.* London: Thames and Hudson, 1989.

Wilson, Colin. *Aleister Crowley: The Nature of the Beast.* Wellingborough: Aquarian Press, 1987.

Wilson, Emma. *Alain Resnais.* Manchester: Manchester University Press, 2006.

Wischhusen, Stephen (ed.). *The Hour of One: Six Gothic Melodramas.* London: Gordon Fraser, 1975.

Wolf, Leonard. *The Annotated Dracula.* London: New English Library, 1976.

Woodward, Christopher. *In Ruins.* London: Chatto & Windus, 2001.

Index

Numbers in **bold italics** *indicate pages with photographs.*

À Bruges (Khnopff) 177
À Rebours (Huysmans) 148, 152
Abbey Church of Iona **58**
Abbott, Bud 232
Abbott and Costello Meet Frankenstein 232
Abtei in Eichwald (Friedrich) 71
Acton, William 136
The Addams Family 242
Adjani, Isabelle ***71***
Adrian, Max 239
Ahmed, Rollo 223
Aida (Verdi) 180
Alastor, or the Spirit of Solitude (Shelley) 83, 88
Albertazzi, Giorgio 177
Albright, Ivan Le Lorraine 124
Aldrich, Robert 238
Alice's Adventures in Wonderland (Carroll) 129
Allan, Maud 183
Alma-Tadema, Sir Lawrence 181, 183
Eine Alpensinfonie (Strauss) 45, 85
An American Werewolf in London 142
Amicus Films 31, 55, 111, 126, 128, 162, 170, 239, 248n
The Anatomy of Melancholy (Burton) 103
And God Created Woman 156
And Now the Screaming Starts 111
Andersen, Hans Christian 128
Andress, Ursula 67, ***68***, 100
Andrews, Dana 206, 208, 209
L'Anglais décrit dans le château fermé (Mandiargues) 176
Anne of the Thousand Days 97
L'Année dernière à Marienbad 22, 177–179, ***178***
Années de pèlerinage (Liszt) 37, 85
The Anniversary 237, ***238***
The Annotated Dracula (Wolf) 136
The Antiquary (Scott) ***70***, 71
Antonioni, Michelangelo 60
Antony and Cleopatra (Shakespeare) 183
Appia, Adolphe 9, 15, 19, 25
Apuleius, Lucius 135
Arabian Adventure 132

An Architectural Description of the Town Hall, Manchester (ed. Axon) 52, ***53***
Arensky, Anton 183
Armstrong, Robert 24
Ashton, Roy 98, 105, 246n
"The Assignation" (Poe) 147, 148, 153
Astley, Edwin 177
Atlantis 206
Atlantis — The Lost Continent 207
Attenborough, Richard 45
Atwill, Lionel 110
Die Augen der Mumie Ma 184
Austen, Jane **57**, 109, 199, 231
The Avengers 238
Avison, Charles 83
The Awakening 133, 196
Axel (Villiers de l'Isle Adam) 150, 156
Aylmer, Felix 21

Bach, Carl Philipp Emanuel 33
Bach, Johann Sebastian 69, 70
Back to Methuselah (Shaw) 167
Bacon, Norman 14
Badham, John 41
Baedeker, Karl 150
Baker, Roy Ward 15, 65, **65**, 106, ***107***, 111, 126, 162, 163, 237–239, ***238***
Baker, Tom 126
Balcombe, Florence 240
Bamberg Rider, Cologne Cathedral 114
Bankhead, Tallulah 96
Banks, Leslie 124
The Barber of Seville (Rossini) 36
The Barbican Centre, London 5
The Bard (Martin) 84
Baring-Gould, Sabine 139
Barry, John 46
Barton, Charles 232
Bass, Alfie 233
Bates, Alan 142
Bates, Ralph 15, 96
Báthory, Countess Elizabeth 24, 140, 179
Batt, Bert 161
Battleship Potemkin 19

Baudelaire, Charles 100, 146–148, 152
Bayreuth 9
BBC 41, 207, 224, 247n
Beacham, Stephanie 111
The Beast in the Cellar 32, 141
The Beatles 60, 213
Beckford, William 13, 25, 50, 185, 186
Bedlam 117
Beethoven, Ludwig van 33, 36, 37
Bellamy, Madge **202**, 203
Belshazzar's Feast (Martin) 84
Belzoni, Giovanni Batista 184
Benson, E(dward) F(rederic) 141
Benson, George 235
Berkeley, George 166
Berlioz, Hector 36, 37, 180
Berna, Maria 120
Bernard, James 9, 15, 37, 41, 50, 63, 152, 155, 210
Bernhardt, Sarah 95
Bernini, Gian Lorenzo 63
Berova, Olinka 215
Beswick, Martine 106, ***107***
The Bible 26, **28**, **29**, 62, 126, 174
Bills, Mark 181
Bioy Casares, Adolfo 179
The Birds 214
"The Birds" (Daphne du Maurier) 240
Birkinshaw, Alan 163
The Birth of Tragedy (Nietzsche) 145
Bishop, Zealia 101
Black, Isobel 153, 156
The Black Art (Ahmed) 223
The Black Cat 11, **12**, 30, 44, 204
The Black Idol (Kupka) 121
Black Park 73–75, **75**, **77**, 80
Blair, Linda 225
Blake, Ann 234
Blavatsky, Helena Petrovna 165, 198, 206–208, 214
Blood from the Mummy's Tomb 30, 127, 194–196, 198, 249n
Blow Up 60
Böcklin, Arnold 114, 115, 117, ***118***, 120–122, 246n
Bogarde, Dirk 73, 105, ***144***, 145, 175, 176

255

Bohn, German von 180
The Book of the Dead 187, 223
The Book of the Penitence of Adam 244n
The Book of Werewolves (Baring-Gould) 139
Boorland, Carroll (aka Carol) 9, *11*, 91
Booth, Harry 237
Bowers, Faubion 206
The Boys from Brazil 209
Bradbury, Ray 44
Brahms, Johannes 117, 204
Bram Stoker's Dracula 121, 146
Bram Stoker's Legend of the Mummy 249n
Branagh, Kenneth 25
Bray Studios 73–75, *77*, 80
Breck, Kathleen *208*, 209
Breugel, Pieter 114
Briant, Shane 30
Bride of Frankenstein 38, 42, 72, 106, 234
The Brides of Dracula 17, *18*, *20*, 22, 80, 150, 222, 235–237, *236*
British Board of Film Censors 4
Britten, Benjamin 111, 112
Broderick, Susan 60
Brommage, Bernard 223
Brontë, Charlotte 204
Brooke, Paul 241
Brookes, Jean *205*
Brooks, Mel 232
The Brotherhood of the Rosy Cross (Waite) 223
Brown, Dr. John 78
Browning, Tod 4, 7, 9, *10*, *11*, 17, 25, 26, 41, 49, 93, 203
Bryan, John 17
Buberl, Brigitte 71, 72
Buckle, Richard 183
Bulwer-Lytton, Edward (Lord Lytton) 207, 208
Buñuel, Luis 93, 113
Burden, Hugh 195
Burke, Edmund 36, 41, 78–80, *79*, 82, 84, 87, 110
Burton, Robert 103
Burton, Tim 241
Byrne, Gabriel 24
Byron, Lord George Gordon 15, 24, 26, 35, *35*, 38, 113, 186, 224, 243n

Cabanne, Christy 186, *188*
The Cabinet of Dr. Caligari 9, 113
Caffé degli Inglesi, Rome 186, 189
Callow, Simon *227*, 228
Camden Society 54
Captain Kronos — Vampire Hunter 238
Carbonnières, Ramond de 71
Carlson, Veronica 94, *95*, 161
"Carmilla" (Le Fanu) 66, 96
Carreras, Sir James 94, 95, 110
Carreras, Michael 17, 40, 96, 194
Carroll, Lewis 128, 129, *130*
Carry On Screaming 110
Carson, John 128, 226, 203, 204, *204*
Carter, Howard 185

"The Case of Charles Dexter Ward" (Lovecraft) 146
"Casting the Runes" (James) 205, 206
The Castle of Otranto (Walpole) 25, 110, 111, 185, 233, 234
The Castle of the Carpathians (Verne) *160*; see also *Le Château des Carpathes*
The Castle Spectre (Lewis) 93
Castro, Adolphe de 191
Cat People 101, 117
Cavalcanti, Cavalcante 3
Cavendish, Richard 138
Ce qu'on entend sur la montagne (Liszt) 85
Cellini, Benvenuto 98
La Cenerentola (Rossini) 36
Chaney, Lon, Jr. *137*, 138, 142
Charlton, Jud 228
Château de Mont-Méry 176
Le Château des Carpathes (Verne) 156
Chemical Wedding *227*, 228
Chéreau, Patrice 246n
Un Chien andalou 113
Childe Harold's Pilgrimage (Byron) 35
Children of the Corn (King) 220
"Children of the Full Moon" 139, *140*
Chirico, Giorgio de 117, 162, 176
Chopin, Frédéric 120
"Christabel" (Coleridge) 103–105, 113
Chronicles (The Bible) 62
Claire Lenoir (Villiers de l'Isle Adam) 152, 164, 165
Clarens, Carlos 203
Clark, Fred 194, 237
Clark, Jim 229
Clarke, Sir Kenneth 9, 54, 78
Clayton, Jack 171
Clegg, Tom 139, *140*
Clemens, Brian 238
Cleopatra 180
Cléopâtre (Diaghilev ballet) 183
Cleopatra (Haggard) 181, *182*
Cleopatra (dir. Mankiewicz) 189, *190*
Cléopâtre (Massenet) 183
Clive, Colin 42
Clouzout, Henri 95
Cocteau, Jean 128, 145
Cole, George *65*
Coleridge, Samuel Taylor 103, 104, 113
Collins, Joan 96
Cologne Cathedral 114
The Coming Race (Bulwer-Lytton) 208
Comus (Milton) 112
Conan Doyle, Sir Arthur 191
Connor, Kevin 55, *131*, 132, 207
Contes cruels (Villiers de l'Isle Adam) 162, 163, 166
Les Contes de Perrault *48*
Constantine the Great 62
Cook, Vera 235

Cooper, James Fenimore 86
Cooper, Merian C(aldwell) 24
"Coppélia" (Hoffmann) 156
Coppola, Francis Ford 121, 146
Corman, Roger 125, *125*, *146*, 147, 168, 169, 229
"Correspondances" (Baudelaire) 147
Corrigan, Lloyd 91
Corruption 133
Costello, Lou 234
Countess Dracula 80, 97, *97*, 140
Court, Hazel 234
Craig, Edward Gordon 9
Craig, Michael 239
Cramer, Marc *118*
The Creeping Flesh 42, 113
Cribbins, Bernard 67, *68*, 237
Crime and Punishment 9
Crippen, Dr. Hawley Harvey 110
Crutchley, Rosalie 112, 127, 198, *227*
Cry of the Werewolf 101
Currie, Finlay 17
The Curse of Frankenstein 80, 161, 234, 237
The Curse of the Mummy's Tomb 17, 21, 30, 191, 194, 237
The Curse of the Werewolf 138, *139*, 142, 145, 176, 235
Curtis, Adam 250n
Curtis, Tony 111
Curtiz, Michael 110, 189
Cushing, Peter 1, 15, 17–19, *18*, 21, 30, 31, 41, 42, 55, 67, *68*, 80, 94, 96, 98, 110, 112, 113, 129, *131*, 132, *158*, 160, 161, *164*, 165, 193, 229, *236*, 244n
Cyr, Miriam 113

"Daisy" wallpaper (Morris) 55, 62, *62*
Dalí, Salvador 113, 117
Daltry, Roger 46
The Damned 163, 248n
Dance of the Vampires see *The Fearless Vampire Killers*
Daniel, Jennifer *153*, *157*
D'Annunzio, Gabrielle 100, 147, 184
Dante Alighieri *2*, 3, *34*, 115, *117*
Dante's Inferno 115–117, *117*
Darwin, Charles 54, 206, 209
Dashwood Mausoleum 73, 225
Daughter of the Dragon 91
Daughters of Darkness 24, 179
Davies, Rupert 14, 41, 80
Davis, Bette 25, 96, 237, *238*
Davis, Geoffrey 239
Davison, Thomas Raffles *52*, *53*
Day, Robert 67, *68*, *75*
DC Comics 163
De praestigiis daemonum (Weyer) 223
De Profundis (Wilde) 167
Dead of Night 129
Dearden, Basil 105
Death as Assassin (Rethel) 114
Death in Venice (dir. Visconti) 143, *144*

Death of Alexander Scriabin (dir. Russell) 207
Debussy, Claude 146, 183
Deception 25
Dee, Francis 204
Dejussieu, Henri 180
Delevoy, Robert L. 148
Delineations of Fonthill Abbey (Rutter) *14*
Delvaux, Paul 162
De Marney, Derrick 123, 125
DeMille, Cecil B(lount) 84, 194
Demons of the Mind 26
Denberg, Susan 94, *158*
Deneuve, Catherine 133
Denham Studios 73
de Quincey, Thomas 35
de Sade, Marquis Donatien Alphonse François 91, 100, 105, 176
de Souza, Edward 152, *153*
Destruction of Sodom and Gomorrah (Martin) 84
de Toth, André 110
Deuteronomy (The Bible) 126
The Devil Rides Out (dir. Fisher) 167, 200, 210, 211, 214, 215, *217*, 224, 225, 227, 237
The Devil Rides Out (Wheatley) 167, 168, 172, 209, 213
The Devil's Elixir (Fitzball) 93
Les Diaboliques 95, 96
Diaghilev, Sergei 183
Dickens, Charles 17, 150
Dickinson, Bruce 228
Dickinson, Desmond 22, 23
Diderot, Denis 67
Dido and Aeneas (Purcell) 186
Diffring, Anton 150
Dillon, Carmen 25
Diodati, Villa 24, 42
Dissent (magazine) 250n
Diverse Ways of ornamenting chimney pieces and all parts of houses taken from Egyptian, Etruscan and Grecian architecture with an Apologia in defense of Egyptian and Tuscan architecture (Piranesi) *187*, *189*
The Divine Comedy (Dante) *2*, 3, 4, *34*, *117*
Dix, William 96
Dr. Jekyll and Mr. Hyde (dir. Mamoulian) 44
Dr. Jekyll and Mr. Hyde (Stevenson) 132, 142
Dr. Jekyll and Sister Hyde 60, 106, *107*, 133, 161, 238
Dr. Mabuse, der Spieler 11
Dr. Terror's House of Horrors 31, 101, 102, 239
Dr. Who 63, 224
Dog Soldiers 142
Dogma et rituel de la haute magie (Lévi) see *Transcendental Magic — Its Doctrine and Ritual*
Donen, Stanley 44
Donner, Richard 225
Doré, Gustave *2*, 3, 26, *28*, *34*, *48*, 115, *117*

Dors, Diana 139, *140*
Dostoyevsky, Fyodor 9
Douglas, Melvyn 44
Doyle, Julian *227*, 228
Dracula (dir. Browning) 4, 7, *10*, 25, 41, 49, *49*, 66, 151, 191, 203, 234
Dracula (dir. Fisher) 7, 13, 30, 41, 50, 151, *151*, 152, 224, 232, 235
Dracula (Stoker) 4, 38, 41, 87–89
Dracula A.D. 1972 *8*, 15, 50, 55, 66, 106, 223, 224
Dracula Has Risen from the Grave 13, 41, 80. 90, 224, 225, *237*
Dracula Is Dead but Alive and Living in London see *The Satanic Rites of Dracula*
Dracula père et fils 232
Dracula Prince of Darkness 13, 22, *75*, 225
Dracula's Daughter 91, *92*
Dragonwyck 24
Dresden 9
Duffell, Peter 94
"The Duke of Portland" (Villiers de l'Isle Adam) 163
du Locle, Camille 180
du Maurier, Daphne 23, 240
Dyer, John 69

Eddington, Paul *217*
Eddy, C(lifford) M(artin) 230
Edison, Thomas Alva 156
Edward I 84
Edwards, Mark 30, 195, 196
The Egyptian 189
An Egyptian Feast (Long) 181
Egyptian Hall, London 183
Egyptian Nights (Arensky) 183
Eiffel, Gustave 121
Einstein, Albert 129
Eisenstein, Sergei 19, 25
Eisner, Lotte H. 9, 12, 170
Eksteins, Modris 122
Eldena Abbey 71
Elès, Sandor 80
Elliot, Denholm 170
Elstree Studios 73
Empire of Lights (Magritte) 162
Endore, Guy 138
Entartung (Nordau) 121
Epstein, Jean 125, 147
Et mourir de plaisir 96
Ethics (Spinoza) 200
Eule vor dem Mond (Friedrich) 114
Eureka (Poe) 168
Evans, Clifford 145
L'Eve future (Villiers de l'Isle Adam) 156, 159, 160, 168
The Evening Standard (newspaper) 5
The Evil of Frankenstein 42, 160
Exclusive Films 160
Exodus (The Bible) 126
The Exorcist 225, 226, 250n
Eye of the Devil 217, *218*, 220
Eyes of the Mummy see *Die Augen der Mumie Ma*

Fairbanks, Douglas, Jr. 186
The Fall of the House of Usher (Debussy) 146
The Fall of the House of Usher (dir. Epstein) 125
"The Fall of the House of Usher" (Poe) 46
The Family Devotional Bible see The Bible
Fanatic 96
Faust (Goethe) 101, 138, 205
Eine Faust Symphonie (Liszt) 101
Fear in the Night 96
The Fearless Vampire Killers 108, 111, 232–234
Ferré, Luis 60
Fiander, Lewis 106, 238
Finch, Jon *65*
Fingal's Cave 71
Fisher, Terence 1, 7, 9, 13, 17, 18, *18*, 21, 22, 30, 37, 41, 42, 69, *75*, 94, *99*, 138, *139*, 142, 143, 145, 150, 151, 153, *158*, 160, 161, 168, 177, 193, 194, 210, *217*, 233, *236*, 246n
Fitzball, Edward 93
Flaming June (Leighton) 55, 121, 129
Fletcher, Bramwell 192
Les Fleurs du mal (Baudelaire) 147
Der fliegender Holländer (Wagner) 37, 90
Foch, Nina 101
Fokine, Mikhail 111, 183
Fontaine, Joan 24, 64
Fontainville Forest (play based on Radcliffe) 33
Fonthill Abbey 13, *14*, 25, 50, 185, 186
Forbes, Bryan 45, 156
France, Anatole 183
Francis, Freddie 13, 31, 41, 42, 55, 96, 138, 177, *237*, 248n
Franju, Georges 160
Frank, Alan 7
Frankel, Cyril 64, 214, *215*
Frankenstein (Shelley) 3, 24, 25, 38, 83, 93, 170
Frankenstein (dir. Whale) 4, 42, *43*, 203, 234
Frankenstein Created Woman 37, 94, 156, *158*, 159, 160, 161, 170, 172, 237
Frankenstein Must Be Destroyed 30, 42, 94, 160, 161, 172, 237
Frankenstein — The True Story 38
Frazer, Sir James 125, 206, 219, 220
Frazer, Robert *202*
Der Freischütz (Weber) 84, 85
Les Frères Kip (Verne) 165
Freud, Sigmund 4, 12, 14, 15, 18, 22, 24, 30, 112
Freund, Karl *127*, 186
Friedkin, William 225
Friedrich, Caspar David 71, 87, 88, 114, 120
From Beyond the Grave 55, 129, *131*
Der Froschkönig (Böcklin) 114
The Frozen Dead *208*, 209
Frülingsreigen (Thoma) 114

Functions and Disorders of the Reproductive Organs (Acton) 136
Furneaux, Yvonne 17, 187
Furse, Roger 25
Fuseli, Henry 113

Galeen, Henrik 114, 141
Gallu, Sam 113
Gamley, Douglas 112
Ganz, Bruno 88
Garber, Frederick 243*n*
Gargantua and Pantragruel (Rabelais) 213, 214
Gates, Tudor 66
Gatiss, Mark 234
Gaugin, Paul 126
Gaunt, William 181
Gautier, Théophile 102, 184
Geeson, Judy 96
Gelée, Claude 82
Genesis (The Bible) **28**
George, Stefan 120
The Ghost Sonata (Strindberg) 120, 191, 192
The Ghoul 31
Gibson, Alan 7, **8**, 15, 31
Gielgud, John 175
Gierke, Henning von 89
Gilbert, W(illiam) S(chwenck) 111
Gilling, John 17, 101, **101**, 127, 191, **197**, 203, 204, **204**
Gilpin, William 74–78, **76**, 83
Glanville, Joseph 168
Godfrey, Derek 215
Godwin, E(dward) W(illiam) **50**
Goethe, Johann Wolfgang von 33, 78, 101, 138
The Golden Ass of Lucius Apuleius 135
The Golden Bough (Frazer) 125, 206, 219
"The Golden Pot" (Hoffmann) 102
Golding, William 224
Der Golem 11
Goodcliffe, Michael 98
Goodrick-Clarke, Nicholas 208, 249*n*
Gordon, Christine 204
The Gorgon 17–19, 55, 60, 62, 97–101, **99**
Gospel According to St. Matthew 94
Gothic 24, 42, 113, 239, 240
The Gothic Revival (Clarke) 9, 54
Götterdämmerung (Wagner) 85, 90, 167
Grant, Arthur 41
Grant, Hugh 240, 241
Grant, Kenneth 213
Grant, Moray 66
Gray, Charles 200, 203, 209, 210, 227
Gray, Thomas 84
The Great Day of His Wrath (Martin) 84
Great Expectations (Dickens) 17, 23
Grebanier, Bernard 21
Green, Nigel 140
Green Hell 186
Griffith, John **62**

The Guardian (newspaper) 5, 113
"Guardian of the Abyss" 226, **226**, 227
Guest, Val 73
The Guildhall, Northampton **50**, **51**, **54**

Hadrian 186
Haggard, H(enry) Rider 67, 68, 72, 100, 181, **182**, 183
Hall, Charles D. 7, 25, 49, 66, 151, 203, 234
Haller, Daniel 146
Halliwell, Leslie 115
Halperin, Victor **202**, 203
Hamer, Robert 129
Hamlet (dir. Olivier) 21, 22, 25, 205
Hamlet (Shakespeare) 22, 33, 36, 230, 233
Hammer Films 1, 5, 7, 13–15, 17, 19, 26, 30, 40, 41, 46, 47, 50, 53, 63–67, 69, 71–73, 75, 79, 80, 82, 83, 87, 90–94, 96–98, 101, 102, 105, 106, 110, 111, 128, 142, 146, 150–153, 161, 162, 167, 176, 189, 193, 194, 196, 200, 203, 210, 211, 213–215, 217, 220, 223–226, 229, 232, 234, 237–240, 249*n*
Hammer House of Horror (T.V. Series) 31, 128, 226
Hammer Presents Dracula with Christopher Lee (LP) 63, 64
Hammerstein, Oscar 60
Hampden House 73
Hands of the Ripper 225, 237
Hardwicke, Edward 247*n*
Hardy, Robert 30
Hardy, Robin 65, 219
Harrington, Michael 250*n*
Hartford-Davis, Rupert 133
Hatfield, Hurd 122, **149**, 150
The Haunted Palace 146
The Haunted Screen (Eisner) 170
Haviland, Theodore 176
Hayden, Linda 15
Haydn, Franz Joseph 33
Hayers, Sidney 25
Hayman, Prudence 98, **99**
Heald, Hazel 98, 165
Hebrides Overture "Fingal's Cave" (Mendelssohn) 71, 85
Hegel, Georg Wilhelm Friedrich 158, 165–168, 170–172, 174, 175, 178, 179, 200, 207
Hellerau, Dresden 9
Hemmings, David 62
Henderson, Don 32
Hendry, Ian 247*n*
Henried, Paul 160
Henry, the Rev. Matthew **29**
Henson, Nicky 221
Herder, Johann Gottfried 33
Herzog, Werner 71, **71**, 72, 87, 88, 114
Heston, Charlton 196
Hickox, Douglas **62**, 229
Highgate Cemetery 15, **16**, 55, **59**
Hill, Benny 238

Hills, Gillian 30
Hillyer, Lambert 91, **92**
Hinds, Anthony 161
Hintertreppen 11
Hitchcock, Alfred 24, 95, 100, 113, 153, 214, 240
Hitler, Adolf 110, 141, 167, 208, 209, 239
Hoffmann, E(rnst) T(heodor) A(madeus) 90, 102, 103, 156
Hofmannsthal, Hugo von 120
Hogarth, William 117
Hollinghurst, Alan 89
Holden, Gloria 91, **92**
Holt, Seth 30, 96, 127, 196
Homer 135
Hooper, Ewan 14
Hooper, Tobe 1
"Hop-Frog" (Poe) 147
Hopkins, Anthony 140
Horror Express **164**, 165
The Horror of Dracula see *Dracula*
The Horror of Frankenstein 232, 238
Houdini, Harry 191
Hough, John 19, **219**
Houghton, Don 63, 64, 224
The Hound of the Baskervilles 50
House of Usher 125, **125**
House of Wax 110
The House That Dripped Blood 94, 170, 239
Houston, Donald 96
Howe, James Wong 9
Howells, Ursula 31, 101
Howlett, Noel 225
Hufeland, Christoph Wilhelm 136, 137
Hume, David 160
Hunt, Martita 17
Huson, Paul 223
Huysmans, Joris Karl 148–150, 152, 201, 206
"Hymn to Intellectual Beauty" (Shelley) 40, 41

I Am Half Sick of Shadows (Meteyard) 126
I Walked with a Zombie 117, **118**, 204
The Illustrated Man 44
The Illustrated Werewolf Movie Guide (Jones) 176
Im Walde (Raff) 85
Imaginary View of the Grand Gallery of the Louvre in Ruins (Robert) 68
"Imprisoned with the Pharaohs" (Lovecraft/Houdini) 191
In a Glass Darkly (Le Fanu) 66
In der Alpen (Raff) 85
"Indian Jones" films 163
Ingram, Rex 201–203
The Innocents 171
The Interpretation of Dreams (Freud) 4
"Intimations of Immortality from Recollections of Early Childhood" (Wordsworth) 229

The Invention of Morel (Casares) 179
The Invisible Man 44
Irwin, Robert 213
Isherwood, Christopher 38, 40
Ishioka, Eiko 121
Isis Unveiled (Blavatsky) 198
The Island of Doctor Moreau (Wells) 179
The Island of Lost Souls 208
Isle of the Dead 115, **118**, 122, 146
The Isle of the Dead (Böcklin) 115, 117, **118**, 120
Israel in Egypt (Poynter) 194
The Italian (Radcliffe) 92, 106, 185, 195, 243n

Jackson, Freda 17
James, Henry 111, 171
James, M(ontague) R(hodes) 25, 205
Jane Eyre (Brontë) 117, 204
Le Jardin des supplices (Mirbeau) 248n
Jarrott, Charles 97
Jessner, Leopold 9, 11
Jessop, Clytie 96
The Jewel of Seven Stars (Stoker) 195
Job (The Bible) 223
Johann, Zita 127, **127**
Johns, Glynis 239
Johns, Stratford 240
Johnson, Dr. Samuel 77
Johnston, Margaret 220
Jones, Darby 204
Jones, Ernest 22
Jones, Stephen 175
Jung, Carl Gustav 91, 100, 132, 201, 223, 245n
Junge, Alfred 26
Justine (de Sade) 106

Kahlert, Karl Friedrich 199
Kandinsky, Wassily 117
Kant, Immanuel 159, 166
Karloff, Boris 4, 5, 12, **12**, 30, **43**, 44, **45**, 72, 117, **118**, 122, 127, **127**, 171, 172, **172**, **173**, 183, 186, 187, 191, 192, 209, 224, 234, 239
Kay, Charles 247n
Keats, George 103
Keats, John 35, 103
Keen, Geoffrey 15
Keir, Anderew 30, 195, 196
Keller, Ferdinand 117
Kelley, James 32
Kelly, Gene 44
Kelly, Walter Keating 136
Kensal Green Cemetery, London 55, **60**, **61**, **62**
Kenton, Erle C. 208
Kerr, Deborah 171
Khamma (Debussy) 183
Khnopff, Fernand 159, 177
Kiersch, Fritz 220
Kind, Johann Friedrich 84
King, Stephen 220
King John (Shakespeare) 136

King Kong 24
King Lear (Shakespeare) 36
Kings (The Bible) 62
Kinski, Klaus **71**, 72, 88, 89
Kinski, Nastassja 170, 225
Kirchner, Ernst Ludwig 87
The Kiss of the Vampire, 106, 150–156, **153**, **157**, 179, 214, 225, 232
Klee, Paul 207
Klimt, Gustav 121
Klinger, Friedrich Maximilian 33
Klinger, Max 117
Kneale, Nigel 215
Knight, Esmond 125
Knights Templars 209, 249n
Knox, Dr. Robert 244n
Köhler, Joachim 167
Korder, Sir Alexander 73
Krauss, Werner 110, 114
Kruger, Otto **92**
Krzywinska, Tanya 211, 213
Kubrick, Stanley 177, 206
Kümel, Harry 24, 179
Kupka, František 121
Der Kuss (Klimt) 121
Kyrou, Alan 93

Là Bas (Huysmans) 201, 202, 206
Lacey, Catherine 127, 171, **173**, 198
Lachman, Harry 115, **117**
"The Lady of Shalott" (Tennyson) 126
The Lair of the White Worm (dir. Russell) 239–241
The Lair of the White Worm (Stoker) 239–241
Lamia (Keats) 103
Landers, Lew 209
Landis, John 142, 143
Landor, Rosalyn 210, 227, 237
Landscape with Psyche Outside the Palace of Cupid (Claude) 82
Lang, Fritz 11, 23, 114
Langella, Frank 41
Langton, Simon 247n
Lanz von Liebenfels, Jörg 208, 249n
Lassalle-Bordes, Gustave 180
The Last Days of Pompeii (Bulwer-Lytton) 208
The Last of the Mohicans (Cooper) 86
"The Last Test" (Lovecraft/de Castro) 191
Last Year at Marienbad see *L'Année dernière à Marienbad*
Laughton, Charles 208
"Laus Virginitatis" (Symons) 159
Laval, Gilles de 139, 140
Lawrence, D(avid) H(erbert) 142, 230
Lawson, Sarah 200, **217**
Lean, David 17
Leder, Herbert J. **208**, 209
Lee, Anna **172**
Lee, Christopher 4, 5, 7, **8**, 15, 17, 21, 24, 26, 43, 63, 89, 96, 98, 113, 132, 151, **164**, 165, 170, **171**, 187, 192, 194, 203, 211, 214, **216**, **217**, 224, 225, 229, 232, 237

Lee, Rowland, V(ance) 12, 13, **45**
Lee-Thompson, J(ohn) 217, **218**
Le Fanu, Sheridan 66, 96, 105, 122
The Legend of the Seven Golden Vampires 239
Legend of the Werewolf 138, 142
Leigh, Andrew 234
Leighton, Frederic, Lord 55, 121, 181
Le Lorraine, Ivan **124**
Leni, Paul 110
Leon, Valerie 30, 195, 196
Leonardo da Vinci 100, 201
The Leopard Man 117
Leroux, Gaston 164
L'Estrange Ewen, C. 223
Leventon, Vladimir see Lewton, Val
Lévi, Éliphas 62, 126, 137, **137**, 138, 207, 208, 210–212, **210**, **211**, **212**, 244n
Levin, Henry 101
Levin, Ira 209
Lewin, Albert 122, **124**, **149**
Lewis, Matthew 23, 91–93, 100, 185, 199, 205, 225
Lewton, Val 115, 117, 122, 204, 217
Ley, Willy 208
"Liebestraum No. 3" (Liszt) 203, 239
Liedtke, Harry 184
"Ligeia" (Poe) 147, 148, 152, 156, 166, 168
Lind, Michael 250n
Linden, Jenny 96
Ling, Barbara Yu 15
Lisbon Earthquake 78, 79
Liszt, Franz 37, 46, 85, 101, 203, 239
Lisztomania 46, 239
Lloyd, Sue 133
Lohengrin (Wagner) 89, 90
Lom, Herbert 112, 163, 177, 246n
London Film Productions 73
Long, Edwin Longsden 181
"The Long Rain" see *The Illustrated Man*
Longinus 79
Lonnen, Ray 227
Lord of the Flies (Golding) 224
The Lord of the Rings 241
Losey, Joseph 163
The Lost Continent 40
"Lot 249" (Conan Doyle) 191
Lovecraft, H(oward) P(hilips) 98, 99, 101, 128, 132, 146, 165, 191, 220, 230
"The Loved Dead" (Lovecraft/Eddy) 230
Low, Prof. A.D. 189
Low, Andrew 189, 194
Lubisch, Ernst 184
Ludwig II of Bavaria 163
Lugosi, Bela 3, 7, 9, **10**, **11**, **12**, 24, 26, 44, **45**, **49**, 89, 91, 142, 152, **202**, 203, 204, 209, 229, 232
Lust for a Vampire 66, 92, 105, 241
Lyndon, Barré 150

Maas, Jeremy 60
Macbeth (Shakespeare) 35, 36, 135, 233, 234
MacGinnis, Niall 21, 205, 206
MacGregor, Scott 66
MacPherson, James 71
Madhouse 229
Maeterlinck, Maurice 120, 146, 246n
Magic — A History of Its Rites, Rituals and Mysteries (Lévi) 244n
The Magician (dir. Ingram) 201, 202
The Magician (Maugham) 201, 202, 206, 228
Magritte, René 162, 176
Mahler, Gustav 85
Maitland, Marne 104
Malchus, Marius 223
Malcolm, Derek 113
Malleson, Miles 235, *236*
Mamoulian, Rouben 44, 142
Man and Superman (Shaw) 167
"The Man of Stone" (Lovecraft/Heald) 98
The Man Who Changed His Mind 172, ***172***
The Man Who Could Cheat Death 93, 150, 161
Manchester Town Hall *52*
Mandiargues, Pandré Pieyre de 176
Maniac 96
Mankiewicz, Joseph L. 24, 189, ***190***
Mann, Thomas 120, 143
Mann und Frau den Mond betrachtend (Friedrich) 114
Marais, Jean 128
Marathon Man 209
Marc, Franz 122
March, Fredric 44, 142
Mark of the Vampire 9, ***11***, 91, 92
"Markheim" (Stevenson) 132
Marshall, Neil 142
Martell, Philip 210
Martin, Eugenio ***164***, 165
Martin, John 26, 84, 87
Martin, Jonathan 84
Mary Shelley's Frankenstein 25
Mason, James 38
The Masque of the Red Death (dir. Birkinshaw) 163
The Masque of the Red Death (dir. Corman) 147
"The Masque of the Red Death" (Poe) 147, 163
Massenet, Jules 183
Massey, Anna 162
Massey, Daniel 162, 163
Massey, Raymond 44
Massie, Paul 143
Mastering Witchcraft (Huson) 223
The Matrix 179
A Matter of Life and Death 26, ***31***
Maturin, Charles 37, 205
Maugham, William Somerset 44, 201, 202, 206, 214, 228
Mayne, Ferdy 108
McCallum, David 38
McCallum, Neil 31
McCormack, W(illiam) J(ohn) 123

McCowan, Alec 64
McLynn, Frank 185
Mearns, William Hughes 26
"Méditation" (Massenet) 183
"Medusa's Coil" (Lovecraft/Bishop) 101
Die Meistersinger von Nürnberg 71
Melly, Andrée ***236***
Melmoth the Wanderer (Maturin) 37, 205
Melrose Abbey ***69***
Melville, H. ***69***, ***70***
Mendelssohn, Felix 69, 71, 85
Mengele, Dr. Josef 208
Mercer, David 175
Meteyard, Sidney 126
Metropolis 11, 114
MGM 9
Michelangelo 68, 102, 105
Middlemass, Frank 161
A Midsummer Night's Dream (dir. Reinhardt) 114
A Midsummer Night's Dream (Shakespeare) 135
The Midwich Cuckoos (Wyndham) 203
Milton, John 26, 82, 84, 112, 221, 223, 224
Mirbeau, Octave 248n
Mist in the Elbe Valley (Friedrich) 87, 88
Mitchell, Yvonne 30
Modern Painters (Ruskin) 36
Molinaro, Edouard 232
Mona Lisa (Leonardo) 110
The Monastery (Scott) ***69***
Mondrian, Piet 207
The Monk (dir. Kyrou) 93
The Monk (Lewis) 91–94, 185, 199, 205
Monlaur, Yvonne 235
"Mont Blanc" (Shelley) 83
Moran, Peggy ***188***
Moreau, Gustave 121
Morell, André 196, 215
Morgan, Terence 21, 194
Morris, Aubrey 249n
Morris, Robert 161
Morris, William 55, 62, ***62***
La Mort de Cléopâtre (Berlioz) 180
The Most Dangerous Game 24
Mower, Patrick 210, ***217***
Mozart, Wolfgang Amadeus 33, 183
Mucha, Alphone 121
Muir, David 66
Muller, Robert 247n
The Mummy (dir. Fisher) 17, 21, 187, 189, 193, 194, 235
The Mummy (dir. Freund) 127, ***127***, 165, 183, 186, 187, 189, 191, 192, 234
The Mummy (dir. Sommers) 189, 242
"The Mummy's Foot" (Gautier) 184
The Mummy's Hand 186, 187, ***188***, 191, 193
The Mummy's Shroud 127, 189, 196, ***197***, 198, 237

Munch, Edvard 117, 120
The Munsters 242
The Muppets 242
Murnau, F(riedrich) W(ilhelm) 23, 71, 72, 87, 88, 90, 114, ***115***
Murray, John 184
Myers, Peter 96
Myerscough-Jones, David 111
Mysteries of the Wax Museum 110
The Mysteries of Udolpho (Radcliffe) 22, 33, 65, 83, 92, 106, 109, 110, 147, 185, 231, 233
The Mysterious Mother (Walpole) 47

Naderman, Henri 185
The Nanny 96
Napoleon 185, 189
Narizzano, Silvio 96
The Narrative of Arthur Gordon Pym (Poe) 148
Nazimova, Alla 115
Neame, Christopher 195
The Necromancer, or The Tale of the Black Forest (Teuthold) 199
Nedwell, Robin 239
Negri, Pola 184
Neuberg, Victor 228
Neuschwanstein Castle 163
Newell, Mike 133, 196
Newton, Sir Isaac 79
Die Nibelungen 23, 114
Nicholas, Paul 46
Nietzsche, Friedrich 37, 143, 145, 201, 214
Night of the Demon 21, 220, 205
Night of the Eagle 25, 220
Nightmare 96
The Nightmare (Fuseli) 113
Nightmare Abbey (Peacock) 230, 231
Niven, David 217, 241
Nordau, Max 121
Northanger Abbey (Austen) 109, 199, 231
Norton, Rictor 82, 83, 106
Nosferatu (dir. Murnau) 23, 87, 90, 114, ***115***
Nosferatu — The Vampyre (dir. Herzog) 71, ***71***, 72, 87, 88, 90, 114
Notes on Designs of the Old Masters in Florence (Swinburne) 102

Oakley Court ***19***, ***20***, ***21***, ***22***, 73, ***74***, 104, 111, ***112***, ***176***
Obrow, Jeffrey 249n
Observations on Several Parts of England (Gilpin) ***76***
The Occult (Wilson) 223
The Occult Arts of Ancient Egypt (Brommage) 223
"Occult Memories" (Villiers de l'Isle Adam) 163, 164
The Occult Roots of Nazism (Goodrick-Clarke) 208
"Ode on Venice" (Byron) ***35***
"Ode to the West Wind" (Shelley) 42
The Odyssey (Homer) 135

Ogilvy, Ian 171
Oland, Warner 91
The Old Dark House 44
Oldman, Gary 121
Olivier, Laurence 21–23, 25, 205, 209
O'Mara, Kate 232
The Omen 225, 226
On the Buses 237
"On the Medusa of Leonardo da Vinci in the Florentine Gallery" (Shelley) 98
On the Nature of the Psyche (Jung) 245n
On the Sublime (Longinus) 79
The 120 Days of Sodom (de Sade) 106
The Order of the Golden Dawn 208, 211, 214, 217
The Origin of Species (Darwin) 206
Orphée 128
Ossian 71
Ostara (magazine) 249n
Othello (Shakespeare) 36
Otterson, Jack 12
"Out of the Aeons" (Lovecraft) 165
"The Outsider" (Lovecraft) 132
"The Oval Portrait" (Poe) 125
Owen, Cliff 170, **217**
Owen, Dickie 194, 217
Owen Wingrave (Britten) 112
"Owen Wingrave" (James) 111, 112
Oxford Companion to Philosophy 166

Pabst, G(eorg) W(ilhelm) 11
Pagett, Nicola 38
Pal, George 207
Palace of Westminster 50
Pandora's Box 11
Paranoiac 96
Paris Opera House 183
Parsifal (Wagner) 129, 175, 90
Pascoe, Richard 98
Pastell, George 193
"Pastoral" Symphony (Beethoven) 36
Pater, Walter 100, 201
Le Pavillion d'Armide (Tcherepnin) 111
Pavlova, Anna 183
Peacock, Thomas Love 230
Pearce, Jacqueline 101, ***101***, 105, 204, 239
Peck, Gregory 113, 209, 225, 226
Peduzzi, Richard 246n
Peel, David 17, **18**
Périer, François 128
Pertwee, Jon 239
The Phantom of the Opera (dir. Fisher) 177, 237
The Phantom of the Opera (Leroux) 164
Phillips, John 196
A Philosophical Enquiry into the Origin of Our Ideas of the Sublime and Beautiful (Burke) 78–80, **79**, 82

"The Philosophy of Furniture" (Poe) 146
The Picture of Dorian Gray (dir. Lewin) 122, **124**, **149**, 150
The Picture of Dorian Gray (Wilde) 122, 148, 149, 161–163
Picturesque Tours (Gilpin) 77
Pierce, Jack 192
Pinewood Studios 73
Pirandello, Luigi 172, 174, 175, 179
Piranesi, Giovanni Battista 68, 184–187, ***187***, ***189***, 191
The Pit and the Pendulum (dir. Corman) 146
"The Pit and the Pendulum" (Poe) 146
Pitoëff, Sacha 178
Pitt, Chris 239
The Plague of the Zombies 203, 204, **204**, 226
Poe, Edgar Allan 24, 46, 125, 141, 146–148, 152, 156, 163, 166, 168, 170, 184, 192, 193, 230
Pogany, Willy 187
Polanski, Roman 106, 108, 111, 133, 232, 233, 234
Polidori, Dr. John 38, 111, 113
Porter, Eric 237
Portrait of an Englishman in His Chateau (Mandiargues) see *L'Anglais décrit dans le château fermé*
Powell, Eddie 170, **197**
Powell, Michael 26, **31**
The Power of Nightmares (BBC documentary) 250n
Powers, Stephanie 96
Poynter, Sir Edward John 181, 194
Praz, Mario 91, 92, 100, 102
Presbury, G. **70**
Pressburger, Emeric 26, **31**
Price, Dennis 217
Price, Vincent 110, 125, **125**, 146, 168, 186, 229, 231
Prinsep, Val 181
Prometheus, the Poem of Fire (Scriabin) 206, 207
Providence 175–177
Prowse, Dave 232
Psycho 113
Psychomania 220–222, **222**
Pugin, Augustus Welby 50
Purcell, Henry 186
Pythagoras 137

Qabalah 137
The Quatermass Xperiment 73
The Quiver, an Illustrated Magazine for Sunday and General Reading **39**, **56**, **57**, **58**, **81**

Rabelais, François 213
Rachmaninoff, Sergei 115, 183
Radcliffe, Ann 22–24, 33, 35, 41, 47, 49, 50, 62–66, 82–84, 92, 106, 108, 110, 147, 177, 185, 186, 195, 199, 233, 234, 237
Raff, Joachim 85
"Rain" (Maugham) 44

Rains, Claude 25, 145
Raitt, A.W. 166
Rank, Otto 12
Rank Organization 73
Raphael 68
Rapper, Irving 25
Raskolnikov 9
The Raven (dir. Corman) 229
The Raven (dir. Landers) 209
Raven's Brood (Benson) 141
Rebecca (du Maurier) 23
"Red Riding Hood" 141
Reed, Anthony 147
Reed, Donna **149**
Reed, Oliver 138, **139**, 142, 145, 207
Rees, Angharad 225
Reeves, Michael 171, **173**
Reid, Beryl 32
Reinhardt, Max. 114
Reizenstein, Franz 189
The Reptile 101–105 **101**, 239, 241
Repulsion 133
Resnais, Alain 22, 175, 176–179, **178**
Rethel, Alfred 114
Retz, Gilles de see Laval, Gilles
The Revenge of Frankenstein 69
The Revolt of Islam (Shelley) 40
Reynolds, John Hamilton 35
Das Rheingold (Wagner) 37, 88, 203
Rhodes, Anthony 147
Rhodes, Marjorie 237
Richardson, Amanda 239, 240
Richardson, John 67, **68**, 215
Richardson, Natasha 113
Rickman, Thomas 54
Rigby, Jonathan 24
Rimsky-Korsakoff, Nicolai 239
Der Ring des Nibelungen (Wagner) 3, 85, 90, 229
"The Ring of Thoth" (Conan Doyle) 191
Rintoul, David 138, 142
Ripper, Michael 196, 235, 237, **237**
Rixens, Jean André 180
RKO 115, 117
Robbe-Grillet, Alain 177
Robert, Hubert 68, 69
Robespierre, Maximilien François Marie Isidore 140
Robinson, Bernard 7, 17, 18, 50, 62, 151, **151**, 152, **153**, **157**, 187, 189, 210, 233
Robinson, Harry 41, 105
Robinson, Margaret 151
Robson, Dame Flora 32
Robson, Mark 115, **118**, 204, **205**
Rodgers, Richard 60
Rogers, Peter 110
Röhrig, Walter 114
The Romance of the Forest (Radcliffe) 33, 36, 47, 62, 64, 83, 106, 195, 234
The Romantic Agony (Praz) 91
Romer, John 184
Rooney, Mickey 114
Rosa, Salvator 82
Rosen, Charles 77

Rossini, Gioachino 36, 37
Rousseau, Jean-Jaques 33
Ruddigore (Gilbert and Sullivan) 111
Ruskin, John 36, 50, 54
Russell, Anna 229
Russell, Ken 24, 42, 46, 113, 142, 207, 239–241
Rutter, John **14**
Rye, Stellan 141

Sadsy, Peter 14, 80, 97, **97**, 225
St. Basil's Cathedral, Moscow 207
St. Botolph's Church, Shenley 73, 225
St. Clement's Church, Leeds 55
St. Irvyne, or The Rosicrucian (Shelley) 40
St. Mary's Church, Whitby 63, **63**
Sanders, George 186, 222
Sands, Julian 42, 113
Sangster, Jimmy 66, 96, 150, 152, 161, 187, 193, 232, 241
Sarrazin, Michael 38
Satan Wants Me (Irwin) 21
The Satanic Rites of Dracula 15, 90, 192, 224, 232
Scars of Dracula 15, 66, 232, 238
Schaffner, Franklin 209
Scheherezade ((Rimsky-Korsakoff) 239
Schiller, Friedrich 75, 87
Schlegel, Friedrich 71
Schlesinger, John 209
Schmidgall, Gary 143
Schnitzler, Arthur 154, 155
Schoedsack, Ernest B(eaumont) 24
Die schöne Melusine (Mendelssohn) 85
Schopenhauer, Arthur 3, 166, 167
Schreck, Max **115**
Schulze-Mittendorf, Walter 114
Schumann, Robert 69, 85
Das Schweigen des Waldes (Böcklin) 114
Scoones, Ian 73
Scott, Sir Walter **69**, **70**, 71, 86
Scriabin, Alexander 206, 207, 224
Séance on a Wet Afternoon 45
The Secret Doctrine (Blavatsky) 165, 206
The Secret Grimoire of Turiel (Malchus) 223
Sellars, Elizabeth 196
Selznick, David O. 115
Sgt. Pepper's Lonely Hearts Club Band (The Beatles) 60, 213
The Seventh Victim 117, 204, **205**, 214, 217, 225
Seymour, Janes 38
Seyrig, Delphine 24, 177, 179
Seyrig, Francis 177
Shakespeare, William 4, 23, 33, 35, 36, 41, 114, 135, 183, 199, 233, 234, 238
Sharp, Don 106, 128, **153**, **157**, 220, **222**, **226**
Shaw, George Bernard 167, 203
She (dir. Day) 67, 68, **68**, 72, 237
She (Haggard) 67, 100

Shelley, Barbara 13, 98
Shelley, Mary 24, 38, 40–42, 83, 84, 93, 106, 170
Shelley, Percy Bysshe 38, 40–42, 83, 84, 88, 98, 100, 113, 230
Shepherd, Elizabeth 168
The Shining 177
Siegfried (Wagner) 85
"The Silent Scream" 31
Simmons, Jean 17, 123
Simon, Simone 101
Singin' in the Rain 44
Siodmak, Robert 14, 137, 138
Six Characters in Search of an Author (Pirandello) 172, 179
Skal, David J. 209
Skeggs, Roy 195, 242
Smight, Jack 38, 44
The Snorkel 96
"Snow White" 126, 133
"The Snow Queen" (Anderson) 128
So Long at the Fair 153, 154, 214
"Some Words with a Mummy" (Poe) 192, 193
Sommers, Stephen 189
Son of Frankenstein 12, 44, **45**
The Sorcerers 171, 172, **173**
The Sound of Music 60
Spellbound 113
Spencer, Jane 106
Spielberg, Steven 163
Spinoza, Baruch de (Benedictus) 78, 199, 200, 201, 205, 213, 214
The Spiral Staircase 14
Spriggs, T. L. S. 200, 205
Stableford, Brian 152, 164
Staines, R. **69**
Stanley, Kim 45
Star Wars 242
Steiger, Rod 44
Steiner, Max 24
Steiner, Rudolf 207, 224
Stensgaarde, Yutte 92, 105
The Stepford Wives 156
Stevenson, Robert 172, **172**
Stevenson, Robert Louis 132, 142
Stimpson Walton Bond (architects) **54**
Stothard, Thomas **29**
A Strange Story (Bulwer-Lytton) 208
Strasberg, Susan 96
Stravinsky, Igor 183
Strindberg, August 1, 3, 117, 191
Stritch, Elaine 175
Stoker, Bram 8, 9, 15, 38, 41, 63, 86–88, 90, 126, 152, 195, 240, 241
Stolen Face 160
The Stones of Venice (Ruskin) 50
Stowitts (Hubert) 203
Strauss, Richard 37, 85, 95, 120
Strawberry Hill 25, **26**, **27**, 50, **51**, 79, **151**
Stuart, Gloria 44
The Student of Prague (dir. Galeen) 114
The Student of Prague (dir. Rye) 141
Stumar, Charles J. 192
Der Stürm 114

Sturm und Drang 33
Sullivan, Sir Arthur 11
Summers, Montague 136, 170
Die Sünde (Stuck) 240
Sunset Blvd. 25, 95, 238
Swanson, Gloria 25, 95
Swedenborg, Emanuel 123
Swinburne, Algernon 100, 102
The Sword of Moses — An Ancient Book of Magic (Gaster) 223
Sykes, Peter 26, 30, 73, **171**, 225
Symons, Arthur 159
Symphonie fantastique (Berlioz) 37

Tales from the Crypt 55, 177
Tannhäuser (Wagner) 148
Taste of Fear 96
Taste the Blood of Dracula 14, 15, 66, 80, 224
Tate, Reginald 123
Taylor, Elizabeth **190**
Tcherepnin, Alexander 111
The Tempest (Shakespeare) 36
Tempi duri per i vampiri 232
The Ten Commandments 194
Tenniel, Sir John **130**
Tennyson, Alfred, Lord 126, 247n
Tenser, Tony 171
Terry, Alice 202
Terry-Thomas 239
Teuthold, Peter 199
The Texas Chainsaw Massacre 1
Thaïs (Massenet) 183
Theater of Death **62**, 113, 229
Theophilus North (Wilder) 230
Die Theosophie und die assyrischen "Menschentiere" (Lanz von Liebenfels) 208
Thesiger, Ernest 38, 234
They Used Dark Forces (Wheatley) 167, 209
Thoma, Hans 114
Thomas, Damien 92, 217, **219**
Thomas, William Luson **39**, **56**, **57**, **58**, **81**
Thorlby, Anthony 174
Thornbury, W. **81**
"The Three Little Pigs" 141
Through the Looking Glass and What Alice Found There (Carroll) 128, 129, **130**
Tierney, Gene 24
Tigon Films 171
The Times Literary Supplement 89
To the Devil a Daughter 73, 170, **171**, 220, 224, 225
Toccata and Fugue in D minor (Bach) 177
Der Tod in Venedig (Mann) 148
Todd, Ann 96
Todd, Bob 238
Toguri, David 210
Toland, John 78
Tom Thumb 184
The Tomb of Böcklin (Keller) 117
The Tomb of Ligeia 168, **169**, 231
Torture Garden 248n
Totentanz (Liszt) 46

Tourneur, Jacques 21, 101, **118**, 204–206
Towers, Harry Alan 163
Townsend, Jill 196
Transcendental Magic — Its Doctrine and Ritual (Lévi) **137**, 207, 210, **210**, **211**, **212**
"The Trap" (Lovecraft) 128
Traumnovelle (Schnitzler) 154–156
Travers, Ben 123
Trionfo della Morte (D'Annunzio) 100
Tristan und Isolde (Wagner) 90, 159
Troughton, Patrick 226, 227
"The Turn of the Screw" (James) 171
Tussaud, Anna Maria 110
Tussaud, François 110
Tutankhamun 185, 187
Twins of Evil 19, 66, 67, 92, 217, **219**
The Two Faces of Dr. Jekyll 142
2001— A Space Odyssey 206
Tyler, Tom 187, **188**

Uberti, Farinata degli 3
Ulmer, Edgar G(eorg) 6, 11, **12**, 31, 204
Uncle Silas (Le Fanu) 122
Uncle Silas (dir. Frank) 123, 125
Universal Studios 1, 5, 17, 23, 25, 30, 44, 49, 66, 71, 90, 127, 138, 145, 151, 165, 183, 186, 189, 191, 192, 203, 228, 229, 234

Vadim, Roger 96, 156
Valentine, Anthony 170, 225
Vampire Circus **75**, 80, 128
The Vampire Lovers 65, **65**, 66, 96
"Vampire Rhapsody" (Bernard) 152, 153
The Vampire's Kiss (Villiers de l'Isle Adam) *see Claire Lenoir*
The Vampyre (Polidori) 110
Vanzina, Stefano 232
Vathek 13, 185, 186
Vault of Horror 126, 162, 239
The Vengeance of She 170, 215, **217**
"Véra" (Villiers de l'Isle Adam) 166, 170
Véra, Augusto 166
Verdi, Giuseppe 180
Verne, Jules 156, **160**, 165
"The Very Image" (Villiers de l'Isle Adam) 162
Victim 105
Victoria and Albert Museum, London 185
Une Ville abandonnée (Khnopff) 177
Villiers, James 30, 195

Villiers de l'Isle Adam, Jean-Marie Mathias Phillipe August 146, 150, 152, 156, 158, 161, 163, 165–168, 170
Virgil 3
Visconti, Luchino 143, **144**, 145
"A Vision of the Sea" (Shelley) 38
Vlad the Impaler 9
Volk, Stephen 24
von Stuck, Franz 240
von Sydow, Max 225
von Weber, Carl Maria 84, 85

Wachowski, Andy 179
Wachowski, Larry 179
Das Wachsfigurenkabinett 100
Wager, Anthony 17
Waggner, George 137
Wagner, Adolf 167
Wagner, Cosima 9
Wagner, Richard 3, 9, 37, 46, 71, 85, 88–90, 120, 121, 129, 141, 148, 156, 159, 167, 168, 175, 203, 229, 231, 239, 243n 246n
Waite, A(rthur) E(dward) 210, 223
Wakeman, Rick 239
Waldscenen (Schumann) 85
Die Walküre (Wagner) 37, 85
Wallis, Jackie 153, **153**
Wallis, Robert **29**
Wallis Budge, E(rnest) A(lfred) 223
Walpole, Horace 25, 26, 30, 47, 79, 110, **151**, 185, 233
Walsh, Kay 214, **215**
Walter, Bruno 85
Walters, Thorley 161, 237
Walton, Sir William 23
Der Wanderer über dem Nebelmeer (Friedrich) 88
Ward, Simon 30
Warlords of Atlantis 207
Warm, Hermann 114
Warner Brothers 25, 114
Warren, Barry 152, **153**
Waterhouse, Alfred **52**, **53**
Waters, Russell 210
Watford, Gwen 31
Waverley (Scott) 86
Waxman, Franz 24, 95
Wegener, Paul 11, 201, 202
Weisse, Christian Herrmann 167
Wells, H(erbert) G(eorge) 179, 208
The Werewolf of Paris (Endore) 138
"The Werewolf Reunion" 247n
Westmore, Wally 142
Weyer, Johann 223
Whale, James 4, 25, 42, **43**, 44, 106, 186, 203, 234, 238, 239

Whatever Happened to Baby Jane? 238
Wheatley, Dennis 167, 170, 208, 209, 211, 213, 223–225, 228
Whitby Abbey **64**
White Zombie **202**, 203–204
Whitelaw, Billie 225, 247n
Whiting, Leonard 38, 41
The Wicker Man 65, 219
Wicking, Christopher 26
Widmark, Richard 170, 224
Wiene, Robert 9, 114
Wilde, Oscar 95, 122, 148–150, 161–163, 166, 240
Wilder, Billy 25
Wilder, Thornton 230
Wilhelm, Richard 223
Will, Peter *see* Teuthold, Peter
William Tell (Rossini) 36
Williams, Kenneth 110
Willman, Noel 101, 150, **157**, 215
Wilmer, Douglas **65**, 66
Wilson, Colin 223
Wilson, Ian 177
Wimbledon Theatre 177
Wimperis, Edmund Morison **39**, **56**, **81**
Winchester Cathedral **57**
The *Witch of Atlas* (Shelley) 40
Witchcraft and Demonianism (L'Estrange Ewen) 223
The Witches 64, 214, 215, **215**
Wolf, Hugo 117
The Wolfman 137, **137**, 188, 142
Women in Love (Lawrence) 142
Women in Love (dir. Russell) 142
Wong, Anna May 91
Woodville, Richard Caton **182**
Woodward, Christopher 67
Wordsworth, William 78, 229
Wuthering Heights (Wyler) 44
Wyler, William 44
Wyndham, John 203
Wyngarde, Peter 25, 171, 220

Yeats, W(illiam) B(utler) 206, 214
The Yellow Book 194
Les Yeux sans visage 160
York Minster 84
Young, Robert 80
Young Frankenstein 232

Zanoni (Bulwer-Lytton) 208
Zastrozzi (Shelley) 40
Die Zauberflöte (Mozart) 183
Zetterling, Mai 246n
Zimbalist, Stephanie 133
Zola, Emile 201, 206
Zucco, George 191

www.ingramcontent.com/pod-product-compliance
Ingram Content Group UK Ltd.
Pitfield, Milton Keynes, MK11 3LW, UK
UKHW050537150426
5217IPUK00026B/1980